1983

MY 6
FAVORITE
PLAYS

J. B. Priestley

MY 6 FAVORITE PLAYS

Eden End
Time and the Conways
When We Are Married
The Linden Tree
An Inspector Calls
Dangerous Corner

STEIN AND DAY/*Publishers*/New York

Library of Congress Cataloging in Publication Data

Priestley, John Boynton, 1894-
   My 6 favorite plays.

   CONTENTS: Dangerous corner.—Eden end.—Time and the
Conways.—An inspector calls.—The linden tree.—When we
are married.
   I. Title.
PR6031.R6A19   1979   822'.9'12   78-8787
ISBN 0-8128-2533-0

CONTENTS

INTRODUCTION

I feel it would be churlish indeed to reprint these plays without saying anything about the leading players who first brought them to life on the stage. And indeed I welcome this opportunity to name them and praise their talent and express my gratitude for their cooperation.

As people say—they did me proud.

Dangerous Corner was less a play of character than one of ingenious theatrical contrivance, but so far as it offered force of character—and here, as elsewhere, I refer to the original production—this force was amply supplied by Flora Robson, then at the beginning of her fine career. With an actress of less psychological weight and power, the total effect would never have been the same. The play and I were lucky to grab Flora.

Eden End was carefully cast and directed by Irene Hentschel but it could not help being dominated by the comic genius of Ralph Richardson, playing the bibulous actor, Charlie Appleby. If they are well done—and sometimes they are dreadful—I cannot help being very fond of drunk scenes, and Ralph offered us a masterpiece in this play. My writing was fairly cunning (I seem to remember that Ralph has paid a public tribute to it), but what he did with it, doing full justice to all the jokes but also suggesting a certain depth and touch of pathos, was close to the miraculous. If I were granted the freedom of the fourth dimension, one of my first demands would be the sight and sound again of this scene from *Eden End*. I have seen revivals of it, but with no Ralph there, the magic has gone.

Time and the Conways brought me Jean Forbes-Robertson, then at the top of her magnificent form, to play Kay Conway. She was then a marvel of a girl, flashing like a bright sword. I can never forget her. Why her dazzling career dimmed and withered away, I shall never understand, and hate to think about. But I love to think about and remember her Kay Conway, which more than brought to life both the girl and then the woman of this family of my imagination. She was a huge piece of luck not only for me, who remembers her as a dear friend, but also for thousands of entranced playgoers.

In *An Inspector Calls,* it is not the Inspector I remember most gratefully—though there was nothing wrong with him—but the two younger members of the family he inspected. These were played by Alec Guinness, still happily hypnotising us, and Margaret Leighton, a fine actress who ran out of luck, as we all can do. I should like to see this play revived, as I believe it well deserves to be, but it would be too much to ask to find these two parts as triumphant again as they were once. On the whole I am a lucky writer but I am not *that* lucky.

The Linden Tree was a smash hit, and this was because the Cassons, Lewis and Sybil, two powerful personalities, were in tremendous form, and never once relaxed their grip on their packed audiences. The writing, by this time that of a fairly old hand, was not without its cunning and force, but it was these two formidable Cassons who really did the trick.

As for *When We Are Married,* all it needs is a cast that understands North-country character and humour, and fortunately for it—and me—it has never been long in want of one.

EDEN END

A Play in Three Acts

TO
MY WIFE

First produced at the Duchess Theatre, London, on September 13*th,* 1934, *with the following cast:*

WILFRED KIRBY	JOHN TEED
SARAH	NELLIE BOWMAN
LILIAN KIRBY	ALISON LEGGATT
DR. KIRBY	EDWARD IRWIN
STELLA KIRBY	BEATRIX LEHMANN
GEOFFREY FARRANT	FRANKLYN BELLAMY
CHARLES APPLEBY	RALPH RICHARDSON

Play produced by IRENE HENTSCHEL

ACT I
Tuesday Afternoon

ACT II
Friday Afternoon

ACT III
SCENE I. Saturday Night
SCENE II. Sunday Afternoon

The action takes place in the sitting-room of Dr. Kirby's house at Eden End in the North of England, the last week in October, 1912.

ACT I

Sitting-room of Dr. Kirby's house, Eden End. An afternoon of early autumn in the year 1912. A comfortable, well-worn room furnished in the taste of an earlier period. A door at the back, preferably up a few steps, leading from the rest of the house. A door on the right leading to a small room, originally the nursery, now used by SARAH *to sit in and to do small jobs. Unless otherwise stated, all characters enter and leave by the main door on the left. A window at left looking out upon a distant grey-green hill of the North-country type. A bookshelf on right wall. A telephone prominently placed in corner near door on left. Upstage on left a cottage piano and old piano stool.* WILFRED *is discovered at this piano, carefully picking out with one finger, and sometimes vamping an accompaniment with left hand, a waltz refrain from "Gipsy Love". He is wearing a tweed suit but a linen collar and dark tie. He is about twenty-four, and though sunburned and in possession of a small moustache, he looks young, unsophisticated, rather weak. After a few moments, during which he can improve a little and even attempt to sing the tune,* SARAH *enters through door on right, carrying some things she has presumably been ironing in her little room.* SARAH *is an old North-country nurse, now about seventy, a queer old creature, at once simple and shrewd, and very earthy. She still slaves for all the family, but her tone toward them is still indulgent, as if they were children.*

WILFRED: I'm getting it, Sarah. I'm getting it.

SARAH: You've been at it long enough.

WILFRED: Now just listen. (*He plays again and she stops in the middle, half-way between doors to listen.*)

WILFRED (*wheeling round*). What do you think of that?

SARAH: It sounds like proper playing—a'most.

WILFRED: Not so much of the *almost*. What more do you want?

SARAH: Well, I'm not saying you're not doing very well with it. But you'll never shape at it like Miss Stella, never in all your born days you won't.

WILFRED: Do you know how many times you've said that?

SARAH: For playing and singing and suchlike——

WILFRED: She was wonderful. I know. Well, I'm wonderful too.

3

SARAH: You're a right untidy lad.

WILFRED: I'm not a lad.

SARAH: Bother I've had wi' your clothes.

WILFRED: Did you do anything to my blue shirt?

SARAH: Ay, that's mended. And two more beside. And two of the doctor's.

WILFRED: When I'm in Africa, Sarah, black women wash my clothes.

SARAH: I remember seeing four black women once at Martinbro Fair. Black as your boots they were. And fuzzy hair.

WILFRED: Where I work, when I go away, there are thousands and thousands of people like that. And I'm the boss. And then when I come home on leave, you call me a lad.

SARAH: These women kept rubbing their teeth with bits of stick, I remember. And I fancy it was the same year you went and fell into that duck pond just outside Martinbro. You wor only a little lad and you had your best sailor suit on. (*Goes to door on left.*)

WILFRED: What would you do if you saw a hippopotamus?

SARAH: I don't know what they are. I've no time to be bothering wi' them things now.

WILFRED: Good old Sarah!

SARAH: You get on wi' your piano playing, and frame a bit better. (*Goes out.*)

> WILFRED *begins playing again, then leaves off, as if in disgust with himself. But hearing somebody coming through the door on left, he hastily plunges into a very noisy, inaccurate rendering of the waltz. LILIAN enters. She is a year or two older than her brother; neither pretty nor ugly; neatly but not well dressed in indoor clothes. She has more sweetness of character than would superficially appear from what she says and does. When she is not taking refuge in sarcasm, she is quick and eager. She goes over to the bookcase and takes a book that is lying open on the top.*

LILIAN: What's that awful row?

WILFRED: That's the waltz from "Gipsy Love".

LILIAN: It sounds a mess.

WILFRED: That's because I can't play it properly.

LILIAN: That's obvious.

WILFRED: You ought to hear it as they do it. Gertie Millar and Robert Michaelis.

LILIAN (*ironically*): Wonderful!

WILFRED (*ignoring this, eagerly*): You know—somehow—it completely carried me away. It's rot, I suppose——

LILIAN (*now trying to read*): Of course it's rot.

WILFRED: Yes, but just think. (*Breaks off.*) You *might* listen, Lilian. Hang it all, I'm not always here to tell you things. And I listen to you.

LILIAN (*looking up from book*): Go on then.

WILFRED (*warming as he goes on*): Just think of it. Back from Africa. London. First night on leave. A jolly good dinner with two other chaps from the Company. Then Daly's. Lights, and everybody in the stalls dressed, stunning girls, the band playing—and then Gertie Millar—and—oh—everything. Do you know, Lilian, I felt quite queer. I nearly cried.

LILIAN: Did you?

WILFRED: I didn't really cry, you know. But I nearly did. Felt like it.

LILIAN: That's the only bit you haven't told me twenty times already.

WILFRED (*hotly*): That's not true.

LILIAN: Sorry, but it is. I can tell you the names of the chaps—as you call them—who went with you that night. One was called Patterson, and he comes from Cumberland and he's a good footballer. The other's called Bell—Bell—Bellingham——

WILFRED (*gloomily*): Bellington.

LILIAN: That's it. Not much difference. He's called Bellington and he comes from Devonshire, and he's got a sister who's married to a Captain in the Navy. There!

WILFRED (*getting up, huffily*): Sorry. Didn't know I'd been boring you.

LILIAN (*beginning to read*): You haven't. Don't apologise. (*She looks at him as he stands looking out of the window.*) By the way, you wouldn't like to walk into the village to give an order to Gregson's, would you?

WILFRED: No thanks.

LILIAN: Then I suppose I'll have to go. Soon. (*Begins reading again.*)

WILFRED (*turning to look at her*): Don't you ever get tired of reading?

LILIAN (*without looking up*): Yes.

WILFRED: You're always reading.

LILIAN (*without looking up*): I'm not. I spend most of the day looking after this house, and Dad, and you when you're at home.

WILFRED: Yes, but the minute you've done you begin reading. What's that?

LILIAN: Wells's new book. *Marriage.* (*Goes on reading.*)

WILFRED: You never seem to stop reading H. G. Wells. I don't know how you can stick him. I can't. He always makes me feel so uncomfortable. Doesn't seem to *like* anything. What's the point of reading if it makes you feel uncomfortable? It's bad enough in real life.

LILIAN (*still reading*): That's stupid.

WILFRED: Why is it stupid? (*She gives no reply but goes on reading.*) Geoffrey Farrant was saying just the same thing the other day. (*She looks up. He guffaws.*) I knew that would make you look up.

LILIAN (*crossly*): Don't be absurd. (*Hesitates.*) Did Geoffrey really say that?

WILFRED (*teasing*): Wouldn't you like to know?

LILIAN: It doesn't matter in the least.

WILFRED: Is Geoffrey coming round to-night?

LILIAN: I don't know. He might.

WILFRED (*wandering about, after lighting a cigarette*): Good old Geoffrey! By jove, when I was a kid, about fourteen, I used to think he was marvellous. That was when he was mad on Stella. He was my hero all right; regular soldier, captain, wounded in the Boer War—I used to follow him round like a little dog. I must have been a nuisance when he wanted to be alone with Stella. She used to tease him and say he came round just to be a hero to me. That's a long time ago. Nearly ten years. I say.

LILIAN (*rather wearily*): Well?

WILFRED: You see a lot of Geoffrey these days. Does he ever talk about Stella?

LILIAN (*shortly*): No, why should he? Give me a cigarette.

WILFRED: What for? You don't smoke.

LILIAN: I do if I want to. Give me one, please. (*Holds out hand.*)

WILFRED: Oh, all right, Christabel Pankhurst. (*Giving her one.*) But mind you don't make yourself sick.

LILIAN: Why should I? I'm better at not being sick than you are. You admit yourself you're always seasick.

WILFRED: That's different. Besides, just you try going through the Bay of Biscay in winter—as I've done, three times now.

LILIAN: And then there was the time when we both went on the swings at Martinbro Fair, and you were horribly sick and I wasn't. (*She awkwardly lights cigarette, and then, when it gets going, takes too deep a breath and coughs.*)

WILFRED: You see. Take it easy. What if Dad marches in?

LILIAN: He won't mind. Mother would have minded, but Dad won't. (*She does not make a success of her smoking.*)

WILFRED: One of our chaps in Nigeria told me his father wouldn't let him do *anything*. Terribly strict. That's why he cleared out.

LILIAN: Lucky chap.

WILFRED (*wandering over to the telephone*): You know, when I came home and saw the telephone, brand new, I thought I'd be able to have a lot of fun with it, but I haven't. There's nobody to ring up here in Eden End.

LILIAN: Who were you ringing up yesterday?

WILFRED (*indignantly*): You were listening!

LILIAN: I wasn't. I happened to hear your voice when I was in the hall, putting some things away. Who was it?

WILFRED: Oh—just somebody I know.

LILIAN: A girl, obviously. You're keeping her very dark, aren't you?

WILFRED: I don't know her very well, and, anyhow, she lives miles away, the other side of Martinbro. Never mind about her.

LILIAN: I'm not minding. But I suspect she's a barmaid and that's why you can get her on the telephone.

WILFRED: You know, Lilian, one thing puzzles me.

LILIAN: And if she's a barmaid, on the telephone, and the other side of Martinbro, she's probably at that big pub at the crossroads near Denly Dene—the "White Hart".

WILFRED (*angrily*): Will you listen?

LILIAN: Do you really like her, Wilfred? Or do you just think that being sweet on a barmaid is very manly and West African?

WILFRED: I'm trying to say something important.

LILIAN: Well, what is it?

WILFRED: You don't really want to know. You'll only laugh.

LILIAN: You've got to risk that. I mightn't. Tell me.

WILFRED (*hesitating*): It's difficult to explain. But I feel as if I'm being done in the eye.

LILIAN: You probably are.

WILFRED: You see, when I'm out there, in Africa, I think of Eden End here—home and you and Dad, and everything, and I long for leave, and when at last it comes—well, of course, it's ripping. But then when I've been here a week or two——

LILIAN: It all begins to look dull. Doesn't it?

WILFRED: Well, not quite as bad as that.

LILIAN: Yes it is. Don't sound so apologetic. I don't blame you.

WILFRED: Anyhow it isn't what I expected. And then I begin to think about Nigeria, and I begin to feel it won't be bad getting back there. But now I know that once I *am* back there I'll be longing to be on leave again, and this place will seem all different. I've got into a sort of life where I'm never in the right place at the right time.

LILIAN: Poor Wilfred. You were just like that when you were at school.

WILFRED: I know. And I thought it would be different when I left school and grew up. Perhaps it will, later on.

LILIAN: Perhaps it will. You've plenty of time.

WILFRED: Things can't stay like this. When I've more money I shall have more fun on leave. And it'll be more amusing out there when I'm promoted. It's Nineteen Twelve now. In three or four years time—say in Nineteen Sixteen, I may have a district of my own.

LILIAN: Could I come out and see you then?

WILFRED: You might. Depends where I'm sent.

LILIAN: You may be married before then.

WILFRED: I don't suppose so. Three or four years isn't really a long time. Hurry up, Nineteen Sixteen. Sounds a nice ripe sort of year, doesn't it?—Nineteen Sixteen.

From the door on left come three deliberate knocks. The two look at it sharply, rather startled—though they must avoid any nervous jump. WILFRED *goes to the door and opens it.* SARAH *enters, carrying a large basket heaped with old clothes.*

SARAH (*breathlessly*): I didn't want to put this down to open the door because I'm not so good at stooping as I was—gives me palpitations—and I've been stooping enough.

LILIAN: What have you been doing?

SARAH: I've been up in the back garret, samming up these old clothes for the doctor. He wants to give 'em away. (*She comes forward as she says this and rests the basket on the table.*) Eh, and look what I found. (*Holds out an old fancy costume.*)

LILIAN: What is it?

SARAH: Don't you remember? It's very same dress Miss Stella wore that time she acted in the Town Hall at Martinbro, and they all clapped her so long, and she came back and told her poor mother she was going on the stage for a living, and we had such a do—all shouting and bawling and crying. Don't you remember it?

WILFRED: I do.

LILIAN: Yes, I do now.

SARAH: And I should think so. I helped her to make it, and right bonny she looked in it. But she never took it with her when she went, and it's been behind some boxes in the back garret. I fancy your mother threw it there. Moths has been at it a bit, but I'm thinking it'ud clean and mend.

LILIAN: What for? It's quite useless.

SARAH: How do you know? We might send it to her and she might be glad of it for her acting.

WILFRED (laughing): You're cracked, Sarah.

SARAH (indignant): What's there to laugh at, I'd like to know?

LILIAN: Nothing. Only, you see, we couldn't send it to Stella— even if it would be useful—because we don't know where she is.

SARAH: Isn't she out—you know—where's it? That big place?

WILFRED: Timbuctoo.

SARAH: Not Timbuctoo neither, you daft lad. It's where she said there was all eucalyptus.

LILIAN: It was Australia. But that was three years ago, and we haven't heard anything from her since.

SARAH: Is it three years since we heard last?

LILIAN: Yes. And she's been away more than eight years.

SARAH (her face working as she fingers the costume): I didn't think it was so long. I'm getting old and I forget. I'm dreaming half my time.

LILIAN (looking at the costume): I remember. It was pretty. I believe I was jealous because I hadn't one like it.

SARAH: Yes, you wor. You wor a jealous little madam in them days, let me tell you. See. I sewed them on myself for her. It was all a secret. She used to sneak in there (pointing to door on right) to try it on. It only seems yesterday. I mun sort these out.

WILFRED: Here, I'll take them.

Picks up basket, etc., and takes them into room on right. SARAH *moves towards door, after him, carrying the costume.*

SARAH (turning): Your father's in. He called at Gregson's. (The *telephone bell rings. She looks at it mistrustfully.*) That wants answering now. Daft thing. Got to wait on a machine, that's what we're coming to. It'll never get me waiting on it, and it can ring its head off.

She goes into room on right. LILIAN *goes to the telephone, but* DR. KIRBY *enters quickly and forestalls her. He is a pleasant homely man about sixty, wearing an old house coat over a dark professional suit. He attends to the telephone rather pompously and proudly.*

DR. KIRBY (*at telephone*): Hello, yes. Yes, Dr. Kirby here. Oh— is that you, William? . . . She's what? . . . Oh I see . . . Well, what do you expect? . . . No pains? . . . I see . . . Yes, keep her warm. And don't worry. Nothing new. It's all happened before. . . . That's right, let me know. And, William, just keep out of the Eden Moor Hotel for a night or two, will you? . . . That's it. You're not in the right state of mind to do yourself any good in the bar of the Eden Moor . . . (*chuckles*). All right. Don't worry. (*Puts down receiver and begins lighting his pipe.*) William Sugden worrying about his wife. She'll be all right. Stronger than he is. Now it just shows you, Lilian, how useful a telephone is here. That little chat across the wires has saved William or me a useless journey. Pity we hadn't it here years ago. We're too old-fashioned round here. Out of date.

LILIAN: You don't think you're out of date, do you?

DR. KIRBY: Me? Years out of date. I've just been trying to understand what some of these young fellows are writing now in the medical journals. Too clever for me. Too Nineteen Twelve altogether. But I could probably give 'em points when it comes to dealing with William Sugden and his wife. (*As* WILFRED *enters from room on right.*) Hello, Wilfred, what have you been doing in there?

WILFRED: Helping Sarah to sort out some old clothes for you.

DR. KIRBY: Good. They can do with some of them down in the village. Lloyd George is going to give 'em ninepence for fourpence soon, with me thrown in, but in the meantime we'll give them some old clothes to be going on with.

WILFRED: Would you like to hear my gramophone, Dad?

DR. KIRBY: No, thank you. I've got to get back to the surgery. But if I was staying I'd just as soon not hear your gramophone. I've got to listen to too many patients to want to hear mechanical music— if it is music. By the way, old Burton tells me they had a fire in the post office at Martinbro late last night. He said they think it's suffragettes. Lot of nonsense. They've got suffragettes on the brain, some of 'em. (*Goes to door on left.*)

WILFRED: Well, it might be, Dad.

DR. KIRBY (*turning at door*): What, at Martinbro! What would they be doing there? Looking for Mr. Asquith! All nonsense. And talking about nonsense, I forgot to tell you I've just been invited to dine at Grosvenor House with the Duke of Westminster.

LILIAN and WILFRED (*together*): Dad, you haven't?

DR. KIRBY: I have. And so has everybody else. The only condition is that we each pay a thousand pounds to Chamberlain's birthday fund for Tariff Reform. I'm not accepting. (*He goes out and* LILIAN *settles down to read again.*)

WILFRED (*restlessly*): We ought to have a billiard table here. If I got more chance to play, I believe I should be good at billiards. I made a break of twenty-seven when I played at the club at Akassa.

LILIAN (*staring at him, quietly*): Isn't it ridiculous that you should go to all these places while I have to stay here?

WILFRED: No, I don't see that.

LILIAN: But I used to be much more adventurous than you, and much keener on exploring and wild places. I'll bet I've read far more about Africa than you have.

WILFRED: What's that? Reading about it! I've been.

LILIAN: I believe I'd rather have gone with Captain Scott to the South Pole than done anything in the world. And if he lectures about it when he comes back I shall go, I don't care where it is.

WILFRED: Well, you can't be so jolly adventurous—as you call it— else you'd have cleared out. After all, Stella did.

LILIAN (*rather bitterly*): Yes, Stella did. And what happened then? Mother died. Father was left, miserable, with nobody to look after him. As soon as I'd done with school I'd obviously got to come back here and look after things. It's easy enough to do what Stella did— just to clear out and do what you want to do.

WILFRED: Yes, but she knew what she wanted to do.

LILIAN: Perhaps I did, too.

WILFRED: You know, that night I went to Daly's, I thought how queer it would be if I suddenly saw Stella come on the stage.

LILIAN (*with slight sardonic emphasis*): Very queer.

WILFRED: I always look at advertisements and programmes and bills to see if she's on. It's silly having a sister on the stage if you've never *seen* her on the stage. Wouldn't it be grand if she became a star—like Gertie Millar or Phyllis Dare?

LILIAN (*sardonically*): Yes. And if the British West African Company suddenly appointed you managing director. And if the King fell ill and they all said, "Send for Dr. Kirby of Eden End." And if

Pierpoint Morgan or Rockefeller said "I must give Lilian Kirby a million pounds, she's been such a good girl."

WILFRED (*guffawing*): And if old Sarah won a prize for doing the Turkey Trot. And if Geoffrey Farrant—what do we do for Geoffrey?

LILIAN: Something with horses or dogs in it.

WILFRED: We'll let him win next year's Derby then. You're not very keen on horses and dogs, are you?

LILIAN (*coldly*): What's that got to do with it?

WILFRED (*grinning*): Nothing.

LILIAN: Don't be an oaf.

WILFRED: One of our chaps in Benin used to own two race-horses when he was in England. Awful nut. What about a good old row on the gramophone?

LILIAN: Must you?

WILFRED (*going over to gramophone*): Yes, I must. I shall take this back with me. (*Putting on record.*) You know, these things are getting awfully good.

> *Plays a tune. If lighting is changed, this is the time to change it. While the record is being played,* WILFRED *can light one lamp and* LILIAN *another. Before record is quite finished* LILIAN, *who is nearer door on left, must listen and hold up her hand.* WILFRED *takes off the record. They hear a voice coming through the door. The voice,* STELLA'S, *must be audible everywhere, but it does not matter if actual words are not caught. Actually she is saying "Yes, put it down there, please. What do I pay you? There you are. Thank you."* STELLA *is five or six years older than* LILIAN, *and looks her age, but is extremely attractive. She is dressed as an actress, hoping to be smart, would be dressed at that time, but her clothes must not be really good or very new, so that it is obvious to an acute feminine spectator that she is not really flourishing. She plays at once in a higher key than the rest of the family, and is obviously an actress as well as a prodigal daughter. All her emotions are quite sincere, but she cannot help being a little larger than life. This gradually wears off during her stay until the scene of her departure, when there are glimpses of the actress again.*

WILFRED: Stella!

STELLA: Oh it's Wilfred. All grown up. And a moustache. (*Embraces and kisses him. Then looks at* LILIAN.) And Lilian. All grown up, too. Here, let me take this damned hat off. (*Hastily takes it off and flings it aside, then rushes over to* LILIAN *and embraces and kisses her.*) Lilian darling, you're not at all what I expected you to look like, and yet you're completely Lilian and just right. Isn't it odd? (*Looking round,*) And everything just the same. Only smaller.

> SARAH *comes in and stands just inside, from door on right, staring at* STELLA *with puckered face.*

STELLA (*seeing her, and rushing over*): Why, Sarah. My precious, precious lovely old Sarah! (*Kisses her.*)

SARAH (*in tears*): Nay—I can't talk.

STELLA (*laughing and crying*): And I can't.

SARAH (*making an effort*): Eh—you haven't altered a bit, love.

STELLA: Oh, but I have. I'm old, Sarah—yes, old. I'll never see thirty again. My hair's turning grey.

SARAH: It isn't.

STELLA: Some of it is. I pulled three grey hairs out yesterday. Where's Dad? Is he—all right?

LILIAN: Yes. He's in the surgery.

WILFRED: Shall I tell him?

STELLA: No, don't disturb him. We'll give him a surprise. Is he just the same?

WILFRED: Of course.

STELLA: *Of course?* There isn't any *of course* about it. Oh Wilfred—that just shows how young you are, in spite of that moustache. People change. Everything changes. Does he still watch birds and collect eighteenth-century engravings?

LILIAN: Yes. Dad hasn't changed at all.

STELLA: Thank God!

LILIAN: But why didn't you tell us you were coming?

STELLA: Oh—my dear—I couldn't. I didn't know. And I couldn't just write. I think I was afraid to. Either I had to stay away or come just like this, with a rush. Don't you understand?

LILIAN: Yes. You'd been away so long.

STELLA: So long. And to so many places.

WILFRED: Where have you been, Stella?

STELLA: Where haven't I been? All over England. Then out East. Then Australia—I wrote to you from there——

SARAH: Yes, you did, love.

STELLA: I was nearly dying of homesickness when I wrote that letter. You can't imagine what it's like.

WILFRED (*proudly*): I can. I'm in Nigeria now. Got a job with the British West African Development Company. I'm on leave.

STELLA (*smiling at him*): Africa and on leave. Wilfred, it's incredible. It seems only yesterday since you were a fat little schoolboy. I'm sorry but it does. I didn't really believe in that moustache. Somehow I thought of you just sticking it on for fun.

WILFRED: I'm twenty-four. I've been four years with the British West African.

STELLA: Isn't that wonderful? And then after Australia, I went to America. We travelled thousands of miles. I seem to have lived in railway trains—with cinders in my eye and a headache—for centuries. None of it real. Like a long stupid dream. And now I'm home. You don't know what it means.

SARAH: Aren't you famished, love? Can't I get you something?

STELLA: No, thank you. Not just now, Sarah. (*She looks about her.*) It's just as I remembered it, only so much smaller. All the time I've been away, it's been shrinking and shrinking. Like life. Oh—(*darting over*)—there's the china castle. Still there. Not broken. All sorts of things can get broken—people can be broken—and yet a thing like this can go on and on. (*Holding it, looking at it.*) I remember how I used to wonder what was happening inside it. Tiny people all made of china.

WILFRED: You used to tell me stories about that castle.

STELLA: And look—the boy's still riding on his goat. What did we used to call him?

LILIAN: Llewellyn. Because he came from Wales.

STELLA: Yes. Dear, dear Llewellyn. His nice silly face has come popping up in dreams. I saw him distinctly once—oh, when was it?—on some long, awful train journey, hot and dusty. And there was Llewellyn riding his goat. (*Goes round touching things.*) And here's Coblentz. (*Looking at old colour print.*) The three soldiers talking. The man carrying the load. The woman with the red petticoat. And the two holding hands. Do you remember how we used to look at it for hours and wonder what was happening round the corner? But where's the other one, you know, Frankfort, with the river and the barges and the little fat woman?

WILFRED: Yes, where is Frankfort? I hadn't noticed it was gone.

SARAH: That's the picture that fell down, isn't it?

LILIAN: Yes, it was broken. About a year ago.

STELLA: Tell me about people. The Mowbrays and the Oldroyds and the Burtons—and everybody. Oh—and my old admirer, Geoffrey Farrant. What's happened to him?

LILIAN: He's still here. His father died.

STELLA: Is he married? Do you ever see him?

LILIAN: He's not married.

WILFRED: And we often see him. He's a great pal of Lilian's now.

LILIAN: Where are your things?

STELLA: My trunk? It's in the hall. I got a trap from the station, but I didn't know the man who brought me. I didn't recognise anybody at the station either. But Eden Moor and Eden End looked just the same. And, coming up, there was a lovely deep rich autumn smell—smoke and dead leaves and the moors all mixed up—and I was absolutely drowned in it and I didn't seem to have been away at all. Millions of smells, mostly beastly, that I've smelt these last eight or nine years were completely washed out. Nothing had really happened. I might have only been in to Martinbro for the day. You were still at school, Wilfred. You'd only just left, Lilian, and you'd still two long plaits. And Dad and Mother—— (*she breaks off, hesitates, then in a low voice.*) Was it awful, Lilian—about Mother?

LILIAN (*quietly*): Yes, for a time. But it's six years ago, you know. She wasn't ill very long, but she'd a lot of pain. It was Dad I was sorry for. (STELLA *begins to cry quietly.*)

SARAH (*going to her*): Miss Stella—love.

STELLA (*through her tears*): Such a silly thing happened in the train. A man sitting opposite me—he looked like Winston Churchill, only fatter—carefully unpacked a lot of sandwiches on the seat, stood up for something, and then suddenly sat down on the sandwiches. There was another woman in the carriage, and we suddenly laughed and laughed, and then the man laughed too. They were very eggy sandwiches. Why are some things so silly?

WILFRED: Do you remember the time when a little man with a very funny face—what was his name?—Flockton—he'd known Dad at college—and we started giggling and then had to go outside in turns to laugh?

STELLA: Yes, Mr. Flockton. And it was much worse for me because I was so much older and I had to be polite. And then the time when poor Aunt Mary brought that new bun flour?

WILFRED: Yes, and the time when the young man called Egg-something came to see you and dropped the tea tray?

LILIAN: And the time when we all went to the Mowbrays for a party on the wrong day?

STELLA: And the snow was so thick we had to stay and they were so cross, and we were so cross, and all the chimneys smoked. (*Laughs.*)

WILFRED (*laughing*): And I broke a huge ornament and put the pieces in the coal scuttle.

STELLA: I was thinking about all those things coming up in the train. And I've got millions of questions to ask.

WILFRED: So have we, haven't we, Lilian?

LILIAN: I suppose you'd like your old room, wouldn't you?

STELLA: I'd love it if it's free.

LILIAN: It's full of odds and ends at the moment——

SARAH (*eagerly*): I'll get it ready, Miss Lilian.

LILIAN: No, I'll do it. Wilfred can give me a hand. There may be some furniture to move.

WILFRED: Rather!

STELLA: Can't I do anything?

LILIAN: No. You're tired. Besides you don't know where things are now. And Dad will be in in a minute. You wait here. (*She goes out.*)

WILFRED: You know, Stella, when you were home I was only a kid and didn't bother about the theatre, but now I'm very keen. I saw "Gipsy Love" at Daly's a few weeks ago—and you've got to tell me all about it.

STELLA: All right. I'll tell you miles and miles of it.

SARAH *goes into room on right.*

WILFRED: Good. I expect you've done jolly well, haven't you? I was telling Lilian only this afternoon how I always looked out for your name, but never saw it.

STELLA: I've been out of England so much, you see.

WILFRED: Yes, that accounts for it. Well, you're looking an awful swell.

STELLA: I should have thought I was looking like nothing on earth.

WILFRED: I expect you've had a marvellous time, haven't you?

STELLA: Well—mixed, you know.

WILFRED: You'll find it pretty dull here.

STELLA: I shan't. (*Draws a long breath.*) It's heavenly. Even though you have been in Africa and come on leave you can't imagine what it means to me to be back again—home. It's real. Everything's real again.

SARAH *re-enters, carrying dress behind her back.*

WILFRED: I'm going to give Lilian a hand with your room. Then I'll come down and ask you thousands of questions. (*Hesitates.*) I say, you don't think this moustache looks silly, do you?

STELLA: Wilfred, it's a *grand* moustache, and you look a real

African adventurer with it. It's tremendously exciting to be a sister to such a moustache. In a year or two it's going to be a terrific heart-breaker.

WILFRED (*smiling*): You're pulling my leg. You always did, you know.

STELLA: Well, isn't it nice that I'm starting all over again?

WILFRED (*shyly*): Yes. (*Smiles.*) Good old Stella! (*Goes out.*)

STELLA *looks after him and smiles. Then she turns and sees* SARAH.

STELLA: I think Wilfred's grown up to be a very nice young man. Don't you?

SARAH: Oh—Master Wilfred's all right. But he's only a bit of a lad, for all his big talk. Miss Lilian's different. She's properly grown up. Always was a bit old-fashioned. Never gave herself away. And there's times now when—dang me!—you'd think she wor fifty—to hear her talk. Not that she talks much.

STELLA: I don't suppose poor Lilian's had a very easy life all these years I've been away. She's a bit—queer. Sort of sunk into herself. On her guard, somehow. Almost as if I were a stranger. Perhaps I am a stranger, Sarah. But I don't seem like one to myself—only Stella Kirby, back home again in Eden End.

SARAH: And look what I found—not an hour since—it might ha' been waiting for you to come home. Look. (*Holds out fancy costume.*)

STELLA: Why it's the one I wore, ages ago, in that show at the Town Hall at Martinbro. The one you and I made, Sarah.

SARAH: I know it is. I was going to clean and mend it. Moths has been at it.

STELLA: The moths have been at us all, Sarah darling. But I never thought I'd see this costume again. The excitement there was here about it! Do you remember?

SARAH: I should think I do.

STELLA: I thought I was a real actress the night I put this on.

SARAH: Well, they clapped you enough.

STELLA: More than some people have clapped me since. That was the night. Look at it. Pathetic!

SARAH: Why, I see nowt wrong wi' it, except where moths has been. It's a right bonny dress. I thowt so then and I think so now.

STELLA: So do I. It's a lovely dress. I must put it on. Oh, I've torn it! The belle and leading juvenile of the Martinbro Amateur Dramatic Society. And fat old Mr. Burton gave me a box of chocolates, do you remember?

Sarah: Ay, and he'd have given a lot more besides chocolates if you'd let him, that chap would. I've heard tales of him since.

Stella *poses and curtsies before* Sarah.

Sarah: Eh, I'm thankful to have seen this day, love. I've prayed to be spared to see you come home.

Stella: I'm sorry I have been so long.

Sarah: You didn't forget me?

Stella: Never, never, never. All over the world, in the oddest places, I've thought about you, longed to see you again. You needn't pray any more. I've come home. (*Kisses her.*)

Sarah (*looking hard at her*): You've always been a bonny piece. You wor a grand baby, and a fine little lass, and a bonny young woman when you grew up.

Stella: Bless you for those kind words.

Sarah: But there's lines in that face that weren't there when I last saw it.

Stella: I'm getting on. And all those years I was away haven't been easy.

Sarah: No, that's it. I can see as much. You've had your troubles, haven't you? (*When* Stella *does not reply.*) Nay, you can tell me even if you never tell another soul. I'll say nowt.

Stella: Yes. I've had my troubles.

Sarah: Disappointments?

Stella: Yes. A fair share.

Sarah (*gently*): Didn't they treat you well on the stage, love?

Stella: Nearly as well as I deserved, I suppose. But—and this is our secret, Sarah—I wasn't the great actress I thought I was going to be. I wasn't bad. I'm not bad. But somehow I've never been able to do what I thought I could do. Something gets in the way. I feel it all inside, but it doesn't come out right. I've disappointed myself. I think even mother would have been sorry for me if she'd known. I don't say I've had wonderful chances, but I have had chances. And somehow I've missed them. Perhaps I came nearer to being a really good actress the night I wore this pathetic thing than I've ever done since. It's all gone wrong, Sarah, my dear. My work, my life. Oh—(*tears off the dress*)—I'm a dismal failure. (*Breaking down.*)

Sarah: Don't worry, love, don't worry. There's plenty of time. You're young.

Stella: No, I'm not.

Sarah: I think I hear the doctor.

STELLA (*springing up, alarmed*): Dad mustn't see me like this. (*Begins doing her face.*) And he mustn't know.

SARAH (*fussing over her*): He won't from me. Nobody will. I'll see if he's there.

> *She goes to door on left.* STELLA *hastily concludes her powdering and begins to look brighter.* SARAH *goes out, leaving the door open, and* DR. KIRBY *comes to the doorway and stands amazed.*

DR. KIRBY: Is it Stella?

STELLA: Yes, Father. (*Then, with a little cry, she runs over to him, and he meets her at the bottom of the steps and they kiss and hug one another.*)

STELLA: You're just the same, Dad. Only a little greyer, that's all.

DR. KIRBY: No, I'm a lot older. And you're older too, you know. I'm not going to flatter you even if you are a famous actress. You look a bit tired. But then I expect you are after your journey. Where did you come from?

STELLA: London. I caught the eleven o'clock to Martinbro.

DR. KIRBY: Ah, yes—the good old eleven o'clock. Why didn't you let us know? We'd have had the fatted calf ready for you.

STELLA: I couldn't. I came—oh—it was a sudden impulse. I'm still impulsive, you know.

DR. KIRBY: We thought you'd forgotten us.

STELLA: I've never forgotten you for a single moment. How could I? But I've been out of England for years—touring, working hard. My plans always seemed so confused. It was difficult to write.

DR. KIRBY: Yes, I can understand that, though in a quiet corner like this we're apt to forget what the hustling and bustling world—*your* world—is like. You know, Stella, I've been thinking a lot just lately—(*his voice trails away.*)

STELLA (*after a pause*): Yes, Father?

DR. KIRBY: Something happened that made me start thinking. You might call it taking stock. Thinking about life—my life—your life. You know, I've come to the conclusion that you were right, and your mother and I were wrong.

STELLA (*hastily, painfully*): No, no——

DR. KIRBY: That's all right. It's all old history now. We can talk frankly and freely now. And you're a grown-up woman, not a bit of a girl. You were right to do what you did. I'm not saying that you didn't cause any pain——

STELLA: I did, I know.

DR. KIRBY: But that wasn't your fault. That's life. Life can't move on without inflicting pain. We can't come into this world without somebody being hurt. As well I know. I shall be lucky if I don't see a bit more of it late to-night. The great cosmic processes have a habit of reaching a climax round here just when I've got comfortably off to sleep.

STELLA: Poor Dad. Who is it this time?

DR. KIRBY: A Mrs. Sugden. I think she's since your time. Well, I think I've done my duty by her and her like in this neighbourhood for nearly forty years.

STELLA: I know you have. And I'm sure they still worship you.

DR. KIRBY: Not they. I only wish they'd pay a bit more attention and then pay a few more bills. But I'm not complaining. I've had a good life here. Your mother and I were happy. We'd all the friends we wanted. This has been a real home. Even to you, it was once.

STELLA (*softly*): Do you think I could forget it?

DR. KIRBY: And then, besides my work and my family, I'd my little hobbies—my birds. (*With sudden animation.*) And by the way, don't let anybody tell you that you can't see a needle-tailed swift in this country, because I saw one myself, only this last summer. A needle-tailed swift. No mistake about it.

STELLA (*affectionately, laughing*): Oh—Dad—I won't let anybody tell me. I'll put them in their place at once.

DR. KIRBY: That's right. There's as much clap-trap talked about birds now as there is about anything else. Why, only the other day——

STELLA (*laughing*): But Dad, you can't go on about birds now. You were just going to tell me something important, something serious.

DR. KIRBY (*with a twinkle*): Well, this is important.

STELLA: Yes, and I'd love to hear it, but that will do any time. Perhaps this other thing won't.

DR. KIRBY (*seriously*): That's true. This is something I wouldn't say to the younger children. What I was going to say was this. Looking back on my life, it's been a reasonably good one——

STELLA: And you wouldn't change it.

DR. KIRBY: That's where you're wrong. I would.

STELLA (*surprised*): Dad!

DR. KIRBY: There was a time when I had to make a choice.

STELLA: Between this—and another kind of life?

DR. KIRBY: Yes. I wasn't always a plodding old G.P., you know, years behind the times. Once, I was thought to be a very clever young man. I had a brilliant career as a student. Then I had to make a choice, between settling down here, quietly and comfortably, or taking a risk in London. I might have failed there. On the other hand, I might have been successful. Men who walked the hospitals when I did, men who hadn't the reputation I had, have been very successful. Some of them—I could give you their names—have been knighted and so forth, are now rich and famous.

STELLA: Pooh!—what's that!

DR. KIRBY: Mere vulgar rewards, if you like.

STELLA: In Harley Street you'd never have seen a bird—except a dirty London sparrow.

DR. KIRBY: I'm not envying them, Stella. Nevertheless, they've had brilliant careers, done original work, met all the great personalities of their time, missed none of the prizes of life.

STELLA: How do you know? They've missed the larks on Eden Moor.

DR. KIRBY: The larks and the moors are there if they want them, and they've probably more leisure now to enjoy such things than I have. And, in addition, they've had all the rest. They've lived as I haven't lived, and as you—I'm glad to say—*are* living. You were right, Stella, to cut and run when you did. And now, looking back when it's all nearly ended——

STELLA (*sharply*): Don't talk like that, Father. You're not old yet.

DR. KIRBY (*firmly*): I say, looking back when it's all nearly ended, I wish now that I'd had the same sort of courage.

STELLA: It's not courage.

DR. KIRBY: I won't envy my—er—distinguished colleagues. But I can envy you, my dear. And I do. You made a bolt for the main road. You're doing what you always wanted to do, and you've made a success of it, gone all over the world, been applauded and admired everywhere, given pleasure to thousands and thousands——

STELLA (*jumping up, in distress*): Oh—Dad—please, please stop.

DR. KIRBY (*astonished*): What's the matter? I never knew actresses suffered from such modesty.

STELLA (*trying to take hold of herself*): It isn't that.

DR. KIRBY: What is it then?

STELLA: Oh—I don't know. Perhaps it's hearing *you* say these things.

DR. KIRBY: Don't try to be kind to me. It's the truth, and you know it.

STELLA (*bursting out*): It's—— (*Checks herself.*) Well, I suppose it's embarrassing.

DR KIRBY: I can talk to you properly. I see you now as a grown-up person.

STELLA (*with irony*): Thank you, Dad.

DR KIRBY: Ah well—it's not easy for a parent. I suppose I ought to see Lilian and Wilfred as grown-up people now, too, but I can't. Not only because they're younger than you, but because there hasn't been the same break. I ought to be frank with them, but it's difficult.

STELLA (*gravely*): You can be frank with me, then?

DR. KIRBY: Yes. I find it quite easy.

STELLA (*after an effort*): Then—then why did you talk about "looking back when it's all nearly ended"? You're not really old, you know.

DR. KIRBY: I'm not young.

STELLA (*relieved*): Oh—is that all?

DR. KIRBY: No, I'm afraid it isn't. There's something I can tell you that I can't tell the other two. You can stand it. They can't. You're older. You have your profession. You're enjoying life. You've really done with us. So you can stand it.

STELLA *laughs bitterly.*

DR. KIRBY: What does that mean?

STELLA: Nothing. Go on. I can stand it. (*Suddenly alert, alarmed.*) Dad—does this mean that there's something wrong with you—that you're ill?

DR. KIRBY: Take it easy, Stella. I'm afraid it does. (*Smiling.*) One advantage of being in my profession is that you get to know what's happening inside you. I've got a bad heart. I had a very nasty bout of influenza a few years ago, and I did a very silly thing, the sort of thing I've warned hundreds of people against doing. I got up and started work again far too early. So I landed myself with a bad heart.

STELLA: But—what's wrong with it?

DR. KIRBY (*easily*): A lot of things. It's worse than my old bike. But you might describe the trouble—shortly—as a valvular lesion with inefficient compensation. Oh—I do what I can about it, of course. I don't work as hard as I used to do, though it's not easy to rest here. And I give myself digitalis—and other things. I get along—but——

STELLA: It's serious—then?

DR. KIRBY (*smiling*): No joke at all. In fact—I'm very glad you've come to see us now.

STELLA (*very distressed*): Dad!

DR. KIRBY: Easy, Stella! It seems a shabby trick landing you with this the minute you arrive, but I think you might have noticed something. And I'm telling you quite frankly so that you won't discuss it with Lilian and Wilfred. It's our little secret. Not much of one—but there you are.

STELLA: I shan't say anything.

DR. KIRBY: That's right. They haven't settled down to their lives yet as you have to yours. In fact, I'm sometimes a bit worried about Lilian. I'm not grumbling about myself. I've had a good run. I'd like to live long enough to see this country settling down a bit better.

STELLA: Oh—bother the country, I don't care about that. It's you.

DR. KIRBY: Yes, but this has been a very unsettling, worrying year so far. Two big strikes. Ulster arming for rebellion. Young women being forcibly fed in gaol. This health insurance business. Everybody wanting to rush about at thirty and forty miles an hour, up in the air as well as on the roads. Not much sunset calm about things. But in a year or two we may have settled down again. I like to think so.

STELLA (*in low voice*): I hope so—for your sake.

DR. KIRBY (*briskly*): Ah well—that's enough about me. Dismal stuff. I've got to hear about all your triumphs. Been all over the place, haven't you?

STELLA (*with forced animation*): Yes, all over. Like a crazy parcel.

DR. KIRBY: And enjoyed it, eh? Constant change, excitement, applause, eh? But don't let it spoil you.

STELLA (*with little ironic smile*): I'll do my best, Dad. Unless I'm spoilt already.

DR. KIRBY: No sign of it. I was against you leaving home and going on the stage, but chiefly, I think, for your mother's sake. I believe it does girls good to go out into the world.

STELLA: Sometimes.

DR. KIRBY (*lowering voice*): I've never said anything to her—and of course I've been glad to have her here—but I've often thought that Lilian's been at home too long. She might have done a lot better for herself if she'd followed your example and found something she wanted to do away from home. Don't tell her that.

STELLA: I won't. But probably she stayed on simply because I went For your sake.

DR. KIRBY (*heartily*): Oh no, I don't think so. I never asked her to stay. She likes being at home. A lot of girls do, of course. Quite natural. (*Looks at his watch.*) Must be nearly supper time. Where's Lilian? (*Goes to door on left.*)

STELLA: I ought to be doing something.

DR. KIRBY: Nonsense. You're a guest. The work here's easy, and we've plenty to do it. Lilian and old Sarah—and a woman from the village comes in every day. (LILIAN *enters.*) Ah, Lilian, I was just wondering about supper. Stella must be hungry.

LILIAN: It'll be ready in about ten minutes.

DR. KIRBY: Good. (*Goes out, closing door behind him,* LILIAN *advancing into the room.*)

LILIAN: Your room's ready now, if you want to go up. And Wilfred's taken your trunk upstairs.

STELLA: Thanks, Lilian. I suppose I ought to go up. I'm probably filthy, but I've been too excited to care.

LILIAN: You look all right.

STELLA: We old travellers know all sorts of dodges. (*Stares at* LILIAN.)

LILIAN: What's the matter?

STELLA: You know—you're different.

LILIAN: Naturally. It's such a long time since you saw me last.

STELLA: Are you happy?

LILIAN (*rather impatiently*): I don't know. Isn't that—rather a silly question?

STELLA: Is it?

LILIAN: I think so. I mean, one isn't always asking oneself about happiness.

STELLA: I am.

LILIAN: Yes, you. You always were.

STELLA: And whether you ask or not, after all, you always know whether you're happy or not.

LILIAN: Most of the time one isn't either happy or unhappy.

STELLA: Like you—now?

LILIAN: Like me—now.

STELLA (*going over to her*): But there's something about you I don't understand.

LILIAN: Well, why bother?

STELLA (*taking her hands*): But, my dear, I want to bother. You talk as if we were strangers.

LILIAN: Aren't we? We haven't set eyes on one another for years.

STELLA: Yes, but I've been thinking about you all the time.

LILIAN: Even if you have, that's not enough. I'd only just left school when you went away. I'm quite different.

STELLA: I see that.

LILIAN (*looking down at* STELLA's *left hand*): We'll get to know one another again—perhaps. But don't force it.

STELLA (*trying to smile*): And that's not meant for a snub, I hope?

LILIAN (*gravely*): No. Tell me something.

STELLA (*lightly*): Anything.

LILIAN (*in low voice*): You're married, aren't you?

STELLA (*startled, but in low voice*): Yes. How did you know?

LILIAN: I saw the mark of the ring. (STELLA *stares at her left hand and rubs the ring finger.*)

STELLA (*troubled*): I'd probably have told you all—later. But please don't say anything—yet.

LILIAN: What happened?

STELLA: I married three years ago—in Australia. He was an actor, in the same company. After the first year it didn't work—very well. We've separated now.

LILIAN: Where is he?

STELLA: A week ago I couldn't have told you. We separated in America. But three days ago I called at my agent's in town—and I saw him there. We have the same agent. It was queer.

LILIAN: What's his name?

STELLA: Charles Appleby. He's not famous or anything. Just a goodish actor. Very nice family. And he can be quite charming—at times. We were very happy together for a little while.

LILIAN: And now you're separated.

STELLA (*with a pitiful smile*): Yes. All bust up. Yet I'm not really Stella Kirby any more, but Mrs. Charles Appleby, not living with her husband.

LILIAN: Is there going to be a divorce?

STELLA: I don't know. (*There is a ring heard through door on left.*) It's all a muddle. Let's stop talking about it. And please, Lilian, don't say anything. We'll talk afterwards, if you like.

Voices heard outside door on left. STELLA *and* LILIAN *look towards it. the latter expectantly.* WILFRED *enters, followed by* GEOFFREY FARRANT *and* DR. KIRBY. FARRANT *is a fair brown-faced man in his late thirties, dressed in tweeds. There is still something of the regular officer in his appearance. He walks with a slight limp.*

WILFRED: Stella, look who's here. Miss Kirby, this is Captain Farrant.

STELLA (*with animation*): Geoffrey! (*Holding out her hand.*)

FARRANT: Stella! (*Shaking hands.*) This *is* a surprise. (*Turning, off-handedly.*) Hello, Lilian.

STELLA: You've hardly changed at all, Geoffrey. How have you managed it?

FARRANT (*pleased and shy*): Oh—I don't know—quiet life—plenty of exercise, riding—that sort of thing. (*Looking at her, smilingly.*) You've not changed much yourself, you know.

STELLA: Not much! I suppose that really means I'm looking a hag?

FARRANT: Of course it doesn't. Anything but——. Matter of fact, you're looking prettier than ever. Isn't she, Dr. Kirby?

STELLA: Well, it's terribly nice seeing you again, Geoffrey. And so soon, too. I'd hardly hoped for that. And still living at the old place, too.

FARRANT: Yes, still at the old place. It's mine now, you know.

STELLA: Do you remember the birthday party you had, just after your leg got better, and we let that enormous pig loose from the farm?

FARRANT (*laughing*): Good lord, yes. Do you remember that?

STELLA: Of course I do. I remember everything. And that time when old Birtley got so drunk when the beagles were meeting at your house?

WILFRED: By jove, I remember that.

FARRANT: I should think you do. So do I. Poor old Birtley. I say, Stella, we *have* got something to talk about. It's going to take us days——

LILIAN (*cutting in*): Supper will be ready in a few minutes. I'll ask Sarah to tell you. (*Moving to door on left.*)

DR. KIRBY: Why, where are *you* going, Lilian?

LILIAN (*shortly*): I'm going to bed. I don't want any supper. I've got a headache. Good night. (*Goes out quickly.*)

FARRANT (*after a pause*): Oh I say—poor old Lilian.

DR. KIRBY: Didn't know she wasn't feeling well.

WILFRED (*carelessly*): She'll be all right. Just one of her moods. She's very queer sometimes. Best to leave her alone.

FARRANT: Excitement, perhaps. Stella coming back, eh?

WILFRED: I say, Stella, did you see "Gipsy Love" at Daly's? I did. Been trying to play bits ever since. (*Going to piano.*) I've got the music of some of the new musical comedies. (*Holds up sheets.*) You're just the person I wanted. Come and play some of them.

STELLA: What, now?

WILFRED: Why not? Just a minute or two.

FARRANT: Go on, Stella. Fine to see you at the piano again. (*With mock air of gallantry, leads her over to the piano.*)

STELLA (*laughing*): All right. (*Sits down.*)

WILFRED: Try this one.

STELLA *begins playing a popular waltz number, with* WILFRED *standing by the piano and* FARRANT *looking on admiringly, and* DR. KIRBY, *seated, beating time. As she gets into the swing of the waltz she begins singing.* SARAH *opens door on left, and stands in doorway, smiling. Slow curtain as the music goes on.*

END OF ACT ONE

ACT II

Same as ACT I. *Afternoon four days later.*

WILFRED *is discovered. He is very uneasy. He approaches the telephone, hesitates, listens, then goes to door on left, looks to see if anybody is about, closes the door and comes back to telephone, reaches out as if to take off the receiver, and then hesitates again. Finally he comes away from it and picks up a copy of "Punch" that is lying on the table. Then the telephone bells rings. He dashes off to the telephone, obviously in high hopes.*

WILFRED (*at telephone, eagerly*): Yes? Yes? Hello. Yes? (*Is obviously disappointed.*) Oh—Dr. Philips. No, Dad—Dr. Kirby—isn't back yet. Yes, I'll see him, I expect. . . . Yes, in a few minutes. . . . At your house—-Monday afternoon, three o'clock. I'll tell him. Good-bye.

As he leaves the telephone, SARAH *enters from right.*

SARAH: It'll be teeming down afore so long.

WILFRED (*gloomily*): Well, let it.

SARAH: Did Miss Stella take her mackintosh?

WILFRED: I don't know. I expect so.

SARAH: She'll want it.

WILFRED: You ought to see it rain in Africa.

SARAH: Does it rain there an' all?

WILFRED: Of course it does.

SARAH: Well I remember young Greenhead—the butcher's lad who went out to fight Kruger—telling me it never rained at all. All dry and dusty, he said it was. Never a drop o' water.

WILFRED: That's a different part of Africa. That's South Africa.

SARAH: Where are you then?

WILFRED: West Africa. Two thousand miles away. Quite different. Very hot and wet. Millions of blacks.

SARAH: Eh, fancy! And it only seems a week since you wor a little lad.

WILFRED: It's years since. And anyhow what's that got to do with it, Sarah, you old chump?

SARAH: A lot more nor you think. But then, lads has no sense. And they don't get ower-loaded with it when they stop being lads.

28

You can't stir up in the doctor's room for daft old birds' eggs.

WILFRED (*accusingly*): Sarah, you've broken some more.

SARAH: Only two. You can't move for 'em, and if you so much as look at 'em, they break.

WILFRED: You've gone and broken the only two specimens of the egg of the Great Spotted Gofoozle we have in the country.

SARAH: How do you know? You didn't see 'em.

WILFRED: I shall tell him.

SARAH: Master Wilfred, if you do that—— But you wouldn't, would you? You see, if you say nowt, he never misses 'em, for he's more eggs nor he knows what to do with. So long as he thinks they're all there, he's contented.

WILFRED: You're a wicked old woman.

SARAH: If you start telling on me, I'll tell on you.

WILFRED: Blackmail, that is. Besides, you've nothing to tell.

SARAH: What about them three cigars I saw you take?

WILFRED (*laughs*): Three cigars? Why, that's ages ago. At least seven years. Dad wouldn't care now. (*Listens.*) I think he's here, isn't he?

SARAH: Yes. I heard him. (*Going to door left.*) Nobody can say I'm hard o' hearing. I can still hear a lot better nor some of you. I'll ask him if he wants owt.

She goes out. WILFRED *settles down with the "Punch".* DR. KIRBY *comes in, wearing an overcoat.*

DR. KIRBY: Hello, Wilfred, any messages for me?

WILFRED: Yes. Dr. Philips of Martinbro just rang up to say that there'd be a meeting at his house next Monday afternoon at three.

DR. KIRBY: Next Monday at three? Well, I've no doubt some of us will be there, if our patients will let us.

WILFRED: What's it about? Health Insurance?

DR. KIRBY: Yes. Where are the girls this afternoon?

WILFRED: Geoffrey Farrant called for Stella, and they've gone out for a walk. And Lilian went out somewhere, I don't know where, about quarter of an hour ago. And I'm here, looking at "Punch".

DR. KIRBY: So I see. Good number?

WILFRED: Not so far. I don't see the point of some of these jokes. (*Turning pages.*) This for instance. (*Reads.*) Candid Friend (to M.F.H.): "I don't think much of your cubhunters, Jack." M.F.H.: "They're very useful horses; you see, we can either ride 'em or eat 'em." What's the point of that?

Dr. Kirby: No idea. I'll have to look at the drawing.

Wilfred (*turning pages*): And here's another. Officer (visiting outpost: "If you saw one of the enemy, what would you do?" Sentry: "I calls 'em to halt." Officer: "Suppose he won't halt?" Sentry (with relish: "I takes and 'unts 'im wiv me bayonnit." I don't think that's very funny.

Dr. Kirby: It wouldn't be very funny for the enemy. I saw some photographs of bayonet wounds once.

Wilfred: My hat, no. I shouldn't like anybody after me with a bayonet.

Dr. Kirby: Well, I shouldn't worry. It isn't very likely that anybody will be. The world's got a lot more sense than it's given credit for in the newspapers. And it's got science now to help it.

Wilfred: Dad, are you sorry I didn't go in for something scientific? That I'm not a doctor, for instance?

Dr. Kirby: Not if you're happy as you are.

Wilfred: Well, I don't know that I'm *happy*.

Dr. Kirby (*hastily*): I didn't mean that. Silly word. Reasonably contented, let us say.

Wilfred: Well it's not bad, you know.

Dr. Kirby: After all, you're seeing the world. More than I've ever done.

Wilfred (*hesitantly*): Yes. Only I don't seem to belong anywhere. I don't seem to belong to this place any more, and yet I can't really fit in with West Africa—nobody could.

Dr. Kirby: Well, that shouldn't bother you at your age. And after all, you've plenty of time. Years and years and years.

Wilfred (*hopefully*): Yes, that's true. Do you often wonder what you'll be like in ten years' time?

Dr. Kirby (*dryly*): Not often, no.

Wilfred: No, of course, naturally you wouldn't.

Dr. Kirby (*grimly amused*): Oh? Why?

Wilfred: Well, being older—you're completely settled, aren't you? You've always been here and——

Dr. Kirby: And I always will be, eh? You talk as if I wasn't so much perishable human stuff, just like yourself, but the Cow Rock up there on Eden moorside. I suppose that's how I seem. I was here, all complete, when you arrived, and I'll simply go on and on. That's the result of being a parent. You're an institution not a human being.

Wilfred: I wouldn't mind if I was a bit more of an institution,

Dad. Everything seems to slide away from me all the time. And I never seem to be in the right place.

DR. KIRBY (*briskly*): Partly liver, and partly boredom. You ought to be having a sharp walk now. (*Moving to door left.*) By the way, now that Stella's here—and looks like stopping a few weeks—I think we might entertain a bit more, don't you?

WILFRED: Good idea. If you can find anybody worth entertaining.

DR. KIRBY: Shouldn't be impossible. Just think of some people— young people, the sort Stella would like—we could have. (SARAH *appears at door on left.*) What is it, Sarah? Do you want me?

SARAH (*handing him note*): That little lad o' Mrs. Hepple's brought it.

DR. KIRBY (*glancing at it*): All right. I'll call. Back in about an hour or so, Wilfred, if anybody wants me.

He goes out, SARAH *standing aside to let him pass. Then* SARAH *comes in, closing door behind her.*

SARAH (*after waiting a moment*): Now I'll tell you what it is——

WILFRED (*picking up "Punch"*): Oh shut up, Sarah. I want to read.

SARAH (*offended*): That's a nice way to talk, isn't it?

WILFRED: No. But I want to be quiet.

SARAH (*moving slowly to door right*): I've seen the time when you'd have got a good slap from me for answering back like that. But now you're a big lad and I'm an old woman. Yes, and I know what you're telling yourself—a silly old woman. Well, old I may be, but I'm not so silly as some folk think——

WILFRED (*deliberately*): I want to read.

SARAH (*a parting shot*): And a lot o' good it'll do you.

She goes out, closing door behind her. WILFRED *looks up, looking at both doors, then gets up. He is rather indecisive. He moves over to the telephone, takes a little book from his pocket rather as if to make doubly sure of the telephone number he wants than to find it for the first time, then stretches out a hand for the instrument, hesitates and listens, is relieved at hearing nothing, then puts his hand on the receiver again.* SARAH *opens the door on right.*

SARAH (*with malicious triumph*): I thought you wanted to read.

WILFRED (*withdrawing from receiver, startled and angry,` shouts*): What's it got to do with you what I want to do?

SARAH: That's not reading, playing about with that thing.

WILFRED (*not so loud*): That's my business.

SARAH: You've been wanting to get at it on the quiet, half the day.

I've seen you. And not for the first time neither. And if you'd any sense you'd let it alone.

WILFRED: You don't know what you're talking about.

SARAH: Oh yes—I do. It may be all right for the doctor—folk being poorly and in a hurry—but no good'll come to you, talking down that thing. If it's worth saying, it's worth saying properly, instead o' gabbling into a daft machine. And if you thought anything o' the lass——

WILFRED (*sulkily*): How do you know it is a lass—as you call it?

SARAH: You wouldn't be making such a palaver if it worn't a lass. And she can't be up to so much when you've got to keep so quiet about her. Leave her alone, I say, and that telly-machine with her.

WILFRED: Oh—rats! And there's somebody coming now. You *are* a nuisance, Sarah.

SARAH: It'll be Miss Lilian.

They look towards door left. It is opened by CHARLES APPLEBY, *who comes in, quite at ease. He is a man about forty, probably wearing rather loud Harris tweeds, very much the actor in the country. At this moment he is also wearing a very large ulster, which is spotted with rain. There are signs that he drinks too much. The evidence of breeding and charm is still there, but it is doubtful how much longer it will be there.*

CHARLES (*smiling*): Beginning to rain. What a lot of rain we've had this autumn, haven't we?

WILFRED (*gaping at him*): Yes.

SARAH: Have you come to see Dr. Kirby?

CHARLES (*enjoying himself*): Not particularly. Now I'm not quite sure about you. But (*to* SARAH) I know who you are. You're Sarah.

SARAH: Well, what if I am?

CHARLES: Recognised you at once, you see. Heard a lot about you.

SARAH: Well, I've never set eyes on you before, young man.

CHARLES (*to* WILFRED): Not quite sure about you. Can't place you. But perhaps you're not one of the family here.

WILFRED: Yes I am. I'm Wilfred Kirby.

CHARLES (*smiling*): Of course. Well, I'm one of the family, too.

SARAH: That you're not.

CHARLES: Sorry, but I am. I'm Charlie Appleby.

SARAH: We're no wiser now.

CHARLES: This won't do. (*Turns and opens door, calling.*) I say—er,

Lilian—Lilian—you'd better come and introduce me. They don't know anything about me in here. We're all very embarrassed.

WILFRED: I say, is this a joke?

CHARLES (*coming in from door*): Not much of one, old boy. (*Turning.*) Here's Lilian.

Enter LILIAN.

LILIAN: Wilfred, this is Mr.——

CHARLES: Whoa, stop! Not Mr. Just Appleby, Charlie Appleby—Charlie.

LILIAN (*rather grimly*): He's our brother-in-law. Stella's husband.

SARAH (*moving forward a step or two*): Never!

CHARLES: Sorry. Know how you feel, Sarah.

WILFRED: But look here—when—when did this happen?

CHARLES: Three years ago. In Australia. Let's complete the ceremony of introduction, shall we? (*Holds out a hand.*) How do you do?

WILFRED (*laughing nervously and shaking hands*): How do you do?

CHARLES (*moving forward and holding out a hand*): Sarah.

SARAH (*moving forward uncertainly*): And you really are Miss Stella's husband?

CHARLES: Mrs. Stella's husband. Yes.

SARAH (*bewildered and suspicious*): But she's never said a single word to me about it, not a single word. I can't understand it.

LILIAN (*rather sharply*): Just a minute, Sarah. I want you to help me.

She moves to door. SARAH *follows slowly, with a puzzled and suspicious look at* CHARLES. *The latter notices it, though he is now lighting a cigarette.* LILIAN *and* SARAH *go out.*

CHARLES: The poor old girl is convinced I'm an impostor. And I must say I never felt so much like one before.

WILFRED: But, you see, we didn't know anything about it.

CHARLES (*dryly*): No, I've gathered that.

WILFRED: She's been home four days, and never said a word.

CHARLES: Didn't know how to break the news, I expect. Difficult, sometimes. I'm not a good news-breaker myself.

WILFRED: Are you on the stage, too?

CHARLES: Such is fame. Am I on the stage!

WILFRED: I'm sorry—but——

CHARLES: Don't apologise. I expect you lead a quiet life. It looks a quiet life, from the little I've seen of it.

WILFRED: Oh—I'm only home on leave. From Africa.

CHARLES: Soldier?

WILFRED: No, I'm with the British West African Trading Company.

CHARLES: This family gets about a bit, doesn't it? And why I'm still wearing this damned thing, I don't know. (*Begins taking off his ulster.* WILFRED *gives him a hand with it.*) I've been on the stage twenty years. Ran away from Oxford to go on the stage. Been all over, played nearly everything. Juvenile leads. Character parts now. Soon I'll be doing the heavies. What a life!

WILFRED: Don't you like it?

CHARLES: Never been able to decide. Do you like Africa?

WILFRED: I'm not sure. (*They both laugh.*) I say, are you staying here?

CHARLES: Looks like it, doesn't it?

WILFRED: I hope you are.

CHARLES: Why?

WILFRED: Well, we might go round a bit. Unless you want to be with Stella all the time.

CHARLES (*dryly*): No, I don't think I shall want to be with Stella all the time, old boy. Certainly let's go round a bit. I can't imagine where we'll go, from the little I've seen of the neighbourhood, but no doubt you know where the lads of the village—the ber-hoys, the ker-nuts—disport themselves. I don't suppose you come all the way from West Africa simply to watch the rain dripping off the old stone walls—do you?

WILFRED: Rather not.

CHARLES: You must take me round, you must show me the sights, and we'll see if we can't have some fun. I've never been to a place yet—and I've been to some dam' rum places—where one couldn't have some fun if one tried.

WILFRED: I'll do my best for you.

CHARLES (*yawning*): Matter of fact, you're a find. I'd forgotten about you. I saw myself simply having some grim chats about appendicitis in the surgery with your governor. What's he like, by the way?

WILFRED: Oh—Dad's all right.

CHARLES: To tell you the truth, I wasn't looking forward to meeting him. After all, it's a bit thick suddenly having a son-in-law thrust on you. Actor, too. Greasy hair, dirty collar. No money. Probably a bad lot.

WILFRED (*enthusiastically*): I think it's going to be fun, having you here.

CHARLES: Thank God somebody thinks so. But I'm not in good form at the moment. Feel half dead. Got up too early to catch that train. And what a train! (LILIAN *enters.*) I'm just saying I feel half dead after that train.

LILIAN: I hope you don't mind a camp bed.

CHARLES: Not at all, so long as it isn't the kind that tries to fold itself up again in the middle of the night.

WILFRED: No, it's all right. But, look here, you can have my bed and I'll have the camp bed.

LILIAN: Well, you can settle it between you, because I've put him in your room, Wilfred.

WILFRED: Good. (*Hesitates.*) Though—I say—oughtn't he to be—you know?

LILIAN (*briskly*): That's all right. I'm running this house.

CHARLES: Running it very well, too, I should think. I'd like to turn in for an hour if nobody's any objection.

LILIAN: No, I expect you're tired. Are you hungry?

CHARLES: No, thanks. I'm not hungry. But I'm devilish thirsty. Could I have a drink?

LILIAN: Would you like some tea?

CHARLES (*with mock gravity*): Sorry, but it doesn't agree with me. If there's such a thing as a whisky and soda going——

WILFRED: There's some in the dining-room.

LILIAN (*moving to door left*): Come along. And I'll show you where your room is. Then I must go out again.

CHARLES (*following her*): I'll take my drink up to my room and not be in anybody's way.

> They go out, and WILFRED *follows them. The room is darker now. The rain can be heard. After a moment* WILFRED *returns, carrying a mackintosh and a cap. He closes the door after him, carefully, then goes to the telephone nervously. Once more he looks at his little book. Then he takes off the receiver. He is very nervous, and catches his breath as he talks.*

WILFRED (*at telephone*): Hello . . . I want *Denly Two Six.* . . . Hello, is that Denly Two Six? Is that the "White Hart"? . . . Could I speak to Miss Alice Murgatroyd, please? . . . Oh, but you could get her, couldn't you? . . . It's—er—a friend. . . . Yes, it's *important*. . . . Oh, thanks very much. . . . Oh (*gasps*) is that you, Alice? It's Wilfred . . . (*Louder*.)   Wilfred—you know—Wilfred Kirby . . . (*Disappointed*.)   Didn't you recognise my voice? . . . Oh, I see. . . . Do you remember the other night? Listen, can I see you to-day? . . . Oh no, it isn't the same thing at all seeing you in the bar. . . . But I must see you alone . . . please, Alice. . . . Oh (*Disappointed*.) . . . But listen, if you don't go on duty until seven, I could see you before then. I'd come over at once. . . . But you can't have so much to do. (*Joyfully*.) Oh, good. I'll come over at once on my bike. . . . (*Desperately again*.) No, honestly, it isn't raining much. It's nothing. Really. And it'll probably be all over by the time I get there. . . . All right. At the bridge, eh? . . . Oh, but you must be there. . . . Hello, hello.

He puts down the receiver, breathes hard, wipes his forehead, and puts on his mackintosh. He hears voices through door on left, so after one glance in that direction hurries out through door on right. The room now is almost dark. The door on left opens and STELLA *and* FARRANT *come in, both wearing wet overcoats or mackintoshes.*

STELLA: Nobody in, thank goodness. We can still go on talking. Will you light the lamps?

FARRANT: Yes. And it won't be the first time I've done it here, either. (*He strikes a match and lights the lamps.*) Aren't you awfully wet?

STELLA: Wettish. (*Takes off her coat.*) I think we'd better put our coats in the nursery to dry. Give me yours.

FARRANT (*taking off his*): No, I'll take them both in. Give me yours.

He takes the coats into room on right. STELLA *tidies her hair, shakes out her skirt, and so forth. She is dressed now in country clothes, different from those in Act One. Then she hums a tune. She is obviously happy.*

FARRANT (*returning*): Nice in here after the rain outside. Looks—cosy.

STELLA (*laughs*): That's very elderly of you, Geoffrey.

FARRANT: I don't see that. Always like to be cosy after I've been out. Did when I was a boy. (*They both sit down.*) This is when a pipe tastes its best, indoors after the wind and the rain. (*Holds up his pipe.*) Do you mind?

STELLA: I've told you before, I adore your pipe. I think I'll smoke, too. Have you a cigarette for me, please?

FARRANT: Yes, of course. (*Holds out a case. She takes one.*)

STELLA (*holding up the cigarette, smiling*): Do you mind?

FARRANT: I admit I *have* objected to women smoking, in my time. But I don't mind when you do it.

STELLA: You mean, it doesn't matter if a tough old hag like me takes to such bad habits?

FARRANT: Don't talk such rot, Stella. You're prettier than ever. And there never was anybody less *tough*—as you call it.

STELLA: You're becoming suspiciously neat at this sort of thing, Geoffrey, much better than you used to be. You've had lots of practice while I've been away. (*He lights her cigarette, and then lights his pipe.*) Well, the walk didn't last long, and there was too much rain —but I loved it.

FARRANT: That's good.

STELLA: The rain suits this country here.

FARRANT: Good thing it does. We get plenty of it.

STELLA (*dreamily*): I wonder if you can understand what it means to come back after being so long away.

FARRANT: Of course I can. I was away over two years during the Boer War. Don't forget that.

STELLA: No, I'm not. But I've been away much longer than that. It seems centuries. Dirty provincial towns. Dozens of 'em. They may not have all been dirty, but looking back on them they seem grimy and dreary. Horsehair sofas, huge double beds in tiny dark bedrooms, landings smelling of cabbage and old blankets. Stinking little dressing-rooms. Stage doors down back streets.

FARRANT: Sounds beastly. Marvel to me how you stuck it.

STELLA: Then London. The real London. Cheap digs in Victoria and Paddington. Meals in tea shops. Fog for days and days. No space, no fresh air.

FARRANT: But it was better when you went away touring?

STELLA: Yes, we saw a lot. Some of the places were lovely. And some—weren't. But, my dear, there was nothing like this anywhere.

FARRANT: There isn't, you know, if it's your own country.

STELLA (*ecstatically*): The grey stone walls climbing up the moors. Geoffrey. The little streams dashing down. The ling and the bracken, The green, green fields. The huge dark brooding hills. That heathery, salty, fresh smell. Oh—lovely, lovely. I feel like someone who's just been let out of prison. I'm alive again. You don't read poetry, do you, Geoffrey?

FARRANT (*apologetically*): Not much. Kipling, y'know. But can't get on with most of the others.

STELLA: Well, there are two lines of Wordsworth's that give me this country as nothing else does. I've repeated them over and over again —in hot dressing-rooms, in railway carriages when I couldn't sleep, in all kinds of hellish places—and they've always brought me back home here.

FARRANT: Good for them! What are they?

STELLA: They're at the very end of some ridiculous poem about a young shepherd coming into an estate. I remember the two lines that come before, so I'll put them in too. (*Quoting, giving the last two lines with deep feeling.*)

> "Love had he found in huts where poor men lie;
>   His daily teachers had been wood and rills;
>   The silence that is in the starry sky,
>   The sleep that is among the lonely hills".

FARRANT: Say the last bit again.

STELLA:
> "The silence that is in the starry sky,
>   The sleep that is among the lonely hills".

FARRANT (*thoughtfully*): I get what he's driving at there, y'know. That's Wordsworth, is it? I must tackle him again.

STELLA *laughs.*

FARRANT: What's the joke?

STELLA: I suddenly saw you—in that den of yours at the Manor— *tackling* Wordsworth.

FARRANT (*after short laugh*): You can understand why I stay on at the old place——

STELLA: Heavens, yes.

FARRANT: There isn't really a lot to do, looking after the estate, and sometimes I've told myself I'm a slacker, just hanging on there, doing a bit of hunting and shooting. I'd have been glad to have stayed in the army, of course, but my leg made that impossible. And, some-how, I've never been attracted to anything else. Probably because I don't want to leave the old place.

STELLA: You must never leave it.

FARRANT: Old Bickley, the shoemaker here in Eden End—he's a Socialist—always tells me that sooner or later he and his pals will have me out of the Manor and the estate. And I always tell him that if they do, he'll have to give me a job—cobbling with him. He's not a bad sort, Old Bickley, though he does talk a lot of hot air.

STELLA: I remember him. A nice old thing. I remember when I was a little girl somebody—it may have been Sarah—told me that Mr.

Bickley didn't believe in God, and after that I used to look at him with horror. He had a fascination for me. I could see him going to Hell. You know, these last few days, I've been thinking again of my child-hood. Things—oh, dozens of things—I'd forgotten have suddenly come back.

FARRANT: Do you like that?

STELLA: Yes. Even though some of the things are unhappy things.

FARRANT: I hope I wasn't one of 'em.

STELLA: No, you come in afterwards, Geoffrey. When I was growing up—or when I thought I was growing up. When I was (*in absurd tone*) a *girl*.

FARRANT: You're still a girl.

STELLA: My dear man, don't be ridiculous. I'm a woman. Very soon—horrors—I shall be an *old girl*.

FARRANT: That puts me well into the decayed class, then, for I'm older than you.

STELLA: It's different for a man. You're merely coming within sight of maturity.

FARRANT: I hope I'm maturing well.

STELLA: You're maturing beautifully, Geoffrey.

FARRANT: Nevertheless, you've changed, and I haven't.

STELLA: How have I changed? (*Hastily.*) If it's something un-pleasant, don't tell me. I won't have to-day spoilt.

FARRANT: It isn't unpleasant.

STELLA: Go on, then, and tell me all about it.

FARRANT: When I've thought about you——

STELLA: Oh, have you thought about me?

FARRANT (*gravely*): I've thought about you a lot. Wondered where you were, what you were doing, and so on, and I've always thought that after being on the stage and knocking up and down——

STELLA: I don't know that I want to be one who has knocked up and down.

FARRANT: Well, you know what I mean. I thought that you'd be much harder. Harder, that is, than you used to be.

STELLA: And I was hard enough to you, wasn't I? Poor Geoffrey. I was a nasty, cocky, little beast.

FARRANT: No, you weren't. But you led me an awful dance sometimes, didn't you?

STELLA: I did. And now I apologise for it. Never mind, Geoffrey. I treated you very badly, and you've been well revenged since.

FARRANT: Oh? How? Who by?

STELLA: Don't look so alarmed. I mean by—well—life. I thought I knew everything then. I knew nothing, and when that fact was forced upon me, it hurt. But go on. You thought I'd be harder still.

FARRANT: Yes. And you're not. You're——

STELLA: Softer. (*Laughs.*) Oh—but I don't want to be softer. It sounds horrid.

FARRANT: I didn't mean that. You know I'm no good at this sort of thing.

STELLA (*gently*): You're much better than you think you are. Besides, I've had the misfortune to meet a lot of men who prided themselves on being good at this sort of thing.

FARRANT: All blighters, I'll bet.

STELLA: Yes, Geoffrey. Mostly blighters.

FARRANT: What I meant to say was, that you're still yourself—Stella—but you're nicer, kinder—dash it, I'll say it—gentler than you used to be. At least to me you are.

STELLA: I'm glad you think so. I should like to be. I've learnt a good deal these last eight years. I've often thought how badly I treated you in the old days here. And—miles away— years away—I've been ashamed. Sometimes, just lately, I've been tempted to write and tell you so. But I didn't know what had happened to you. You might easily have forgotten all about me.

FARRANT (*in a low voice*): I've tried hard enough.

STELLA: I can understand that.

FARRANT: I wanted to get on with my own life. You'd got on with yours. That's reasonable, isn't it?

STELLA: Yes. And I should think that's what was the matter with it. Too reasonable.

FARRANT: Yes, too reasonable. I knew that the moment I came in here, the other night, and saw you again. I hadn't been doing badly the last year or two.

STELLA: At forgetting me?

FARRANT: Yes. I'd even been able to come here a good deal—sometimes to see your father, and Wilfred when he was on leave, but chiefly to see Lilian. I've seen a lot of her, you know.

STELLA: Yes, I gathered that.

FARRANT: Lilian's a fine girl, you know.

STELLA: I'm sure she is. That sounds absurd, doesn't it, when I'm her sister. But the fact is, I don't know her very well now. She's grown-up, and she's changed in the process, I suppose. But I'm sure there's something very strong and fine about her. She always had more courage and strength and honesty than I had. (*As he is about to protest.*) No, I mean that. Do you think I don't know myself now? I'm changeable, I'm weak, and I'm a coward.

FARRANT: You're not.

STELLA: You don't know, my dear. I'm being weak and cowardly at this very moment.

FARRANT: I don't believe you.

STELLA (*almost in tears, but smiling*): I don't want you to believe me. (*Smiling at him.*) Dear Geoffrey.

FARRANT: You may be changeable. I don't know. But I know this. I'm not changeable. (*Goes over and takes her hands.*) I loved you years ago. I love you now, just the same. I see why nobody's ever meant anything all this time. It's because of you. There's only you. I love you, Stella.

He looks down at her. She raises her face to him and he kisses her. Then she rests her head against his sleeve, closing her eyes. Nothing is said. Then she makes a little gesture with her hand that releases her.

FARRANT: I may not be able to read poetry, Stella, but I've imagined that—over and over again.

STELLA (*with a tiny smile*): I've thought of it too—sometimes.

FARRANT: By jove, have you? If I'd known that I'd have come charging all over Australia and the United States looking for you. See what I've missed!

He threatens to kiss her again, but she holds up a hand and shakes her head.

No, probably you're right. Now we've got to talk.

STELLA: Yes, but not the kind of talk you mean, Geoffrey. No plans, no arrangements, no time tables, no—"seeing how we stand". Nothing like that.

FARRANT (*bewildered*): Oh!

STELLA: We can't be always arranging ourselves in the world's eye, like goods in a smart shop window. Not that sort of talk at all. Just idle, foolish talk that gets you nowhere, that means nothing and yet can mean everything. It doesn't matter now who we are or how we stand, or anything like that. Just think of the two of us here, in a cosy little room, lost in the moorland rain. We're lost too. There isn't anybody else. Just us. And time's stopped for us.

FARRANT: I see. At least I think I do.

STELLA (*dreamily*): Or we needn't talk at all, if you like. Just be quiet. Trying to make time stand still for us. It flies at a terrible speed really, Geoffrey.

Farrant: Oh, I don't know. Things don't change much.

Stella: They do. Even in ten years time—in Nineteen Twenty-two —what a queer year that sounds, doesn't it——

Farrant: We shall only be in our forties.

Stella: I know. And yet everything may be different. You never know. We might look back at this year and see it—oh, a thousand years away. In another world, a lost world.

Farrant: But things don't change much here.

Stella: Yes, they do. I haven't been away so long, yet it's all different really. Mother gone. Wilfred and Lilian grown-up—half strangers. Father much older—too old. I sound like Stevenson's Wanderer. Do you remember the verse I used to keep saying over and over again?

She repeats the verse beginning " Home was home then, my dear",
very softly.

"Home was home then, my dear, full of kindly faces.
Home was home then, my dear, happy for the child.
Fire and the windows bright glittered on the moorland.
Song, tuneful song, built a palace in the wild."

Just before the end the door on left opens quietly and Charles *stands there, looking like a man who has just had a nap.* Farrant *stares at him in surprise. When* Stella *sees him she gives a sharp cry and stands with a hand pressed against her heart.*

Charles: Sorry if I startled you, Stella, but I didn't want to interrupt the performance.

Stella (*with an enormous effort*): Charles!

Charles (*cheerfully*): Didn't they tell you I was coming? Too bad. Wanted to make a surprise of it, I suppose. Something to pass the long autumn evening.

Stella: But how did you get here?

Charles: Train, my dear. Train from town. Hours and hours and hours of it, and started about dawn. I'm feeling a bit muzzy too. (*Indicating* Farrant, *who is standing rigid.*) I'm afraid we're embarrassing your friend—this gentleman. Hadn't you better introduce me?

Stella (*silent a moment, then making a big effort*): Geoffrey, this is Charles Appleby—my husband. Captain Farrant.

Charles: How d'you do? An old friend of my wife's, I expect. Think I've heard her mention you. (*Looks shrewdly from one to the other*.) If you'll excuse me one minute, I'll go and get myself a drink. Always get thirsty on trains, most curious thing.

He goes out. FARRANT *stares at* STELLA.

FARRANT: Is this true?

STELLA: Yes.

FARRANT: But why didn't you tell me?

STELLA (*with a miserable smile*): I told you I was weak and cowardly, didn't I?

FARRANT (*contemptuously*): Yes, but I didn't know it was as bad as that.

STELLA: Please, Geoffrey, don't try to hurt me. I'm hurt enough as it is.

FARRANT: What about me? I suppose you think I'm enjoying myself.

STELLA (*in tears*): Please, Geoffrey. It isn't as bad as it seems. We were married three years ago. We've been separated for nearly a year now. I don't know why he's here. I didn't ask him here.

FARRANT: I don't think I want to hear any more about it just now. I must go.

STELLA: Only a few minutes ago I was happy. I thought it couldn't last long. It didn't even last as long as I thought.

FARRANT: It didn't deserve to last a second. I'll get my coat.

Goes to room on right. STELLA *makes a great effort to avoid breaking down altogether. As* FARRANT *re-appears with his cap and coat,* CHARLES *appears in the other doorway with a whisky and soda in his hand.*

CHARLES: What? Going?

FARRANT (*curtly*): Yes. Good-bye.

STELLA *turns away from them.* CHARLES *stands aside to let* FARRANT *pass.* FARRANT *goes out. You hear the outer door bang outside.* STELLA *is still turned away.*

CHARLES (*who has no malice in him, an insensitive, good-humoured chap*): I'm sorry, Stella. Didn't mean to barge in at the wrong moment like that. Always putting my foot in it. No tact. It's just cost me a job. You'll laugh when I tell you about it.

STELLA *sits down, away from him, and stares straight in front of her. She is not sulking, but is temporarily oblivious of anything at the moment but her own misery.*

Shall I tell you? Perhaps I'd better keep it. No good spoiling the story. But you will laugh when I tell you.

He takes a good gulp of his whisky and soda, and looks across at her rather wistfully.

STELLA (*in a muffled voice*): Why have you come here?

CHARLES (*trying to keep it light*): Oh—well—you see, I was resting and a bit fed up with town. Thought the change might do me good. All in order, you know. I had an invitation to come down here. I thought it might have come—indirectly—from you.

STELLA: It didn't.

CHARLES: No, I'm gathering that. Nobody seems to know much about me here. Haven't met your father yet.

STELLA: No—that's not going to be easy.

CHARLES: Why?

STELLA: I can't explain.

CHARLES: I'm beginning to feel like a baby that's turned up at a wedding. A warm welcome was given to Mr. Charles Appleby, always a favourite in the North of England. Good old Charlie, they cried.

STELLA (*wearily*): Oh—don't be funny, Charlie.

CHARLES: Well, I've got to be something. Damn it, look at it from my point of view. I've got feelings as well as you and your old friend, the bronzed, clean-living English gentleman who's just pushed off in a temper. I come here because I'm invited. I imagine you've something to do with it. After all, you're still my wife. I get up at some unearthly hour this morning—in pitch darkness—travel most of the day, and then when I arrive here, I'm treated as if I were a bad dose of small-pox.

STELLA: Oh, I know. It's not your fault.

CHARLES: By the way, what's the telephone number here?

STELLA: I don't know. It's there.

CHARLES (*goes over to telephone, and notes number*): I must send it to the agents. They may want me in a hurry. One or two new tours going out. Somebody said something about *Old Heidelberg* touring again. And *The Monk and the Woman*. A title like that ought to bring 'em in. You know that Hilda Moore's touring in *Bella Donna*. If she wants to get back to town and they want to keep the tour going, there might be a chance for you there—you've played Hilda Moore parts.

STELLA: I've finished with the theatre.

CHARLES: Don't believe it. I've heard that before. Nobody's finished with the theatre until the theatre's finished with them. You'll be working again in a month.

STELLA (*shaking her head*): I shan't.

CHARLES: I've said that, you know. We all have. Meant it too when we've said it. I remember once—it was about two years before I met you—I was out in *A Message From Mars*—and——

Enter LILIAN, *carrying account books, etc.*

CHARLES: Hullo! You look business-like.

LILIAN: I have to do Dad's accounts.

STELLA (*with hostility*): Why?

LILIAN: He's so forgetful now.

STELLA: Oh. I haven't noticed it.

LILIAN: You haven't been here long enough to notice it.

CHARLES (*looking from one to the other*): Er . . . no. I think I'll have a look round. (*He escapes. Nothing is said for a moment.*)

STELLA: It was you, of course, who asked Charles to come here.

LILIAN: Yes.

STELLA: How did you find him?

LILIAN: You'd told me his name and you said that you both had the same agent. When I was helping to turn out your room, I saw a letter from your agent——

STELLA: I see. Quite simple. These things usually are if you don't mind going into other people's rooms and reading their letters.

LILIAN: Perhaps if you'd condescended to do your own room—instead of going out for a walk with Geoffrey, I shouldn't have seen the letter.

STELLA: I wasn't asked to help with the housework here, was told, in fact, not to do anything. On the other hand, I *was* asked to go for a walk by Geoffrey. But that has nothing to do with it. You read my letter, probably read all my letters.

LILIAN: I've not the least desire to read your letters. That particular one happened to be lying open on your dressing-table. Your agent's name and address on it were big enough to be read a yard away.

STELLA: I'm glad he saved your eyesight. Why did you ask Charles to come here? It was no business of yours. I'd told you that we had separated. We haven't lived together for over a year. We haven't spoken to one another, haven't seen one another—except the other day at the agent's—for months and months. If I'd wanted him here, I would have asked him myself. You'd no right to interfere. And if it had been anybody else but Charles—who's a fool—he'd never have come here on such an invitation.

LILIAN: Three years ago, you were sufficiently in love with him to marry him. Now you can't stand him in the same house.

STELLA: That's my affair.

LILIAN: By the way, I've put him in Wilfred's room.

STELLA: I suppose I ought to be grateful you haven't put him into my bed.

LILIAN: You needn't be disgusting.

STELLA: And you needn't be such a beastly little hypocrite. Why did you send for him?

LILIAN: He was your husband. You weren't happy, I could see that. I thought you'd like another chance.

STELLA: All lies. You're still talking like a beastly little hypocrite. You're lying, Lilian, you're lying. *Why did you send for him?*

LILIAN: I've told you.

STELLA: You've told me nothing, and you know it. But I'll make you tell the truth. You made me confess about my marriage, you've read my letters, you've interfered in my private affairs—and now you imagine you can put me off with a few silly lies. (*Going nearer.*) Do you think I'm a fool?

LILIAN (*contemptuously*): Yes.

> STELLA, *blazing with fury, slaps her face, hard. The effect is very marked on each.* LILIAN *stands rigid, filled with a cold anger.* STELLA *steps back and then turns away, trembling, her anger rapidly vanishing. She sits down.*

STELLA: I oughtn't to have done that. I'm sorry, Lilian.

LILIAN (*contemptuously*): It doesn't make me think you any less of a fool. It's like nearly everything else you do—violent and silly and useless.

STELLA (*roused again*): Is it? Well, I'll tell you now why you sent for Charles. It had nothing to do with me and my marriage. You don't care a rap about that. Do you?

LILIAN (*calmly*): Not much. Why should I?

STELLA: No, you did it because you're in love with Geoffrey Farrant. What's the use of pretending? You know. And I know. You're in love with Geoffrey, and you're terrified of losing him. I knew that the very first night I came back, when you went sulking off to bed, pretending you'd a headache. Even before that, before Geoffrey called, the moment I arrived, I knew there was *something*. You didn't really want me back here. I felt at once there was something resentful about you.

LILIAN (*herself roused now, but still colder and harder than the other*):

And why should there be anything else? Why should you expect us all to fall on your neck the minute you condescended to come home again?

STELLA: That's unfair——

LILIAN: It isn't. And if you didn't think about yourself all the time, you'd soon see that. You always had more of everything than Wilfred and I had. Before you went away, you let Geoffrey fall in love with you, made him follow you round, laughed at him—yes, and to us, and even then I hated you for it——

STELLA: I cared more for Geoffrey then than you think.

LILIAN: I don't believe you know what it is to love anybody properly. You think being sentimental is caring for people. It isn't. Then you insisted on going on the stage, although you knew very well that mother had a horror of theatres. She couldn't help it. That's how she'd been brought up. You went away, without caring how much mother and father were worrying.

STELLA: That's not true. I cared terribly. You can't begin to understand——

LILIAN: That helped to kill mother.

STELLA (breaking down): Oh—you're cruel, Lilian. That's not true.

LILIAN: Yes, it is. You said you'd make me tell the truth, and here it is. Mother died. Father was left lonely and miserable. I didn't want to stay here all my life. I had plans of my own. But I had to stay then, to look after the house and father. He needed me.

STELLA (through her tears): He didn't. If you'd decided to do something away from home he wouldn't have tried to stop you. He simply thought you wanted to stay at home.

LILIAN: How do you know?

STELLA: He—oh it doesn't matter. The point is, you stayed at home because you wanted to stay at home. And now you're making a great virtue out of it. You're one of these self-appointed martyrs.

LILIAN: I'm not pretending to be a martyr. I'm simply explaining why I didn't think you were so very wonderful. You went off, not caring about us, to do what you wanted to do. And while you were enjoying yourself, you didn't bother about us. You could even get married without telling us. Then, when you thought you'd had enough of the stage and had made a mess of your marriage, you decided to come home.

STELLA: Yes, and you seem to forget that, after all, it's my home just as much as it's yours.

LILIAN: No, it isn't, and you know very well it isn't. It stopped being your home when you ran away from it years ago. And it's my home, more than ever, because I've stuck to it and helped to keep it going. We'd made a life here without you, and now you have to come charging back into it, upsetting everyone.

STELLA: Upsetting everyone? You seem to forget that everybody here was glad to see me again—except you.

LILIAN: Yes, and a lot of good it'll do them.

STELLA: All you're thinking about is Geoffrey, only you won't admit it.

LILIAN: I'm not afraid of admitting it. I do love Geoffrey—I have done for years—and I believe I could make him happy. And I know you couldn't, and wouldn't even try very long.

STELLA: So you made up your mind at once that he must see for himself that I have a husband. Oh—yes, they've met already. I'm sorry you weren't here.

LILIAN: It wasn't just that. You have a life of your own—a life that you've made quite apart from us—you can't run away from it.

STELLA: But you see, I'm away from it now. And I'm not running back to it. You've done your best. Charles is here—and he's a nuisance—but he won't stay long. But I'm staying. You've played your trick, Lilian—and a very dirty little trick it was—but you haven't won. Nothing has happened except that now I realise that either you've changed completely or I never really knew you.

LILIAN: I can't see that it matters which it is.

STELLA (distressed): What does matter to me is that you and I could have talked to one another as we have done. I've never even tried to hurt you, and you've deliberately hurt me. I'd looked forward so much to seeing you again. We'd shared so many things before. I thought we'd be able to have a wonderful time together. If you'd been open and friendly from the first, I couldn't have taken anything, anybody, away from you. I could have been happy just because you were happy. Oh—Lilian—you wouldn't be so hard if you hadn't been shut up here so long in a safe little corner. It's because you don't know how much misery there is in the world, how circumstances and time can change and hurt us.

LKLIAN: You're not really unhappy now. In a way you're enjoying it. You see, I'm not made like that. I can't enjoy my emotions.

CHARLES appears in doorway on left.

CHARLES (to STELLA): I say, Stella, your father's just come in. He thinks I'm a patient. You'd better come and explain. (He goes out.)

STELLA (*in a low voice*): I hope you don't think I'm going to enjoy this.

LILIAN (*scornfully*): You're not afraid of Dad, are you?

STELLA: I'm afraid for him. You can't begin to understand how hateful this is going to be for me. (*She goes to the door and calls, with assumed cheerfulness.*) Dad!

DR. KIRBY (*off*): Yes.

STELLA: Just a minute.

She goes off, banging the door to behind her. LILIAN sits down to her accounts and gradually loses control of herself. As the curtain falls, she is crying.

END OF ACT TWO

ACT III

SCENE I

As before. Late on Saturday night. When the curtain rises, the room is empty. Lamps are lit, but turned low. There is a good fire. On the table are a tray, holding a thermos flask, small bottle of brandy, a glass and some biscuits, and another tray with whisky decanter and soda syphon and glasses on it. A clock outside in the hall strikes twelve. Before it has finished striking the voices of CHARLES *and* WILFRED *are heard outside.* CHARLES *enters first and begins turning up the lights. He is dressed as in* ACT II. WILFRED *staggers in, with a folded mackintosh slung over one shoulder, and he sticks to this for some time. They are both drunk.* WILFRED *is the worse of the two. It should be quite obvious that they are drunk, but they must not indulge in the usual antics, and though their voices are thick, they must be clearly heard. There must be no hiccupping.*

CHARLES (*looking round the room*): Nice. Very nice. I call this very snug, old boy.

WILFRED: Not bad qua'ers, not bad qua'ers at all. Wish I'd something like this in Bri'sh West.

CHARLES (*solemnly*): In where, old boy?

WILFRED (*solemnly*): Bri'sh West.

CHARLES: Never heard of it.

WILFRED (*deliberately*): Bri-tish West—Africa.

CHARLES: Oh—yes. Africa. I've been to Africa—South Africa. It's all right, Africa is, old boy.

WILFRED (*very seriously*): It's fine. I like Africa, Charlie.

CHARLES (*wandering round*): Quite right. We pass Africa. (*Going to table.*) Hello, drinks. But what's this business?

WILFRED (*peering at the thermos flask*): That's for my father.

CHARLES: Where is he?

WILFRED (*waving a hand*): Out—working. Somebody somewhere must be very ill. Having a baby p'r'aps. Or pegging out.

CHARLES: And your poor old governor's looking after 'em.

WILFRED: Yes, and that's for when he comes in. Hot milk. Brandy. Biscuits. And he deserves 'em, Charlie.

CHARLES: He does, old boy. He's a noble fellow. As soon as I saw

50

him—yesterday afternoon—I said to myself: "Stella's father—my father-in-law—he's a noble old fellow." I think we ought to drink his health.

WILFRED (*solemnly*): I ag-agree.

CHARLES *pours out two whiskies and sodas during the next two speeches.*

CHARLES (*with air of profundity*): If my old man had been a doctor, a lot of things would have been different—very different. But he wasn't.

WILFRED: What was he—your old man?

CHARLES (*very solemnly*): Nothing, old boy—nothing. Just a bloody English gentleman. But never mind him. (*Sternly, raising glass.*) Here's to Dr. Kirby—a noble old fellow.

WILFRED (*raising glass*): Here's to him—good old Dad.

CHARLES (*still solemnly*): Let's sit down.

WILFRED: Yes.

They sit down. CHARLES *lights a cigarette.* WILFRED *looks rather sleepy.*

CHARLES: You know, old boy—we've had a good evening. I told you yesterday—when we first met—I said then "We can go out—you and I—and have a good evening here." Didn't I?

WILFRED: You did.

CHARLES: Well, we've had one. What was the name of the fellow that gave us a lift in the trap?

WILFRED: Harper.

CHARLES: Harper. A very nice fellow—Harper. But he was badly screwed, y'know, old boy. He ought to have let us drive.

WILFRED: I met a fellow on the boat coming home called Harper. He came from Manchester and he had a glass eye. I hate glass eyes.

CHARLES: And I hate Manchester. If I'd to choose between a glass eye and Manchester, I'd rather have a glass eye. You meant a glass eye, old boy, didn't you—and not an eye glass?

WILFRED: Yes, glass eye. One of our chaps in the Company——

CHARLES: What company? You're not on the stage, you're in Africa.

WILFRED: Yes, I mean the Bri'sh West African Company. He has an eye glass. He says he used to own two racehorses when he was home. Awful nut.

CHARLES: Probably lying, old boy. There's a terrible lot of lying about. When you're my age you'll have found that out. Everybody lies like the devil. Women worse than men.

WILFRED: That's true, Charlie. A girl on the boat told me a lot of lies. (*With sudden energy.*) Absolute lies.

CHARLES: I know, I know. If I'd had a sovereign for every lie that girls on boats have told me, I'd be rich man now. And I'll tell you another thing about women, old boy. Women—and I don't care who they are—all women—can't stand seeing men enjoy themselves *by* themselves. It annoys 'em. It makes 'em furious. They like to think they're indis-indispensable. We've had a good evening, haven't we?

WILFRED: Yes.

CHARLES: All right then. We've had a good evening. No harm in it, no harm in it at all. A few pubs. A few rounds of drinks. A talk with some of the local boys. Social harmony and innocent mirth, as somebody said somewhere. A good evening. But do you think you could get any woman to admit we'd had a good evening? No, old boy. Take it from me. You couldn't. Stella's a nice girl. Would she admit we'd had a good evening? No. Your other sister—Lilian—would she admit it? No. Old boy, they'd turn it down flat. "Where have you been? Look at you."

WILFRED: Well, I don't know. There's a girl I could mention—lives round here—and I don't think she——

CHARLES (*holding up his hand*): She's different. Don't you believe it. They're all different—they don't mind anything—no, not until they've got hold of you. But once they've got you, they won't have this, they won't have that. The thing—the very thing—they told you once they liked you for—that's what they want you to change, old boy. If they liked your little jokes before you were married, then after you're married they ask you why you're always trying to be funny. See what I mean?

WILFRED: Yes, I suppose so. One of our chaps in Africa——

CHARLES: Just a minute. Tell me afterwards. Don't forget. I want to hear about that chap. But what I was going to say was this. It doesn't matter what women do, or who tells you lies, or whether you go to Africa or not, life's a very wonderful thing. Do you realise that, old boy?

WILFRED: By jove—yes. I was just thinking coming along——

CHARLES: A wonderful thing. You can't get away from that.

WILFRED: You can't get away from it, Charlie.

CHARLES: I've had my troubles. Even you've had your troubles——

WILFRED: I should think I have. Do you know when I first went out to Nigeria——

CHARLES: You had a hell of a time. Yes, and I've had a hell of a time. But in spite of everything, I think—I *know*—life's a wonderful thing.

WILFRED: There's *something* about it, isn't there?

CHARLES: You've hit it. There's *something* about it. Here I am—in —where is it?

WILFRED: Where's what?

CHARLES: Here—this place.

WILFRED: Eden End.

CHARLES: Here I am in Eden End. Never been here before—may not ever come here again——

WILFRED: I hope you will, Charlie.

CHARLIE: I hope so, too, old boy. But you never know. That's another thing about life (*very solemnly*)—you never know. A week ago I didn't know I was going to be here—sitting here with you.

WILFRED: And I didn't know you existed.

CHARLES: Didn't you? Dam' shame. But there you are, you see. Here I am. And here you are. Having a drink together. Everything's quiet. Women asleep upstairs—or I hope they are. Your governor out there somewhere—helping some poor devil out of the world—or perhaps helping some other poor devil into the world—and here we are. And you'll go back to Ceylon——

WILFRED: Africa.

CHARLES: It's all the same, old boy. This isn't geography. And I'll go back to town. Get a job. Go on tour again perhaps. People will come to see me. They don't know much about me. I don't know anything about them. Never mind. Perhaps I make 'em cry. Perhaps I make 'em laugh. And, mind you, old boy, give me a part with the ghost of a bit of comedy fat in it, and I *can* make 'em laugh. I can make 'em yell. Weedon Grossmith—Weedon Grossmith, mind you— once said to me: "You've got a touch, Appleby, old boy. You've *got* something." And I have. The trouble is—and this is where *luck* comes in—most of the time I've had to make something out of nothing.

WILFRED: I'll bet you're awfully good, Charlie. Do you know what old Stansted—one of the Company's chief men out there—said about me?

CHARLES: No?

WILFRED: He didn't say it *to* me, but he told one of the other fellows. He said that of all the young men who'd come out lately I'd got the best idea of handling the niggers.

CHARLES: I'm not surprised, old boy. It doesn't surprise me at all.

That's because you've got sympathy. You're human. You're like me. You've either got it or you haven't got it. We've got it.

WILFRED (*sleepily*): We've got it. I think—you're an awfully fine chap, Charlie. And I'm glad you came to stay with us.

CHARLES: Thanks, old boy. So am I. All the best. (*Drains his glass.*)

WILFRED: All the best. (*Drains his.*)

CHARLES (*getting up*): We'd better be getting upstairs. What was the name of that biggish place at the crossroads?

WILFRED: That's the "White Hart". My favourite.

CHARLES: Quite right. Best of the lot. We'll concentrate on that one next time. Did you notice the little barmaid there, the little fair one?

WILFRED: Yes. That's Alice.

CHARLES: Alice, is it? Well, she's all right. A promising little tart, that. (*Puts his glass back on the table humming or singing "Where My Caravan has Rested".*)

WILFRED (*suddenly rigid with attention*): Why do you call her that?

CHARLES (*carelessly*): Didn't you notice her? Something doing there, old boy. Can't miss it. Quite pretty and absolutely asking for it. Didn't you see her giving me enormous glad eyes? Wanted me to come round and see her when it was quieter.

WILFRED (*suddenly shouting*): She didn't. You're a liar.

CHARLES (*good-humouredly*): Here, steady, steady.

WILFRED (*not so loud now, but with intensity*): I tell you she didn't, and you're a dirty liar.

CHARLES: You're screwed, old boy. Take it easy.

WILFRED (*half shouting, half crying*): Tell me it isn't true.

CHARLES: Anything you like so long as you stop making that row. What the devil does it matter whether it's true or not?

WILFRED: It matters to me.

CHARLES: Oh—I see.

WILFRED: It's the only thing that matters to me.

CHARLES: Don't be a damned fool. Of course it isn't.

WILFRED (*vehemently, clutching hold of the other*): She didn't ask you to come round and see her, did she? Tell me she didn't. (*Raising his voice.*)

CHARLES: Not so much noise, you young ass.

WILFRED: Tell me she didn't, Charles.

CHARLES: She didn't, then. It must have been somebody else—one of the others.

WILFRED (*distressed*): Are you sure?

CHARLES: What I am sure of, old boy, is that you're badly screwed and that it's time I got you up to bed.

LILIAN *in night things and a dressing-gown, stands in the doorway on left, looking at them.*

LILIAN: You're making a frightful noise. (*She comes into room.*)

CHARLES: Sorry—Lilian. Just been having a little argument, that's all. I'm taking Wilfred up to bed now. He's a bit—tired.

LILIAN (*contemptuously*): You mean he's drunk. You both are.

CHARLES (*indignantly*): Oh—no, no, no, no.

STELLA, *also in night things and dressing-gown, appears in open doorway.*

STELLA: What's the matter?

WILFRED (*miserably*): I think—I'm going—to be sick.

CHARLES (*putting arm round him*): That's all right, old boy. That's all right. You stick to me. Steady, steady. (*To* STELLA, *who comes in and clears the doorway, and* LILIAN.) I'll look after him. (*To* WILFRED, *who is groaning.*) That's all right, old boy. I've got you. Steady, steady. (*To the* GIRLS.) Don't worry. He's all right.

He escorts him through the doorway. He can be heard, repeating his "All right" and "Steady" outside. STELLA *stands near the doorway, watching them.* LILIAN *stands in the middle of the room, watching* STELLA. *Finally the latter closes the door, and comes in, looking troubled.* LILIAN *picks up* WILFRED'S *glass, which is on the floor, and puts it on the table, then picks up his mackintosh, which is sprawling over a chair, and begins to fold it.*

LILIAN: Thank God, Dad's still out, that's all.

STELLA: That's what I was thinking.

LILIAN: He hates drunkenness. So do I.

STELLA: He needn't know anything about this.

LILIAN: Don't imagine that I shall tell him. But this has never happened before. Wilfred does go into the local pubs sometimes, but he's never had much to drink. As a matter of fact, I believe he thinks he's fallen in love with a barmaid somewhere. But he's never been like this before.

STELLA: No, this comes of going out with Charles—the very first night too.

LILIAN: And—I hope—the last.

STELLA: I didn't ask Charles to come here. He's your guest.

LILIAN: He's your husband.

STELLA: He was.

LILIAN: He still is. (*A pause.*) Why did you marry him, Stella?

STELLA: For the usual reasons. I was in love with him. Queer, no doubt—but true. As a matter of fact, I was very much in love with him.

LILIAN: Were you?

STELLA: Poor Charlie! I suppose it does seem incredible to you. I think I'll have one of Dad's biscuits. (*Takes one.*) You have one. (LILIAN *has one.*)

LILIAN: Has he changed very much?

STELLA: No, he hasn't—really. But it's one thing seeing him here, quite out of his element, not working, rather depressed. And it's quite another thing seeing him—as I did for months when we were touring the East and Australia—as the most amusing and charming person in the company. And to be working and travelling and laughing with him month after month, thousands of miles from home. It's no use, Lilian, you can't begin to understand my life. We were very happy for a time. Poor Charlie.

LILIAN: Why do you say "Poor Charlie"?

STELLA: Because—although he doesn't deserve it—I can't help feeling sorry for him. I suppose I'm still fond of him.

LILIAN: Then why don't you look after him?

STELLA: Why should I?

LILIAN: He belongs to you.

STELLA: I can't think about people like that. I'm not possessive. (*Startled.*) What's that?

> It is CHARLES, *looking in at the door. He is soberer than he was, but still ripe—and very sleepy.*

CHARLES: Are you two quarrelling again? You're always quarrelling. Why don't you take it easy? Live and let live.

STELLA (*sharply*): Never mind about us. What about Wilfred?

CHARLES: That's what I came down to say. He's been sick. He's in bed. He's fast asleep.

STELLA: Well, you get to bed now, Charles, and you can both sleep as long as you like in the morning.

CHARLES: It was his own fault, you know. He would mix them. I said to him, right at the first, I said "Now, take my tip, and don't mix 'em." But he wouldn't——

STELLA (*wearily*): Oh—get to bed, Charlie. And don't make a noise. Father may be in any minute.

CHARLES: A noble old fellow. Wouldn't disturb him for the world. Good night, girls. (*Withdraws.*)

STELLA: Poor Charlie. Nobody knows better than I do how maddening he can be, but there's something rather sweet about him. He's only a great child. There are dozens of them—great children, just like him—in the theatre.

LILIAN: Well, if he's a child, all the more reason why you should look after him.

STELLA: Don't nag at me, Lilian.

LILIAN: And child or no child, he can't be allowed to spend any more evenings like this with Wilfred.

STELLA: Well, if Wilfred is developing a passion for barmaids, he's quite capable of getting drunk by himself.

LILIAN: No, he isn't. Wilfred's only a silly baby yet. Besides, it's Dad I'm really thinking about.

STELLA: Yes, there's Dad.

LILIAN: Well?

STELLA: You're just trying to drive me out, aren't you, Lilian? I can't understand you. I don't mean what you're doing—I understand that. But you—yourself. You seem to have no feeling for me at all, less than a stranger would have. It doesn't seem to matter to you that I've been desperately unhappy these last months and that when I came home it was like beginning a wonderful new life. Doesn't that mean anything to you, Lilian?

LILIAN: Yes. And it would mean a lot more if I really believed in it.

STELLA: You think it's all insincere, made-up stuff, an actress letting herself go—don't you?

LILIAN: I think you encourage your emotions, so that whatever they are—in a way—you enjoy them.

STELLA: We shall never agree, of course. We've grown up to be thousands of miles away from each other. We live in different worlds. I think you're rather like mother.

LILIAN: I think I am.

STELLA: But what hurts me is that, underneath all this difference, there isn't, with you, any affection or friendship. If you'd lived so long among strangers, in places where nobody knew or cared about you at all, you'd understand how this can hurt. You've behaved very badly to me—you've deliberately set yourself against me—and yet to me you're still Lilian, my sister, and I'm longing all the time to talk properly with you, to remember all the silly old things we did, to laugh and cry together. Can't you see?

LILIAN: The trouble is, Stella, you can afford to feel like that. I can't.

STELLA: What do you mean?

LILIAN: It hasn't been fun for me—treating you like this. It's not true that I don't care at all. I do. But I know—and I knew it the moment you came back—that if I gave in, you'd overwhelm me, sweep me away——

STELLA: And why not?

LILIAN: Because you'd knock down everything I've built up here. You'd take Geoffrey again, without really wanting him. You'd unsettle Dad, Wilfred, everybody and everything. And just when they'd all come to depend on you again, you'd run away—as you did before. People like you, Stella, don't want to make other people unhappy——

STELLA: I don't. Never, never. I know too much about it myself.

LILIAN: But, for all that, you *do* make people unhappy. You can't help it, I suppose. But there's no real responsibility in you.

STELLA (*in despair*): But why are you so responsible—so old and wise? You say I make people unhappy. I may do. I don't know. But I can make them happy too. Can you?

LILIAN: Yes, in my own way.

STELLA: And a dull and dusty way it seems, too.

LILIAN: No it isn't. What do you know about me?

STELLA: How can I know anything about you when you're all shut up inside yourself and won't come out? Oh—it's no use.

LILIAN: We'll never agree.

STELLA: I don't want us to agree. That doesn't matter. But we could at least be *real* together. Even that's impossible, it seems.

LILIAN: It's years too late. Let's be reasonable.

STELLA (*wearily*): Go on, then, let's be reasonable.

LILIAN: You saw what happened to-night? Wilfred—and your Charles. What are you going to do?

STELLA: I don't know. I want to think.

LILIAN: You'll go sooner or later, you know.

STELLA: Why should you say that? You don't know. You don't know what my life's been like. You don't realise what it's meant—coming back—home.

LILIAN: You'll soon get tired of it.

STELLA (*uncertainly*): No. No. I'm sure I shouldn't.

LILIAN (*mercilessly*): Just as you did before. You'd go on smashing things, other people's lives as well as your own. Dad thinks you've had a wonderful time on the stage, that you're going to be a famous actress, that you're happily married——

STELLA (*in distress*): I know. Please, Lilian. I want to think.

LILIAN (*without malice, but forcefully*): If you wanted to stay, you'd have to tell him that you'd failed in everything. And that's only the beginning. You'd never get back into this life properly. You'd be restless. You'd be a person without a real life anywhere. You'd think yourself a failure.

STELLA (*stopping her*): Oh—stop, stop! I won't listen to any more. (*The front door shuts rather noisily.*)

LILIAN: There's Dad coming in.

STELLA: You go to bed, Lilian. I want to talk to him for a minute.

LILIAN: Don't keep him up. He'll be awfully tired.

STELLA (*wearily*): No, no, I know. But I must talk to him. It may be for the last time.

DR. KIRBY *enters. He looks very tired.*

DR. KIRBY: Mrs. Sugden's been delivered of a man-child so big and so like William Sugden that I felt like offering it a pipe of tobacco. Ah, well—I'm tired.

STELLA: You must be, Dad.

LILIAN: Your hot milk and brandy's here.

DR. KIRBY: Thanks. But what are you two doing up?

STELLA: We both heard a noise. It was Charles, and Wilfred. They went to bed but we stayed on, talking.

LILIAN: But I'm going now. Good night.

DR. KIRBY and STELLA: Good night.

LILIAN *goes out.* DR. KIRBY *pours out the hot milk and puts some brandy in it, sits down and nibbles a biscuit.*

DR. KIRBY: I'm getting a bit tired of the human body, Stella. I shall be glad to get back to my birds. I don't know that the behaviour of birds is much better than that of people. They can be as greedy and quarrelsome and vindictive as we can. But they're not so heavy and lumpy. They do things with more style. There's more enchantment about them. They ought to have had the fairy tales, not us.

STELLA: Perhaps they have their own. Was Mrs.—Sugden—difficult?

DR. KIRBY: Not really. Though it's always a worrying job,

especially when you've had to wait overtime. But it's done now. And there's another of us arrived in the village.

STELLA: Poor little chap.

DR. KIRBY: Oh—you needn't be sorry for him. To begin with, he looks a fine healthy specimen—the Sugdens are. And then again, with any luck he'll see a better world than you and I will ever know. That's certainly true of me. I'm not one of these elderly men—and I meet enough of 'em—who think everything's going to the dogs. There's a better world coming, Stella—cleaner, saner, happier. We've only to turn a corner—and it's there. I don't suppose I shall turn it, but you will. And this baby of Sugden's won't know anything else. When he grows up—sometime in the Nineteen Thirties—he simply won't understand the muddle we lived in.

STELLA (*sitting at his feet*): It is a muddle, isn't it?

DR. KIRBY (*sipping his drink*): Yes, and it's mostly our own fault. Yet it isn't either. Have you noticed—or are you too young yet—how one part of us doesn't seem to be responsible for our own character and simply suffers because we have that character? You see yourself *being* yourself, behaving in the old familiar way, and though you may pay and suffer, the real you, the one that watches, doesn't seem to be responsible.

STELLA (*eagerly*): Yes, I was thinking about that only to-night. It's true.

DR. KIRBY (*tenderly*): Queer to see you looking like that again, with your hair down. It makes the last twenty years seem like nothing. You might be a child again. (*He puts a hand on her hair, in an awkward caress. She takes his hand and leans her face against his arm.*)

STELLA (*gently*): Dad, I'm afraid Charles and I must go to-morrow.

DR. KIRBY: That's bad news, my dear. I'd hoped you were staying a long time.

STELLA: So had I. But—well—we've just been offered two very good parts.

DR. KIRBY: And you're right to take them. Though I think you could do with a longer holiday than you've had. But if the English Theatre won't even let go of you for a few weeks, we must put up with it, that's all.

STELLA: I don't want to go.

DR. KIRBY: You mustn't mind us. I'm proud of you. I like to think of you forging ahead in your profession, getting all you can out of life. You know, you're doing it for me, as well as for yourself. As I told you before, I think I made a mistake. Your mother wanted me to settle down here, so I did. Nobody knows but you that I've ever regretted it. That's our secret.

STELLA (*distressed, deeply affectionate, pressing her face against his arm*): Dad!

DR. KIRBY: You're rectifying that mistake, my dear. And only you. Lilian's your mother over again. As long as she's a house of her own—and a man in it—she'll be happy in her own way. Wilfred's a good lad, but he's a bit weak and easy-going. He'll never do much. But you're going on, living as I could have lived. I'm glad. I'm proud. (*Putting a hand gently on her face.*) So there can't be anything to cry about.

STELLA (*jumping up*): Of course not. I'm stupid. And it's bedtime.

DR. KIRBY (*briskly*): Sunday to-morrow. Only one train to London. The Four Twenty. And a brute.

STELLA (*going to door*): That's nothing. We're used to brutal Sunday trains. They're almost the only kind we know. (*Turning at door, trying to smile at him.*) Good night, Dad.

DR. KIRBY: Good night, Stella. (*He finishes his milk and brandy as the curtain falls.*)

SCENE II

Same as before. Sunday afternoon. It is a dark afternoon. The door on the left is open. DR. KIRBY *enters, followed closely by* SARAH, *who is talking volubly and dividing her attention between the window and him. He is trying as best he can to search through the drawers at the table.*

SARAH: If you'd a bit o' sense you wouldn't let her stir out to-day, let alone go to London. Sunday an' all. Travelling o' Sunday in a fog. Nowt good'll come of that. It's as thick as ever it wor. Nay, thicker. It'll be worse afore it's better. What they want to run trains at all for o' Sundays, I don't know. Why can't they let folks have a bit o' peace and quiet for one day in the week? (*Taking advantage of her back being turned,* DR. KIRBY *escapes.* SARAH *does not notice or turn round.*) Stop at home and sit by the fire. London 'ull still be there to-morrow. It'll keep, London will. Unless it goes rotten. Daft, I call it.

WILFRED *pops his head round the corner.*

WILFRED: I say, Sarah. Who do you think you're talking to?
SARAH: Not to you.

WILFRED: Well, you're not talking to anybody else, because there's nobody else here.

SARAH: Then I'm wasting my breath.

WILFRED (*entering*): The car'll be here in another quarter of an hour

SARAH: Are they having a motor-car to take 'em to the station?

WILFRED: Yes, old Thompson's Arrol-Johnston.

SARAH: I call it tempting providence.   .

WILFRED: I can't find my records. Have you seen them?

SARAH: Do you mean the things for that talking machine?

WILFRED: Yes. I can't find them anywhere.

SARAH: I'll go and help Miss Stella to finish her packing. (*Moves towards door.*)

WILFRED: I believe you know where they are.

SARAH: You shall have 'em in the morning.

WILFRED: I thought as much. Cheek! Where've you put them?

SARAH: .Where you won't find them. We don't want no talking machines on a Sunday. You can play it to-morrow all day if you like.

WILFRED (*shouting*): I don't want to play it all day to-morrow. I want those records now.

SARAH: If I gave 'em you, you wouldn't have time to play 'em. (DR. KIRBY *bustles in. He is in a very fussy mood.* SARAH *darts at him.*) What you're letting Miss Stella go for to-day, Sunday, and wi' this fog and in a motor-car too, I don't know.

DR. KIRBY (*very fussily*): Don't be fussy, Sarah. Don't be fussy. I left a little book somewhere round here this morning. (*Ring at door.* DR. KIRBY *calls through open door left.*) See who that is, Sarah. (*Almost to himself.*) And I hope to goodness I'm not going to be called away now.

SARAH (*calling off*): It's Captain Farrant.

DR. KIRBY (*calling to her*): All right then, send him in, send him in. (*To* WILFRED.) It's a little book—about that size—called *Moorland Bird Life.* Have you seen it?

WILFRED: No. And Sarah's hidden my gramophone records away somewhere, because it's Sunday. Damned cheek!

FARRANT *appears in doorway.*

DR. KIRBY: Hello, Geoffrey. Come into the surgery with me, will you? I want to get something for Stella to take away with her.

DR. KIRBY *bustles him out.* WILFRED, *muttering "Too much fuss," lights a cigarette.* CHARLES *enters.*

CHARLES: How's the head now?

WILFRED: Getting better, thanks.

CHARLES: You mixed 'em too much, old boy. (*Comes in and looks out of window.*) God!—what a beast of a day. And I don't feel too crisp.

WILFRED (*not without gloomy satisfaction*): You'll have a rotten journey.

CHARLES: I know we shall. You can't tell me anything about long train journeys on foggy Sundays. If we'd any sense, we'd stay here and sit in front of the fire and talk about West Africa and wild birds and operations and Gaby Deslys and the Bunny-Hug.

WILFRED: Can you do the Bunny-Hug?

CHARLES: No. Nor the Turkey Trot. Nor the Tango. Not my line—thank God! At the moment, I feel that my line is playing old family solicitors, rheumaticky, toothless old scoundrels. (*Imitates one.*) "I have been instructed, Sir Rupert, to acquaint you with the te-r-r-rms of your uncle's will."

WILFRED (*laughs*): Jolly fine, I wish I was an actor.

CHARLES (*gloomily*): And I wish I was in West Africa—the hottest and blackest bit. (*Coming closer, and lowering voice.*) By the way, just let me give you a tip, while I've a chance, old boy. Take it or leave it. But I think, if I were you, I should give that pub—you know the one—the "White Hart"—a miss, and give the little girl Alice a miss with it. I don't want to interfere, old boy—and couldn't preach if I tried. But they're no good, those bits. Not to a youngster like you. She'll only lead you up and down the garden. I know. I've had some in my time. Give it a miss, old boy.

WILFRED (*sullen*): Yes—but you don't understand——

CHARLES: Absolutely understand everything. I've been there. I've had some. Just think it over, old boy.

WILFRED (*wearily*): The trouble is—— I'm having a hell of a time.

CHARLES (*patting him on the shoulder*): It'll pass. I know. Try and find another little girl. There must be plenty round here. Squires' daughters with round red cheeks who'll sing the Indian Love Lyrics to you after dinner. (*Sings, in burlesque manner.*) "Ler-hess than the der-hust, Be-neath thy chariot whee-heel".

STELLA *enters, dressed as in* ACT I. *She carries a small case which she puts on the table.*

STELLA: Oh, Wilfred, Lilian wants you.

WILFRED (*gloomily*): All right. (*Goes off.*)

CHARLES: Haven't you finished packing yet, old girl?

STELLA: Very nearly. All but some needlework and a couple of books. Charles, I want to talk to you.

CHARLES: And I want to talk to you. Haven't had a chance yet to-day. Look here, what's happening? I get up——

STELLA: At lunch time.

CHARLES: Admitted. And not feeling very bright. And I find we're leaving this afternoon. I gather, from what your father said, that we're supposed to have just been offered two wonderful parts.

STELLA (*hastily*): That's what I told him. I hope you didn't——

CHARLES: Now, now. You know me better than that. I murmured something about Tree and His Majesty's Theatre—big new production. Nearly convinced myself.

STELLA (*relieved*): That's all right, then.

CHARLES: Yes, as far as it goes. But I want to know what's happening.

STELLA (*smiling faintly*): Well, we're both getting on the same train for town and sitting in the same compartment. Once we're out of sight, if you don't want to talk to me, you needn't, Charles.

CHARLES: I see. We're putting on a performance for these people here.

STELLA: Yes. It's probably the only performance we shall put on for some time, so we'd better make the best of it.

CHARLES: Look here, Stella, couldn't we go on with it when we get to town?

STELLA: Do you want to?

CHARLES: I do. You ought to know that. But do you, that's the point?

STELLA (*gravely*): I think I'd like to try again, Charles.

CHARLES (*happily*): That's wonderful of you, it really is, old girl.

STELLA (*half laughing, but sharp*): And you mustn't call me "old girl".

CHARLES: Sorry, I forgot.

STELLA: How much money have you?

CHARLES (*humorously*): Now I know we *have* joined up again. Quite like old times. Yes, I've some money. About seventeen pounds. And then there's a fellow at the club who owes me a tenner——

STELLA: I haven't forgotten him. He still doesn't count. You haven't much, have you? And I've only about twenty left. We shall have to get a job quick, Charles.

CHARLES: We'll walk into one to-morrow, now that we're together again. Might pick up a couple of leads for the road. What about trying for one of God's own countries again, eh?

STELLA: Yes, I wouldn't mind. In fact, I'd like it. If I'm going away, I might as well go a long way.

CHARLES: You're right, y'know, to clear out. You'd never settle here. All right for a break, but that's all. You're doing the right thing.

STELLA (*indulgently*): And am I doing the right thing—taking you back again?

CHARLES: It's a risk, I know—I'm no catch—but I won't let you down. We've had some fun together. We'll have some more yet. What do you say?

STELLA (*after a pause*): You've got the wrong tie on. Why do you keep wearing that tie?

CHARLES: It's the only one I brought. What's the matter with it?

STELLA: It's awful.

FARRANT *opens the door.*

FARRANT: Oh—sorry.

CHARLES: That's all right. Come in, old boy. We're just having a chat about ties.

FARRANT *comes in.*

STELLA: We haven't long now. (*To* CHARLES.) Will you and Wilfred get my trunk down?

CHARLES: All baggage will be stacked in the hall—immediately. (*Goes out, whistling.*)

STELLA: Well—Geoffrey?

FARRANT: You're going.

STELLA: Very soon. Back to town.

FARRANT: I'm going too.

STELLA: You're going? Where? When?

FARRANT: I'm going out to New Zealand for a year or two, perhaps longer. To my cousin.

STELLA: But, Geoffrey, you were saying, only the other day, that you were so fond of this place you couldn't bear to leave it.

FARRANT: So I thought. Then I found I was wrong. I wanted to get away.

STELLA: And you've really made your mind up?

FARRANT: Yes. I cabled my cousin yesterday. I shall take the next boat.

STELLA (*involuntarily*): Poor Lilian!

FARRANT: Why do you say that?

STELLA: Don't you realise that Lilian's in love with you, and has been for years?

FARRANT (*embarrassed*): Awful question to ask a chap!

STELLA: Well, she is, you know.

FARRANT (*embarrassed*): I'm sorry. Matter of fact, I'm very fond of Lilian. She's a fine girl. We've seen a lot of one another.

STELLA (*softly*): Then why don't you marry her, Geoffrey?

FARRANT: Because I don't want to, Stella. And I don't understand why you should ask me to. I don't understand women, at all, I'm afraid. I can't make you out—for instance.

STELLA: Then don't try.

FARRANT: I was angry with you when I left the other afternoon.

STELLA: I know you were, my dear. I'm sorry.

FARRANT: In a way, I'm still angry. But it's no use.

STELLA: It isn't any use being angry with people—like that. I'm beginning to see that.

FARRANT: I don't mean that—quite. I mean—well, here I am, you see. And I didn't know you were going when I called. I just couldn't keep away.

STELLA: But you were determined to go yourself—and a long way, too?

FARRANT: That was your doing, of course. I knew you'd be leaving us soon, and I felt you'd just leave me and the whole place as flat as a pancake. I couldn't stand the thought of that. I had to do something.

STELLA (*distressed*): I'm sorry. It's all such a muddle, Geoffrey, and I seem to be muddle-maker in chief. For years, while I stayed away, I had the thought of this place—home—always in my mind, and here, I felt, it was different—no muddle. For an hour—no, only for half an hour—it was all I had thought it was, and I was so happy. Then I found it was all mixed up with the rest of the world. And now I haven't even got this to think about.

FARRANT: You talk too much about happiness, Stella.

STELLA (*with a faint smile*): I think I do, Geoffrey. I must be a braver traveller. We have our lives to get on with, to live them as best we can. There's no running away. No escape. No miracles.

There is a burst of talking, off, as if the kitchen door had been opened.

CHARLES (*off*): I'll carry the tray.

FARRANT: I think the others are coming. Good-bye, Stella.

STELLA (*quickly*): But you're coming to the station?

FARRANT (*very quietly*): Yes, but this is the real good-bye. And good luck. I—well—I shall always love you.

STELLA: It's more than I deserve. Good-bye, my dear.

She kisses him, lightly, quickly. SARAH *enters, followed by* CHARLES *carrying a tray on which are cups of tea. A car can be heard hooting outside.* DR. KIRBY *and* LILIAN *follow* CHARLES.

WILFRED *arrives a moment later. They are all wearing or carrying overcoats, etc., and are ready for the journey.*

CHARLES: Enter ye butler!

SARAH: I don't care if all the motor-cars in England is blowing and puffing and tooting outside, you're all going to have a good hot cup o' tea afore you go.

STELLA: Of course we are. Lovely tea. Thank you, Sarah.

WILFRED (*entering*): The car's here. You haven't much time. (*The tray is on the table and they are now grouped round it.*)

SARAH (*going off right, grumbling*): Plenty o' time. Let the thing wait.

CHARLES (*trying tea, in low voice*): Strong stuff, isn't it?

DR. KIRBY (*also in low voice*): Far too strong. But she's made it specially. Must try and drink some just to please her.

CHARLES: Rather.

STELLA: Of course. (*In loud ringing tone.*) Lovely tea.

FARRANT: Hello, Lilian!

LILIAN (*smiling charmingly*): Hello, Geoffrey. Isn't it a horrible day?

FARRANT: Beastly.

LILIAN: How's the roan?

FARRANT: Better than I thought. The vet says it's a sprain. (*Moves away negligently.*)

Enter SARAH *from right, carrying small parcel.*

SARAH: I'd nearly forgotten this, Miss Stella.

STELLA: What is it, darling?

SARAH: Why, your fancy dress I found the other day—very day you came home.

WILFRED: She doesn't want it, Sarah.

STELLA: Of course, I do. I shall hang it up in my dressing-room—always, wherever I am. A lovely present, Sarah. And the tea's so good.

CHARLES: Extraordinary.

DR. KIRBY: Now, Sarah, you must stop in, y'know. No station for you.

STELLA: Good gracious, no! Much too cold and foggy for you. Besides I can say good-bye to you much better here.

SARAH: All right, then. Won't you have a drop more tea, love?

STELLA: No, thank you, darling.

WILFRED: Time we were off.

There is a vague stir but no definite move towards the door.

CHARLES (*idly*): If that telephone rings when we've gone, I'll bet it's to offer me the biggest part I've ever known—and I'll miss it.

WILFRED: More likely to ask me to go shooting rabbits with the Mowbrays.

DR. KIRBY (*heartily*): Don't you worry. I'll be the person who'll be wanted. And I've a good idea who'll be wanting me—poor soul. Well, all ready?

They straggle out, first WILFRED and DR. KIRBY, then LILIAN and FARRANT.

CHARLES (*with STELLA's parcel*): Now, Sarah, old girl, you stay here and keep warm. And I'm delighted to have met you. Heard a lot about you from Stella, y'know. Good-bye. (*Holds out his hand.*)

SARAH: Good-bye. (*Shaking hands timidly.*) And—look after her.

CHARLES (*with mock salute of sword*): With my life! Good-bye. (*He goes out.*)

SARAH: He's not a bad sort for an actor chap, though I'll bet he takes a bit o' watching But you look after him, too, love. He's nowt but a big daft lad—like 'em all.

STELLA (*whispering*): Oh, Sarah. I don't know what to say. There aren't any words.

SARAH: Nay, love. Nay, little love. (*Fondling her face.*) And don't catch cold when you're coming out o' the theatres. (*Very softly.*) I'm an old woman now, a'most past my time. Happen I shan't see you again.

STELLA (*crying*): Yes, you will. You must.

SARAH: Oh, I'll see you sometime. There's a better place than this, love.

Noise of motor engine starting up outside.

CHARLES (*off, calling*): Come on, Stella.

STELLA (*breaking loose*): I must go. Good-bye, Sarah, darling. (*She takes a last look round.*) Good-bye—everything.

She hurriedly kisses SARAH, *then runs out blindly. The door bangs to behind her. Then the outer door is heard closing with a bang. Noise of car going away.* SARAH *goes to the window, stares out for a moment, then closes the curtains, so that there is no light but that from the fire. She goes over to the fire and lights a taper. The telephone bell begins ringing.* SARAH *goes to the telephone with the lighted taper in her hand, holds the light close to it for a second, staring at it in bewilderment, then slowly withdraws into her own room. The telephone ringing is fainter, the firelight fades, until at last there is silence and there is darkness, and we find that the curtain has fallen and the play has ended.*

END OF ACT THREE

TIME AND THE CONWAYS

A Play in Three Acts

For IRENE and IVOR BROWN with
affection

"Time and the Conways" *was first produced in London on August 26th, 1937, at the Duchess Theatre, with the following cast:*

HAZEL	ROSEMARY SCOTT
CAROL	EILEEN ERSKINE
ALAN	RAYMOND HUNTLEY
MADGE	MOLLY RANKIN
KAY	JEAN FORBES-ROBERTSON
MRS. CONWAY	BARBARA EVEREST
JOAN HELFORD	HELEN HORSEY
GERALD THORNTON	WILFRED BABBAGE
ERNEST BEEVERS	MERVYN JOHNS
ROBIN	ALEXANDER ARCHDALE

The Play produced by IRENE HENTSCHEL

ACT I
That Night. Kay's Twenty-first Birthday

ACT II
Another Night. And Another Birthday

ACT III
That Night Again. Her Twenty-first Birthday

ACT III is continuous with ACT I

The scene throughout is a sitting-room in Mrs. CONWAY's house, a detached villa in a prosperous suburb of a manufacturing town, Newlingham. ACTS I and III take place on an autumn night in 1919. ACT II on an autumn night at the present time. (1937)

ACT I

There is a party at the Conways, this autumn evening of 1919, but we cannot see it, only hear it. All we can see at first is the light from the hall coming through the curtained archway on the right of the room, and a little red firelight on the other side. But we can hear young voices chattering and laughing and singing, the sharp little explosion of a cracker or two, and a piano playing popular music of that period. After a moment or two, a number of voices begin to sing the tune we hear on the piano. It is all very jolly indeed.

Then we hear a girl's voice (it is HAZEL CONWAY'S) *calling, loud and clear: "Mother, where shall we put them?" The voice that replies, further off, can only be* MRS. CONWAY'S, *and she says: "In the back room. Then we'll act out here." To this,* HAZEL, *who is obviously very excited, screams: "Yes, marvellous!" and then calls to some-body still further away, probably upstairs: "*CAROL—*in the back room."*

And now HAZEL *dashes in, switching on the light. We see at once that she is a tall, golden young creature, dressed in her very best for this party. She is carrying an armful of old clothes, hats, and odds and ends, all the things that happy people used to dress up in for charades. The room looks very cosy, although it has no doorway, only the large curtained archway on the right. At the back is a window with a step up to it, and a cushioned seat. The curtains are drawn. On the left is a fireplace or an anthracite stove, glowing red. There are several small bookcases against or in the walls, some pieces of fairly good furniture, including a round table and a small bureau, and some passable pictures. It is obviously one of those nondescript rooms, used by the family far more than the drawing-room is, and variously called the Back Room, the Morning Room, the School-room, the Nursery, the Blue, Brown or Red Room. This might easily have been called the Red Room, for in this light it seems to range from pink to plum colour, and it makes a fine cosy setting for the girls in their party dress.*

Another one has arrived, while HAZEL *is dumping her charade things on a round settee in the middle of the room. This is* CAROL, *the youngest of the Conways—perhaps sixteen—and now terrifically excited, breathless, and almost tottering beneath a load of charade stuff, including a cigar-box gloriously filled with old false whiskers and noses, spectacles, and what not. With all the reckless haste of a*

73

child she bangs down all this stuff, and starts to talk, although she has no breath left. And now—after adding that CAROL *is an enchanting young person—we can leave them to explain themselves.*

CAROL (*gasping but triumphant*): I've found—the box—with all the false whiskers and things in——

HAZEL (*triumphantly*): I knew it hadn't been thrown away.

CAROL: Nobody'd *dare* to throw it away. (*Holds it out, with lid open.*) Look! (HAZEL *makes a grab at it.*) Don't *snatch*!

HAZEL (*not angrily*): Well, I must *look*, mustn't I, idiot? (*They both, like children, eagerly explore the contents of the box.*) Bags I this one. (*She fishes out a large drooping moustache.*) Oo—and this! (*Fishes out very bulbous false nose.*)

CAROL (*an unselfish creature*): All right, but don't take *all* the good ones, Hazel. Kay and Madge will want some. I think Kay ought to have *first* choice. After all, it's *her* birthday—and you know how she adores charades. Mother won't want any of these because she'd rather look grand, wouldn't she? Spanish or Russian or something. What are you doing?

HAZEL *has turned aside to fasten on the nose and moustache, and now has managed it, though they are not very secure. She now turns round.*

HAZEL (*in deep voice*): Good morning, good morning.

CAROL (*with a scream of delight*): Mr. Pennyman! You know, Hazel, at the paper shop? The one who hates Lloyd George and wags his head very slowly all the time he tells you Lloyd George is no good. Do Mr. Pennyman, Hazel. Go on.

HAZEL (*in her ordinary voice, incongruous*): I couldn't, Carol. I've only seen him about twice. I never go to the paper shop.

ALAN *looks in, grinning when he sees* HAZEL. *He is a shy, quiet, young man, in his earlier twenties, who can have a slight stammer. He is dressed, rather carelessly, in ordinary clothes.* CAROL *turns and sees him.*

CAROL: Alan, come in, and don't let the others see. (*As he does.*) Isn't she *exactly* like Mr. Pennyman at the paper shop, the one who hates Lloyd George?

ALAN (*grinning shyly*): She is—a bit.

HAZEL (*in a fantastic deep voice*): "I hate Lloyd George."

ALAN: No, he doesn't talk like that, Hazel.

CAROL: Not the least little bit. He says (*with a rather good imitation of a thick, semi-educated man's voice*): "I'll tell you what it is—Mish

Conway—that there Lloyd George—they're going to be shorry they ever put 'im where they did—shee?"

ALAN (*grinning*): Yes, that's him. Very good, Carol.

CAROL (*excitedly*): I think I ought to be an actress. They said at school I was the best Shylock they'd ever had.

HAZEL (*taking off the nose and moustache*): You can have these if you like, Carol.

CAROL (*taking them*): Are you sure you don't want them? I don't think you ought to dress up as a silly man because you're so pretty. Perhaps I could wear these and do Mr. Pennyman. Couldn't we bring him into the third syllable somehow? Instead of a general. I think we've had enough generals.

ALAN: We have. Ask Kay to work in Mr. Pennyman instead.

HAZEL: Kay ought to be here now, planning everything.

ALAN: She's coming in. Mother told me to tell you not to make too much of a mess in here.

CAROL: You *must* have a mess with charades. It's part of it.

HAZEL: And just wait till mother starts dressing up. She makes more mess than anybody. (*To* ALAN.) I hope some of the old ones are going now. Are they?

ALAN: Yes.

HAZEL: It's much more fun without them. And mother daren't let herself go while they're still here. Tell Kay and Madge to come in, Alan.

ALAN: Right.

> *Goes out. The two girls begin turning the clothes over.* HAZEL *picks out some old-fashioned women's things and holds them up or against herself.*

HAZEL: Look at these! Could you believe people *ever* wore such ridiculous things?

CAROL: I can just remember mother in that, can't you?

HAZEL: Of course I can, infant!

CAROL (*more soberly, looking at man's old-fashioned shooting or Norfolk coat*): That was Daddy's, wasn't it?

HAZEL: Yes. I believe he wore it—that very holiday.

CAROL: Perhaps we ought to put it away.

HAZEL: I don't think mother would mind—now.

CAROL: Yes she would. And I know I would. I don't want anybody to dress up and be funny in the coat father wore just before he was drowned. (*She has now folded the coat, and puts it on the window-seat. Then, as she returns.*) I wonder if it's very horrible being drowned.

HAZEL (*impatiently*): Oh, don't start that all over again, Carol. Don't you remember how you used to go on asking that—until mother was furious?

CAROL: Yes—but I was only a kid then.

HAZEL: Well, now that you think you aren't a kid any longer, just stop it.

CAROL: It was the coat that made me remember. You see, Hazel, to be talking and laughing and all jolly, just the same as usual—and then, only half an hour afterwards—to be drowned—it's so horrible. It seemed awfully quick to us—but perhaps to him, there in the water, it may have seemed to take ages——

HAZEL: Oh, stop it, Carol. Just when we're having some fun. Why do you?

CAROL: I don't know. But don't you often feel like that? Just when everything is very jolly and exciting, I suddenly think of something awfully serious, sometimes horrible—like Dad drowning—or that little mad boy I once saw with the *huge head*—or that old man who walks in the Park with that great lump growing out of his face——

HAZEL (*stopping her ears*): No, I'm not listening. I'm not listening.

CAROL: They pop up right in the middle of the jolly stuff, you know, Hazel. It happens to Kay, too. So it must be in the family—a bit.

Enter MADGE. *She is a year or two older than* HAZEL, *not so pretty, and a far more serious and responsible person. She has been to Girton, and already done a little teaching, and you feel all this in her brisk, decided, self-confident manner. She is, too, an earnest enthusiast.*

MADGE: You found them? Good. (*Looks over the things.*) I didn't think we'd have so many old things left. Mother ought to have given them away.

HAZEL: I'm glad she didn't. Besides, who'd have had them?

MADGE: Lots of people would have been glad of them. You never realise, Hazel, how wretchedly poor most people are. It just doesn't occur to you, does it?

HAZEL (*not crossly*): Don't be schoolmistressy, Madge.

CAROL (*who is trying things on, turning to point at* MADGE *impishly*): Has Gerald Thornton arrived?

MADGE: As a matter of fact, he has—a few minutes ago.

CAROL (*triumphantly*): I knew it. I could see it in your eye, Madge.

MADGE: Don't be absurd. He's brought another man with him, a new client of his, who's desperately anxious to know this family.

HAZEL: So he ought to be. Nice?

MADGE: Oh—a funny little man.

CAROL (*dancing about*): That's just what we want—a funny little man. Perfect for charades.

MADGE: No, not that kind. In fact, he probably hasn't any sense of humour. Very shy, so far, and terrified of mother. Very much the little business man, I should think.

CAROL: Is he a profiteer—like the ones in *Punch*?

MADGE: He looks as if he might be, some day. His name's Ernest Beevers.

HAZEL (*giggling*): What a silly name! I'm sorry for his wife, if he has one.

MADGE: I gather he hasn't. Look here, we ought to be starting. (*Enter* KAY, *whose twenty-first birthday party this is. An intelligent, sensitive girl, who need not be as pretty as* HAZEL. *She has a sheet of paper.*) Kay, we ought to be starting.

KAY: I know. The others are coming. (*Begins rooting among the things.*) Some good costumes here, ladies. Oo—look! (*She has fished out some absurd old-fashioned woman's cape, cloak or coat, and hat, and throws them on ridiculously, then stands apart and strikes absurd melodramatic attitude and speaks in false stilted tone.*) One moment, Lord What's-your-name. If I am discovered here, who will believe that my purpose in coming here to-night—visiting your—er—rooms— er unaccompanied—was solely to obtain the—er papers—that will enable me to clear—er—my husband's name, the name of a man who —er—has asked nothing better than the—er privilege of serving his country—and ours too, Lord Thingumtibob—one who—that is—to whom—— (*In ordinary tone.*) No, I'm getting all tied up. You know, we ought to have had a scene like that, all grand and dramatic and full of *papers*.

MADGE: Well, what *are* we to have?

HAZEL (*coolly*): I've forgotten the word.

CAROL (*indignantly*): Hazel, you're the *limit*! And we spent hours working it out!

HAZEL: I didn't. Only you and Kay, just because you fancy yourselves as budding authoresses and actresses.

KAY (*severely*): The word—idiot!—is *Pussyfoot*. Puss. See. Foot. Then the whole word.

MADGE: I think four scenes are too many. And they'll easily guess it.

KAY: That doesn't matter. It makes them happy if they guess it.

CAROL (*rather solemnly*): The great thing is—to *dress up*.

Enter MRS. CONWAY. *She is a charming woman in her middle forties, very nicely dressed, with an easy, vivacious manner.*

MRS. C.: Now I'm ready—if you are. What a mess you're making. I knew you would. Let me see. (*Dives into the clothes, and scatters them far more wildly than the others have done. She finally fishes out a Spanish shawl and mantilla.*) Ah—here they are. Now I shall be a Spanish beauty. I know a song for it, too. (*Begins putting the Spanish things on.*)

HAZEL (*to* KAY): What did I tell you?

MRS. C. (*who is specially fond of* HAZEL): What did you tell her, darling?

HAZEL: I told Kay, whatever she arranged, you'd insist on doing your Spanish turn.

MRS. C.: Well, why not?

KAY: It doesn't come into the scenes I'd thought of, that's all.

MRS. C. (*busy with her costume*): Oh—you can easily arrange that, dear—you're so clever. I've just been telling Dr. Halliday and his niece how clever you are. They seemed surprised, I can't imagine why.

HAZEL: It's the first time I've seen Monica Halliday out of her land girl costume. I'm surprised she didn't turn up to-night in her trousers and leggings.

KAY: She looks quite queer out of them, doesn't she? Rather like a female impersonator.

MADGE: Oh, come on, Kay. What do we do?

KAY: The first scene, *Puss*, is an old lady who's lost her cat. She's really a kind of witch.

CAROL (*happily*): I'm to be the old lady.

CAROL *begins finding suitable clothes—an old shawl, etc.—and some white hair—for the old lady. And during following dialogue, converts herself into a very creditable imitation.*

KAY: Mother, you and Hazel are her two daughters who are visiting her—

HAZEL: I know my bit. I keep saying "I always hated that terrible cat of yours, Mother." What can I wear? (*Pokes about.*)

MRS. C. (*now Spanish*): Well, that's all right, dear. I'll be the Spanish daughter, you see.

KAY (*resignedly*): She didn't have a Spanish daughter, but I suppose it doesn't matter.

MRS. C.: Not in the least. Nobody cares. And then I think I'd better not appear in the others, because I suppose you'll be wanting me to sing afterwards.

KAY: Of course. But I'd put you down for two more. Madge and Joan Helford will have to do those.

MRS. C.: What a pity Robin isn't here! You know, Madge, he wrote and said he might be demobbed any day now, and it seems such a shame just to miss Kay's party. Robin loves parties. He's like me. Your father never cared for them much. Suddenly, right in the middle, just when everything was getting along, he'd want to be quiet—and take me into a corner and ask me how much longer people were staying—just when they were beginning to enjoy themselves. I never could understand that.

KAY: I can. I've often felt like that.

MRS. C.: But why, dear, why? It isn't sensible. If you're having a party, you're having a party.

KAY (*earnestly*): Yes, it isn't that. And it isn't that you suddenly dislike the people. But you feel—at least I do, and I suppose that's what father felt too—you feel, quite suddenly, that it isn't *real* enough —and you want something to be *real*. Do you see, Mother?

MRS. C.: No I don't, my dear. It sounds a little morbid to me. But your father could be quite morbid sometimes—you mightn't think so, but he could—and I suppose you take after him.

KAY (*very gravely*): Do you think that sometimes, in a mysterious sort of way, he *knew*?

MRS. C. (*not too attentive to this*): Knew *what*, dear? Look at Hazel, doesn't she look rather sweet? I can remember where I first wore those things. Absurd! Knew *what*?

KAY: Knew what was going to happen to him. You know, Alan said that some of the men he knew who were killed in the trenches seemed to know sometimes that they were going to be killed, as if a kind of shadow fell over them. Just as if—now and then—we could see round the corner—into the future.

MRS. C. (*easily*): You have the most extraordinary ideas. You must try and put some of them into your book. Are you happy, darling?

KAY: Yes, Mother. Very happy.

MRS. C.: That's all right then. I want you to have a lovely birthday. I feel we all can be happy again, now that the horrible war's all over and people are sensible again, and Robin and Alan are quite safe. I forgot to ask—did Robin send you anything, Kay?

KAY: No. I didn't expect him to.

MRS. C.: Oh—but that isn't like Robin, you know, Kay. He's a most generous boy, much too generous really. Now that may mean he thinks he's coming home very soon.

Enter ALAN *with* JOAN HELFORD, *who is* HAZEL's *friend and the same age, pretty and rather foolish.*

KAY: Alan, tell them we're beginning—and it's three syllables.

ALAN *goes.*

JOAN: I think you all look marvellous. I'm rotten at this, you know, Kay Don't say I didn't warn you.

KAY: Now then, Carol, you start. And remember, only say "Puss" once. Don't you two say it—only Carol. (ALAN *returns.* CAROL *goes out—and there can be the sound of distant laughing and clapping.*) Good old Carol. Now then—you two. (*Almost pushes them off.*) Now the next syllable is *S.Y.* So I thought it wouldn't be cheating too badly if we called that "sy". Y'know, Cockney—"I sy, Bert." So this is an East End scene. Madge, you're the old mother.

MADGE (*who has started putting on very droll shabby clothes*): Yes, I remembered.

ALAN: What am I? I forget.

KAY: You're Bert. Just put something silly on. Is there anything here you can wear, Joan?

During following dialogue, they all dress up.

JOAN: I was in London last week, staying with my uncle, and we went to the theatre *three times.* We saw *Tilly of Bloomsbury* and *Cinderella Man* and *Kissing Time.* I liked *Cinderella Man* best—Owen Nares, y'know. I thought Robin was coming home soon.

KAY: He is.

JOAN: He's an officer, isn't he? You weren't an officer, were you, Alan?

ALAN: No, I was a lance-corporal. One stripe, y'know. Nothing at all.

JOAN: Didn't you want to be anything better than that?

ALAN: No.

KAY: Alan has no ambition at all. Have you, my pet?

ALAN (*simply*): Not much.

JOAN: If I were a man, I'd want to be very important. What are you doing now, Alan? Somebody said you were at the Town Hall.

ALAN: I am. In the Rate Office. Just a clerk, y'know.

JOAN: Isn't it dull?

ALAN: Yes.

KAY: Alan never minds being dull. I believe he has tremendous long adventures inside his head that nobody knows anything about.

JOAN: Hazel says you've started to write another novel, Kay. Have you?

KAY (*rather curtly*): Yes.

JOAN: I don't know how you can—I mean, I think I'd be all right once I'd started properly—but I can't see how you start. What did you do with the last one?

KAY: Burnt it.

JOAN: Why?

KAY: It was putrid.

JOAN: But wasn't that an awful waste of time?

KAY: Yes, I suppose so.

ALAN: Still, look at the time you and I waste, Joan.

JOAN: Oh—no—I'm always doing *something*. Even though I haven't to go to the canteen any more, I'm always busy. (MADGE, *who has withdrawn herself a little, now laughs.*) Why do you laugh, Madge?

MADGE: Can't a girl laugh?

JOAN (*humbly*): You always did laugh at me, Madge. I suppose because I'm not clever, like you.

HAZEL *returns, letting in noise—laughing and clapping—from outside.*

HAZEL: Well, you can imagine what happened. Mother let herself go, and of course it became all Spanish. I don't believe they'll ever remember hearing "puss" mentioned. What are you supposed to be, Joan?

JOAN (*hopefully*): A sort of Coster girl.

HAZEL: You look a sort of general mess. Oh—(*to* KAY) Carol wants to do Mr. Pennyman at the paper shop instead of a general for the third syllable.

KAY: How can she? If it's soldiers drilling, you can't have Mr. Pennyman. Unless we make him another soldier—and get Gerald Thorton or somebody to be a general.

CAROL *returns, very hot and flushed, and begins taking off her old woman's disguise.*

CAROL: Mother's still on. Golly!—it's baking being an old witch.

KAY: Do you insist on being Mr. Pennyman in the third syllable?

CAROL (*brightening up*): Oo—I'd forgotten that. Yes, please let me do Mr. Pennyman, Kay—my lamb, my love, my precious——

KAY: All right. But he'll have to be a soldier. Just joined up, you see.

> *Enter* MRS. C. *very grand, flushed, triumphant. She is carrying a glass of claret cup.*

MRS. C.: Well—really—that was *very* silly—but they seemed to enjoy it, and that's the great thing. I thought you were very good, Carol. (*To* KAY.) Carol was sweet, Kay. Now don't ask me to do any more of this, because really I mustn't, especially if you want me to sing afterwards. So leave me out, Kay. (*Begins to sip cup.*)

KAY: All right. Now come on. (*Begins shepherding her players,* MADGE, ALAN, JOAN.)

JOAN: Honestly, Kay, I'll be *awful.*

KAY: It doesn't matter. You've nothing to do. Now then—Madge.

MADGE (*loudly, in laborious imitation of Cockney mother*): Nah then, Bert. End yew, Dy-sy. Cem along or we'll be lite. (*Leads the way off, followed by other three.*)

HAZEL: How on earth did you get that claret cup, Mother?

MRS. C. (*complacently*): Got Gerald Thornton to hand it to me—and it rounded off my little scene nicely. I don't want any more. Would you like it?

> HAZEL *takes it, and sips while removing things. They are all removing things.*

CAROL: Mother, you weren't going to be an *actress*, were you—just a singer?

MRS. C.: I don't know what you mean by *just* a singer. I was a singer certainly. But I did some acting too. When the Newlingham Amateur Operatic first did *Merrie England*, I played Bess. And I'd had all you children then. *You* were only about two, Carol.

HAZEL: Mother, Joan *did* stay in London last week, and she went to three theatres.

MRS. C.: She has relatives there, and we haven't. That makes a great difference.

HAZEL: Aren't we *ever* going?

MRS. C.: Yes, of course. Perhaps Robin will take us—I mean, just you and me—when he comes back.

CAROL (*solemnly*): It says in the paper this morning that We Must All Get On With Our Jobs. This Mere Rush For Amusement has gone on long enough now. There's Work Waiting To Be Done.

HAZEL (*indignantly*): A fat lot of rushing for amusement we've done, haven't we? I think that's frightfully unfair and idiotic. Just when we *might* have some fun, after washing up in canteens and hospitals and queueing for foul food, with *nobody* about at all, they go and say we've had enough amusement and must get on with our jobs. What jobs?

CAROL: Rebuilding a shattered world. It said that too.

MRS. C. (*half lightly, half not, to* HAZEL): Your job will be to find a very nice young man and marry him. And *that* oughtn't to be difficult —for you.

CAROL (*now getting into trousers to play Mr. Pennyman*): Hurry up, Hazel, and then I can be a bridesmaid. I believe you're my *only* chance. Kay says she won't get married for *ages*, if ever, because her Writing—Her Work—must come first.

MRS. C.: That's nonsense, my dear. When the proper young man comes along, she'll forget about her writing.

CAROL: I don't believe she will, Mother. And anyhow, she won't have bridesmaids. And if Madge ever marries, I know it will be to some kind of Socialist in a tweed suit, who'll insist on being married in a Register Office——

HAZEL: I'm not so sure about that. I've had my eye on Madge lately.

CAROL (*now as Mr. Pennyman*): And I've 'ad my eye on Lloyd George. An' what for, Mish Conway? Bee-corsh yew can't trusht that little Welshman. Yew watch 'im, that'sh all I shay——

MRS. C.: That's *very* good, dear. You're rather like Mr. Worsnop —do you remember him—the cashier at the works? Every New Year's Eve, your father used to bring Mr. Worsnop here, after they'd done all the books at the office, and used to give him some port. And when I went in, Mr. Worsnop always stood and held his glass like this (*she holds glass close to herself in a rather cringing attitude*) and say "My respects, Mrs. Conway, my deepest respects." And I always wanted to laugh. He's retired now, and gone to live in South Devon.

After slight pause, MADGE, *still in absurd old Costerwoman disguise, enters with* GERALD THORNTON. *He is in his early thirties, a solicitor and son of a solicitor, and is fairly tall and good-looking, and carefully dressed. He has a pleasant, man-of-the-world air, very consciously cultivated.* MADGE *is arguing hotly, with all the fiery slapdash of enthusiastic youth.*

MADGE: But what the miners want and ask for is simply nationalisation. They say, if coal is as important as you say it is, then the mines shouldn't be in the hands of private owners any longer. Nationalise them, they say. That's the fairest thing.

GERALD: All right. But supposing we don't want them nationalised.

What then? Some of us have seen enough of Government mismanagement already.

MRS. C.: Quite so, Gerald. Everybody knows how ridiculous they were. Sending bags of sand to Egypt!

MADGE (*hotly*): I don't believe half those stories. Besides they had to improvise everything in a hurry. And anyhow it wasn't a *Socialist* Government.

GERALD (*mildly*): But you don't know they'd be any better. They might be worse—less experience.

MADGE (*same tone*): Oh—I know that *experience*! We're always having that flung in our faces. When all that's wanted is a little intelligence—and enthusiasm—and—and decency.

GERALD (*to* MRS. C. *rather as one adult to another at children's party*): I've been conscripted for the next scene. To be a general or something.

HAZEL: We haven't fancy dress for you.

GERALD: Good!

MRS. C.: I really mustn't neglect them any longer, must I? And most of them will be going soon. Then we can have a nice cosy little party of our own.

Goes out.

CAROL (*to* GERALD): Well, you must look different somehow, you know. You could turn your coat inside out.

GERALD: I don't think that would be very effective.

CAROL (*impatiently*): Wear an overcoat then. Oh—and—— (*Fishes out a large false moustache and gives it to him.*) Put this on. That's a *very* good one.

GERALD *takes and looks at it dubiously.* JOAN *rushes in, more animated now her ordeal is over.*

JOAN (*excitedly, girlish*): Hazel, d'you know who's here? You'll never guess!

HAZEL: Who?

JOAN (*ignoring this*): That *awful* little man who always stares at you —the one who followed us once all round the Park——

HAZEL: He's *not*!

JOAN: He is, I tell you. I distinctly saw him, standing at the side, near the door.

GERALD: This sounds like my friend Beevers.

HAZEL: Do you mean to say the man you brought is *that* awful little man? Well, you're the absolute limit, Gerald Thornton! He's a *dreadful* little creature. Every time I go out, he's somewhere about, staring and staring at me. And now you bring him here!

GERALD (*not worried by this outburst*): Oh—he's not so bad. He insisted on my bringing him, and your mother said it was all right. You shouldn't be so devastating, Hazel.

JOAN (*giggly*): I told you he must be mad about you, Hazel.

HAZEL (*the haughty beauty now*): I swear I won't speak to him. He just would butt in like this!

CAROL: Why shouldn't he, poor little manny?

HAZEL: Shut up, Carol, you don't know anything about him.

Enter KAY *and* ALAN.

KAY: That wasn't much good. The Costers were a wash-out. Oh—that's all right, Carol. Now you're a general, Gerald, and the others are recruits. Hurry up, Alan, and put something different on. Gerald, you're inspecting them—you know, make up something silly—and then say to one of them: Look at your *foot*, my man." Anyhow, bring in "foot".

GERALD: Have I only two recruits, Carol and Alan?

KAY: No, mother's sending in another man. They aren't guessing anything yet, but that's simply because it's all such a muddle. I don't think I like charades as much as I used to do. Dad was marvellous at them. (*To* GERALD.) He always did very fat men. You'd better be a fat general. And you can be fat, too, Alan.

Piano can be heard playing softly off. As the men are stuffing cushions under coats, and JOAN *and* KAY *and* MADGE *are finishing removing their last things,* ERNEST BEEVERS *enters slowly and shyly. He is a little man, about thirty, still socially shy and awkward, chiefly because his social background is rather lower in the scale than that of the* CONWAYS, *but there is a suggestion of growing force and self-confidence in him. He is obviously attracted towards the whole family, but completely fascinated by* HAZEL.

ERNEST (*shyly, awkwardly*): Oh—er—Mrs. Conway told me to come in here.

KAY: Yes, of course. You've to be one of the recruits in this next bit.

ERNEST: I'm—not much good—at this sort of thing—you know——

KAY: It doesn't matter. Just be silly.

GERALD: Oh—Beevers—sorry! I'd better introduce you. (*Carries off slightly awkward situation with determined light touch.*) This—is Mr. Ernest Beevers, a rather recent arrival in our—er—progressive city. Now all these are Conways, except this young lady—Miss Joan Helford——

ERNEST (*seriously*): How d'you do?

JOAN (*faintly giggly*): How d'you do?

GERALD: This is Kay, who decided to be twenty-one to-day so that we could have this party——

ERNEST: Many happy returns.

KAY (*nicely*): Thank you.

GERALD: She's the literary genius of this distinguished family. Over there is Madge, who's been to Girton and will try to convert you to Socialism.

ERNEST: I'm afraid she won't succeed.

GERALD: This strange-looking middle-aged person is young Carol——

CAROL (*nicely*): Hello!

ERNEST (*grateful for this, smiling*): Hello!

GERALD: Alan I think you've met already. (*Teasing.*) Oh—and let me see—yes, this is Hazel. She creates such havoc that when the Leicesters were stationed here the Colonel wrote and asked her to stay indoors when they had route marches.

ERNEST (*solemnly*): How d'you do?

HAZEL (*crossly*): Don't be idiotic, Gerald. (*Very quickly to* ERNEST.) How d'you do?

Faint giggle from JOAN.

ALAN (*to* ERNEST): You'd better do something funny to yourself. Is there anything here you'd like?

ERNEST *pokes about in the things, while* HAZEL *looks disdainfully on and* JOAN *wants to giggle.* ERNEST *is very clumsy now.*

KAY: Carol and Alan, you start. You're recruits. Carol can do bits of Mr. Pennyman to fill in.

CAROL, *followed by* ALAN, *goes out.* GERALD *is waiting for* BEEVERS. KAY *goes out.*

JOAN: What did your mother say, Hazel, about removing?

HAZEL: Oh, of course, she won't think of it. And she's been offered five thousand pounds—*five thousand*—for this house!

ERNEST (*the business man*): Tell her to take it. I'll bet in ten years she couldn't get two thousand. It's only this temporary shortage that's forced prices of property up. You'll see 'em come down with a bang yet.

HAZEL (*snubbing him*): But she adores being here, of course, and so it's hopeless.

ERNEST *realises he has been snubbed. He has now made a few ridiculous changes in his clothes. He looks hard at* HAZEL, *who will not return his look.* JOAN *still giggly.*

ERNEST (*with dignity which ill assorts with his appearance*): If I spoke out of my turn, I'm sorry.

KAY (*looking in*): Hurry up, Mr. Beevers.

ERNEST (*hurrying forward*): I'm no good at this, you know, Miss Conway, and it's no use pretending I am——

But she rushes him and GERALD *off, and follows them.* JOAN *bursts into a peal of laughter.*

HAZEL (*indignantly*): I don't think it's funny, Joan. I'm *furious.*

JOAN (*between gurgles and gasps*): He—looked—so—silly.

HAZEL *begins laughing, too, and they laugh together, rocking round.*

HAZEL (*hardly distinguishable*): Did you hear him? "If I spoke out of my turn, I'm sorry."

JOAN (*hardly distinguishable*): We ought to have said "Pleased to meet you," and then he'd have said "Granted."

KAY *comes back, and looks rather severely at these two.*

KAY (*severely*): I think you were rather beastly to that little man.

They still laugh, and as she looks at them KAY *begins to laugh too. They all laugh.*

HAZEL (*coming to*): Oh—dear! Oh—dear! But that's the little man I told you about, Kay, who always stared, and once followed us round.

KAY: Well, now he'll be able to raise his little hat.

HAZEL (*vehemently*): And that's all he'll jolly well get out of this, I'll tell you. And I think Gerald Thornton had the cheek of the devil to bring him here. Just because he's a new client.

JOAN (*still giggly*): You don't think you'll marry him then, Hazel?

HAZEL: Ugh! I'd just as soon marry a—a ferret.

KAY (*rather loftily*): I don't believe you two ever think or talk about anything but clothes and going to London and young men and marriage.

HAZEL (*not too rudely*): Oh, don't you start being so grand! (*Quotes dramatically.*) *The Garden of Stars.*

KAY (*hastily*): Now, shut up, Hazel!

HAZEL (*to* JOAN): That's what she called the last novel she started.

The Garden of Stars. And there were so many bits of paper with the opening words on that I know them off by heart. (*Quotes dramatically. As soon as she begins* KAY *makes a rush at her, but she dodges, still quoting.*) "Marion went out into the still smooth night. There was no moon but already—already—the sky was silver-dusted with stars. She passed through the rose garden, the dying scent of the roses meeting the grey moths——"

KAY (*shouting her down*): I know it's all wrong, but I tore it up, didn't I?

HAZEL (*mildly*): Yes, my duck. And then you cried.

KAY (*fiercely*): I've just began a real one. With some *guts* in it. You'll see.

HAZEL: I'll bet it's about a girl who lives in a town just like Newlingham.

KAY (*still fierce*): Well, why shouldn't it be? You wait, that's all.

GERALD, *plus false moustache,* ALAN *and* ERNEST *in their absurd get-up come in slowly and solemnly.*

GERALD: That's true, Alan.

ERNEST (*seriously*): But they can't expect people to behave differently when they've still got their war restrictions on everything. They can't have it both ways.

GERALD: Well, there's still a lot of profiteering.

ERNEST: You've got to let business find its own level. The more interference the worse it is.

ALAN: The worse for everybody?

ERNEST (*decidedly*): Yes.

ALAN (*stoutly, for him*): I doubt it.

ERNEST (*not too unpleasantly*): You're working in the Town Hall, aren't you? Well, you can't learn much about these things there, y'know.

KAY (*with tremendous irony*): I say! You three must have been terribly good in the charade, weren't you?

ALAN: No, we weren't very amusing.

CAROL (*who has just entered*): Oh—they were awful. No, you weren't *too* bad, Mr. Beevers, especially for a man who was doing a charade in a strange house.

ERNEST: Now I call that handsome, Miss Carol.

KAY (*briskly*): The whole word now. *Pussyfoot.* It's supposed to be a party in America, and we can't have anything to drink. We won't bother dressing up for this. Just some good *acting.* I'll say the word.

Joan, tell Madge, she's in this. Just the girls, for the grand finale.

JOAN *goes.*

GERALD (*now normal again*): So we're sacked?

KAY: Yes. No good.

GERALD: Then we can give ourselves a drink. We've earned a drink. Any dancing afterwards?

KAY: There might be, after mother's done her singing.

GERALD: Do you dance, Beevers?

ERNEST: No, never had time for it.

HAZEL (*significantly, in loud clear tone*): Yes, we *must* have some dancing, Gerald.

> ERNEST *looks hard at her. She gives him a wide innocent stare of complete indifference. He nods, turns and goes.* GERALD, *after distributing a smile or two, follows him.* CAROL *is busy getting out of her Mr. Pennyman disguise.*

CAROL (*excitedly*): Kay, we could have done the Prince of Wales in America for this last scene. Why didn't we think of it? You could be the Prince of Wales, and you could fall in love with Hazel, who could turn out to be Pussyfoot's daughter.

KAY (*laughing*): Mother'd be shocked. And so would some of the others.

CAROL: I'd hate to be a Prince of Wales, wouldn't you?

HAZEL (*with decision*): I'd *love* it.

CAROL: Old Mrs. Ferguson—you know, the one with the queer eye—the rather frightening one—told me there was an old prophecy that when King David came to the throne of Britain everything would be *wonderful*.

> *Sound off of a loud shout, then confused voices and laughter.*

KAY: What's that?

HAZEL (*excitedly*): It's Robin.

> *They all look up with eager interest.* HAZEL *moves, but before she gets very far,* ROBIN *dashes in. He is twenty-three, and a rather dashing, good-looking young man in the uniform of an R.A.F. officer. He is in tremendous spirits. He carries a small package.*

ROBIN (*loudly*): Hello, kids! Hazel! (*Kisses her.*) Kay, many happies! (*Kisses her.*) Carol, my old hearty! (*Kisses her.*) Gosh! I've had a dash to get here in time. Did half the journey on one of our lorries. And I didn't forget the occasion, Kay. What about that? (*Throws her the parcel, which she opens and finds is a silk scarf.*) All right, isn't it?

KAY (*gratefully*): It's lovely, Robin. Lovely, lovely!

ROBIN: That's the stuff to give 'em. And I've finished. Out! Demobbed at last!

HAZEL: Oo—grand! Have you seen mother?

ROBIN: Of course I have, you chump. You ought to have seen her face when I told her I was now a civilian again. Golly! we'll have some fun now, won't we?

KAY: Lots and lots.

CAROL: Have you seen Alan?

ROBIN: Just for a second. Still the solemn old bird, isn't he?

CAROL (*very young and solemn*): In my opinion, Alan is a very wonderful person.

ROBIN (*rattling on*): I know. You always thought that, didn't you? Can't quite see it myself, but I'm very fond of the old crawler. How's the writing, Kay?

KAY: I'm still trying—and learning.

ROBIN: That's the stuff. We'll show 'em. This is where the Conways really begin. How many young men, Hazel?

HAZEL (*calmly*): Nobody to speak of.

CAROL: She'd worked her way up to Colonels, hadn't you, Haze?

KAY (*affectionately*): Now that it's civilians, she's having to change her technique—and she's a bit uncertain yet.

ROBIN: All jealousy that, isn't it, Hazel? (MRS. C. *appears, carrying a tray laden with sandwiches, cake, etc., and some beer.*) A-ha, here we are! (*Rushes to take the tray from her.* MRS. C. *is very happy now.*)

MRS. C. (*beaming*): Isn't this nice! Now we're *all* here. I knew somehow you were on your way, Robin, even though you didn't tell us—you naughty boy.

ROBIN: Couldn't, Mother, honestly. Only wangled it at the last minute.

MRS. C. (*to* KAY): Finish your charade now, dear.

ROBIN: Charade! Can I be in this? I used to be an ace at charades.

MRS. C.: No, dear, they're just finishing. We can have as many charades as we want now you're home for good. Have something to eat and talk to me while they're doing the last bit.

KAY (*to* HAZEL *and* CAROL): Come on, you two. We can collect Madge out there. Remember, it's an American party, and we can't have anything to drink, and then, after kicking up a row, you ask who's giving the party, and then I'll say *Pussyfoot*.

She is going off and the others following her as she is saying this.

MRS. C. *hastily puts some of the old clothes together, while* ROBIN *settles down to the tray.* MRS. C. *then comes and watches him eat and drink with maternal delight. Both are happy and relaxed, at ease with each other.*

MRS. C.: Is there anything you want there, Robin?

ROBIN (*mouth full*): Yes thanks, Mother. Gosh, you don't know what it feels like to be out at last!

MRS. C.: I do, you silly boy. What do you think I feel, to have you back at last—for good?

ROBIN: I must get some clothes.

MRS. C.: Yes, some really nice ones. Though it's a pity you can't keep on wearing that uniform. You look so smart in it. Poor Alan— he was only a corporal or something, y'know, and had the most hideous uniform, nothing seemed to fit him—Alan never looked *right* in the Army.

ROBIN: He's got a piffling sort of job at the Town Hall, hasn't he?

MRS. C.: Yes. He seems to like it, though. And perhaps he'll find something better later on.

ROBIN (*eagerly*): I've got all sorts of plans, y'know, Mother. We've all been talking things over in the mess. One of our chaps knows Jimmy White—you know, *the* Jimmy White—you've heard of him— and he thinks he can wangle me an introduction to him. My idea is something in the car and motor-bike line. I understand 'em, and I've heard people are buying like mad. And I have my gratuity, you know.

MRS. C.: Yes, dear, we'll have to talk about all that. There's plenty of time now, thank goodness! Don't you think all the girls are looking well?

ROBIN (*eating and drinking away*): Yes, first-rate, especially Hazel.

MRS. C.: Oh—of course Hazel's the one everybody notices. You ought to have seen the young men. And Kay—twenty-one—I can hardly believe it—but she's *very* grown-up and serious now—I don't know whether she'll make anything out of this writing of hers—but she is trying very hard—don't tease her too much, dear, she doesn't like it——

ROBIN: I haven't been teasing her.

MRS. C.: No, but Hazel does sometimes—and I know what you children are. Madge has been teaching, you know, but she's trying for a much better school.

ROBIN (*indifferently*): Good old Madge. (*With far more interest.*) I think I ought to go up to town for my clothes, Mother. You can't get anything really decent in Newlingham, and if I'm going to start selling cars I've got to look like somebody who knows a good suit when he sees one. Lord!—it's grand to be back again, and not just on a filthy little leave. (*Breaks off, as he looks at her, standing quite close to him.*) Here, Mother—steady!—nothing to cry about now.

MRS. C. (*through her tears, smiling*): I know. That's why. You see, Robin—losing your father, then the war coming—taking you—I'm not used to happiness. I've forgotten about it. It's upsetting! And Robin, now you are back—don't go rushing off again, *please!* Don't leave us—not for years and years. Let's all be cosy together and happy again, shall we?

JOAN *enters, then stands awkwardly as she sees them together.* MRS C. *turns and sees her. So does* ROBIN, *and his face lights up.* MRS C. *sees* ROBIN'S *face, then looks again at* JOAN. *This should be played for as long as it will stand.*

JOAN (*rather nervously*): Oh—Mrs. Conway—they've finished the charade—and some people are going—and Madge asked me to tell you they're expecting you to sing something.

MRS C.: Why didn't she come herself?

JOAN (*rather faltering*): She and Kay and Carol began handing people sandwiches and things as soon as they finished the charade.

ROBIN (*rising*): Hello, Joan!

JOAN (*coming forward, thrilled*): Hello, Robin! Is it—nice to be back again?

ROBIN (*smiling, rather significantly*): Yes, of course.

MRS. C. (*rather irritably*): Really this room's a dreadful mess. I knew it would be. Hazel and Carol brought all these things down here. Joan, go and tell them they must take these things upstairs at once. I can't have this room looking like an old clothes' place. Perhaps you'd like to help them, dear.

JOAN: Yes—rather.

Smiles at ROBIN *and goes.* MRS. C. *turns and looks at him. He smiles at her. She has to smile back.*

ROBIN: You're looking very artful, Mother.

MRS. C.: Am I? I'm not feeling very artful. (*Carefully just.*) Joan's grown up to be a very nice-looking girl, hasn't she?

ROBIN (*smiling*): Quite.

MRS. C. (*same careful tone*): And I think she's got a pleasant easy disposition. Not very clever or go-ahead or anything like that. But a thoroughly *nice* girl.

ROBIN (*not eagerly*): Yes. I'll bet she is.

HAZEL *sails in, to begin packing up the things. This should be done as quickly as possible.*

HAZEL: They're all panting for a song, Mother. They don't even mind if it's German.

MRS. C.: Thank goodness, I was never so stupid as to stop singing German songs. What have Schubert and Schumann to do with Hindenburg and the Kaiser?

CAROL *comes in, followed by* JOAN. HAZEL *goes with her armful* ROBIN *helps* JOAN *to collect her lot.* MRS. C. *stands rather withdrawn from them.*

CAROL (*loudly and cheerfully as she collects her stuff*): Everybody guessed the charade, just because it was Pussyfoot—though they hadn't guessed *any* of the syllables. All except Mr. James, who thought it was *Kinema*. (*Hard "k".*) When they say "Kinema" I can't believe I've ever been to one. It sounds like some other kind of place. Robin, have you seen William S. Hart?

ROBIN: Yes.

CAROL (*pausing with her armful, very solemnly*): I *love* William S. Hart. I wonder what "S." stands for.

ROBIN: Sidney.

CAROL (*turning, in horror*): Robin, it *doesn't*!

Goes out. JOAN *now has the remainder of the things.*

MRS. C.: Come along, Robin, I may want you and Alan to move the piano for me.

ROBIN: Righto.

They all go out. Nearly all the things have been cleared now. Sounds of the party—vague applause and laughter—off. Then KAY *enters quickly and eagerly, and finds a bit of paper and pencil in some convenient drawer or cupboard. She frowns and thinks, then makes some rapid notes, not sitting down but standing against table or bookshelf. A few chords and runs can be heard from the piano.* CAROL *looks in, to remove the last of the charade things.*

CAROL (*with awe, very charming*): Kay, have you suddenly been *inspired*?

KAY (*looking up, very serious*): No, not really. But I'm bursting with all kinds of feelings and thoughts and impressions—you know——

CAROL (*coming close to her favourite sister*): Oh—yes—so am I. Millions and millions. I couldn't possibly *begin* to write them.

KAY (*that eager young author*): No, but in my novel, a girl goes to a party—you see—and there are some things I've been feeling—very subtle things—that I *know* she'd feel—and I want my novel to be very real this time—so I had to scribble them down——

CAROL: Will you tell me them afterwards?

KAY: Yes.

CAROL: Bedroom?

KAY: Yes, if you're not too sleepy.

CAROL: I couldn't be. (*She pauses happily, one earnest young creature staring at the other. And now we can just hear* MRS. CONWAY *in the drawing-room beginning to sing Schumann's "Der Nussbaum". * CAROL *is now very solemn, a little awed.*) Kay, I think you're *wonderful.*

KAY (*awed herself*): I think *life's* wonderful.

CAROL: Both of you are.

CAROL *goes out, and now we can hear the lovely rippling Schumann better than before.* KAY *writes for another moment, then moved by both the music and the sudden ecstasy of creation, she puts down pencil and paper, drifts over to the switch and turns out the lights. The room is not in darkness because light is coming in from the hall.* KAY *goes to the window and opens the curtains, so that when she sits on the window-seat, her head is silvered in moonlight. Very still, she listens to the music, and seems to stare not* at *but* into *something, and as the song goes soaring away, the curtain creeps down.*

END OF ACT ONE

ACT II

*When the curtain rises, for a moment we think nothing has happened
since it came down, for there is the light coming in from the hall, and
there is KAY sitting on the window-seat. But then ALAN comes in
and switches on the central light, and we see that a great deal must
have happened. It is the same room, but it has a different wall-
paper, the furniture has been changed round, the pictures and books
are not altogether the same as before. We notice a wireless set.
The general effect is harder and rather brighter than it was during
the party in 1919, and we guess at once that this is present day (1937).
KAY and ALAN are not quite the same, after nearly twenty years.
KAY has a rather hard, efficient, well-groomed look, that of a
woman of forty who has earned her own living for years. ALAN, in
his middle forties, is shabbier than he was before—his coat does not
match the rest of his suit and really will not do—but he is still the
rather shy, awkward, lovable fellow, only now there is about him a
certain quiet poise, an inward certainty and serenity, missing from
all the others we shall see now.*

ALAN (*quietly*): Well—Kay.

KAY (*happily*): Alan!

*She jumps up and kisses him. Then they look at one another,
smiling a little. He rubs his hands in embarrassment, as he always
did.*

ALAN: I'm glad you could come. It was the only thing about this
business that didn't make me hate the thought of it—the chance *you*
might be able to come. But mother says you're not staying the night.

KAY: I can't, Alan. I must get back to London to-night.

ALAN: Work?

KAY: Yes. I have to go to Southampton in the morning—to write
a nice little piece about the newest little film star.

ALAN: Do you often have to do that?

KAY: Yes, Alan, quite often. There are an awful lot of film stars
and they're always arriving at Southampton, except when they arrive
at Plymouth—damn their eyes! And all the women readers of the
Daily Courier like to read a bright half-column about their glamorous
favourites.

ALAN (*thoughtfully*): They look very nice—but all rather alike.

KAY (*decidedly*): They *are* all rather alike—and so are my bright interviews with 'em. In fact, sometimes I feel we're all just going round and round, like poor old circus ponies.

ALAN (*after a pause*): Are you writing another novel?

KAY (*very quietly*): No, my dear, I'm not. (*Pauses, then gives short laugh.*) I tell myself too many people are writing novels.

ALAN: Well, it does look like that—sometimes.

KAY: Yes. But that's not the real reason. I still feel mine wouldn't be like theirs—anyhow, not the next, even if the last was. But—as things are—I just can't . . .

ALAN (*after a pause*): The last time you wrote, Kay—I mean to me —you sounded rather unhappy, I thought.

KAY (*with self-reproach*): I was. I suppose that's why I suddenly remembered you—and wrote. Not very flattering—to you—is it?

ALAN (*with cheerful modesty*): In a way it is, y'know. Yes, Kay, I'd take that as a compliment.

KAY (*with sudden burst of affection*): Alan! And I loathe that coat you're wearing. It doesn't match the rest of you, does it?

ALAN (*stammering, apologetic*): No—well, you see—I just wear it in the house—an old coat—just as a house coat—it saves my other one— I oughtn't to have put it on to-night. Just habit, y'know. I'll change it before the others come. . . . Why were you so unhappy then—the last time you wrote?

KAY (*in broken painful phrases*): Something—that was always ending—really did come to an end just then. It had lasted ten years— off and on—and eating more of one's life away when it was off than when it was on. He was married. There were children. It was the usual nasty muddle. (*Breaks off.*) Alan, you don't know what day it is to-day?

ALAN (*chuckling*): But I do, I do. And, of course, Mother did, too. Look!

He pulls small package out of his pocket and holds it out to her.

KAY (*after taking it and kissing him*): Alan, you're an angel! I never thought I'd have another single birthday present. And you know how old I am now? Forty. *Forty!*

ALAN (*smiling*): I'm forty-four. And it's all right, y'know. You'll like it. (*Front door bell rings.*) Look at your present. I hope it's all right.

Goes to front door. KAY hastily unwraps her parcel and takes out a hideous cheap little handbag. She looks at it and does not know whether to laugh or cry over the thing. Meanwhile ALAN has brought in JOAN, now Joan Conway, for she married ROBIN. Time has not been very kind to her. She is now a rather sloppy, querulous woman of forty-one. Her voice has a very irritating quality.

JOAN: Hello, Kay. I didn't think you'd manage to be here—you hardly ever do come to Newlingham now, do you? And I must say I don't blame you. (*Breaks off because she notices the awful handbag.*) Oh—what a——

KAY (*hastily*): Nice, isn't it? Alan has just given it to me. How are the children?

JOAN: Richard's very well, but the doctor says Ann's tonsils ought to come out—though he doesn't tell me who's going to pay for the operation, never thinks about that. They did enjoy those things you sent at Christmas, Kay—I don't know what they'd have done without them, though I did my best.

KAY: I'm sure you did, Joan.

JOAN: Alan was very good to them, too, weren't you, Alan? Though, of course, it's not like their having a father. (*Breaks off and looks miserably at* KAY.) You know, I haven't seen Robin for months. Some people say I ought to divorce him—but—I don't know—— (*With sudden misery.*) Honestly, isn't it awful? Oh—Kay. (*Suddenly giggles.*) Doesn't that sound silly—*Oh—Kay.*

KAY (*wearily*): No, I've stopped noticing it.

JOAN: Richard's always saying Okay—he's heard it at the pictures—and, of course, Ann copies him. (*Breaks off, looks anxiously at them both.*) Do you think it's all right, my coming here to-night? It was Hazel who told me you were having a sort of family meeting, and she thought I ought to be here, and I think so too. But Granny Conway didn't ask me——

KAY (*with a sudden laugh*): Joan, you don't call mother Granny Conway?

JOAN: Well, I got into the habit, y'know, with the children.

KAY: She must loathe it.

ALAN (*apologetically, to* JOAN): I think she does, you know.

JOAN: I must try and remember. Is she upstairs?

ALAN: Yes. Madge is here, too.

JOAN (*nerving herself*): I think—I'll go up and ask her if it's all right—my staying—otherwise I'd feel such a fool.

KAY: Yes, do. And tell her we think you ought to be here—if you *want* to be——

JOAN: Well, it isn't that—but—you see—if it's about money—I must know something, mustn't I? After all, I'm Robin's wife—and Richard and Ann are his children——

ALAN (*kindly*): Yes, Joan, you tell mother that, if she objects. But she won't, though.

JOAN *looks at them a moment doubtfully, then goes. They watch her go, then look at one another.*

KAY (*lowering her voice a little*): I suppose Robin's pretty hopeless —but really, Joan's such a fool——

ALAN: Yes, but the way Robin's treated her has made her feel more of a fool than she really is. It's taken away all her confidence in herself, you see, Kay. Otherwise she mightn't have been so bad.

KAY: You used to like Joan, didn't you?

ALAN (*looking at her, then slowly smiling*): You remember when she and Robin told us they were engaged? I was in love with her then. It was the only time I ever fell in love with anybody. And I remember— quite suddenly hating Robin—yes, really hating him. None of this loving and hating lasted, of course—it was just silly stuff. But I remember it quite well.

KAY: Suppose it had been you instead of Robin?

ALAN (*hastily*): Oh—no, that wouldn't have done at all. Really it wouldn't. Most unsuitable!

KAY *laughs in affectionate amusement at his bachelor's horror.* MADGE *enters. She is very different from the girl of* ACT I. *She has short greyish hair, wears glasses, and is neatly but severely dressed. She speaks with a dry precision, but underneath her assured schoolmistress manner is a suggestion of the neurotic woman.*

MADGE (*very decisively, as she bustles about the room, finding an envelope and filling her fountain-pen*): I've just told mother that if I hadn't happened to be in the neighbourhood to-day—I've applied for a headship at Borderton, you know, Kay, and had my interview there this afternoon—nothing would have induced me to be here to-night.

KAY: Well, I don't know why you bothered telling her, Madge. You *are* here, that's all that matters.

MADGE: No it isn't. I want her to understand quite clearly that I've no further interest in these family muddles, financial or otherwise. Also, that I would have thought it unnecessary to ask for a day away from my work at Collingfield in order to attend one of these ridiculous hysterical conferences.

KAY: You talk as if you'd been dragged here every few weeks.

MADGE: No I haven't. But I've had a great many more of these silly discussions than you have—please remember, Kay. Mother and Gerald Thornton seem to imagine that the time of a woman journalist in London is far more precious than that of a senior mistress at a large girls' public school. Why—I can't think. But the result is, I've been dragged in often when you haven't.

KAY (*rather wearily*): All right. But seeing we're both here now, let's make the best of it.

ALAN: Yes, of course.

MADGE: Joan's here. I hope there's no chance of Robin coming too. That's something you've missed so far, I think, Kay. I've had one experience of their suddenly meeting here—Robin half drunk, ready to insult everybody. Joan weeping and resentful—the pair of them discussing every unpleasant detail of their private life—and it's not an experience I want to repeat.

KAY (*lightly, but serious underneath*): I don't blame you, Madge. But for the Lord's sake be human to-night. You're not talking to the Collingfield common room now. This is your nice brother, Alan. I'm your nice sister Kay. We know all about you——

MADGE: That's just where you're wrong. You know hardly anything about me, any of you. The life you don't see—call it the Collingfield common room if that amuses you—is my real life. It represents exactly the sort of person I am now, and what you and Alan and mother remember—and trust mother not to forget anything foolish and embarrassing—is no longer of any importance at all.

KAY: I'd hate to think that, Madge.

ALAN (*shyly, earnestly*): And it isn't true. It really isn't. Because—— (*Hesitates, and is lost.*)

MADGE: I heard your extraordinary views the last time I was here, Alan. I also discussed them with Herrickson—our senior Maths. mistress and a most brilliant woman—and she demolished them very thoroughly.

KAY (*to cheer him up*): You tell *me*, Alan, if there's time later on. We're not going to be trampled on by any of Madge's Miss What's-her-names. And we don't care how brilliant they are, do we, Alan?

ALAN *grins and rubs his hands.* MADGE *deliberately changes the subject.*

MADGE: I hope you're doing something besides this popular journalism now, Kay. Have you begun another book?

KAY: No.

MADGE: Pity, isn't it?

KAY (*after a pause, looking steadily at her*): What about you, Madge? Are you building Jerusalem—in England's green and pleasant land?

MADGE: Possibly not. But I'm trying to put a little knowledge of history and a little sense into the heads of a hundred and fifty middle-class girls. It's hard work and useful work. Certainly nothing to be ashamed of.

KAY (*looking hard, speaking very quietly*): Then—why be ashamed?

MADGE (*instantly, loudly*): I'm not.

> HAZEL *enters, from outside. She is extremely well dressed, the best dressed of them all, and has not lost her looks, but there is something noticeably subdued, fearful, about her.*

HAZEL: Hello, Madge! (*Sees* KAY.) Kay! (*Kisses her.*)

KAY: Hazel, my dear, you're grander every time I see you.

HAZEL (*preening*): Do you like it?

KAY: Yes—and you didn't get that in Newlingham. At the *Bon Marché.* Do you remember when we used to think the *Bon Marché* marvellous?

HAZEL (*brightening up at this*): Yes—and now they seem ghastly. Well, that's something, isn't it? (*Realises that this gives her away, so hastily asks*): Is Joan here?

ALAN: Yes. She's upstairs with mother. Is Ernest coming to-night?

HAZEL (*hesitating*): I—don't—know.

MADGE: I thought it was understood he was coming. Mother thinks he is. I believe she's rather counting on him.

HAZEL (*hastily*): Well, she mustn't. I've told her not to. I don't even know yet if he'll be here at all.

MADGE (*annoyed*): But this is ridiculous. We're told that things are desperate. Kay and I have to leave our work, travel miles and miles, stop thinking about anything else, and now you don't even know if your own husband will walk down the road to be here.

HAZEL: But you know what Ernest is. He said he *might* come to-night. I asked him again only at lunch time to-day—and he said he didn't know—and then I didn't like——

MADGE (*cutting in sharply*): Didn't like! You mean you *daren't.* That miserable little——

HAZEL: Madge! Please stop.

> MADGE *looks at her in contempt, then walks off.* HAZEL *looks very miserable.*

KAY: How are the children?

HAZEL: Peter has a cold again—poor lamb—he's always getting colds. Margaret's all right. Never *any* trouble with her. She's been doing some ballet dancing, y'know, and the teacher thinks she's *marvellous* for her age. Oh—you forgot her last birthday, Kay. The child was *so* disappointed.

KAY: I'm sorry. Tell her I'll make up for it at Christmas. I must have been away on a job or something——

HAZEL (*eagerly*): I read your article on Glynia Foss—you know, about three months ago—when she came over from Hollywood. Did she really say all those things to you, Kay, or did you make them up?

KAY: She said some of them. The rest I made up.

HAZEL (*eagerly*): Did she say anything about Leo Frobisher—her husband, y'know, and they'd just separated?

KAY: Yes, but I didn't print it.

HAZEL (*all eagerness now*): What did she say?

KAY: She said (*imitating very bad type of American voice*), "I'll bet that God-forgotten left-over ham husband of mine gets himself poured out o' the next boat." (*Normal voice, dryly.*) You'd like her, Hazel. She's a sweet child.

HAZEL: She sounds awful, but I suppose you can't judge by the way they talk, using all that slang. And I know you don't think you're very lucky, Kay——

KAY: I vary. Sometimes when I manage to remember what most women go through, all kinds of women all over the world, I don't think, I *know* I'm lucky. But usually—I feel clean out of luck.

HAZEL: I know, that's what I say. But I think you're *very* lucky, meeting all these people, and being in London and all that. Look at me, still in Newlingham, and I *loathe* Newlingham, and it gets worse and worse. Doesn't it, Alan—though I don't suppose you notice?

ALAN: I think it's about the same—perhaps we get worse, that's all.

HAZEL (*looking at him in a sort of impersonal fashion*): Somebody was saying to me only the other day how queer they thought you were, Alan, and you are—really, aren't you? I mean you don't seem to bother about everything as most people do. I've often wondered whether you're happy inside or just dull. But I often wonder about people like that—(*to* KAY) don't you? Though I suppose being so clever now, and a writer and everything, you *know* about them. But I don't. And I simply can't tell from what people look like. We had a maid, y'know, Jessie, and she seemed such a cheerful little thing—always smiling and humming—Ernest used to get quite cross with her —she was *too* cheerful really—and then suddenly she took over twenty aspirins all at once, we had to have the doctor and everything, and she said it was simply because she couldn't bear it any longer—she'd had enough of *everything*, she said. Isn't it strange?

KAY: But you must feel like that sometimes, don't you?

HAZEL: Yes, I do. But I'm always surprised when other people do, because somehow they never *look* it. Oh——(*gets up and lowers her voice*) Robin rang me up yesterday—he's living in Leicester just now, you know—and I told him about to-night—and he said he might look in because he wouldn't be far away.

ALAN: I hope he doesn't.

KAY: What's he doing now, Hazel?

HAZEL: I don't know really—he's always changing, y'know—but it's something to do with commission. Shall I tell Joan he might be coming here?

KAY: No. Risk it.

> *Doesn't say any more because* MRS. CONWAY *comes in now, followed by* JOAN. MRS. CONWAY *is now a woman of sixty-five, and has not gone neat and modern, but kept to her full-blown Edwardian type.*

MRS. C. (*who is still very brisk*): Now then, Hazel, haven't you brought Ernest with you?

HAZEL: No, Mother. I hope—he'll be here soon.

MRS. C.: Of course he will. Well, we can't do anything until Gerald arrives. He knows how things are—exactly. Where's Madge?

KAY: I thought she went upstairs.

MRS. C. (*as she goes to turn on more lights*): She's probably taking something in the bathroom. I've never known anybody who took so many things as poor Madge. She's given herself so many lotions and gargles and sprays that no man has ever looked twice at her—poor thing. Alan, I think we ought to have both port and whisky out, don't you? I told the girl to leave it all ready in the dining-room. Better bring it in. (ALAN *goes out, returning, during following dialogue, carrying a tray, with port and small glasses, whisky and soda and tumblers.*) Now what I'm wondering is this—should we all sit round looking very stiff and formal—y'know, make it a proper business affair, because, after all, it *is* a business affair—or should we make everybody comfortable and *cosy*? What do you think?

KAY: I think—Mother—you're enjoying this.

MRS. C.: Well, after all, why shouldn't I? It's nice to see all you children at home again. Even Madge. (MADGE *enters.* MRS. C. *probably saw her before, but undoubtedly sees her now.*) I say it's nice to see all you children home again—even you, Madge.

MADGE: I'm not a child and this is no longer my home.

MRS. C. (*sharply*): You were a child once—and a very troublesome one too—and for twenty years this was your home—and please don't talk in that tone to me. You're not in a classroom now, remember.

HAZEL: Now—Mother—please—it's not going to be easy to-night —and——

MADGE (*coldly*): Don't worry, Hazel. Mother *enjoys* things not being easy.

> *She sits down.* MRS. C. *observes her maliciously, then turns to* KAY.

MRS. C.: Kay, *who* was the man the Philipsons saw you dining with at the—what's the name of that restaurant?

KAY: The Ivy, Mother. And the man is a man called Hugo Steel. I've told you already.

MRS. C. (*smoothly*): Yes, dear, but you didn't tell me much. The Philipsons said you seemed awfully friendly together. I suppose he's an old friend?

KAY (*sharply*): Yes.

MRS. C. (*same technique*): Isn't it a pity—you couldn't—I mean, if he's a really nice man.

KAY (*trying to cut it short*): Yes, a great pity.

MRS. C.: I've so often hoped you'd be settled with some nice man— and when the Philipsons told me——

KAY (*harshly*): Mother, I'm forty to-day. Had you forgotten?

MRS. C. (*taking it well*): Of course I hadn't. A mother *always* remembers. Joan——

JOAN (*whose attention has been elsewhere, turning*): Yes, Grannie Conway?

MRS. C. (*crossly*): Don't call me that ridiculous name.

JOAN: I forgot, I'm sorry.

MRS. C.: Didn't I tell you it was Kay's birthday? I've something for you too——

KAY: No, Mother, you mustn't—really——

MRS. C. (*producing small diamond brooch*): There! Your father gave me that, the second Christmas after we were married, and it's a charming little brooch. Brazilian diamonds. It was an old piece then. Look at the colour in the stones. You always get that in the old South American diamonds. There now!

KAY (*gently*): It's very sweet of you, Mother, but really I'd rather not take this from you.

MRS. C.: Don't be absurd. It's mine and now I give it to you. Take it or I'll be cross. And many happy returns, of course. (KAY *takes the brooch, then, suddenly rather moved, kisses her mother.*) When you were younger, I never liked you as much as I did Hazel, but now I think I was wrong.

HAZEL: Oh—Mother!

MRS. C.: I know, Hazel dear, but you're such a *fool* with that little husband of yours. Why, if he were mine——

HAZEL (*sharply for her*): Well he isn't—and you really know very little about him.

MRS. C. (*as she looks about her*): It's time the men were here. I've always hated seeing a lot of women sitting about, with no men. *They* always look silly, and then I feel silly myself. I don't know why. (*Notices* ALAN. *With some malice.*) Of course you're here, Alan. I was forgetting you. Or forgetting you were a man.

ALAN (*mildly*): I must grow a shaggy beard and drum on my chest and ro-o-ar!

JOAN (*doing her best*): When their Uncle Frank—you know, Freda's husband, they live in London—took the children to the Zoo for the first time, little Richard was only five—and there was an enormous monkey—what Alan said reminded me of it—and——

MRS. C. (*cutting this ruthlessly*): Would anybody like a glass of port? Kay? Hazel? What about you, Madge? It's a scholarly wine. You remember what Meredith wrote about it in *The Egoist*. But nobody reads Meredith now and nobody takes port. I used to read Meredith when I was a girl and thought I was very clever. But I didn't like port then. Now I don't care about Meredith, but I rather like port. (*She has poured herself a glass of port, and now sips it.*) It's not good port this—even I know that, though men always say women don't know anything about it—but it's rich and warming, even this— like a handsome compliment. That's gone too. Nobody pays compliments any more—except old Doctor Halliday, who's well over eighty and has no memory at all. He talked to me for half an hour the other day, thinking I was Mrs. Rushbury—— (*Ring at bell.*) There! That's probably Gerald.

MADGE (*wearily*): At last!

MRS. C. (*maliciously*): Yes, Madge, but you mustn't be so impatient.

> MADGE *glares at her.* ALAN *is now ushering in* GERALD THORNTON, *who carries a brief-case, and* ERNEST BEEVERS. GERALD *is over fifty now, and though careful of his appearance, he looks it. He is grey and wears glasses. He is much drier and harder than he was in* ACT I. ERNEST BEEVERS *looks far more prosperous than*

he did before, and has lost his early shyness. With the arrival of these two, the party is apparently complete, so that there is no longer the feeling of waiting about.

MRS. C.: Well, Gerald, will you have a drink before you begin talking?

GERALD: No, thank you. (*He turns to* KAY.) How are you, Kay?

KAY: Quite well, thank you, Gerald. (*Stares at him.*) I'm sorry, but it's true.

GERALD: What is?

KAY: I always remember your saying, years ago, that you didn't mind living in Newlingham but you were determined to be as different as possible from the Newlingham type of man.

GERALD (*hastily, frowning a little*): I don't remember saying that——

KAY: Yes, you did. And now—I'm sorry, Gerald, but it's true— you suddenly look like *all* those Newlingham men rolled into one——

GERALD (*rather shortly*): What do I do? Apologise?

Turns away, leaving her regarding him speculatively.

HAZEL (*who has managed to get* ERNEST *to herself a moment*): Oh— Ernest—I'm so glad you're here——

ERNEST (*not pleasantly*): You are, eh?

HAZEL (*who knows him by this time*): I suppose that means you won't stay now—just to show me——

ERNEST: I don't need to show you. You know, by this time.

HAZEL (*lowering voice*): Ernest—please—be nice to them to-night— especially to Mother—you could be such a help if you wanted to be——

ERNEST (*cutting through this*): I don't know what you're talking about.

They both notice then that MADGE *is quite near, regarding them with a contemptuous smile.* ERNEST *gives her a sharp look, then turns away.* HAZEL *looks deeply embarrassed, then looks as if she was about to appeal to* MADGE.

MADGE (*coolly*): I shouldn't say a word, if I were you, Hazel. I mean, to me. It would only make it worse.

MRS. C. (*loud cheerful tone*): Now then, everybody, please be quiet and pay attention. We must be very business-like, mustn't we, Gerald? I'm so glad you were able to come, Ernest. You'll help us to be business-like, won't you?

ERNEST (*grimly*): Yes.

MADGE: And that doesn't mean you're at liberty to make yourself unpleasant.

MRS. C. (*sharply*): Be quiet, Madge. (*Turning, with smile and great social air, to* GERALD.) Now then, Gerald, we're all waiting. Tell us all about it.

GERALD, *who has been glancing at his papers, looks up at her and, round the waiting circle with a sort of despair, as if to ask what could be done with such people.*

GERALD (*in dry legal tone*): Acting under instructions from Mrs. Conway, after it was decided you should all meet here, I have prepared a short statement of Mrs. Conway's present financial position——

MRS. C. (*protesting*): Gerald.

GERALD (*rather despairing*): Yes?

MRS. C.: Must you talk in that awful dry inhuman way? I mean, after all, I've known you since you were a boy, and the children have known you all their lives, and you're beginning to talk as if you'd never seen any of us before. And it sounds so horrid.

GERALD: But I'm not here now as a friend of the family, but as your solicitor.

MRS. C. (*with dignity*): No. You're here as a friend of the family who also happens to be my solicitor. And I think it would be much better if you told us all in a simple friendly way what the position is.

ALAN: I think that would be better, you know, Gerald.

KAY: So do I. When you turn on that legal manner, I can't take you seriously—I feel you're still acting in one of our old charades.

HAZEL (*with sudden warmth*): Oh—weren't they fun! And you were so good in them, Gerald. Why can't we have some more——

ERNEST (*brutally*): What—at your age?

HAZEL: I don't see why not. Mother was older than we are now when she used to play——

GERALD (*not amused by all this*): You're not proposing to turn this into a charade, are you, Hazel?

KAY: What a pity it isn't one!

ALAN (*very quietly*): Perhaps it is.

MRS. C.: Now don't *you* start being silly, Alan. Now then, Gerald, just tell us how things are—and don't read out a lot of figures and dates and things—I know you've brought them with you—but keep them for anybody who wants to have a look at them—perhaps *you*'d like to have a look at them afterwards, Ernest——

ERNEST: I might. (*To* GERALD.) Go ahead.

GERALD (*dryly*): Well, the position is this. Mrs. Conway for a long time now has derived her income from two sources. A holding in Farrow and Conway Limited. And some property in Newlingham, the houses at the north end of Church Road. Farrow and Conway were hit badly by the slump and have not recovered yet. The houses in Church Road are not worth anything like what they were, and the only chance of making that property pay is to convert the houses into flats. But this would demand a substantial outlay of capital. Mrs. Conway has received an offer for her holding in Farrow and Conway Limited, but it is a very poor offer. It would not pay for the reconstruction of the Church Road property. Meanwhile that property may soon be a liability instead of an asset. So, you see, the position is very serious.

MADGE (*coldly*): I must say I'm very much surprised. I always understood that mother was left extremely well provided for.

MRS. C. (*proudly*): Certainly I was. Your father saw to that.

GERALD: Both the shares and the property have declined in value.

MADGE: Yes, but even so—I'm still surprised. Mother must have been very extravagant.

GERALD: Mrs. Conway hasn't been as careful as she might have been.

MRS. C.: There were six of you to bring up and educate——

MADGE: It isn't that. I know how much *we* cost. It's since then that the money's been spent. And I know who must have had most of it—Robin!

MRS. C. (*angry now*): That'll do, Madge. It was my money——

MADGE: It wasn't. It was only yours to hold in trust for us. Alan, you're the eldest and you've been here all the time, why didn't you do something?

ALAN: I'm afraid—I—haven't bothered much about—these things——

MADGE (*with growing force*): Then you ought to have done. I think it's absolutely wicked. I've been working hard earning my living for over twenty years, and I've looked forward to having something from what father left, enough to pay for a few really good holidays or to buy myself a little house of my own—and now it's all gone—just because mother and Robin between them have flung it away——

MRS. C. (*angrily*): You ought to be ashamed of yourself, talking like that! What if I have helped Robin? He needed it, and I'm his mother. If you'd needed it, I'd have helped you too——

MADGE: You wouldn't. When I told you I had a chance to buy a partnership in that school, you only laughed at me——

MRS. C.: Because you were all right where you were and didn't need to buy any partnerships.

MADGE: And Robin did, I suppose?

MRS. C : Yes, because he's a man—with a wife and children to support. This is just typical of you, Madge. Call yourself a Socialist and blame people for taking an interest in money, and then it turns out you're the most mercenary of us all.

MADGE: I don't call myself a Socialist—though that's nothing to do with it——

ERNEST (*who has been glancing at an evening paper, breaking in brutally*): How long does this go on? Because I've something else to do.

MRS. C. (*trying hard to placate him*): That's all right, Ernest. Look what you've done now, Madge. Made Joan cry.

JOAN (*suddenly weeping quietly in the background*): I'm sorry—I just —remembered—so many things—that's all——

GERALD: At the present moment, Mrs. Conway has a considerable overdraft at the bank. Now there are two possible courses of action. One is to sell the houses for what they'll fetch, and to hold on to the Farrow and Conway shares. But I warn you that the houses won't fetch much. The alternative is to sell the shares, then to raise an additional sum—probably between two or three thousand pounds— and to convert the houses into flats——

MRS. C. (*hopefully*): We've had a sort of scheme from an architect, and really it looks most attractive. There'd be at least thirty nice flats, and you know what people will pay for flats nowadays. Don't you think it's a splendid idea, Ernest? (*He does not reply. She smiles at him and then her smile falters, but she returns hopefully to the theme.*) I felt if we all discussed it in a nice friendly way, we could decide something. I know you business men like everything cut-and-dried, but I believe it's better to be nice and friendly. It isn't true that people will only do things for money. I'm always being surprised about that. People are very nice and kind, really—— (*Breaks off, then looks at the women, more intimate tone.*) Only last week, I went to old Mrs. Jepson's funeral, and I was walking back through the cemetery with Mrs. Whitehead—I hadn't been round there for years—and I saw Carol's grave—and, of course, I was rather upset, suddenly coming on it like that—but it was so beautifully kept, with flowers—lovely flowers— growing there. And I thought, now there's an instance—nobody's told them to do that or paid them for it—it's just natural kindness——

MADGE (*harshly*): No it isn't. Somebody must have been paying for it.

KAY (*turning*): Alan! It must be you. Isn't it?

ALAN: Well—I do send them something—once every year, y'know —it isn't much.

HAZEL: Oh, Mother—I'd forgotten about Carol—it's sixteen years ago.

ALAN: Seventeen.

HAZEL (*in melancholy wonder*): Why, my Margaret's nearly as big as she was. Doesn't that seem strange, Kay?

KAY: I'd nearly forgotten about Carol too.

MRS. C. (*with some emotion*): Don't think I had—because I was so stupid about that grave. I'm not one of those people who remember graves, it's human beings I remember. Only the other day, when I was sitting upstairs, I heard Carol shouting "Mo-ther, mo-ther"—you know how she used to do. And then I began thinking about her, my poor darling, and how she came in that awful day, her face quite greyish, and said, "Mother, I've the most sickening pain," and then it was too late when they operated——

HAZEL: Yes, Mother, we remember.

ERNEST (*harsh and astonishing*): I'll tell you what you don't remember—and what some of you never even knew. She was the best of the lot—that one—little Carol—worth all the rest of you put together.

HAZEL (*a shocked wife*): Ernest!

ERNEST: Yes, and I'm counting you in. You were the one I wanted —that's all right, I got the one I wanted—but it didn't take me two hours to see that little Carol was the best of the lot. (*Adds gloomily.*) Didn't surprise me when she went off like that. Out! Finish! Too good to last.

MRS. C. (*now near to tears*): Ernest is quite right. She was the best of you all. My darling baby, I haven't forgotten you, I haven't forgotten you. (*Rising.*) Oh, why isn't Robin here? (*Begins weeping, also moves away.*) Go on, Gerald, explaining to them. I shan't be long. Don't move.

Goes out in tears. There is silence for a moment or two.

MADGE: Surely, under the circumstances, it's absurd that mother and Alan should continue living in this house. It's much too large for them.

ALAN (*mildly*): Yes. We could do with something much smaller now.

MADGE: Then this house could be sold, that would help. It's mother's freehold, isn't it?

GERALD: I think it would be better to move into something smaller, just to cut down living expenses. But this house wouldn't fetch very much now.

HAZEL: Why, mother was offered thousands and thousands for it just after the War.

ERNEST (*dryly*): Yes, but this isn't just after the War. It's just before the next War.

GERALD: How much do *you* think, Ernest?

ERNEST: Take anything you can get for it.

KAY: Well, what are we supposed to do? If the worst comes to the worst, we can club together to keep mother going——

MADGE: But it's monstrous. When I was at home—and knew about things—we were considered quite well off. There were all the shares and property father left, not simply for mother but for all of us. And now not only has it nearly all been frittered away, but we're expected to provide for mother——

KAY (*rather wearily*): But if the money's gone, it's gone.

GERALD: No, the point is this——

He is stopped by a loud ring at bell. They turn and look. ALAN *moves, then stops.* ROBIN *has marched in. He is wearing an old raincoat. He is shabbily smart, and looks what he is, a slackish, hard-drinking unsuccessful man of forty-two.*

ROBIN: Hello! All here? Where's mother?

ALAN: She'll be back in a minute.

ROBIN *takes off his raincoat and negligently gives it to* ALAN, *who characteristically accepts it and puts it away.* ROBIN *takes no notice of this, but looks at* JOAN.

ROBIN: Well, Joan. How are the offspring?

JOAN (*stiffly*): They're quite well, Robin.

ROBIN: Still telling them what an awful man their father is?

MADGE: Are we going to have this all over again?

ROBIN: No, you're not—dear old Madge. Do I see a drink over there? I do. Have a drink, Gerald. Ernest, have a drink. No? Well, I will. (*Goes and helps himself liberally to whisky and soda. Turns after first quick drink, faces them and grins.*) Hello, Kay. Condescending to visit the provinces again, eh?

KAY: Yes, but I've got to be back sometime to-night.

ROBIN: Don't blame you. Wish I was going back to town. That's the place. I've half a mind to chuck what I'm doing and try my luck there again. Know several decent chaps there.

KAY: What are you doing now, Robin?

ROBIN (*rather gloomily*): Trying to sell a new heavy motor oil. I ought to have tried your stunt—writing. Might, one day. I could tell 'em something—my oath I could. (*Finishes his drink rather noisily.*) Well, don't let me interrupt the business. Or are you waiting for mother?

MADGE: No, we're better without her.

ROBIN (*belligerently*): Yes, you would think that! But don't forget, it's her money——

He stops because MRS. C. *reappears, all smiles.*

MRS. C. (*joyfully*): Robin! Now this is nice! (*Sweeps across and kisses him. There is perhaps a touch of defiance to the others in the warmth of her welcome.*) Are you staying the night?

ROBIN: I wasn't, but I could do—(*with a grin*) in Alan's best pyjamas.

They settle themselves.

MADGE: We were just saying, Mother, that it was absurd for you to keep on living here. The house is much too big and expensive now.

ROBIN: That's for mother to decide——

MRS. C.: No, that's all right, dear. It is too big now, and, of course, if I sold it I could probably raise enough to convert the Church Road houses into flats.

ERNEST: No you couldn't. Nothing like.

MRS. C. (*with dignity*): Really, Ernest! I was offered four thousand pounds for it once.

ERNEST: You ought to have taken it.

GERALD: I'm afraid you can't count on getting much for this house, though, of course, you'll save money by living in a smaller place.

ROBIN: Not much, though. She'd have to pay rent for the smaller house, and this is hers.

GERALD (*rather impatiently for him, probably because* ROBIN *is here*): But rates and taxes are fairly heavy on this house. I want you all to understand that the present situation is very unsatisfactory. The over-draft can be paid off, of course, simply by selling shares or some of the houses, but after that Mrs. Conway would be worse off than ever. If the money for the conversion scheme could be raised, then the Church Road property would bring in a decent income.

MRS. C.: And I'm sure that's the thing to do. Flats. I might live in one of them myself—a nice, cosy little flat. Delightful!

GERALD: But after you've sold your shares you've still to find another two or three thousand to pay for the conversion into flats.

MRS. C.: But couldn't I borrow that?

GERALD: Not from the bank. They won't accept the Church Road houses as security for a loan to convert them into flats. I've tried that.

HAZEL (*hopefully, and a shade timidly*): Ernest—could lend you the money.

ERNEST (*staggered by this*): *What!*

HAZEL (*rather faltering now*): Well, you could easily afford it, Ernest.

MRS. C. (*smiling*): From what I hear, you're very well off indeed these days, Ernest.

GERALD: Oh—there's no doubt about that.

MRS. C. (*hoping this will win him over*): And it only seems yesterday, Ernest, that you first came here—a very shy young man from nowhere.

ERNEST (*grimly*): It's twenty years ago, to be exact—but that's just what I was—a shy young man from nowhere. And when I managed to wangle myself into this house I thought I'd got somewhere.

MRS. C.: I remember so well feeling that about you at the time, Ernest.

ERNEST: Yes. I was made to feel I'd got somewhere, too. But I stuck it. I've always been able to stick it, when I've had my mind on something I badly wanted. That's how I've managed to get on.

ROBIN (*who doesn't like him, obviously*): Don't begin to tell us now that you landed here with only a shilling in your pocket——

MRS. C. (*warning, reproachful, yet secretly amused*): Now, now Robin!

ERNEST (*in level unpleasant tone*): I wasn't going to. Don't worry, you're not going to have the story of *my* life. All I was about to say was—that as far as I'm concerned, you can whistle for your two or three thousand pounds. You won't get a penny from me. And I might as well tell you—while I'm making myself unpleasant—that I could lend you the two or three thousand without feeling it. Only, I'm not going to. Not a penny.

HAZEL (*indignation struggling with her fear of him*): You make me feel ashamed.

ERNEST (*staring hard at her*): Oh! Why? (*She does not reply, but begins to crumple under his hard stare.*) Go on. Tell 'em why I make you feel ashamed. Tell *me.* Or would you like to tell me later when *I'm* telling *you* a few things?

HAZEL *crumples into tears.* ROBIN *jumps up, furious.*

ROBIN: I never did like you, Beevers. I've half a mind to boot you out of this house.

ERNEST (*no coward*): You do, and I'll bring an action for assault. *And* I'd enjoy it. My money or the boot, eh? I told Hazel a long time ago that not one of you would ever get a penny out of me. And I'm not mean. Ask her. But I swore to myself after the very first night I came here, when you were all being so high and mighty—especially you—that you'd never see a penny that I ever made.

ROBIN (*with a lurking grin*): I see.

ERNEST (*very sharply*): What's that mean? By God, she *has*! She's been giving you money—*my* money.

HAZEL (*terribly alarmed now*): Oh—Robin, why did you?

ROBIN (*irritably*): What does it matter? He can't eat you.

ERNEST (*very quietly and deadly, to* HAZEL): Come on.

Goes out. HAZEL *looks terrified.*

MADGE: Don't go, if you don't want to.

KAY: Hazel, there's nothing to be afraid of.

HAZEL (*sincere, quiet, desperate*): There is. I'm frightened of *him*. Except right at the first—I've always been frightened of him.

ROBIN (*noisily*): Don't be silly. This little pipsqueak! What can *he* do?

HAZEL: I don't know. It isn't that. It's just something about him.

ERNEST (*returning with his overcoat on, to* HAZEL): Come on. I'm going.

HAZEL (*summoning up all her courage*): N-no.

He waits and looks at her. She slowly moves towards him, fearful and ashamed. MRS. C. *moves hastily over towards* ERNEST.

MRS. C. (*excitedly*): You sneaked your way in here, Ernest Beevers, and somehow you persuaded or bullied Hazel, who was considered then one of the prettiest girls in Newlingham, into marrying you——

HAZEL (*imploring her*): No, Mother—please don't——

MRS. C.: I'll tell him now what I've always wanted to tell him. (*Approaching* ERNEST *with vehemence.*) I was a fool. My husband wouldn't have had such a bullying mean little rat near the house. I never liked you. And I'm not surprised to hear you say you've always hated us. Don't ever come here again, don't ever let me see you again. I only wish I was Hazel for just one day, I'd show you something. What—you—my daughter——! (*In a sudden fury she slaps him hard across the face, with a certain grand magnificence of manner.*) Now bring an action for that!

Stands there, blazing at him. He rubs his cheek a little, backs a step or two, looking at her steadily.

ERNEST (*quietly*): You've done a lot of dam' silly things in your time, Mrs. Conway, but you'll find that's the dam' silliest. (*Turns and walks to door. At door he turns quickly to* HAZEL.) Come on.

Goes out. HAZEL *is wretched.*

HAZEL: Oh—Mother—you shouldn't.

ROBIN (*rather grandly*): She did quite right. And you just let me know—if he gives you any trouble.

HAZEL (*tearfully, shaking her head as she wanders towards door*): No, Robin. You don't understand . . . you don't understand. . . .

She goes out slowly. A strained silence. MRS. C. *goes back to her place.*

MRS. C. (*with a short laugh*): Well—I suppose that was a silly thing to do.

GERALD (*gravely*): I'm afraid it was, y'know.

KAY: You see, it's Hazel who will have to pay for it.

ROBIN: Well, she needn't. She's only to let me know what he's up to.

JOAN (*surprisingly*): What's the good of talking like that? What could *you* do ? He can make her life a misery, and you couldn't stop it.

MADGE: Well, it's her own fault. I've no patience with her. I wouldn't stand it ten minutes.

JOAN (*with plenty of spirit, for her*): It's no use you talking, Madge. You simply don't understand. You've never been married.

MADGE: No, and after what I've seen here, I think I'm lucky.

MRS. C. (*with energy*): You're not lucky—never were and never will be—and as you haven't the least idea what a woman's real life is like, the less you say the better. You're not among schoolgirls and silly teachers now. Robin, give me a glass of port. Won't you have a drink too?

ROBIN *pours her a port and himself another whisky.*

GERALD (*rising. He has already put his papers away in case*): I don't think there's any point in my staying any longer.

MRS. C.: But we haven't settled anything.

GERALD (*rather coldly*): I thought there was a chance that Ernest Beevers might have been persuaded to lend you the money. As I don't think anybody else here has three thousand pounds to spare——

ROBIN (*turning on him*): All right, Thornton, you needn't be so damned supercilious about it. Seems to me you've not made a particularly bright job of handling my mother's affairs.

GERALD (*annoyed*): I don't think that comes too well from you.

For years I've given good advice, and never once has it been acted upon. Now I'd be only too delighted to hand over these affairs.

ROBIN: I believe I could make a better job of it myself.

GERALD (*stiffly*): I can't imagine a possible worse choice. (*Moves with his case.*) Good night, Kay. Good night, Alan.

JOAN (*moving*): I think I'll come along too, Gerald.

GERALD *and* ALAN *go out.*

ROBIN: You'll be able to have a nice little chat about me on the way.

JOAN *stands still now and looks across at him.*

JOAN (*very quietly*): It doesn't hurt so much as it used to do, Robin, when you say such bitter things. I suppose one day it won't hurt at all.

ROBIN (*who is sorry at the moment*): Sorry, old girl. And give my love to the kids. Say I'm coming to see them soon.

JOAN: Yes, come and see us soon. Only remember—we're very poor now.

ROBIN: Thanks for that. And then you talk about being bitter.

They look at one another for a moment, lost and hopeless. Then JOAN *moves away, slowly.*

KAY (*rather painfully*): Good night, my dear.

JOAN (*painfully turning and producing little social smile*): Good night, Kay. It's been nice—seeing you again.

She goes out. KAY, *who is moved, withdraws herself.*

ROBIN (*after another drink, an optimist*): Well, now we ought to be able to settle something.

MADGE (*coldly*): So far as I'm concerned, this has simply been a waste of time—and nervous energy.

MRS. C. (*with malice*): You know, Madge, when I think of Gerald Thornton as he is now, a dreary, conceited middle-aged bachelor, I can't help thinking its perhaps a pity you *didn't* marry him.

ROBIN (*with a guffaw*): What, Madge! I never knew you fancied Gerald Thornton.

MRS. C. (*in light but significant tone*): She did—once. Didn't you, dear? And I believe he was interested—oh, a long time ago, when you children were all still at home.

KAY (*sharply*): Mother, if that's not true, then it's stupid silly talk. If it *is* true, then it's cruel.

MRS. C.: Nonsense! And not so high-and-mighty, please, Kay.

MADGE (*facing them bravely*): It *was* true, a long time ago, just after the War. When I still thought we could suddenly make everything better for everybody. Socialism! Peace! Universal Brotherhood!

All that. And I felt then that Gerald Thornton and I together could—help. He had a lot of fine qualities, I thought—I believe he had then, too—and only needed to be pulled out of his rut here, to have his enthusiasm aroused. I was remembering to-night—when I was looking at him. It came back to me quite quickly. (*This last was more to* KAY *than the other two. Now she takes her mother in.*) One evening—just one evening—and something you did that evening—ruined it all. I'd almost forgotten—but seeing us all here again to-night reminded me—I believe it was at a sort of party for you, Kay. (*Accusingly to her mother.*) Do you remember?

MRS. C.: Really, Madge, you *are* absurd. I seem to remember some piece of nonsense, when we were all being foolish.

MADGE: Yes, you remember. It was quite deliberate on your part. Just to keep a useful young man unattached or jealousy of a girl's possible happiness, or just out of sheer nasty female mischief. . . . And something went for ever. . . .

MRS. C.: It can't have been worth very much then.

MADGE: A seed is easily destroyed, but it might have grown into an oak tree. (*Pauses, looks solemnly at her mother.*) I'm glad I'm not a mother.

MRS. C. (*annoyed*): Yes, you may well say that.

MADGE (*with deadly deliberation*): I know how I'd have despised myself if I'd turned out to be a bad mother.

MRS. C. (*angrily, rising*): So that's what you call me? (*Pauses, then with more vehemence and emotion.*) Just because you never think of anybody but yourselves. All selfish—selfish. Because everything hasn't happened as you wanted it, turn on me—all my fault. You never really think about me. Don't try to see things for a moment from my point of view. When you were children, I was so proud of you all, so confident that you would grow up to be wonderful creatures. I used to see myself at the age I am now, surrounded by you and your own children, so proud of you, so happy with you all, this house happier and gayer even than it was in the best of the old days. And now my life's gone by, and what's happened? You're a resentful soured schoolmistress, middle-aged before your time. Hazel—the loveliest child there ever was—married to a vulgar little bully, and terrified of him. Kay here—gone away to lead her own life, and very bitter and secretive about it, as if she'd failed. Carol—the happiest and kindest of you all—dead before she's twenty. Robin—I know, my dear, I'm not blaming you now, but I must speak the truth for once—with a wife he can't love and no sort of position or comfort or anything. And Alan—the eldest, the boy his father adored, that he thought might do anything—what's he now? (ALAN *has come in now and is standing there quietly listening.*) A miserable clerk with no prospects, no ambition, no self-respect, a shabby little man that nobody would look at twice. (*She sees him standing there now, but in her worked-up fury does not care, and lashes out at him.*) Yes, a shabby clerk that nobody would look at twice.

KAY (*in a sudden fury of loyalty*): How dare you, Mother, how dare you! Alan of all people!

ALAN (*with a smile*): That's all right, Kay. Don't you get excited. It's not a bad description. I am a shabby little clerk, y'know. It must be very disappointing.

MRS. C.: Oh—don't be so forgiving! Robin, you've always been selfish and weak and a bit of a good-for-nothing——

ROBIN: Here, steady, old girl. I've had some rotten bad luck, too, y'know, and a lot of it's just luck. I've come to see that.

MRS. C. (*exhausted now*): All right—add the bad luck, too, my dear. The point is, whatever they may say about you, Robin my darling, you're my own boy and my own sort, and a great comfort. So you and I will go upstairs and talk.

ROBIN (*as she takes his arm*): That's the spirit!

They move off together.

MADGE (*very quietly*): Mother! (MRS. C. *stops but does not turn.*) We've both said what we want to say. There isn't any more to be said. And if you decide to have any more of these family conferences, don't trouble to ask me to attend them, because I shan't. I don't expect now to see a penny of father's money. And please don't expect to see any of mine.

ROBIN: Who wants yours?

MRS. C.: Come on, my dear, and we'll talk like human beings.

They go out. The other three are quiet and still.

MADGE: I have an idea I wasn't too pleasant to you, Kay, earlier when we met to-night. If so, I'm sorry.

KAY: That's all right, Madge. Are you going back to Collingfield to-night?

MADGE: No, I can't. But I'm staying with Nora Fleming—you remember her? She's Head of Newlingham High now. I've left my things there. I'll go now. I don't want to see mother again.

KAY: Good-bye, Madge. I hope you collar one of these headships.

MADGE: Good-bye, Kay. And do try and write a good book, instead of doing nothing but this useless journalism.

They kiss. MADGE *goes off, accompanied by* ALAN. KAY, *left to herself, shows that she is deeply moved. She moves restlessly, then hastily pours herself a whisky and soda, lights a cigarette, tastes the whisky, then sits down, ignores the cigarette burning in her hand and the whisky, stares into the past, and then begins to cry.* ALAN *returns, filling his pipe.*

ALAN (*cheerfully*): You've a good half-hour yet, Kay, before you need set out for the London train. I'll take you to the station. (*Comes up to her.*) What's the matter? Has all this—been a bit too much for you?

KAY (*ruefully*): Apparently. And I thought I was tough now, Alan.
. . . See, I was doing the modern working woman—a cigarette and a whisky and soda . . . no good, though. . . . You see, Alan, I've not only been here to-night, I've been here remembering other nights, long ago, when we weren't like this. . . .

ALAN: Yes, I know. Those old Christmasses. . . . birthday parties. . . .

KAY: Yes, I remembered. I saw all of us then. Myself, too. Oh, silly girl of Nineteen Ninteen! Oh, lucky girl!

ALAN: You mustn't mind too much. It's all right, y'know. Like being forty?

KAY: Oh no, Alan, it's hideous and unbearable. Remember what we once were and what we thought we'd be. And now this. And it's all we have, Alan, it's *us*. Every step we've taken—every tick of the clock—making everything worse. If this is all life is, what's the use? Better to die, like Carol, before you find it out, before Time gets to work on you. I've felt it before. Alan, but never as I've done to-night. There's a great devil in the universe, and we call it Time.

ALAN (*playing with his pipe, quietly, shyly*): Did you ever read Blake?

KAY: Yes.

ALAN: Do you remember this? (*quotes quietly, but with feeling*):

> Joy and woe are woven fine,
> A clothing for the soul divine;
> Under every grief and pine
> Runs a joy with silken twine.
> It is right it should be so;
> Man was made for joy and woe;
> And when this we rightly know,
> Safely through the world we go. . . .

KAY: Safely through the world we go? No, it isn't true, Alan—or it isn't true for me. If things were merely mixed—good and bad—that would be all right, but they get worse. We've seen it to-night. Time's beating us.

ALAN: No, Time's only a kind of dream, Kay. If it wasn't, it would have to destroy everything—the whole universe—and then remake it again every tenth of a second. But Time doesn't destroy anything. It merely moves us on—in this life—from one peep-hole to the next.

KAY: But the happy young Conways, who used to play charades here, they've gone, and gone for ever.

ALAN: No, they're real and existing, just as we two, here now, are real and existing. We're seeing another bit of the view—a bad bit, if you like—but the whole landscape's still there.

KAY: But, Alan, we can't be anything but what we are *now*.

ALAN: No . . . it's hard to explain . . . suddenly like this . . . there's a book I'll lend you—read it in the train. But the point is, now, at this moment, or any moment, we're only a cross-section of our real selves. What we *really* are is the whole stretch of ourselves, all our time, and when we come to the end of this life, all those selves, all our time, will be *us*—the real you, the real me. And then perhaps we'll find ourselves in another time, which is only another kind of dream.

KAY: I'll try to understand . . . so long as you really believe—and think it's possible for me to believe—that Time's not ticking our lives away . . . wrecking . . . and ruining everything . . . for ever. . . .

ALAN: No, it's all right, Kay. I'll get you that book. (*Moves away towards door, then turns.*) You know, I believe half our trouble now is because we think Time's ticking our lives away. That's why we snatch and grab and hurt each other.

KAY: As if we were all in a panic on a sinking ship.

ALAN: Yes, like that.

KAY (*smiling at him*): But you don't do those things—bless you!

ALAN: I think it's easier not to—if you take a long view.

KAY: As if we're—immortal beings?

ALAN (*smiling*): Yes, and in for a tremendous adventure.

> *Goes out.* KAY, *comforted, but still brooding, goes to the window and stands there looking out, with head raised. No sooner is she settled there than the curtain comes down.*

END OF ACT TWO

ACT III

KAY *is sitting just as we left her at the end of* ACT I, *and we can still hear* MRS. CONWAY *singing Schumann's "Der Nussbaum". Nothing happens until the song has ended and we have heard some applause and voices from the party, but then* ALAN *enters and switches on the lights. We see that the room and everything in it is exactly as they were before. Only* KAY *herself has changed. Something—elusive, a brief vision, a score of shadowy presentiments—is haunting her. She is deeply disturbed. She throws a look or two at the room, as if she had just seen it in some other guise. She looks at* ALAN, *puzzled. He grins and rubs his hands a little.*

ALAN: Well, Kay?

KAY (*as if to break into something important*): Alan—— (*Breaks off.*)

ALAN: Yes?

KAY (*hurriedly*): No—nothing.

ALAN (*looking more closely at her*): I believe you've been asleep—while mother was singing.

KAY (*confusedly*): No. I was sitting here—listening. I turned the light out. No, I didn't fall asleep—I don't know, perhaps I did—just for a second. It couldn't have been longer.

ALAN: You'd know if you'd been asleep.

KAY (*looking about her, slowly*): No, I wasn't asleep. But—quite suddenly—I thought I saw . . . we were. . . . Anyhow, you came into it, I think, Alan.

ALAN (*amused and puzzled*): Came into *what*?

KAY: I can't remember. And I know I was listening to mother singing all the time. I'm—a bit—wuzzy.

ALAN: Most of the people are going now. You'd better go and say good night.

HAZEL *enters, carrying plate on which is enormous piece of sticky, rich, creamy cake. She has already begun to tackle this as she moves in.*

KAY (*seeing her*): Hazel, you greedy pig!

KAY *deftly swoops up a bit of the cake and eats it.*

HAZEL (*talking with her mouth rather full*): I didn't come in here just to eat this.

KAY: Course you did!

HAZEL: They're all saying good night now, and I'm dodging that little horror Gerald Thornton brought.

KAY (*hastily*): I must say my piece to them.

Hurries off. ALAN *lingers.*

ALAN (*after a pause*): Hazel!

HAZEL (*mouth full*): Um?

ALAN (*with elaborate air of casualness*): What's Joan Helford going to do now?

HAZEL: Oh—just mooch round a bit.

ALAN: I thought I heard her saying she was going away—I was wondering if she was leaving Newlingham.

HAZEL: She's only going to stay with her aunt. Joan's always staying with aunts. Why can't *we* have aunts planted all over the place?

ALAN: There's Aunt Edith.

HAZEL: And a doctor's house in Wolverhampton! Ghastly! (*Quick change of tone. Teasingly.*) Anything else you'd like to know about Joan?

ALAN (*confused*): No—no. I—just wondered. (*Turns to go and almost bumps into* ERNEST, *who is wearing a very shabby mackintosh-raincoat and carrying a bowler hat. As soon as* HAZEL *sees who it is, she turns away and has another dab at her cake.* ALAN *stops and so does* ERNEST.) Oh!—you going?

ERNEST (*a man who knows his own mind*): In a minute. (*He obviously waits for* ALAN *to clear out.*)

ALAN (*rather confused*): Yes—well—— (*Makes a move.*)

HAZEL (*loudly and clearly*): Alan, you're not going?

She looks across, completely ignoring ERNEST, *who waits, not perhaps quite as cool as he would appear on the surface, for the hat he is clutching moves a bit.*

ALAN (*not at home in this*): Yes—have to say good night and get their coats and things—you know——

Goes out. HAZEL *attends to her cake, and then looks, without a smile, at* ERNEST.

ERNEST: I just looked in to say good night, Miss Conway.

HAZEL (*blankly*): Oh—yes—of course. Well——

ERNEST (*cutting in*): It's been a great pleasure to me to come here and meet you all.

He waits a moment. She finds herself compelled to speak.

HAZEL (*same tone*): Oh—well——

ERNEST (*cutting in again*): Especially you. I'm new round here, y'know. I've only been in the place about three months. I bought a share in that paper mill—Eckersley's—out at West Newlingham—you know it?

HAZEL (*no encouragement from her*): No.

ERNEST: Thought you might have noticed it. Been there long enough. Matter of fact it wants rebuilding. But that's where I am. And I hadn't been here a week before I noticed you, Miss Conway.

HAZEL (*who knows it only too well*): Did you?

ERNEST: Yes. And I've been watching out for you ever since. I expect you've noticed me knocking about.

HAZEL (*loftily*): No, I don't think I have.

ERNEST: Oh—yes—you must have done. Come on now. Admit it.

HAZEL (*her natural self coming out now*): Well, if you must know, I have noticed you——

ERNEST (*pleased*): I thought so.

HAZEL (*rapidly and indignantly*): Because I thought you behaved very stupidly and rudely. If you want to look silly yourself—that's your affair—but you'd no right to make me look silly too——

ERNEST (*rather crushed*): Oh! I didn't know—it'ud been as bad as that——

HAZEL (*feeling she has the upper hand*): Well, it has.

He stares at her, perhaps having moved a little closer. She does not look at him at first, but then is compelled to meet his hard stare. There is something about this look that penetrates to the essential weakness of her character.

ERNEST (*coming up again now*): I'm sorry. Though I can't see anybody's much the worse for it. After all, we've only one life to live, let's get on with it, I say. And in my opinion, you're the best-looking girl in this town, Miss Hazel Conway. I've been telling you that—in my mind—for the last two months. But I knew it wouldn't be long before I got to know you. To tell you properly. (*Looks hard at her. She does not like him but is completely helpless before this direct attack. He nods slowly.*) I expect you're thinking I'm not much of a chap. But there's a bit more in me than meets the eye. A few people have found that out already, and a lot more'll find it out before so long— here in Newlingham. You'll see. (*Changes his tone, because he is uncertain on purely social matters, almost humble now.*) Would it be all right—if I—sort of—called to see you—some time soon?

HAZEL (*coming to the top again*): You'd better ask my mother.

ERNEST (*jocularly*): Oh!—sort of *Ask Mamma* business, eh?

HAZEL (*confused and annoyed*): No—I didn't mean it like that at all.
I meant that this is mother's house——

ERNEST: Yes, but you're old enough now to have your own friends,
aren't you?

HAZEL: I don't make friends with people very quickly.

ERNEST (*with appalling bluntness*): Oh! I'd heard you did.

HAZEL (*haughtily, angrily*): Do you mean to say you've been
discussing me with people?

ERNEST: Yes. Why not?

> They stare at one another, ERNEST *coolly and deliberately and*
> HAZEL *with attempted hauteur, when* MADGE *and* ROBIN *enter
> together, in the middle of a talk.*

ROBIN (*who is in great form*): Golly yes! It was a great lark. We
weren't in uniform, y'know. I did some stoking. Hard work, but a
great stunt.

MADGE (*hotly*): It wasn't. You ought to have been ashamed of
yourselves.

ROBIN (*surprised*): Why?

MADGE: Because helping to break a strike and being a blackleg
isn't a lark and a stunt. Those railwaymen were desperately anxious
to improve their conditions. They didn't go on strike for fun. It was a
very serious thing for them and for their wives and families. And then
people like you, Robin, think it's amusing when you try to do their
work and make the strike useless. I think it's shameful the way the
middle classes turn against the working class.

ROBIN (*rather out of his depth now*): But there had to be some sort of
train service.

MADGE: Why? If the public had to do without trains altogether,
they might realise then that the railwaymen have some grievances.

ERNEST (*sardonically*): They might. But I've an idea they'd be too
busy with their own grievance—no trains. And you only want a few
more railway strikes and then half their traffic will be gone for ever,
turned into road transport. And what do your clever railwaymen do
then? (*Pauses.* MADGE *is listening, of course, but not quite acknowledg-
ing that he had any right to join in.*) And another thing. The working
class is out for itself. Then why shouldn't the middle class be out for
itself?

MADGE (*coldly*): Because the middle class must have already been
"out for itself"—-as you call it——

ERNEST: Well, what do you call it? Something in Latin?

MADGE (*with chill impatience*): I say, the middle class must have already been successfully out for itself or it wouldn't be a comfortable middle class. Then why turn against the working class when at last *it* tries to look after itself?

ERNEST (*cynically*): That's easy. There's only so much to go round, and if you take more, then I get less.

MADGE (*rather sharply*): I'm sorry, but that's bad economics as well as bad ethics.

ROBIN (*bursting out*): But we'd have Red Revolution—like Russia —if we began to listen to these wild chaps like this J. H. Thomas.

HAZEL (*moving*): Well, I think it's all silly. Why can't people agree?

ERNEST (*seeing her going*): Oh!—Miss Conway——

HAZEL (*her very blank sweetness a snub*): Oh—yes—good night.

She goes out. ERNEST *looks after her, a rather miserable figure. Then he looks towards* ROBIN *just in time to catch a grin on his face before it is almost—but not quite—wiped off.*

MADGE (*to* ROBIN): I came in here for something. What was it?

Looks about her and through ERNEST, *whom she obviously dislikes.*

ROBIN (*still a grin lurking*): Don't ask me.

MADGE *goes, ignoring* ERNEST, *though rather absently than pointedly.* ROBIN *still looking vaguely mocking, lights a cigarette.*

ROBIN (*casually*): Were you in the army?

ERNEST: Yes. Two years.

ROBIN: What crush?

ERNEST: Army Pay Corps.

ROBIN (*easily, not too rudely*): That must have been fun for you.

ERNEST *looks as if he is going to make an angry retort when* CAROL *hurries in.*

CAROL: Mr. Beevers—— (*As he turns, looking rather sullen,* ROBIN *wanders out.*) Oh!—you look *Put Out.*

ERNEST (*grimly*): That's about it. Put out!

CAROL (*looking hard at him*): I believe you're all hot and angry inside, aren't you?

ERNEST (*taking it as lightly as he can*): Or disappointed. Which is it?

CAROL: A mixture, I expect. Well, Mr. Beevers, you mustn't. You were very nice about the charade—and very good in it too—and I don't suppose you've ever played before, have you?

ERNEST: No. (*Grimly.*) They didn't go in for those sort of things in my family.

CAROL (*looking at him critically*): No, I don't think you've had enough Fun. That's your trouble, Mr. Beevers. You must come and play charades again.

ERNEST (*as if setting her apart from the others*): You're all right, y'know.

MRS. C.'*s voice, very clear, is heard off saying, "But surely he's gone, hasn't he?"*

CAROL: We're *all* all right, you know. And don't forget that, Mr. Beevers.

ERNEST (*liking her*): You're a funny kid.

CAROL (*severely*): I'm not very funny and I'm certainly not a kid——

ERNEST: Oh—sorry!

CAROL (*serenely*): I'll forgive you this time.

MRS. C. *enters with* GERALD. *She looks rather surprised to see* ERNEST *still there. He notices this.*

ERNEST (*awkwardly*): I'm just going, Mrs. Conway. (*To* GERALD.) You coming along?

MRS. C. (*smoothly, but quickly in*): No, Mr. Thornton and I want to talk business for a few minutes.

ERNEST: I see. Well, good night, Mrs. Conway. And I'm very pleased to have met you.

MRS. C. (*condescendingly gracious*): Good night, Mr. Beevers. Carol, will you——

CAROL (*cheerfully*): Yes. (*To* ERNEST, *who looks rather bewildered by it, in imitation Western American accent.*) I'll set you and your hoss on the big trail, pardner.

She and ERNEST *go out.* MRS. C. *and* GERALD *watch them go. Then* GERALD *turns and raises his eyebrows at her.* MRS. C. *shakes her head. We hear a door slammed to.*

MRS. C. (*briskly*): I'm sorry if your little friend thought he was being pushed out, but really, Gerald, the children would never have forgiven me if I'd encouraged him to stay any longer.

GERALD: I'm afraid Beevers hasn't been a success.

MRS. C.: Well, after all, he is—rather—isn't he?

GERALD: I did warn you, y'know. And really he was so desperately keen to meet the famous Conways.

MRS. C.: Hazel, you mean.

GERALD: Hazel, especially, but he was determined to know the whole family.

MRS. C.: Well, I do think they're an attractive lot of children.

GERALD: Only outshone by their attractive mother.

MRS. C. (*delighted*): Gerald! I believe you're going to flirt with me.

GERALD (*who isn't*): Of course I am. By the way, there *wasn't* any business you wanted to discuss, was there?

MRS. C.: No, not really. But I think you ought to know I've had another *enormous* offer for this house. Of course I wouldn't dream of selling it, but it's nice to know it's worth so much. Oh!—and young George Farrow would like me to sell him my share in the firm, and says he's ready to make an offer that would surprise me.

GERALD: I believe it would be pretty handsome too. But, of course, there's no point in selling out when they're paying fifteen per cent. And once we're really out of this war-time atmosphere and the government restrictions are off, there's going to be a tremendous boom.

MRS. C.: Isn't that lovely? All the children back home, and plenty of money to help them to settle down. And, mind you, Gerald, I shouldn't be a bit surprised if Robin doesn't do awfully well in some business quite soon. *Selling* things, probably—people find him so attractive. Dear Robin! (*Pauses. Then change of tone, more depth and feeling.*) Gerald, it isn't so very long ago that I thought myself the unluckiest woman in the world. If it hadn't been for the children, I wouldn't have wanted to go on living. Sometimes—without *him*—I didn't want to go on living. And now—though, of course, it'll never be the same without *him*—I suddenly feel I'm one of the luckiest women in the world. All my children round me, quite safe at last, very happy. (ROBIN'S *voice, shouting, off,* "It's hide and seek all over the house.") Did he say "all over the house"?

GERALD: Yes.

MRS. C. (*calling*): Not in my room, Robin, please.

ROBIN (*off, shouting*): Mother's room's barred.

JOAN'S VOICE (*further off, shouting*): Who's going to be It?

ROBIN'S VOICE (*off*): I am. Mother, come on. Where's Gerald?

MRS. C. (*as she prepares to move*): Just to hear him shouting about the house again—you don't know what it means to me, Gerald. And you never will know.

They go out. As MRS. C. *passes switch, she can switch off half the lights in the room, perhaps leaving right half unilluminated and perhaps standard lamp on left half.*

ROBIN'S VOICE (*loud, off*): I'll go into the coat cupboard and count fifty. Now then—scatter.

After a moment JOAN *enters, happy and breathless, and after looking about chooses a hiding-place to the right—behind a chair, end of bookcase or sofa, or curtain. No sooner has she installed herself than* ALAN *enters and moves across to that end. She peeps out and sees him.*

JOAN (*imploring whisper*): Oh—Alan—don't hide in here.

ALAN (*humbly*): I came specially. I saw you come in.

JOAN: No, please. Go somewhere else.

ALAN (*wistfully*): You look so pretty, Joan.

JOAN: Do I? That's sweet of you, Alan.

ALAN: Can I stay, then?

JOAN: No, please. It's *so* much more fun if you go somewhere else. Alan, don't spoil it.

ALAN: Spoil what?

JOAN (*very hurriedly*): The game—of course. Go on, Alan, there's a pet. Oh—you can't go out that way now. You'll have to go out of the window and then round. Go on.

ALAN: All right. (*Climbs out of window, then looks closely at her a moment, then softly.*) Good-bye, Joan.

JOAN (*whispering, surprised*): Why do you say that?

ALAN (*very sadly*): Because I feel it *is* good-bye.

ROBIN'S *voice, humming, is heard off.* ALAN *goes through the curtains at the window.* ROBIN, *half humming, half singing, a popular song of the period, enters slowly. He moves to the edge of the lighted half, looking about him, still singing. Finally he turns away and begins to move, when* JOAN *joins in the song softly from her hiding-place.*

ROBIN (*with satisfaction*): A-ha! (*Very quickly he closes the curtains but as he turns his back,* JOAN *reaches out and turns off the switch of the standard lamp in her corner. The room is now almost in darkness.*) All right, Joan Helford. Where are you, Joan Helford, where are you? (*She is heard to laugh in the darkness.*) You can't escape, Joan Helford, you can't escape. No, no. No, no. No escape for little Joan. No escape.

They run round the room, then she goes to the window and stands on the seat. He pulls her down, and then, in silhouette against the moonlight we see them embrace and kiss.

JOAN (*really moved*): Oh—Robin!

ROBIN (*mocking, but nicely*): Oh—Joan!

JOAN (*shyly*): I suppose—you've been—doing this—to dozens of girls?

ROBIN (*still light*): Yes, Joan, dozens.

JOAN (*looking up at him*): I thought so.

ROBIN (*a trifle unsteadily*): Like that, Joan. But not—like this——

Now he kisses her with more ardour.

JOAN (*deeply moved, but still shy*): Robin—you *are* sweet.

ROBIN (*after pause*): You know, Joan, although it's not so very long since I saw you last, I couldn't believe my eyes to-night—you looked so stunning.

JOAN: It was because I'd just heard that you'd come back, Robin.

ROBIN (*who does*): I don't believe it.

JOAN (*sincerely*): Yes, it's true—honestly—I don't suppose you've ever thought about me, have you?

ROBIN (*who hasn't*): Yes, I have. Hundreds of times.

JOAN: I have about you too.

ROBIN (*kissing her*): Joan, you're a darling!

JOAN (*after pause, whispering*): Do you remember that morning you went away so early—a year ago?

ROBIN: Yes. But you weren't there. Only mother and Hazel and Kay.

JOAN: I was there too, but I didn't let any of you see me.

ROBIN (*genuinely surprised*): You got up at that filthy hour just to see me go?

JOAN (*simply*): Yes, of course. Oh—it was awful—trying to hide and trying not to cry, all at the same time.

ROBIN (*still surprised and moved*): But Joan, I'd no idea.

JOAN (*very shyly*): I didn't mean to give myself away.

ROBIN (*embracing her*): But Joan—oh gosh!—it's marvellous.

JOAN: You don't love me?

ROBIN (*now sure he does*): Of course I do. Golly, this is great! Joan, we'll have a scrumptious time!

JOAN (*solemnly*): Yes, let's. But Robin—it's terribly *serious*, y'know.

ROBIN: Oh—yes—don't think I don't feel that, too. But that's no reason why we shouldn't enjoy ourselves, is it?

JOAN (*crying out*): No, no, no. Let's be happy for ever and ever.

They embrace fervently, silhouetted against the moonlit window. Now the curtains are suddenly drawn by CAROL, *who sees them and calls out to people behind her.*

CAROL (*with a sort of cheerful disgust*): I thought so! They're in here—*Courting!* I knew there was a catch in this hide-and-seek.

ROBIN *and* JOAN *spring apart but still hold hands as* CAROL *switches on all the lights and comes into the room, followed by* MADGE *and* GERALD. MADGE *is rather excited—and rather untidy, too, as if she had been hiding in some difficult place.*

ROBIN (*grinning*): Sorry! Shall we start again?

MADGE (*crossing towards window*): No, thank you, Robin.

CAROL: You'd better explain to mother. I'm going to make tea.

She goes. ROBIN *and* JOAN *look at one another, then go out.* GERALD *watches* MADGE, *who now draws the curtains and then returns to him.*

GERALD: Well, Madge, it sounds all right. And I know Lord Robert Cecil's a fine chap. But I don't quite see where I come into it.

MADGE: Because in a few weeks' time there'll be a branch of this League of Nations Union here in Newlingham. It's no use my doing much about it—though I'll join, of course—because I'll be away. But you could be organising secretary or something, Gerald.

GERALD: Don't know that I'd be much good.

MADGE: You'd be perfect. You understand business. You know how to handle people. You'd make a good public speaker. Oh, Gerald—you're maddening!

GERALD (*smiling, not without affection*): Why, Madge? What have I done now?

MADGE: We're friends, aren't we?

GERALD: I consider you one of my very best friends, Madge, and I hope I'm not flattering myself.

MADGE (*warmly*): Of course not.

GERALD (*smiling*): Good! So?

MADGE: You're not doing enough, Gerald.

GERALD (*mildly*): I'm kept pretty busy, y'know.

MADGE: Yes, I don't mean you're lazy—though I'm not sure that you aren't a bit, y'know, Gerald—I mean you're not doing enough with yourself. You're not *using* yourself to the utmost. I could be *tremendously* proud of you, Gerald.

GERALD: That's—almost overwhelming—coming from you, Madge.

MADGE: Why from me?

GERALD: Because I know very well that you've got a very good brain and are a most critical young woman. Rather frightening.

MADGE (*rather more feminine here*): Nonsense! You don't mean that. I'd much rather you didn't, y'know.

GERALD: All right, I don't. As a matter of fact, I'm very fond of you, Madge, but don't often get a chance of showing you that I am.

MADGE (*lighting up at this*): I've always been fond of you, Gerald, and that's why I say I could be tremendously proud of you. (*With more breadth and sweep and real warm enthusiasm.*) We're going to build up a new world now. This horrible War was probably necessary because it was a great bonfire on which we threw all the old nasty rubbish of the world. Civilisation can really begin—at last. People have learned their lesson——

GERALD (*dubiously*): I hope so.

MADGE: Oh—Gerald—don't be so pessimistic, so cynical——

GERALD: Sorry, but a lawyer—even a young one—sees a lot of human nature in his office. There's a procession of people with their quarrels and grievances. And sometimes I wonder how much people are capable of learning.

MADGE: That's because you have to deal with some of the stupidest. But *the* people—all over the world—have learned their lesson. You'll see. No more piling up armaments. No more wars. No more hate and intolerance and violence. Oh—Gerald—I believe that when we look back—in twenty years time—we'll be staggered at the progress that's been made. Because things happen quickly now——

GERALD: That's true enough.

MADGE (*begins to orate a little, sincerely*): And so is all the rest. Under the League, we'll build up a new commonwealth of all the nations, so that they can live at peace for ever. And Imperialism will go. And so in the end, of course, will Capitalism. There'll be no more booms and slumps and panics and strikes and lock-outs, because the people themselves, led by the best brains in their countries, will possess both the political and economic power. There'll be Socialism at last, a free, prosperous, happy people, all enjoying equal opportunities, living at peace with the whole world. (*Quotes with great fervour and sincerity.*)

> Bring me my bow of burning gold:
> Bring me my Arrows of desire:
> Bring me my Spear: O clouds unfold!
> Bring me my Chariot of fire.

I will not cease from Mental Fight,
Nor shall my Sword sleep in my hand
Till we have built Jerusalem
In England's green and pleasant Land . . .

GERALD (*genuinely moved by her fervour*): Madge—you're inspired to-night. I—I hardly recognise you—you're——

MADGE (*warmly, happily*): This is the real me. Oh!—Gerald—in this New World we're going to build up now, men and women won't play a silly little game of cross-purposes any longer. They'll go forward together—sharing everything——

MRS. C. *enters with* HAZEL. MADGE *breaks off, looking rather untidy.* GERALD, *who has been genuinely dominated by her, looks round, recovering himself.*

MRS. C. (*with maddening maternal briskness*): Madge dear, your hair's all over the place, you've made your nose all shiny, you're horribly untidy, and I'm sure you're in the middle of a Socialist speech that must be boring poor Gerald.

The generous mood is shattered. MADGE *might have been hit in the face. She looks at her mother, then looks quickly at* GERALD, *reads something in his face—a sort of withdrawal from her—that is somehow final, and then in complete silence walks straight out of the room.*

MRS. C. (*lightly, but knowing what has happened*): Poor Madge!

HAZEL (*with sudden reproach*): Mother!

MRS. C. (*with wide innocence*): What, Hazel?

HAZEL (*significantly, indicating* GERALD): *You* know!

GERALD (*not half the man he was*): I think—I'd better be going.

MRS. C.: Oh—no, Gerald, don't go. Kay and Carol are making some tea and we're all going to be nice and cosy together in here.

GERALD: I fancy it's rather late, though. (*Glances at his watch, while* HAZEL *slips out.*) After eleven. I *must* go. I've an early appointment in the morning, and one or two things to look through before I turn in to-night. So—— (*With slight smile.* KAY *enters with folding legs of small Oriental table. She puts them down, to turn to* GERALD, *and* MRS. CONWAY *arranges them.*) Good night, Kay. Thank you for a very nice party. And now that you're properly grown-up, I hope you'll be happy.

KAY (*with a slight smile*): Thank you, Gerald. Do you think I will?

GERALD (*his smile suddenly vanishing*): I don't know, Kay. I really don't know.

Smiles again and shakes hands. Nods and smiles at HAZEL, *who enters with tray of tea things.*

MRS. C.: No. I'll see you out, Gerald.

They go out. HAZEL *and* KAY *can rearrange things a little while talking.*

HAZEL (*thoughtfully*): I've always thought it must be much more *fun* being a girl than being a man.

KAY: I'm never sure. Sometimes men seem quite hopelessly dull, like creatures made out of wood. And then at other times they seem to have all the fun.

HAZEL (*very seriously for her*): Kay, just now—this very minute—I wish I wasn't a girl. I'd like to be a man—one of those men with red faces and loud voices who just don't care what anybody says about them.

KAY (*laughingly*): Perhaps they do, though.

HAZEL: I'd like to be one of those who don't.

KAY: Why all this?

HAZEL *shakes her head.* CAROL *and* ALAN *enter with the rest of the tea things.*

CAROL: Alan says he wants to go to bed.

KAY: Oh—no, Alan. Don't spoil it.

ALAN: How could I?

KAY: By going to bed. It's my birthday, and you're not to leave us until I say you can.

CAROL (*severely*): Quite right, Kay. (*Going up to* ALAN.) And that's because we're very very fond of you, Alan, though you are such a chump. You must smoke your pipe too—for cosiness. (*Generally.*) Robin and Joan are courting in the dining-room now. I can see they're going to be an awful nuisance.

KAY (*as* HAZEL *and* CAROL *settle down*): If you had to fall in love with somebody, would you like it to be at home or somewhere else?

HAZEL: Somewhere else. Too ordinary at home. On a yacht or the terrace at Monte Carlo or a Pacific Island. Marvellous!

CAROL: That would be using up too many things at once. Greedy stuff!

HAZEL (*coolly*): I *am* greedy.

CAROL: I should think so. (*To the other two.*) Yesterday morning, she was in the bath, reading *Greenmantle*, and eating nut-milk chocolate.

KAY (*who has been thinking*): No, it wouldn't be too ordinary, falling in love at home here. It would be best, I think. Suppose you were suddenly unhappy. It would be awful to be desperately unhappy and in love miles away in a strange house. . . . (*Suddenly stops, shivers.*)

CAROL: Kay, what's the matter?

KAY: Nothing.

CAROL: Then it must have been a goose walking over your grave.

KAY *abruptly turns away from them, going towards the window.* HAZEL *looks at her—as the other two do—then raises her eyebrows at* CAROL, *who shakes her head sternly.* MRS. C. *enters and looks cheerful at the sight of the tea.*

MRS. C. (*cheerfully*): Now then, let's have some tea and be nice and cosy together. Where's Robin?

HAZEL: Spooning with Joan in the dining-room.

MRS. C.: Oh!—hasn't Joan gone yet? I really think she might leave us to ourselves now. After all, it's the first time we've all been together in this house for—how long? It must be at least three years. I'll pour out. Come on, Kay. What's the matter?

CAROL (*in tremendous whisper, seriously*): Sh! It's a *Mood*.

But KAY *returns, looking rather strained. Her mother looks at her carefully, smiling.* KAY *manages an answering smile.*

MRS. C.: That's better, darling. What a funny child you are, aren't you?

KAY: Not really, Mother. Where's Madge?

ALAN: She went upstairs.

MRS. C.: Go up, dear, and tell her we're all in here, with some tea, and ask her—very nicely, dear, specially from me—to come down.

HAZEL (*muttering, rather*): I'll bet she's doesn't.

ALAN *goes.* MRS. C. *begins pouring out tea.*

MRS. C.: This is just like old times, isn't it? And we seem to have waited so long. I ought to tell fortunes again—to-night.

HAZEL (*eagerly*): Oh—yes—Mother, do.

KAY (*rather sharply*): No.

MRS. C.: Kay! Really! Have you had too much excitement to-day?

KAY: No, I don't think so. Sorry, Mother. Somehow, I hated the idea of you messing about with those cards to-night. I never did like it much.

CAROL (*solemnly*): I believe only the Bad Things come true.

MRS. C.: Certainly not. I clearly saw Madge's Girton scholarship, you remember. I said she was going to get one, didn't I? And I always said Robin and Alan would come back. I saw it every time in the cards.

Enter JOAN *and* ROBIN.

JOAN: I—I think I ought to go now, Mrs. Conway. (*To* KAY, *impulsively.*) Thank you so much, Kay, it's been the loveliest party there ever was. (*Suddenly kisses her with great affection, then she looks solemnly at* MRS. C. *who is considering the situation.*) I really have had a marvellous time, Mrs. Conway.

Standing close to her now. MRS. C. *looks quite searchingly at her.* JOAN *meets her look quite bravely, though a little shaky.*

ROBIN: Well, Mother?

MRS. C. *looks at him, then at* JOAN, *and suddenly smiles.* JOAN *smiles back.*

MRS. C.: Are you two children *serious*?

ROBIN (*boisterously*): Of course we are.

MRS. C.: Joan?

JOAN (*very solemnly, nervously*): Yes.

MRS. C. (*with an air of capitulation*): I think you'd better have a cup of tea, hadn't you?

JOAN *flings her arms round* MRS. C. *and kisses her excitedly.*

JOAN: I'm so happy.

CAROL (*loudly, cheerfully*): Tea. Tea. Tea.

Passing of cups, etc. ALAN *enters.*

ALAN: Madge says she's too tired, Mother.

Goes and sits down near KAY.

MRS. C.: Well, I think we can get on very nicely without Madge. Kay ought to read us some of the new novel she's writing——

Exclamations of agreement and approval from JOAN *and* ROBIN *and a groan from* HAZEL.

KAY (*in horror*): I couldn't possibly, Mother.

MRS. C.: I can't see why not. You always expect me to be ready to sing for you.

KAY: That's different.

MRS. C. (*mostly to* ROBIN *and* JOAN): Kay's always so solemn and secretive about her writing—as if she were ashamed of it.

KAY (*bravely*): I am—in a way. I know it's not good enough yet. Most of it's stupid, stupid, *stupid*.

CAROL (*indignantly*): It isn't, Kay.

KAY: Yes, it is, angel. But it won't always be. It *must* come right if I only keep on trying. And then—you'll see.

JOAN: Is that what you want to do, Kay? Just to write novels and things?

KAY: Yes. But there's nothing in simply writing. The point is to be *good*—to be sensitive and sincere. Hardly anybody's both, especially women who write. But I'm going to try and be. And whatever happens, I'm never *never* going to write except what I want to write, what I feel is true to me, deep down. I won't write just to please silly people or just to make money. I'll——

But she suddenly breaks off, The rest wait and stare.

ALAN (*encouragingly*): Go on, Kay.

KAY (*confusedly, dejectedly*): No—Alan—I'd finished really—or if I was going to say something else, I've forgotten what it was—nothing much——

MRS. C. (*not too concernedly*): You're sure you're not over-tired, Kay?

KAY (*hastily*): No, Mother. Really.

MRS. C.: I wonder what will have happened to you, Hazel, when Kay's a famous novelist? Perhaps one of your majors and captains will come back for you soon.

HAZEL (*calmly*): They needn't. In fact, I'd rather none of them did.

ROBIN (*teasingly*): Thinks she can do much better than them.

HAZEL (*calmly*): I know I can. I shall marry a tall, rather good-looking man about five or six years older than I am, and he'll have plenty of money and be very fond of travel, and we'll go all over the world together but have a house in London.

MRS. C.: And what about poor Newlingham?

HAZEL: Mother, I couldn't possibly spend the rest of my life here. I'd die. But you shall come and stay with us in London, and we'll give parties so that people can come and stare at my sister, Kay Conway, the famous novelist.

ROBIN (*boisterously*): And what about your brother, Robin, the famous—oh! famous something-or-other, you bet your life.

JOAN (*rather teasingly*): You don't know what you're going to do yet, Robin.

ROBIN (*grandly*): Well, give me a chance. I've only been out of the Air Force about twelve hours. But—by jingo—I'm going to do *something*. And none of this starting-at-the-bottom-of-the-ladder, pushing-a-pen-in-a-corner business either. This is a time when young men get a chance, and I'm going to take it. You watch.

MRS. C. (*with mock alarm, though with underlying seriousness*): Don't tell me you're going to run away from Newlingham, too!

ROBIN (*grandly*): Oh—well—I don't know about that yet, Mother. I might make a start here—there's some money in the place, thanks to some jolly rotten profiteering, and we're pretty well known here, so that would help—but I don't guarantee to take root in Newlingham, no fear! Don't be surprised, Hazel, if I'm in London before you. Or even before you, Kay. *And* making plenty of money. (*To* HAZEL.) Perhaps more than this tall, good-looking chap of yours will be making.

CAROL (*sharply, pointing*): Hazel will always have plenty of money

MRS. C. (*amused*): How do you know, Carol?

CAROL: I just do. It came over me suddenly then.

MRS. C. (*still amused*): Well now! I thought I was the prophetic one of the family. I suppose it wouldn't be fair if I sent my rival to bed.

CAROL: I should jolly well think it wouldn't. And I'll tell you another thing. (*Points suddenly at* ALAN.) Alan's the happy one.

ROBIN: Good old Alan!

ALAN: I—rather think—you're wrong there, y'know, Carol.

CAROL: I'm not. I *know*.

MRS. C.: Now I'm not going to have this. I'm the one who *knows* in this family. Now wait a minute. (*Closes her eyes, then half playfully, half seriously.*) Yes. I see Robin dashing about, making lots of money and becoming very important and helping some of you others. And a very devoted young wife by his side. And Hazel, of course, being very grand. And her husband *is* tall and *quite* good-looking, nearly as good-looking as she thinks he is. I believe he comes into a title.

ROBIN: Snob!

MRS. C.: I don't see Madge marrying, but then she'll be head-mistress of a big school quite soon, and then she'll become one of these women who are on all sorts of committees and have to go up to London to give evidence, and so becomes happy and grand that way.

ROBIN: I'll bet she will, too, good old Madge!

MRS. C. (*gaily*): I'll go and stay with her sometimes—*very* important, the headmistress's mother—and the other mistresses will be invited in to dine and will listen *very* respectfully while I tell them about my other children——

JOAN (*happily, admiringly*): Oh—Mrs. Conway—I can just imagine that. You'll have a *marvellous* time.

Mrs. C. (*same vein*): Then there's Carol. Well, of course, Carol will be here with me for years yet——

Carol (*excitedly*): I don't know about that. I haven't exactly decided *what* to do yet, there are so many things to do.

Joan: Oh—Carol—I think you could go on the stage.

Carol (*with growing excitement*): Yes, I could, of course, and I've often thought of it. But I shouldn't want to be on the stage *all* the time—and when I wasn't playing a part, I'd like to be painting pictures —just for myself, y'know—daubing like mad—with lots and lots and lots of the very brightest paint—tubes and tubes of vermilion and royal blue and emerald green and gamboge and cobalt and Chinese white. And then making all kinds of weird dresses for myself. And scarlet cloaks. And black crêpe-de-Chine gowns with orange dragons all over them. And cooking! Yes, doing sausages and gingerbread and pancakes. And sitting on the top of mountains and going down rivers in canoes. And making friends with all sorts of people. And I'd share a flat or a little house with Kay in London, and Alan would come to stay with us and smoke his pipe, and we'd talk about books and laugh at *ridiculous* people, and then go to foreign countries——

Robin (*calling through*): Hoy, hoy, steady!

Mrs. C. (*affectionately amused*): How are you going to *begin* doing all that, you ridiculous child!

Carol (*excitedly*): I'd get it all in somehow. The point is—to live. Never mind about money and positions and husbands with titles and rubbish—I'm *going to live*.

Mrs. C. (*who has now caught the infection*): All right, darling. But wherever you were, all of you, and whatever you were doing, you'd all come back here sometimes, wouldn't you? I'd come and see you, but you'd all come and see me, too, all together, perhaps with wives and husbands and lovely children of your own, not being rich and famous or anything but just being yourselves, as you are now, enjoying our silly old jokes, sometimes playing the same silly old games, all one big happy family. I can see us all here again——

Kay (*a terrible cry*): Don't!

> *She is standing, deeply moved. The others stare in silent consternation.*

Mrs. C.: But what is it, Kay?

> Kay, *still moved, shakes her head. The others exchange puzzled glances, but* Carol *hurries across, all tenderness, and puts an arm round her.*

Carol (*going to her with the solemnity of a child*): I won't bother with any of those things, Kay, really I won't. I'll come and look after you wherever you go. I won't leave you ever if you don't want me to. I'll look after you, darling.

Kay stops crying. She looks—half-smiling—at Carol in a puzzled, wistful fashion. Carol goes back to her mother's side.

Mrs. C. (*reproachful but affectionate*): Really, Kay! What's the matter?

Kay shakes her head, then looks very earnestly at Alan.

Kay (*struggling with some thought*): Alan . . . please tell me. . . . I can't bear it . . . and there's something . . . something . . . you could tell me. . . .

Alan (*troubled, bewildered*): I'm sorry, Kay. I don't understand. What is it?

Kay: Something you know—that would make it different—not so hard to bear. Don't you know *yet*?

Alan (*stammering*): No—I don't—understand.

Kay: Oh—hurry, hurry, Alan—and then—tell me—and comfort me. Something—of Blake's—came into it—— (*Looks hard at him, then struggling, remembers, saying brokenly*):

> Joy . . . and woe . . . are woven fine,
> A clothing for the . . . soul divine. . . .

I used to know that verse, too. What was it at the end? (*Remembers, as before*):

> And, when this . . . we rightly know,
> Safely through the world we go.

Safely . . . through the world we go. . . .

Looks like breaking down again, but recovers herself.

Mrs. C. (*almost a whisper*): Over-excitement. I might have known. (*To Kay, firmly, cheerfully.*) Kay, darling, all this birthday excitement's been too much. You'd better go to bed now, dear, and Carol shall bring you some hot milk. Perhaps an aspirin, too, eh? (*Kay, recovering from her grief, shakes her head.*) You're all right now, aren't you, darling?

Kay (*in muffled voice*): Yes, Mother, I'm all right.

But she turns and goes to the window, pulling back the curtains and looking out.

Mrs. C.: I know what might help, it did once before. Robin, come with me.

JOAN (*rather helplessly*): I ought to go, oughtn't I?

MRS. C.: No, stay a few minutes, Joan. Robin.

She and ROBIN *go out.*

CAROL (*whispering as she moves*): She's going to sing, and I know what it will be.

CAROL *switches out the lights and returns to sit with* HAZEL *and* JOAN, *the three girls making a group, dimly but warmly lit by the light coming in from the hall. Very softly there comes the opening bars of Brahms' "Wiegenlied".* ALAN *joins* KAY *at the window, so that his face, too, like hers, is illuminated by the moonlight.*

ALAN (*quietly through the music*): Kay.

KAY (*quietly*): Yes, Alan?

ALAN: There will be—something—I can tell you—one day. I'll try—I promise.

The moonlight at the window shows us ALAN *looking at her earnestly, and we just catch her answering smile, as the song swells out a little. And then the lights begin to fade, and very soon the three girls are no more than ghosts and all the room is dark, but the moonlight—and the faces of* KAY *and* ALAN—*still lingers; until at last there is only the faintest glimmer, and the Conways have gone, the curtain is down, and the play over.*

END OF PLAY

WHEN WE ARE MARRIED

A Yorkshire Farcical Comedy

Produced at the St. Martin's Theatre, London, on October 11th, 1938, with the following cast:

RUBY BIRTLE	PATRICIA HAYES
GERALD FORBES	RICHARD WARNER
NANCY HOLMES	BETTY FLEETWOOD
HELLIWELL	LLOYD PEARSON
MRS. HELLIWELL	MURIEL GEORGE
PARKER	RAYMOND HUNTLEY
MRS. PARKER	HELENA PICKARD
SOPPITT	ERNEST BUTCHER
MRS. SOPPITT	ETHEL COLERIDGE
MRS. NORTHROP	BEATRICE VARLEY
FRED DYSON	ALEXANDER GRANDISON
HENRY ORMONROYD	FRANK PETTINGELL
LOTTIE GRADY	MAI BACON
REV. CLEMENT MERCER	NORMAN WOOLAND

Produced by BASIL DEAN

The sitting-room of Alderman Helliwell's house in Cleckleywyke, a town in the West Riding, on a September evening about thirty years ago.

ACT I

The sitting-room in HELLIWELL'S *house, a solid detached late-Victorian house. On left (actor's left) wall is a window. Left of centre in back wall is a door to rest of house, leading directly into the hall. On right wall is a small conservatory, with door leading into this, and then into garden. The room is furnished without taste in the style of about thirty years ago. There is an upright piano. Little cupboards, drawers, small tables, etc. At rise, evening sunlight coming through window. Nobody on stage.*

We hear the front door bell ring. A moment later, RUBY BIRTLE *ushers in* GERALD FORBES. RUBY *is a very young "slavey" of the period, who looks as if her hair has just gone "up".* FORBES *is a pleasant young man, in the smart clothes of the period, and unlike* RUBY *and most of the other characters does not talk with a marked West Riding accent.*

RUBY: You'll have to wait 'cos they haven't finished their tea.

GERALD: Bit late, aren't they?

RUBY (*approaching, confidentially*): It's a do.

GERALD: It's what?

RUBY: A do. Y'know, they've company.

GERALD: Oh—I see. It's a sort of party, and they're having high tea.

RUBY (*going closer still*): Roast pork, stand pie, salmon and salad, trifle, two kinds o' jellies, lemon cheese tarts, jam tarts, swiss tarts, sponge cake, walnut cake, chocolate roll, and a pound cake kept from last Christmas.

GERALD (*with irony*): Is that all?

RUBY (*seriously*): No, there's white bread, brown bread, currant teacake, one o' them big curd tarts from Gregory's, and a lot o' cheese.

GERALD: It *is* a do, isn't it?

RUBY (*after nodding, then very confidentially*): *And* a little brown jug.

GERALD (*astonished*): A little brown jug?

RUBY (*still confidentially*): You know what that is, don't you? *Don't* you? (*Laughs.*) Well, I never did! Little brown jug's a drop

143

o' rum for your tea. They're getting right lively on it. (*Coolly*) But you don't come from round here, do you?

GERALD (*not disposed for a chat*): No.

A distant bell rings, not front door.

RUBY: I come from near Rotherham. Me father works in t' pit, and so does our Frank and our Wilfred.

Distant bell sounds again.

GERALD: There's a bell ringing somewhere.

RUBY (*coolly*): I know. It's for me. Let her wait. She's run me off me legs to-day. And Mrs. Northrop's in t' kitchen—she can do a bit for a change. There's seven of 'em at it in t' dining-room—Alderman Helliwell and missus, of course—then Councillor Albert Parker and Mrs. Parker, and Mr. Herbert Soppitt and Mrs. Soppitt —and of course, Miss Holmes.

GERALD: Oh—Miss Holmes *is* there, is she?

RUBY: Yes, but she's stopped eating. (*Giggles. Coolly*) You're courting her, aren't you?

GERALD (*astonished and alarmed*): What!

RUBY (*coolly*): Oh—I saw you both—the other night, near Cleckley Woods. I was out meself with our milkman's lad.

GERALD *turns away.*

Now don't look like that, I won't tell on you.

GERALD (*producing a shilling, then rather desperately*): Now—look here! What's your name?

RUBY: Ruby Birtle.

GERALD: Well, Ruby, you wouldn't like Miss Holmes to get into a row here with her uncle and aunt, would you?

RUBY: No, I wouldn't like that. But I'd like that shilling.

GERALD (*after giving it to her*): You said Miss Holmes had finished eating.

RUBY: Yes. She can't put it away like some of 'em. I'd rather keep Councillor Albert Parker a week than a fortnight. D'you want to see her?

GERALD: Yes. Could you just give her the tip quietly that I'm here—if the rest of them aren't coming in here yet?

RUBY: Not them! You'd think they'd been pined for a month— way they're going at it! I'll tell her. She'd better come round that way—through t' greenhouse——

Before she can actually move, MRS. NORTHROP, *an aggressive but humorous working-woman of about fifty puts her head in the door.*

MRS. NORTHROP (*aggressively*): Oh—'ere y'are!

RUBY (*coolly*): That's right, Mrs. Northrop.

MRS. NORTHROP (*aggressively*): I see nought right about it—you gassin' in 'ere as if you owned t' place instead o' gettin' on wi' your work. She's rung for yer twice, an' I've just taken another lot o' hot water in. Nah, come on, yer little crackpot!

Holds door open, and RUBY *goes to it—turns and grins. Exit* RUBY.

MRS. NORTHROP: Aren't you t' organist at chapel?

GERALD: Yes.

MRS. NORTHROP (*cheerfully*): Ay, well, they've got it in for you.

GERALD (*astonished*): How do you know?

MRS. NORTHROP: 'Cos I 'eard 'em say so. (*Complacently*) I don't miss much.

GERALD: So that's why Mr. Helliwell asked me to come round and see him.

MRS. NORTHROP: That's right. There's three of 'em 'ere to-night, d'you see—all big men at chapel. You've been enjoyin' yerself a bit too much, I fancy, lad.

GERALD: So that's it—is it?

MRS. NORTHROP (*with very confidential air*): Ay—and d'you know what I say? I say—to 'ell with 'em!

Goes out, leaving GERALD *looking a little worried. He moves about restlessly, takes cigarette-case out of his pocket mechanically, then puts it back again. He keeps an eye on the door into conservatory. After a few moments,* NANCY HOLMES, *an attractive girl in her early twenties, hurries in through this door.*

NANCY (*in breathless whisper*): Gerald!

GERALD: Nancy! (*Makes as if to kiss her.*)

NANCY (*breathlessly*): No, you mustn't, not here—no, Gerald—please——

But he does kiss her and no harm has been done.

Now, listen, Gerald, and be sensible. This is serious. You know why Uncle Joe sent for you?

GERALD (*with a slight grin*): They've *got it in for* me. I've just been told.

NANCY: It's serious, Gerald. They've been grumbling about you some time, and now, as far as I can gather, one of these miserable old beasts saw you late one night—with *me*——

GERALD (*serious now*): Oh—I say—you weren't recognised, were you?

NANCY: No. But *you* were.

GERALD: Well, that's not so bad, as long as they can't drag you into it. I know how strict your aunt is, and you can't afford to quarrel with them here until we're ready to be married——

NANCY (*earnestly*): No, but you can't either, Gerald. And they're going to be very cross with you, and you'll have to be awfully careful what you say to them. And there's that beastly Councillor Parker here too, and you loathe him, don't you?

GERALD: Absolutely. And I'll loathe him more than ever now that he's full of roast pork and trifle. I think I'd better give them time to recover from that huge ghastly tuck-in they're having.

NANCY: I should. Though they've nearly finished now.

GERALD: If I clear out for half an hour or so, could you slip away too?

NANCY: I might. They don't really want me. I'm in the way. You see, it's an anniversary celebration, and I don't come into it at all.

GERALD: What are they celebrating?

Before she can reply, RUBY *opens door, announcing:*

RUBY: It's *Yorkshire Argus*—two of 'em.

GERALD *rises, moves down right.* NANCY *rises up to door.*

Enter FRED DYSON, *a cheerful, rather cheeky youngish reporter, and* HENRY ORMONROYD, *who carries a large and old-fashioned newspaperman's camera and a flash-light apparatus.* ORMONROYD *is a middle-aged man with an air of beery dignity and wears a large drooping moustache.* DYSON *walks down to* NANCY.

RUBY: This is Miss Holmes, Alderman Helliwell's niece. T'others is still having their tea.

RUBY *goes out.*

DYSON (*cheerfully*): 'Evening, Miss Holmes. (*To* GERALD) How d'you do? This is Mr. Henry Ormonroyd, our photographer.

ORMONROYD (*bowing*): Pleased to meet you, I'm sure. Delightful weather we're having for the time of year.

GERALD: Isn't it?

ORMONROYD (*profoundly*): It is.

DYSON: We seem to have come too early.

NANCY: I'm afraid you have——

ORMONROYD (*with dignified reproach*): What did I tell you, Fred? Always wanting to rush things. We could have had at least a couple more—with my friend at the *Lion*. He's a chap who used to have a very good little peppermint-rock business on the Central Pier, Blackpool at the time I had my studio—there. Old times, y'know, Mr.—er, and happy days, happy days! (*Hums.*)

DYSON (*briskly*): All right, Henry. I'm sorry we're early. Matter of fact, I don't know yet what this is about. I just got a message from the office to come up here and bring a photographer.

NANCY: You see, it's their Silver Wedding.

DYSON: Henry, it's Alderman Helliwell's *Silver Wedding*.

ORMONROYD: Very nice, I suppose.

NANCY: Yes, but not only my uncle and aunt's. There were three couples—my uncle and aunt, Mr. and Mrs. Soppitt, Mr. and Mrs. Parker——

DYSON: Is that Councillor Albert Parker?

NANCY (*pulling a little face*): Yes. You know him?

DYSON (*gloomily*): Yes, we know him.

ORMONROYD: Every time he opens his mouth at the Town Hall, he puts his foot in it, so they call him "the foot and mouth disease". Ha. Ha. Are all three happy couples here?

NANCY: Yes, because they were all married on the same morning at the same chapel. They have a photograph—a combined wedding group. (*She goes to find it—top of piano.*)

GERALD: You'll have to interview 'em, and they'll tell you how happy they've been——

DYSON: Oh—yes. I see the idea now.

NANCY (*returning with old photograph*): Here you are. All six of them on their wedding morning. Don't they look absurd in those clothes?

ORMONROYD (*solemnly*): To you—yes. To me—no. I was married myself about that time. (*Holding photograph at arm's length*) Now, you see, Fred, what's wanted is another group in the very same positions. After twenty-five years' wear and tear. Very nice.

DYSON: You're holding it upside down.

ORMONROYD: I know, lad. I know, that's the way we always look at 'em professionally. Either flies 'ave been at this or somebody's touched up Albert Parker with a screw-driver. Well, if we're too early, we're too early. Might nip back to the *Lion*, Fred lad, eh?

ORMONROYD *takes camera from top of settee left.*

DYSON: We'll come back in about an hour.

ORMONROYD: They're keeping a very nice drop of beer down at the *Lion* now.

DYSON *and* ORMONROYD *go out,* NANCY *going towards the door with them, and shutting it behind them.* GERALD *looks at the photograph, then at the back of it, and is obviously interested and amused.*

GERALD: This was when they were all married then—September the fifth, Eighty-Three?

NANCY: Yes—why? What's the matter, Gerald? (*He has started laughing.*) Gerald, what is it? Oh—don't be so mean. They'll be here in a minute.

As he shakes his head, still laughing softly, we hear voices behind door into hall.

GERALD: They're coming in. Nancy, let's dodge out that way.

Puts photograph on table behind settee right, picks up his straw hat, while she has gone to door into conservatory, and they hurry out that way, shutting door behind them.

Voices outside door into hall are louder now, and after a moment the PARKERS, *the* SOPPITTS, *the* HELLIWELLS *enter. They are dressed in their best, and obviously crammed with high tea.* ALBERT PARKER, *is a tall, thin, conceited, sententious man, his wife* ANNIE, *a hopeful kind of woman.* HERBERT SOPPITT *is a smallish neat man, clearly dominated by his wife* CLARA, *a noisy woman. The* HELLIWELLS *are high-coloured, rather bouncing, rather pompous, very pleased with themselves. Their ages are all between forty-five and fifty-five.* HERBERT SOPPITT *and* MRS. PARKER *talk a rather genteel ordinary English; the other four have pronounced north-country accents, with particularly broad "a" sounds.*

HELLIWELL (*very much the host*): Now what's wanted now's a good cigar, an' I've got the very thing. (*Goes to get box from drawer or table.*)

MARIA (*indignantly*): That Mrs. Northrop! When she's finished her washing-up to-night she goes—and goes for good.

CLARA: And quite right too! They're all the same. Answering back—if you say anything.

MARIA: Trouble with her is—she likes a drop. I've smelt it before to-day.

CLARA *sits below sofa left.* MARIA *to corner.* ANNIE *drops down right to sofa down right.*

HELLIWELL (*offering cigar-box to* PARKER): Now then, Albert! You'll find that's a good cigar, La Corona.

PARKER (*taking one*): Thanks, Joe. As you know, I don't smoke a lot, but when I do, I like a good cigar.

HELLIWELL (*offering to* SOPPITT): Herbert?

SOPPITT: I don't think—er—I will—thanks, Joe.

MARIA (*expansively*): Nay, Herbert, 'ave one o' Joe's cigars.

CLARA: If he'd had it to pay for himself, he'd have been wanting one.

SOPPITT (*rather nervously*): I think—I'd rather not smoke just now —I believe I ate too much at tea.

ANNIE (*to keep him company*): I know *I* did.

PARKER (*severely*): Yes, an' you'll be complaining before the night's out.

CLARA: An' so will Herbert.

PARKER (*complacently*): Now that's something that never bothers me.

HELLIWELL: No, we've noticed that, Albert.

PARKER (*offended*): How d'you mean?

MARIA: Go on, Albert, you know what Joe is—must 'ave his little joke.

ANNIE: I know *I* ought to have stopped long before I did—I mean, at tea—but, Maria, everything was *so* nice.

CLARA: 'Ere, 'ere.

MARIA (*complacently accepting this*): Well, I said to Joe "Now, Joe," I said, "we'll only have just the six of us, but we'll make it an occasion an' do it well while we're at it," I said. Didn't I, Joe?

HELLIWELL (*busy attending to his cigar, though he does not remove the band*): Did you?

MARIA (*indignantly*): You know very well I did.

HELLIWELL (*still not interested*): All right, you did then.

MARIA (*same indignant tone*): You know quite well I did, Joe Helliwell.

HELLIWELL (*suddenly annoyed himself*): All right, all right, all right, you did then.

CLARA (*pats* MARIA'S *hand*): They're all alike. Wait till somebody else's with you, and then try to make you out a liar.

PARKER (*severely*): Speak for yourself! I don't try to make my wife out a liar, do I, Annie?

ANNIE (*rather timidly, hesitantly*): Well—no—Albert, not— really——

PARKER (*very severely*): How d'you mean—*not really*—I just don't, that's all. (*Changing the subject, in rather lordly style*) A good smoke, Joe, quite a good smoke. It reminds me of that cigar Sir

Harold Watson gave me not so long since at the club. I was standing near the fireplace, and Sir Harold came up——

ANNIE (*gathering courage to interrupt*): Albert—you told them before.

PARKER (*glaring*): Well, I can tell 'em again, can't I?

SOPPITT: Maria, have you got a copy of that old photograph we had taken? I couldn't find ours.

MARIA: Yes. Where is it, Joe? (*While he looks round*) Aaa, I laugh many a time when I think o' that morning—six of us, all so nervous——

HELLIWELL: And the parson worse still. He was only like two-pennorth o' copper, an' I could ha' given him a few years myself.

CLARA: I think we were about first he'd ever married.

ANNIE: I'm sure we were. I didn't feel I'd been married properly——

PARKER (*severely*): Of course you'd been married properly. If he'd been ninety and doing it all his life, you wouldn't ha' been married any better, would you?

MARIA: I've forgotten his name now. He was only a temporary, wasn't he?

SOPPITT: I remember! (*A pause.*) It was a tree. Beech.

HELLIWELL: That's right—Beech—an' he'd a funny squint. (*Has found photograph.*) And here's the old photo.

> Hands it to his wife and the ladies look at it, with exclamations, while the men remain aloof.

PARKER (*the business man now*): I see Crossbreds are down again.

HELLIWELL (*another business man*): Ay—and they'll stay down with Australian market as it is. If I've said it once, I've said it a thousand times—if Merinos is down and staying down, then your Crossbreds'll have to follow. Now, look at Merinos——

MARIA (*looking up to expostulate*): Here, Joe, we didn't come here to talk about Merinos. This isn't Wool Exchange. Take a look at yourselves and see what we took on.

> He ignores her. She puts photograph on table back of settee.

HELLIWELL: Now wait a minute. 'Ealths!

MARIA: That's right, Joe. Ring!

> HELLIWELL *rings.* MARIA *turns to others.*

We ought to do it in proper style, an' drink our healths before we go any further.

SOPPITT (*attempting a joke*): Further—where?

CLARA (*severely*): That'll do, Herbert. A bit o' fun's all right, but you go too far.

SOPPITT: I didn't mean——

CLARA (*cutting in*): That'll do.

MRS. NORTHROP *looks in.*

MRS. NORTHROP (*aggressively*): Well?

MARIA (*rather grandly*): There's a tray with glasses on—just bring it in——

MRS. NORTHROP (*indignantly*): What—me? How many pairs of 'ands——

HELLIWELL (*peremptorily*): *Now then*—just tell thingumptyite—Ruby—to bring in the port wine.

MRS. NORTHROP: What—on top o' your tea? You'll be poorly. *She withdraws.* HELLIWELL *is furious.*

HELLIWELL (*angrily*): Now did you 'ear that——

MARIA (*hastily*): All right, Joe, we don't want any trouble. She goes to-night, an' she doesn't come back.

CLARA: I don't know what things are coming to! All the same! Answering back!

PARKER (*sententiously*): They're all alike, that class of people. We have the same trouble at mill. Don't know when they're well off. Idle, that's what they are—bone idle!

CLARA: *And* impudent! Back-answers!

ANNIE (*timidly*): Yes—but I suppose they don't know any better——

PARKER (*severely*): They know a lot better. And what you want to stick up for 'em for, I can't think.

HELLIWELL (*heartily*): Now then, Albert, don't start fratching, but try an' enjoy yourself for once. This is an anniversary. Which reminds me, Charlie Pearson told me, t' other day, they built a new Wesleyan Methodist Chapel up at Thornton, and they opened with an anniversary. Anyhow, this is ours, so let's have peace an' goodwill all round. Now I thought we'd first drink a bit of a toast to ourselves——

MARIA: That was *my* idea.

HELLIWELL (*ignoring this, but only just*): Then I thought we'd have a bit of a chat about old times, an' then we'd settle down to a game o' Newmarket——

MARIA: That was my idea too.

HELLIWELL (*annoyed*): What the hangment does it matter whose idea it was, so long as we get on with it and enjoy ourselves!

SOPPITT: That's the great thing. (*Controlled belch. Catches his wife's eye and falters.*) Enjoy ourselves. (*Rises. Moves to door. Looks miserable and a bit sick.*)

CLARA (*severely*): I told you to leave that salmon alone.

HELLIWELL: Nay, Clara, why can't he have a bit o' salmon if he fancies it?

CLARA (*sharply*): 'Cos it doesn't fancy him, Joe Helliwell, that's why. Look at that time we all went to Scarborough!

SOPPITT (*turns*): It was Bridlington.

CLARA: It was both! And what did that doctor say? *You're digging your grave with your teeth, Mr. Soppitt.*

HELLIWELL: Hahaha!

> *Enter* RUBY, *carrying tray with six small glasses on it, and three bottles of port.*

Here, what did you want to bring 'em all for? One bottle at a time's enough.

RUBY (*putting down tray*) Mrs. Northrop said you'd better 'ave t'lot while you was at it.

HELLIWELL: In future, just take your orders from me and not from Mrs. Northrop. Now just trot along—an' no lip. (*Starts to take cork out of bottle.*)

RUBY (*turning at door*): Mrs. Northrop says she's not coming 'ere again——

HELLIWELL (*heatedly*): We know all about it. (*Moves after her, cigar in mouth, bottle in hand.*)

MARIA (*cutting in*): Now let it be, Joe.

> HELLIWELL *stands, draws cork with an effort.*
>
> RUBY *has now gone and closed door.* HELLIWELL *begins pouring out the port.*

D'you know what we ought to do for this? We ought to get just in the same places we were in that old photo. Where is it? (*Finds it and directs them from it.*) Now here we are. (*Uses a sofa.*) I was in the middle. You were here, Clara. You this side, Annie. Now come on, Albert—behind Annie. Herbert.

> MARIA *sits last. These five have now arranged themselves in grouping of old photograph.* HELLIWELL *hands them their glasses of port, then takes up a position himself.*

HELLIWELL (*facetiously*): Here's to me and my wife's husband!

MARIA: Let's have none o' that silly business, Joe!

PARKER (*solemnly*): A few serious words is what's needed.

ANNIE (*rather plaintively*): Oh—must you, Albert?

PARKER: How d'you mean—must I? What's wrong with a few serious words on an occasion like this? Marriage—is a serious business.

CLARA: That's right, Albert. Where'd we be without it?

SOPPITT: Single.

CLARA: That'll do, Herbert.

PARKER (*sententiously*): Marriage—well—marriage—to begin with, it's an institution, isn't it?

MARIA (*solemnly*): That is so. (*Sighs profoundly.*)

PARKER (*getting into his stride*): One of the *oldest* institutions. It goes back—right back to—well, it goes right back. And it's still going strong to-day. Why?

HELLIWELL (*hastily*): Well, because——

PARKER (*sharply cutting in*): Let me finish, Joe, let me finish. Now why is it still going strong to-day? Because it's the backbone of a decent respectable life.

HELLIWELL (*solemnly*): True, Albert, true.

PARKER: Where would women be without marriage?

CLARA (*sharply*): And where'd some o' you men be?

PARKER: All right, I'm coming to that.

HELLIWELL: Well, don't be too long, Albert. I want to try this port.

PARKER (*solemnly*): Marriage may be a bit more necessary to women than it is to men——

ANNIE: Why?

PARKER (*annoyed at this*): *Why?*

HELLIWELL: Children, you see, Annie.

ANNIE (*abashed*): Oh—yes—I'd forgotten. Still——

PARKER: I'm talking now, *if* you please. But if a woman wants a 'ome and security and a respectable life, *which* she gets from marriage, a man wants something to——

CLARA (*quickly*): He wants all he can get.

PARKER: He wants a nice comfortable 'ome, somebody to tell his troubles to and so forth——

HELLIWELL (*facetiously*): That's good, Albert, the *and so forth*.

PARKER: Now, Joe——

HELLIWELL: Well, cut it short——

PARKER (*slowly and solemnly*): So, as we're all gathered 'ere to celebrate the anniversary of our joint wedding day, friends, I give you—the toast of *Marriage!*

Maria: Very nice, Albert.

They all drink.

Annie (*confidentially*): It'll go straight to my head. D'you re-member that time at Harrogate? I could have sunk through the floor when that waiter laughed.

Helliwell (*producing bottle again*): Now wait a minute. That's all right as far as it goes—but—nay—damn it!——

Maria (*reproachfully*): Joe!

Helliwell: We must have another toast, just for ourselves. I bet it isn't often there's three couples can meet like this who were all wed on same morning together. Now then——

Insists on filling the glasses again as they still hold them in their hands.

Maria (*confidentially*): I don't act silly, but my face gets so red.

Helliwell: Now—here's to all of us—and the Reverend Mr. What's his name—Beech—who tied us up—wherever he is——

The Others: Here's to us. Here's to him. (*Etc.*)

They drink. When they have finished, front-door bell is heard.

Maria: Front door! Who'll that be?

Helliwell (*rather importantly*): Well, I told *Yorkshire Argus* to send somebody round to have a word with us.

Clara (*delighted*): What—are you going to have a piece in the papers?

Parker: They don't want to catch us like this.

Parker swallows rest of his port hastily. The others do the same. The group breaks up.

Ruby looks in.

Maria: Is it *Yorkshire Argus?*

Ruby: No, it's Mr. Forbes, t'organist from t'chapel. He came afore, an' then went away again.

Helliwell: Tell him to wait.

Ruby goes. Helliwell turns to the others.

You know about this business, Albert. You too, Herbert.

Soppitt (*hesitantly*): Yes—but—— (*crosses to Helliwell.*)

Helliwell (*sharply*): But, nothing. You're too soft, Herbert.

Clara: I'm always telling him so.

Helliwell: He's chapel organist—he's paid for t'job—an' either he behaves himself properly or he goes.

Parker (*severely*): He'll go anyhow, if I've *my* say.

ANNIE: No, Albert, he's not a bad young fellow——

PARKER: Now you shut up, Annie. You don't know half of what we know. An' I'll bet we don't know half there is to know about that chap. Never should ha' been appointed. I said so then. I say so now. I know my own mind.

ANNIE (*rebelliously*): I wish sometimes you'd keep a bit of it to yourself.

PARKER: What's that mean?

NANCY *now appears at door from conservatory.*

MARIA: Hallo, love, where've you been?

NANCY (*who seems a trifle giggly*): Just out a minute. You don't want me, do you, Auntie? Because if you don't, I thought I'd put my hat and coat on and see if Muriel Spencer's in. (*Crosses up to door.*)

MARIA (*rises*): All right. There's that Gerald Forbes waiting outside—your uncle has something to say to him—now don't go talking to him.

HELLIWELL: I should think not. Just say "Hello" or "Good evening" and leave it at that. The less you have to do with that chap the better, Nancy.

NANCY *suddenly explodes into giggles.*

Now what's funny about that?

NANCY (*still giggling*): I'm sorry, Uncle. I just remembered—something that amused me——

NANCY *goes out, giggling.*

HELLIWELL: Now what's got hold of her?

MARIA: Oh—she's at silly age. They don't know half the time whether to laugh or cry when they're that age. Now, Clara—Annie —we'll leave the men to it. I expect that's what they want——

PARKER (*solemnly*): Certainly. After all, it's chapel business.

MARIA: Well, we want to go upstairs anyhow!

HELLIWELL: That's right.

CLARA *glares at him.*

MARIA: You haven't seen what Joe bought me yet. But don't take too long over him.

PARKER: *Him!* It wouldn't take *me* long——

HELLIWELL: It'll take me less long, 'cos I don't make speeches. Here, we'll put these out o' t'way—— (*at sideboard.*)

The women go out, and HELLIWELL *puts the glasses back on the tray. A certain primness now descends on them.*

Parker: I said from first—it's a bad appointment. To start with, he's too young.

Soppitt (*rather timidly*): I don't think that matters much.

Parker (*severely*): Trouble with you, Herbert, is you don't think anything matters much, and that's just where you're wrong.

Helliwell: Young Forbes is a southerner an' all.

Parker (*with grim triumph*): Ah—I was coming to that.

Soppitt: Oughtn't we to have him in?

Helliwell: No, let him wait a bit.

Parker: Do him good. No, as soon as they told me he's a southerner and his name's Gerald, I said: "We don't want him." I said: "La-di-dah. That's what you're going to get from him," I said. "La-di-dah. What we want at Lane End—biggest chapel for miles— wi' any amount o' money in congregation—what we want is a bit o' good old Yorkshire organ-playing and choir training," I said. "We don't want la-di-dah." (*With awful imitation of ultra-refined accents.*) "Heow d'yew dew. Sow chawmed to meek your acquaintance. Eoh, dee-lateful wethah!" Grr. You know what I call that stuff?

Soppitt (*who has a sense of humour*): Yes. (*Broadly.*) La-di-dah.

Helliwell: Albert's right. We made a mistake. Mind you, he'd good qualifications, an' he seemed a nice quiet lad. But I must say, after old Sam Fawcett, chapel didn't seem right with an organist who goes round wearing one o' these pink shirts and knitted ties and creases in his trousers——

Parker: It's all——

Here Soppitt *joins in.*

Parker and Soppitt: La-di-dah!

Parker (*in disgusted tone*): Then look at his *Messiah!* We warned him. I said to him myself: "I know it's a Christmas piece, but you've got to get in quick, afore the others."

Helliwell: Right, Albert. After t'end o' November, there's been so many of 'em you might as well take your Messiah an' throw it into t'canal.

Parker: And look what happened. Hillroad Baptist gave *Messiah.* Salem gave *Messiah.* Tong Congregational gave *Messiah.* Picklebrook Wesleyans gave *Messiah.* And where was Lane End?

Soppitt: Well, when we did get it—it was a good one.

Helliwell: I'm not saying it wasn't, but by that time who cared? But anyhow all that's a detail. Point is, we can't have any carrying on, can we?

SOPPITT ((*gravely*)): Ah—there I agree, Joe.

PARKER (*indignantly*): An' I should think so. Organist at Lane End Chapel *carrying on!* That sort o' game may do down south, but it won't do up 'ere.

HELLIWELL: We're all agreed on that.

SOPPITT *and* PARKER *nod.*

Right then! We'll have 'im in.

HELLIWELL *goes to the door, the other two sitting up stiffly and looking official and important.*

(*Rather grimly through open door.*) All right, come in.

GERALD FORBES *follows him in, closing but not latching the door behind him.* GERALD *looks cool and self-possessed, with a twinkle in his eye.* HELLIWELL *sits down and looks as official and important as the other two. All three stare severely at* GERALD, *as he sits down.* GERALD *pulls out a cigarette-case, but no sooner has he taken a cigarette from it than* ALBERT PARKER *remonstrates with him.*

PARKER (*severely*): I wouldn't do that.

GERALD (*rather startled*): Do what?

PARKER (*severely*): Well, what 'ave you got in your 'and?

GERALD (*still surprised*): This? Cigarette. Why?

PARKER: Under the circumstances, young man, don't you think it might be better—more—more suitable—more fitting—if you didn't smoke that just now?

The three men look at each other.

GERALD (*with a shrug*): Oh—all right, if that's how you feel about it. (*Puts case away. A pause.*) Well? You wanted to talk about something, didn't you?

HELLIWELL (*firmly*): We did. We do.

PARKER: And if I'd 'ad *my* way, we'd have been talking to you long since.

GERALD: Well, not very long since, because I haven't been up here very long.

PARKER: No, you haven't been up here very long, and I don't think you'll be up here much longer.

HELLIWELL: Here, Albert, let *me* get a word in. Mr. Forbes, you're organist of our Lane End Chapel, and that's the biggest place o' worship round here, and this is a very respectable neighbourhood, with a lot o' money behind it. You have a paid appointment as organist and choir-master.

GERALD: Yes, though it doesn't keep me, y'know, Mr. Helliwell.

HELLIWELL: No, but because you *are* our organist, you're able to get pupils and various extra jobs, so you don't do so bad out of it, eh?

GERALD (*a trifle dubiously*): No, I'm quite satisfied—for the time being.

PARKER (*annoyed*): *You're* satisfied! For the time being! You're satisfied!

GERALD (*quietly*): That's what I said, Mr. Parker.

PARKER (*with dignity*): Councillor Parker. (*Pointing.*) Alderman Helliwell. Councillor Parker. *Mr.* Soppitt.

GERALD (*indicating himself*): Plain mud!

PARKER (*explosively*): Now listen——

HELLIWELL (*cutting in noisily*): Nay, let me finish, Albert. We want to keep calm about this—just keep calm.

GERALD: I'm quite calm.

HELLIWELL (*explosively*): You're a damn sight too calm for my liking, young man. You ought to be sitting there looking right ashamed of yourself, instead of looking—looking—well, as you do look.

GERALD: But you haven't told me what's wrong yet.

PARKER (*angrily*): Wrong? You're wrong. And carrying on's wrong.

HELLIWELL (*loftily*): In some chapels they mightn't care what you did—I don't know—but Lane End's got a position to keep up. We're respectable folk, and naturally we expect our organist to behave respectably.

SOPPITT (*apologetically*): I think you have been very careless, Mr. Forbes, and there really has been a lot of grumbling.

PARKER: For one thing—you've been seen out—late at night—wi' girls.

GERALD: Girls?

HELLIWELL: It may be t'same lass each time, for all I know, but if what I hear is true, whoever she is, she ought to be ashamed of herself. My word, if she'd owt to do wi' me, I'd teach her a sharp lesson.

PARKER: Somebody saw you once gallivanting away late at night, at Morecambe. And it gets round, y'know—oh—yes—it gets round.

GERALD (*beginning to lose his temper*): Yes, so it seems. But I didn't think you'd find it worth while to listen to a lot of silly gossip——

PARKER (*sharply*): Now don't start taking that tone——

GERALD: What tone can I take? I say, a lot of silly gossip——

SOPPITT: Now, steady, steady.

GERALD: Silly gossip. Old women's twaddle——

HELLIWELL (*heavily*): That'll do. Just remember, you're not much more than a lad yet. We're nearly twice your age, and we know what's what——

GERALD (*angrily*): Well, what is what then?

HELLIWELL (*angrily*): This is what. We're not going to have any more of this. Either behave yourself or get back to where you came from. You're not going to make us a laughing-stock and a byword in t'neighbourhood. Now this is a fair warning——

GERALD (*steadily*): I haven't done anything I'm ashamed of.

PARKER: What's that prove? If a chap's got cheek of a brass monkey, he never need do aught he's ashamed of.

SOPPITT: Careful, Albert.

PARKER: Why should I be careful? I'll tell him to his face what I've said behind his back. He never ought to have been appointed, and now he's been carrying on and not caring tuppence what respectable folk might think, he oughtn't to be given any warnings but told to get back to where he came from, and then he can carry on as much as he likes.

> Both GERALD *and* HERBERT SOPPITT *start to protest, but* HELLIWELL *loudly stops them.*

HELLIWELL: Now, Albert, we mustn't be too hard. We must give young men just another chance. (*Severely and patronisingly to* GERALD) I'm not sure I should if this were any other time. But nay—damn it this is a festive occasion an' we must take it easy a bit. So I'm giving you a last chance to mend yourself. And you can think yourself lucky catching me i' this humour. Just happens we're all celebrating anniversary of our wedding day—all three of us—ay, we've all been married twenty-five years to-day. (*Blows nose.*)

> GERALD *shakes his head rather sadly.*

What're you shaking your head about?

GERALD (*quietly, gently*): Well, you see, Mr. Helliwell—I beg your pardon, Alderman Helliwell—I'm rather afraid you haven't been married twenty-five years.

HELLIWELL (*roaring*): Do you think we can't count, lad?

GERALD (*same quiet tone*): No, I don't mean that. But I'm afraid you've only been living together all this time.

HELLIWELL (*jumping up angrily*): *Living together!* I'll knock your head right off your shoulders, lad, if you start talking like that to me.

GERALD (*also standing up*): No, no, no. I'm not trying to insult you. I mean what I say.

PARKER (*rises, angrily*): Mean what you say! You're wrong in your damned 'ead.

SOPPITT (*authoritatively, for him*): Wait a minute—Albert, Joe. We must listen. He means it.

HELLIWELL (*angrily*): Means it! Means what?

GERALD (*impressively*): If you'll just be quiet a minute I'll explain.

PARKER (*explosively*): I don't want to——

GERALD (*sharply*): I said—*quiet.*

HELLIWELL: Leave him be, Albert.

GERALD (*sits*): Thanks. Mind if I smoke now?

All sit. With maddening slowness, GERALD *takes out and lights cigarette.* HELLIWELL *and* ALBERT PARKER *watch him with impatience and look as if about to explode.*

I went to North Wales for my holiday this summer——

HELLIWELL (*impatiently*): Is this part of it, 'cos *I* don't care *where* you went for your holidays!

GERALD (*calmly*): I went to North Wales, and only came back about a fortnight ago. While I was there I made the acquaintance of a parson, who'd been in Africa for the last twenty years. When he learnt that I was the organist of Lane End Chapel, Cleckleywyke, he became very excited, and then it turned out that he'd been at Lane End himself for a short time. About twenty-five years ago.

SOPPITT: What was his name.

GERALD: Beech. Francis Edwin Beech.

HELLIWELL (*boisterously*): Oh—yes—Beech! We were only talking about him to-night. We remember Mr. Beech. He married us, y'know. Yes, he married us, five-and-twenty years ago—all three couples. That's what we're celebrating——

His voice suddenly dies away because he realises what the other two have realised for the last minute, that there might be something wrong. So as he mutters the end of his sentence now, he glances unhappily at the others.

Y'know—being—married—twenty-five years——

GERALD *looks at them over his cigarette.*

PARKER (*swallowing*): Go on. Go on.

GERALD: I could see that something he remembered about Cleckley-wyke and Lane End worried him. (*With obvious relish.*) You might say, gentlemen, it was *preying* on his mind, it was *gnawing* at his conscience, it was *haunting* him, it was——

HALLIWELL (*angrily*): What is this—a recitation?

GERALD: I must apologise if I'm boring you, gentlemen——

PARKER (*in sudden passion, jumps up*): La-di-dah! La-di-dah! (*As* GERALD *stares at him in astonishment.*) Now if you've anything to tell us, for God's sake tell us—and don't la-di-dah!

HELLIWELL: Quite right, Albert. (*To* GERALD, *impatiently*) Well, what did Mr. Beech say?

GERALD: He didn't *say* anything.

> HELLIWELL *and* PARKER *are at once relieved and annoyed. They breathe more freely, but then feel they have been needlessly alarmed.* HERBERT SOPPITT *waits to learn more and looks steadily at* GERALD.

HELLIWELL: Well, what are you nattering on about him for——?

SOPPITT: Just a minute, Joe. (*To* GERALD) That's not all, is it?

GERALD: All? I should think not! Only you won't give me a chance. I said he didn't *say* anything, but he *wrote* something. The letter only came two days ago. I have it here. (*Produces one rather small sheet of notepaper, written on both sides. He now reads it impressively.*) From the Reverend Francis Edwin Beech. "*Dear Mr. Forbes, Before returning to Africa I feel I owe it both to you and to myself to explain what you must have found puzzling in my many references to Cleckleywyke and Lane End Chapel. Although I was only temporarily at Lane End, I could not forget it for there I was guilty of the most culpable negligence.*"

> *The three men look at each other.*

"*I went to Cleckleywyke straight from college, and during those first few months I did not realise that there were various forms I ought to have signed, and had witnessed by church officers, so that one may be recorded as an authorised person to perform the ceremony of marriage——*"

HELLIWELL (*rises, shouting*): What? (*Grabs the letter from* GERALD, *stares at it, then reads himself, slowly.*) . . . "*the ceremony of marriage. The result was, I was not then an authorised person. Fortunately during that short period I was only called upon twice to marry people, but the first time there were no less than three hopeful young couples who imagined—poor souls—that I was joining them in holy wedlock—when —I—was completely—unauthorised—to—do—so——*"

PARKER (*yelling and snatching the letter*): Let's have a look. (*He looks and* HERBERT SOPPITT *joins him.*) It's signed all right too— Francis Edwin Beech.

GERALD: And if you compare that signature with the one in the chapel register, you'll see it's the same man. No deception.

HELLIWELL (*dazed and bitter*): Why—the bloody donkey!

HELLIWELL, PARKER *and* SOPPITT *look at each other in silent consternation.*

SOPPITT (*slowly, thoughtfully*): Why, if we've never been married at all, then——

HELLIWELL: Don't start working it out in detail, Herbert, 'cos it gets very ugly—very ugly. There's that lad o' yours at grammar school, for instance—I wouldn't like to have to give him a name now——

SOPPITT (*indignantly*): Here, steady, Joe——

HELLIWELL: Well, you see, it gets very ugly. Keep your mind off t'details.

PARKER (*bitterly*): Silver wedding!

HELLIWELL: Now don't you start neither, Albert.

PARKER (*solemnly*): Joe, Herbert, when them three poor women upstairs gets to know what they really are——

HELLIWELL (*grimly*): Then t'balloon goes up properly. Talk about a rumpus. You'll 'ear 'em from 'ere to Leeds.

PARKER (*gravely*): Joe, Herbert, they mustn't know. Nobody must know. Why—we'd be laughed right out o' town. What—Alderman Helliwell—Councillor Albert Parker—Herbert Soppitt—all big men at chapel too! I tell you, if this leaks out—we're done!

HELLIWELL: We are, Albert.

SOPPITT (*horrified*): If once it got into the papers!

HELLIWELL (*even more horrified*): *Papers!* Oh—Christmas!—it's got to be kept from t'papers.

GERALD, *who has been leaving them to themselves to digest this news, now turns to them again.*

GERALD (*holding out his hand*): You'd better give me that letter, hadn't you?

PARKER and HELLIWELL (*rising*): Oh no!

They stand together as if protecting it.

PARKER (*holding it out*): This letter——

HELLIWELL (*snatching it*): Here——

PARKER (*angrily*): Nay, Joe—give it back——

HELLIWELL: I'm sorry, Albert, but I don't trust nobody wi' this letter but meself. Why—it's—it's dynamite!

GERALD: Yes, but it's addressed to me, and so it happens to be my property, you know.

SOPPITT: I'm afraid he's right there!

HELLIWELL (*turning on him, annoyed*): You would have to put that in, wouldn't you? Dang me, you're in this mess just as we are, aren't you?

PARKER (*severely*): Anyhow, *we've* a position to keep up even if you haven't, Herbert.

SOPPITT (*apologetically*): I was only saying he's right when he says it's his property. We had a case——

HELLIWELL (*aggressively*): Never mind about that case. Think about this case. It's a whole truck-load o' cases, this is.

GERALD: My letter, please.

HELLIWELL (*ingratiatingly*): Now listen, lad. I know you only want to do what's right. And we happened to be a bit 'asty with you, when you first came in. We didn't mean it. Just—a way o' talking. When Herbert Soppitt there gets started——

SOPPITT (*indignantly*): What—me!

PARKER (*severely*): You were 'asty, y'know, Herbert, you can't deny it. (*To* GERALD) Mind you, I'll say now to your face what I've often said behind your back. You gave us best *Messiah* and best *Elijah* we've ever had at Lane End.

HELLIWELL: Easy, easy! Best i' Cleckleywyke! And why? I've told 'em when they've asked me. "That young feller of ours is clever," I said. "I knew he had it in him," I said.

SOPPITT (*hopefully*): Yes, you did, Joe. (*To* GERALD) And so did I. I've always been on your side.

GERALD: I believe you have, Mr. Soppitt. (*To all three of them*) You can keep that letter to-night—on one condition. That Mr. Soppitt has it.

SOPPITT (*eagerly, holding out his hand*): Thank you, Joe.

HELLIWELL (*uneasily*): What's the idea o' this?

GERALD: That happens to be the way I feel about it. Now either give it back to me at once—or hand it over to Mr. Soppitt, who'll be answerable to me for it.

SOPPITT (*eagerly*): Certainly, certainly.

HELLIWELL *silently and grudgingly hands it over.* SOPPITT *puts it carefully in his inside pocket. The others watch him like hawks. There is a pause, then we hear a knocking from upstairs.*

HELLIWELL: Knocking.

PARKER (*grimly*): I 'eard.

HELLIWELL: That means she's getting impatient.

PARKER: I expect Clara's been ready to come down for some time

HELLIWELL (*bitterly*): They want to get on with the celebration.

PARKER (*bitterly*): Chat about old times.

HELLIWELL (*bitterly*): Nice game o' cards.

GERALD (*after a pause*): I'd better be going.

HELLIWELL (*hastily*): No, no. No. Take it easy.

PARKER: No 'urry, no 'urry at all. I expect Joe has a nice cigar for you somewhere.

HELLIWELL (*with forced joviality*): Certainly I have. And a drink of anything you fancy——

GERALD: No, thanks. And I must be going.

HELLIWELL: Now listen, lad. We've admitted we were 'asty with you, so just forget about it, will you? Now you see the mess we're in, through no fault of ours—— (*Goes up to get cigars.*)

GERALD: I do. And it *is* a mess, isn't it? Especially when you begin to think——

PARKER (*hastily*): Yes, quite so, but don't you bother thinking. Just—— (*rather desperately*) try an' forget you ever saw that letter.

HELLIWELL (*who now comes with the cigars*): We're all friends, the best of friends. Now you've got to have a cigar or two, lad—I insist—— (*he sticks several cigars into* GERALD'S *outside pocket, as he talks*) and you're going to promise us—on your word of honour—not to tell anybody anything about this nasty business, aren't you?

All three look at him anxiously. He keeps them waiting a moment or two.

GERALD: All right.

They breathe again. HELLIWELL *shakes his hand.*

HELLIWELL: And you won't regret it, lad.

The knocking from upstairs is heard again.

PARKER (*miserably*): 'Ear that?

HELLIWELL: It's wife again.

SOPPITT (*thoughtfully*): Curious thing about wives. They're always telling you what poor company you are for them, yet they're always wanting to get back to you.

HELLIWELL (*darkly*): That isn't 'cos they enjoy your company. It's so they can see what you're doing.

PARKER: Well, what are we doing?

HELLIWELL (*sharply now*): Wasting time. (*To them*) Now listen, chaps, we're in no proper shape yet to face t'wives. They'd have it all out of us in ten minutes, and then fat'll be in t'fire.

PARKER: I know. We've got to put our thinking caps on.

SOPPITT: I suppose Mr. Beech couldn't have been mistaken, could he?

PARKER: We might take that letter and get expert advice——

HELLIWELL (*hastily*): What! An' 'ave it all over the town?

PARKER (*quickly*): We might put a case—without mentioning names——

HALLIWELL (*with decision*): I know what we'll do. We'll nip down to t'club, 'cos we can talk it over there in peace an' quiet. Come on, chaps. Just as we are, straight down t'club. (*To* GERALD) Now, young man, you promised. You won't go back on your word?

GERALD: No. You're safe with me.

HELLIWELL (*urgently*): Good lad! Now, wait till we've got off, then go out front way. Come on, Albert, Herbert, we've no time to lose an' we go this way—— (*bustling them towards exit through conservatory*) straight to t'club.

> They go out. GERALD *looks at his watch, smiles, lights a cigarette, then makes for door, which has never been quite closed. When he opens it suddenly,* MRS. NORTHROP, *still holding a towel and a large glass dish, which she is wiping perfunctorily, is discovered just behind door. She is in high glee and not at all abashed at being found there.*

GERALD (*with mock sternness*): Have you been listening?

MRS. NORTHROP (*who may have had a drink or two*): Listening! I should think I have been listening! I wouldn't have missed this lot even if it means 'aving earache for a week. None of 'em rightly married at all! Not one of 'em properly tied up! (*She begins laughing quite suddenly, and then goes off into peals of laughter, rolling against the door. The dish she holds seems to be in danger.*)

GERALD (*amused as he goes past her, out*): Look out—or you may break that dish.

MRS. NORTHROP (*calling to him*): Brek a dish! If I want to, I'll brek a dozen now.

GERALD (*just off, challengingly*): Not you! I dare you!

MRS. NORTHROP (*coolly*): Well, here's a start, any road. (*Tosses the dish down and it smashes noisily in hall.*)

> We hear GERALD *give a laughing shout, then bang the front door.*

MRS. NORTHROP *now starts laughing helplessly again, still leaning against the door.*

MRS. NORTHROP: Nay—dammit!—— *(laughing)* Oh dear—oh dear—oh dear——

She is still roaring with laughter as the curtain briskly descends.

END OF ACT ONE

ACT II

About half an hour later. The lights are on. MARIA *is drawing curtains,* ANNIE *and* CLARA *are laying out the cards and counters for New-market on a card-table, and they continue doing this throughout the scene that follows, chiefly counting the coloured counters and putting them into piles.*

CLARA (*with much discontent*): Well, I must say—this is a queer way o' going on.

MARIA: They'll have just gone outside to finish their smokes.

CLARA (*grimly*): When Herbert takes me out to enjoy myself, I don't expect him to be outside finishing any smokes.

ANNIE (*at table*): Perhaps they'd something they wanted to talk over.

CLARA: Well they can talk it over here, can't they?

RUBY *enters from conservatory.*

MARIA: Well, Ruby, are they out there?

RUBY: No, they aren't.

MARIA (*sharply*): Have you looked properly?

RUBY: Well I couldn't miss three grown men in a garden that size.

MARIA: Did you look up and down the road like I told you?

RUBY: Yes, but they aren't there.

The three wives look at each other, puzzled.

CLARA: Didn't you hear them go?

RUBY: No. I was back in t'kitchen all time, doing t'washing up. That Mrs. Northrop left me to it.

MARIA: Where was she then?

RUBY: Out 'ere somewhere, I fancy. I know she's gone like a dafthead, ever since she come back. Laughin' to herself—like a proper barmpot.

MARIA: Well, ask Mrs. Northrop if she knows where they went.

RUBY *goes.*

That noise you heard upstairs was a bit o' this Mrs. Northrop's work —one o' my best dishes gone. An' Ruby says she just laughed.

CLARA: Stop it out of her wages and see if she can get a good laugh out o' that. I've no patience with 'em.

ANNIE: I thought she didn't look a nice woman.

167

CLARA: One o' them idle drinking pieces o' nothing from back o' t'mill.

MARIA: Well, I was in a hurry and had to have somebody. But she goes—for good—to-night.

RUBY *appears.*

RUBY: Mrs. Northrop says they wanted to have a nice quiet talk, so they went down to their club.

RUBY *disappears.*

CLARA (*angrily*): Club! *Club!*

ANNIE: And to-night of all nights—I do think it's a shame.

MARIA (*indignantly*): I never 'eard o' such a thing in me life.

CLARA (*furiously*): *Club!* I'll club him.

ANNIE: Nay, I don't know what's come over 'em.

CLARA (*angrily*): I know what'll come over one of 'em.

MARIA: Perhaps there's something up.

CLARA: Something down, you mean—ale, stout, an' whisky. Drinks all round! Money no object!

MARIA: They're 'ere.

The three of them immediately sit bolt upright and look very frosty. The men file in from the conservatory, looking very sheepish.

HELLIWELL (*nervously*): Ay—well——

MARIA (*grimly*): Well what?

HELLIWELL: Well—nowt—really.

SOPPITT (*nervously*): We didn't—er—think you'd be down yet. Did we, Joe? Did we, Albert?

HELLIWELL: No, we didn't, Herbert.

ALBERT: That's right, we didn't.

CLARA (*cuttingly*): Herbert Soppitt, you must be wrong in your head. *Club!*

ANNIE: And to-night of all nights!

HELLIWELL: Well, you see, we thought we'd just nip down for a few minutes while you were talking upstairs.

MARIA: What for?

PARKER: Oh—just to talk over one or two things.

CLARA: What things?

SOPPITT: Oh—just—things, y'know—things in general.

PARKER (*coming forward, rubbing his hands*): Well—I see the table's all ready—so what about that nice little game o' Newmarket?

CLARA: You'll get no Newmarket out o' me to-night.

ANNIE: You're—you're—selfish.

CLARA: Have you just found that out? Never think about anything but their own comfort and convenience.

MARIA: I'm surprised at you, Joe Helliwell—and after I'd planned to make everything so nice.

CLARA: Lot o' thanks you get from them! Club! (*Looking hard at* SOPPITT) Well, go on—say something.

The men look at each other uneasily. Then the women look indignantly.

ANNIE: Just think what day it is!

CLARA: And after giving you best years of our life—without a word o' thanks.

MARIA: An' just remember, Joe Helliwell, there were plenty of other fellows I could have had besides you.

ANNIE: You seem to think—once you've married us you can take us for granted.

PARKER (*uneasily*): Nay, I don't.

CLARA (*very sharply*): Yes, you do—all alike!

MARIA: If some of you woke up to-morrow to find you weren't married to us, you'd be in for a few big surprises.

HELLIWELL (*uneasily*): Yes—I dare say—you're right.

MARIA (*staring at him*): Joe Helliwell, what's matter with you to-night?

HELLIWELL (*uneasily*): Nowt—nowt's wrong wi' me, love.

CLARA (*looking hard at* SOPPITT): You'll hear more about this when I get you 'ome.

SOPPITT (*mildly*): Yes, Clara.

The women look at the men again, then at each other. Now they turn away from the men, ignoring them.

MARIA: What were you saying about your cousin, Clara?

CLARA (*ignoring the men*): Oh—well, the doctor said: "You're all acid, Mrs. Foster, that's your trouble. You're making acid as fast as you can go."

ANNIE: Oh—poor thing!

CLARA: Yes, but it didn't surprise me, way she'd eat. I once saw her eat nine oyster patties, finishing 'em up after their Ethel got married. I said: "Nay, Edith, have a bit o' mercy on your inside," but of course she just laughed.

The men have been cautiously moving to the back towards the door. As HELLIWELL *has his hand on the handle,* MARIA *turns on him.*

MARIA: And where're you going now?

HELLIWELL (*uneasily*): Into t'dining-room.

MARIA: What for?

HELLIWELL: Well—because—well—— (*Gathers boldness.*) We've summat to talk over. Albert, 'Erbert, quick!

They file out smartly, without looking behind them. The women stare at them in amazement. The door shuts. The women look at each other.

MARIA: Now what's come over 'em?

ANNIE: There's something up.

CLARA: What can be up? They're just acting stupid, that's all. But wait till I get his lordship 'ome.

ANNIE: Suppose we went home now——

CLARA: No fear! That's just what they'd like. Back to t'club!

MARIA: I'd go up to bed now and lock me door, if I didn't think I'd be missing something.

ANNIE: It's a pity we can't go off just by ourselves—for a day or two.

CLARA: And what sort o' game are they going to get up to while we're gone? But I've a good mind to go in and tell mine: "Look, I've been married to you for five-and-twenty years and it's about time I had a rest."

MARIA: And for two pins I'll say to Joe: "If you got down on your bended knees and begged me to, I wouldn't stay married to you if I didn't have to."

Door opens slowly, and MRS. NORTHROP *comes just inside, carrying large string bag, with clothes, two stout bottles in, etc. She is dressed to go home now.*

MRS. NORTHROP: I've done.

MARIA (*suspiciously*): It hasn't taken you very long.

MRS. NORTHROP (*modestly*): No—but then I'm a rare worker. Many a one's said to me: "Mrs. Northrop, I can't believe you've just that pair of 'ands—you're a wonder."

MARIA (*acidly*): Well, I don't think I want a wonder here, Mrs. Northrop. I'll pay you what I owe you to-night, and then you needn't come again.

MRS. NORTHROP (*bridling*): Ho, I see—that's it, is it?

MARIA: Yes, it is. I don't consider you satisfactory.

CLARA: I should think not!

MRS. NORTHROP (*annoyed*): Who's asking you to pass remarks? (*To* MARIA) And don't think I want to come 'ere again. Me 'usband wouldn't let me, anyhow, when he 'ears what I 'ave to tell him. We've always kept ourselves respectable.

MARIA: And what does that mean?

CLARA: Don't encourage her impudence.

MRS. NORTHROP: An' *you* mind your own .interference. (*To* MARIA) I was beginnin' to feel sorry for you—but now——

MARIA (*coldly*): I don't know what you're talking about.

CLARA: What's she got in that bag?

MRS. NORTHROP (*angrily*): I've got me old boots an' apron an' cleanin' stuff in this bag——

MARIA: I can see two bottles there——

MRS. NORTHROP (*angrily*): Well, what if you can? D'you think you're the only folk i' Cleckleywyke who can buy summat to sup? If you must know, these is two stout empties I'm taking away 'cos they belong to me—bought an' paid for by me at Jackson's off-licence an' if you don't believe me go an' ask 'em.

MARIA (*stopping* CLARA *from bursting in*): No, Clara, let her alone —we've had enough. (*To* MRS. NORTHROP, *rather haughtily*) It's twenty-four shillings altogether, isn't it?

MRS. NORTHROP (*aggressively*): No, it isn't. It's twenty-five and six—if I never speak another word.

MARIA (*going for her purse on side-table*): All right then, twenty-five and six, but I'm going to take something off for that dish you broke——

MRS. NORTHROP (*angrily*): You won't take a damned ha'penny off!

CLARA: Language now as well as back-answers!

MARIA (*giving* MRS. NORTHROP *a sovereign*): Here's a pound and that's all you'll get.

MRS. NORTHROP (*angrily*): I won't 'ave it. I won't 'ave it.

MARIA (*leaving it on nearest table to* MRS. NORTHROP): There it is, Mrs. Northrop, and it's all you'll get. (*Sitting down in stately fashion and turning to* CLARA.) Let's see, Clara, what were you saying? (*All three women now ignore* MRS. NORTHROP, *which makes her angrier than ever.*)

MRS. NORTHROP (*drowning any possible conversation*): An' don't sit there tryin' to look like duchesses, 'cos I've lived round 'ere too long an' I know too much about yer. Tryin' to swank! Why—— (*pointing to* MARIA) I remember you when you were Maria Fawcett an' you

G

were nobbut a burler and mender at Barkinson's afore you took up wi' Joe Helliwell an' he were nobbut a woolsorter i' them days. And as for you—— (*pointing to* CLARA) I remember time when you were weighin' out apples an' potatoes in your father's greengrocer's shop, corner o' Park Road, an' a mucky little shop it wor an' all——

MARIA (*rising, angrily*): I'll fetch my husband.

MRS. NORTHROP: He isn't your husband. I was goin' to say I'm as good as you, but fact is I'm a damn sight better, 'cos I'm a respectable married woman an' that's more than any o' you can say——

CLARA (*angrily*): Get a policeman.

MRS. NORTHROP (*derisively*): Get a policeman! Get a dozen, an' they'll all 'ave a good laugh when they 'ear what I 'ave to tell 'em. Not one o' you properly married at all. I 'eard that organist o' yours tellin' your 'usbands—if I can call 'em your 'usbands. I wor just be'ind t'door—an' this lot wor too good to miss—better than a turn at t'Empire.

CLARA (*angrily*): I don't believe a word of it.

MRS. NORTHROP: Please yourself. But 'e give 'em a letter, an' that's why they went down to t'club to talk it over—an' I can't say I blame 'em 'cos they've plenty to talk over. An' by gow, so 'ave you three. It's about time yer thought o' getting wed, isn't it?

They stare in silence. She gives them a triumphant look, then picks up her sovereign.

And now you owe me another five an' six at least—an' if you've any sense you'll see I get it—but I can't stop no longer 'cos I've said I meet me 'usband down at '*Are an*' '*Ounds*, 'cos they're 'aving a draw for a goose for Cleckleywyke Tide an' we've three tickets—so I'll say *good night*.

She bangs the door. The three women stare at each other in consternation.

MARIA: That's why they were so queer. I knew there was something.

CLARA (*bitterly*): The daft blockheads!

ANNIE *suddenly begins laughing.*

CLARA: Oh—for goodness' sake, Annie Parker!

ANNIE (*still laughing*): I'm not Annie Parker. And it all sounds so silly.

MARIA (*indignantly*): Silly! What's silly about it?

CLARA (*bitterly*): Serves me right for ever bothering with anybody so gormless. Isn't this Herbert Soppitt all over! Couldn't even get us married right!

MARIA (*looking distressed*): But—Clara, Annie—this is *awful!* What are we going to do?

CLARA: I know what we're *not* going to do—and that's play *Newmarket*. (*Begins putting things away, helped by other two.*)

ANNIE: Eee—we'll look awfully silly lining up at Lane End Chapel again to get married, won't we?

CLARA (*angrily*): Oh—for goodness' sake——!

MARIA (*bitterly*): Better tell them three daftheads in t'dining-room to come in now.

CLARA: No, just a minute.

MARIA: What for?

CLARA: 'Cos I want to think, an' very sight of Herbert'll make me that mad I won't be able to think. (*Ponders a moment.*) Now if nobody knew but us, it wouldn't matter so much.

MARIA: But that fool of a parson knows——

CLARA: And the organist knows——

ANNIE: And your Mrs. Northrop knows—don't forget that—and you wouldn't pay her that five-and-six——

MARIA: Here, one o' them men must fetch her back.

CLARA: I should think so. Why, if people get to know about this —we're—we're——

RUBY (*looking in, announcing loudly*): Yorkshire Argus.

CLARA (*in a panic*): We don't want any *Yorkshire Argus* here—or God knows where we'll be——

She is interrupted by the entrance of FRED DYSON, *who has had some drinks and is pleased with himself.*

DYSON (*very heartily*): Well, here we are again. At least I am. Fred Dyson—*Yorkshire Argus*. Mrs. Helliwell?

MARIA (*rather faintly*): Yes.

DYSON (*same tone*): And Mrs. Albert Parker and Mrs. Soppitt— three lucky ladies, eh?

They are looking anything but fortunate.

DYSON: Now, you'd never guess my trouble.

ANNIE (*who can't resist it*): You'd never guess ours, either.

MARIA (*hastily*): Shut up, Annie. What were you saying, Mr. Dyson?

DYSON: I've gone and lost our photographer—Henry Ormonroyd. Brought him with me here earlier on, then we went back to the *Lion*, where he'd met an old pal. I left 'em singing *Larboard Watch* in the tap-room, not twenty minutes since, went into the private bar five

minutes afterwards, couldn't find old Henry anywhere, so thought
he must have come up here. By the way, where's the party?

ANNIE: This is it.

MARIA (*hastily*): Shut up, Annie. (*Rather desperately, to* DYSON)
You see, my husband—Alderman Helliwell—you know him of
course?

DYSON (*heartily*): Certainly. He's quite a public figure, these days.
That's why the *Argus* sent me up here to-night—when he told 'em
you were all celebrating your silver wedding——

CLARA (*unpleasantly*): Oh—he suggested your coming here, did he?

DYSON: He did.

CLARA (*unpleasantly*): He would!

MARIA: Well, he didn't know then—what—I mean—(*her voice
alters and dies away.*)

DYSON: Our readers 'ud like to know all about this affair.

CLARA (*grimly*): An' I'll bet they would!

MARIA: Now 'ave a bit o' sense, Clara——

CLARA (*quickly*): Why, you nearly gave it away——

ANNIE (*coming in*): What on earth are you saying, you two? (*Smiles
at* DYSON, *who is looking rather mystified.*) It's all right, Mr. Dyson.
What Mrs. Helliwell was going to say was that there was only just
us six, y'know. It wasn't a real party. Just a little—er—private—
er—sort of—you know.

DYSON (*looking about him, thirstily*): I know. Just a cosy little do
—with—er—a few drinks.

MARIA: That's it.

DYSON: A few drinks—and—er—cigars—and—er—so on.

> But they do not take the hint, so now he pulls out pencil and bit
> of paper.

Now, Mrs. Helliwell, wouldn't you like to tell our readers just what
your feelings are now that you're celebrating twenty-five years of
happy marriage?

MARIA (*her face working*): I—er—I—er——

DYSON: You needn't be shy, Mrs. Helliwell. Now, come on.

> To his astonishment, MARIA *suddenly bursts into tears, and then
> hurries out of the room.*

CLARA (*reproachfully*): Now, look what you've done, young man.

DYSON (*astonished*): Nay, dash it—what have I done? I only asked
her——

ANNIE (*hastily*): She's a bit upset to-night—you know, what with all the excitement. It's no use your staying now—you'd better go and find your photographer.

CLARA (*angrily*): Now, Annie, for goodness' sake! We want no photographers here.

ANNIE (*to* DYSON): That's all right. She's upset too. Now you just pop off.

> ANNIE *almost marches* DYSON *to the door and sees him through it. We hear him go out.* CLARA *sits breathing very hard.* ANNIE *returns, leaving door open behind her.*

ANNIE: Well, we're rid of him.

CLARA: For how long?

ANNIE (*annoyed*): You can't sit there, Clara, just saying: "For how long?" as if you're paying me to manage this business. If we want it kept quiet, we'll have to stir ourselves and not sit about shouting and nearly giving it all away as you and Maria did when that chap was here.

CLARA (*bitterly*): If we hadn't said we'd marry a set o' numskulls, this would never 'ave happened. If my poor mother was alive to see this day——

> MARIA *returns, blowing her nose and sits down miserably.*

MARIA (*unhappily*): I'm sorry—Clara, Annie—but I just couldn't help it. When he asked me that question, something turned right over inside—an' next minute I was crying.

CLARA (*severely*): Well, crying's not going to get us out of this mess.

ANNIE (*sharply*): You're never satisfied, Clara. First you go on at me for laughing and now you blame poor Maria for crying——

CLARA (*loudly, sharply*): Well, what do you want to go laughing an' crying for? What do you think this is? *Uncle Tom's Cabin?*

MARIA: They're coming in.

> *The women sit back, grimly waiting.* HELLIWELL, PARKER, SOPPITT *enter, and the women look at them.*

PARKER (*uneasily*): Who was that?

> *No reply. He exchanges a glance with* SOPPITT *and* HELLIWELL.

I said, who was it came just then?

CLARA (*suddenly, fiercely*): *Yorkshire Argus!*

PARKER (*resigned tone*): They know.

ANNIE (*sharply*): Course we know.

> HELLIWELL *looks at them, then makes for the door again.*

MARIA: And where are you going?

HELLIWELL: To fetch t'whisky.

MARIA: And is whisky going to 'elp us?

HELLIWELL: I don't know about you, but it'll help me. (*Goes out.*)

MARIA (*hopefully*): It's not all a tale, is it?

PARKER: No, it's right enough. We put case to a chap at club—no names, of course—and he said it 'ad 'appened a few times—when a young parson thought he was qualified to marry folk—an' it turned out he wasn't. But of course it 'asn't happened often.

CLARA: No, but it has to 'appen to *us*. (*Fiercely to* SOPPITT) I blame you for this.

SOPPITT (*unhappily to* PARKER): Didn't I tell you she would?

CLARA (*sharply*): She! Who's *she*? The cat? Just remember you're talking about your own wife.

PARKER: Ah—but you see, he isn't—not now.

CLARA (*angrily*): Now, stop that, Albert Parker.

> HELLIWELL *returns with large tray, with whisky, soda and glasses.*

HELLIWELL: Any lady like a drop?

MARIA: State I'm in now, it 'ud choke me.

> *The other women shake their heads scornfully.*

HELLIWELL: Albert?

PARKER: Thanks, I think I will, Joe. (*Goes to him.*)

HELLIWELL (*busy with drinks*): 'Erbert?

CLARA (*quickly*): He mustn't 'ave any.

HELLIWELL: '*Erbert?*

CLARA (*confidently*): You 'eard what I said, Herbert. You're not to 'ave any.

SOPPITT (*the rebel now*): Thanks, Joe, just a drop.

> *He goes up, looks at his wife as he takes his glass and drinks, then comes away, still looking at her, while she glares at him.*

HELLIWELL: 'Ere, but I'd never ha' thought young Forbes ud' have gone back on his word like that, when he promised solemnly not to tell another soul.

MARIA: But he didn't tell us.

HELLIWELL (*staggered*): Eh? (*Exchanges alarmed glance with other men.*) Who did then?

MARIA: Charwoman—Mrs. Northrop. She 'eard you, behind that door.

HELLIWELL (*alarmed*): 'Ere, where is she?

MARIA: Gone.

ANNIE (*with some malice*): Maria's just given her the push.

PARKER (*angrily*): If she's gone off with this news you just might as well play it on Town Hall chimes.

HELLIWELL (*angrily*): Why didn't you say so at first? If this woman gets round wi' this tale about us, we'll never live it down. Did she go 'ome?

ANNIE: No, to the *Hare and Hounds*.

HELLIWELL (*masterfully*): Herbert, swallow that whisky quick—an' nip down to t'*Hare an' Hounds* as fast as you can go, an' bring her back——

SOPPITT: But I don't know her.

HELLIWELL: Nay, damn it, you saw her in here, not an hour since——

SOPPITT: An' she doesn't know me.

HELLIWELL: Now, don't make difficulties, Herbert. Off you go. (*Moves him towards conservatory.*) And bring her back as fast as you can and promise her owt she asks so long as you get back. (*He is now outside, shouting.*) An' make haste. We're depending on you.

HELLIWELL *returns, blowing, carrying* SOPPITT'S *glass. He is about to drink out of this when he remembers, so takes and drinks from his own, then breathes noisily and mops his brow. They are all quiet for a moment.*

You know, Albert lad, it feels quite peculiar to me.

PARKER: What does?

HELLIWELL: This—not being married.

MARIA (*rising, solemn*): Joe Helliwell, 'ow can you stand there an' say a thing like that?

CLARA: } He ought to be ashamed of himself.
ANNIE: } I'm surprised at you, Joe.

HELLIWELL (*bewildered*): What—what are you talking about?

MARIA (*solemnly*): After twenty-five years together. Haven't I been a good wife to you, Joe Helliwell?

HELLIWELL: Well, I'm not complaining, am I?

PARKER (*tactlessly*): You've been the *same* as a good wife to him, Maria.

MARIA (*furiously*): The *same!* I haven't been the same as a good wife, I've been a good wife, let me tell you, Albert Parker.

ANNIE: } Nay, Albert!
CLARA: } (*angrily to* PARKER): I never 'eard such silly talk.

PARKER (*aggressively*): Oh—an' what's silly about it, eh?

CLARA: Everything.

HELLIWELL (*tactlessly*): Nay, but when you come to think of it—Albert's right.

PARKER (*solemn and fatuous*): We must face facts. Now, Maria, you might *feel* married to him——

MARIA (*scornfully*): I might *feel* married to him! If you'd had twenty-five years of him, you wouldn't talk about *might*. Haven't I——

HELLIWELL (*cutting in noisily*): 'Ere, steady on, steady on—with your *twenty-five years of 'im*. Talking about me as if I were a dose o' typhoid fever.

MARIA (*loudly*): I'm not, Joe. All I'm saying is——

PARKER (*still louder*): Now let me finish what I started to say. I said—you might *feel* married to him—but strictly speaking—and in the eyes of the law—the fact is, you're *not* married to him. We're none of us married.

CLARA (*bitterly*): Some o' t'neighbours ha' missed it, couldn't you shout it louder?

PARKER: I wasn't that loud.

HELLIWELL (*reproachfully*): You were bawling your 'ead off.

ANNIE: Yes, you were.

MARIA (*reproachfully*): You don't know who's listening. I'm surprised you haven't more sense, Albert.

PARKER (*irritably*): All right, all right, all right. But we shan't get anywhere till we face facts. It's not our fault, but our misfortune.

MARIA: I don't know so much about that either.

HELLIWELL: Oh? (*To* ALBERT) Goin' to blame us now.

MARIA: Well, an' why not?

HELLIWELL (*irritably*): Nay, damn it—it wasn't *our* fault.

MARIA: If a chap asks me to marry him and then he takes me to chapel and puts me in front of a parson, I expect parson to be a real one an' not just somebody dressed up.

HELLIWELL: Well, don't I?

MARIA: You should ha' found out.

HELLIWELL: Talk sense! 'Ow could I know he wasn't properly qualified?

MARIA (*sneering*): Well, it's funny it's got to 'appen to us, isn't it?

PARKER: But that's what I say—it's not our fault, it's our misfortune. It's no use blaming anybody. Just couldn't be 'elped. But fact remains—we're——

CLARA (*interrupting angrily*): If you say it again, Albert Parker, I'll throw something at yer. You needn't go on and on about it.

MARIA (*bitterly*): Mostly at top o' your voice.

PARKER (*with air of wounded dignity*): Say no more. I've finished. (*Turns his back on them.*)

> *All three women look at him disgustedly.* MARIA *now turns to* JOE.

MARIA: But, Joe, you're not going to tell me you feel different—just because of this—this accident?

JOE (*solemnly*): I won't tell you a lie, love. I can't help it, but ever since I've known I'm not married I've felt *most peculiar*.

MARIA (*rising, sudden temper*): Oo, I could knock your fat head off.

> MARIA *goes hurriedly to the door, making sobbing noises on the way, and hurries out.*

ANNIE (*following her*): Oh—poor Maria!

> ANNIE *goes out, closing door.*

CLARA: Well, I 'ope you're pleased with yourself now.

HELLIWELL (*sententiously*): Never interfere between 'usband and wife.

CLARA: You just said you weren't 'usband an' wife.

HELLIWELL (*angrily*): 'Ere, if I'm going to argue with a woman it might as well be the one I live with.

> HELLIWELL *hurries out. A silence.* PARKER *remains sulky and detached.*

CLARA (*after pause*): Well, after all these ructions, another glass o' port wouldn't do me any 'arm. (*Waits, then as there is no move from* PARKER) Thank you very much. (*Rises, with dignity, to help herself.*) Nice manners we're being shown, I must say. (*Fills her glass.*) I said *nice manners*, Councillor Albert Parker!

PARKER (*turning, angrily*): Now if I were poor Herbert Soppitt, I'd think twice before I asked you to marry me again.

CLARA (*just going to drink*): Ask me again! There'll be no asking. Herbert Soppitt's my husband—an' he stays my husband.

PARKER: In the eyes of the law——

CLARA (*cutting in ruthlessly*): You said that before. But let me tell you, in the sight of Heaven Herbert and me's been married for twenty-five years.

PARKER (*triumphantly*): And there you're wrong again, because in the sight of Heaven nobody's married at all——

> HELLIWELL *pops his head in, looking worried.*

HELLIWELL: Just come in the dining-room a minute, Albert. We're having a bit of an argument——

PARKER: Yes, Joe.

HELLIWELL *disappears.* PARKER *goes out, leaving door a little open.* CLARA, *left alone, finishes her port, then picks up the old photograph and glares with contempt at the figures on it. A house bell can be heard ringing distantly now.*

CLARA (*muttering her profound contempt at the figures in the photograph*): Yer silly young softheads! (*Bangs it down in some prominent place, face up.*)

RUBY *now looks in.*

RUBY: Mrs. Soppitt——

CLARA (*rather eagerly*): Yes?

RUBY: Mrs. Helliwell says will you go into t' dining-room.

As CLARA *moves quickly towards door,* RUBY *adds coolly:*
Aaa—they're fratchin' like mad.

CLARA *goes out quickly, followed by* RUBY. *We hear in distance sound of door opening, the voices of the three in the dining-room noisily raised in argument, the shutting of the door, then a moment's silence. Then several sharp rings at the front door. After a moment,* RUBY'S *voice off, but coming nearer.*

(*Off*) Yes, I know . . . All right . . . 'Ere, mind them things . . . This way . . .

RUBY *ushers in* ORMONROYD, *who is carrying his camera, etc., and is now very ripe.*

ORMONROYD (*advances into room and looks about him with great care, then returns to* RUBY): Nobody here. (*Gives another glance to make sure.*) Nobody at all.

RUBY: They'll all be back again soon. They're mostly in dining-room—fratchin'.

ORMONROYD: What—on a festive occasion like this?

RUBY: That's right.

ORMONROYD: Well, it just shows you what human nature is. Human nature! T-t-t-t-t. I'll bet if it had been a funeral—they'd have all been in here, laughing their heads off. (*He goes over and looks closely at the cigars.*) There isn't such a thing as a cigar here, is there?

RUBY: Yes, yer looking at 'em. D'you want one? 'Ere. (*As he lights it*) Me mother says if God had intended men to smoke He'd have put chimneys in their heads.

ORMONROYD: Tell your mother from me that if God had intended men to wear collars He'd have put collar studs at back of their necks. (*Stares at her.*) What are you bobbing up an' down like that for?

RUBY: I'm not bobbing up an' down. It's you. (*Laughs and regards him critically.*) You're a bit tiddly, aren't yer?

ORMONROYD (*horror-struck*): Tidd-ldly?

RUBY: Yes. Squiffy.

ORMONROYD (*surveying her mistily*): What an ex't'rornry idea! You seem to me a mos' ex't'rornry sort of—little—well, I dunno, really—what's your name?

RUBY: Ruby Birtle.

ORMONROYD (*tasting it*): Umm—Ruby——

RUBY: All right, I know it's a silly daft name, you can't tell me nowt about Ruby I 'aven't been told already—so don't try.

ORMONROYD (*solemnly*): Ruby, I think you're quite ex't'rornry. How old are you?

RUBY (*quickly*): Fifteen—how old are you?

ORMONROYD (*waving a hand, vaguely*): Thousands of years, thousands and thousands of years.

RUBY (*coolly*): You look to me about seventy.

ORMONROYD (*horrified*): *Seventy!* I'm fifty-four.

RUBY (*severely*): Then you've been neglectin' yerself.

ORMONROYD *looks at her, breathing hard and noisily.* Too much liftin' o' t' elbow.

ORMONROYD (*after indignant pause*): Do you ever read the *Police News?*

RUBY: Yes. I like it. All 'orrible murders.

ORMONROYD: Then you must have seen them pictures of women who've been chopped up by their husbands——

RUBY (*with gusto*): Yes—with bloody 'atchets.

ORMONROYD (*impressively*): Well, if you don't look out, Ruby, you'll grow up to be one of them women. (*Wanders away and then notices and takes up old photograph.*)

RUBY (*looking at it*): Aaaaa!—don't they look soft? (*Looks suspiciously at him, dubiously.*) How d'you mean—one o' them women?

ORMONROYD: Don't you bother about that, Ruby, you've plenty of time yet.

RUBY (*puzzled*): Time for what?

ORMONROYD (*intent on his art now*): Now what I'm going to do— is to take a flashlight group of the three couples—just as they were in the old photograph. Now—let me see—— (*Very solemnly and elaborately he sets up his camera.*)

RUBY (*who has been thinking*): 'Ere, d'you mean I've plenty of time yet to grow up an' then be chopped up?

ORMONROYD (*absently*): Yes.

RUBY (*persistently*): But what would 'e want to chop me up for?

ORMONROYD: Now you sit there a minute.

RUBY: I said, what would 'e want to chop me up for?

ORMONROYD (*putting her into a chair and patting her shoulder*): Perhaps you might find one who wouldn't, but you'll have to be careful. Now you stay there, Ruby.

RUBY (*hopefully*): Are yer goin' to take my photo?

ORMONROYD (*grimly*): Not for a few years—yet—— (*Is now fiddling with his camera.*)

RUBY (*after thoughtful pause*): D'you mean you're waiting for me to be chopped up? (*Cheerfully, not reproachfully.*) Eeeee!—you've got a right nasty mind, 'aven't you? (*A pause.*) Are *you* married?

ORMONROYD: Yes.

RUBY: Yer wife doesn't seem to take much interest in yer.

ORMONROYD: How do you know?

RUBY: Well, I'll bet yer clothes hasn't been brushed for a month. (*Going on cheerfully.*) Yer could almost make a meal off yer waist-coat—there's so much egg on it. (*After pause.*) Why doesn't she tidy you up a bit?

ORMONROYD (*busy with his preparations*): Because she's not here to do it.

RUBY: Doesn't she live with yer?

ORMONROYD (*stopping to stare at her, with dignity*): Is it—er—essential—you should know all about my—er—private affairs?

RUBY: Go on, yer might as well tell me. Where is she?

ORMONROYD: Mrs. Ormonroyd at present is—er—helping her sister to run a boarding-house called *Palm View*—though the only palm you see there is the one my sister-in-law holds out.

RUBY: Where? Blackpool?

ORMONROYD: Not likely. There's a place you go to live in—not to die in. No, they're at Torquay. (*With profound scorn*) *Torquay!*

RUBY (*impressed*): That's right down South, isn't it?

ORMONROYD (*with mock pompousness*): Yes, my girl, Torquay is on the South Coast of Devonshire. It is sheltered from the northerly and easterly winds, is open to the warm sea breezes from the South, and so is a favourite all-year-round resort of many delicate and re-fined persons of genteel society. In other words, it's a damned miserable hole. (*Surveys his arrangements with satisfaction.*) There we are, all ready for the three happy couples.

RUBY (*sceptically*): Did yer say 'appy?

ORMONROYD: Why not?

RUBY: Well, for a start, go an' listen to them four in t' dining-room.

ORMONROYD (*beginning solemnly*): Believe me, Rosie——

RUBY (*sharply*): Ruby.

ORMONROYD: Ruby. Believe me, you're still too young to under-stand.

RUBY: I've 'eard that afore, but nobody ever tells what it is I'm too young to understand. An' for years me brother kept rabbits.

ORMONROYD (*solemnly but vaguely*): It's not a question of rabbits —thank God! But marriage—marriage—well, it's a very peculiar thing. There's parts of it I never much cared about myself.

RUBY: Which parts?

ORMONROYD: Well—now I'm a man who likes a bit o' company. An' I like an occasional friendly glass. I'll admit it—I like an occasional friendly glass.

RUBY: It 'ud be all t' same if you didn't admit it. We could tell. (*Sniffs.*)

ORMONROYD: If these three couples here have been married for twenty-five years and—er—they're still sticking it, well, then I call 'em three happy couples, an' I won't listen to you or anybody else saying they're not. No, I won't have it. And if you or anybody else says "Drink their health" I say "Certainly, certainly, with pleasure——" (*Gives himself a whisky with remarkable speed.*) Wouldn't dare to refuse, 'cos it would be dead against my principles. Their very good health. (*Takes an enormous drink.*)

RUBY: Eeee!—you are goin' to be tiddly.

ORMONROYD (*ignoring this, if he heard it, and very mellow and senti-mental now*): Ah—yes. To be together—side-by-side—through all life's sunshine and storms—hand-in-hand—in good times and bad ones—with always a loving smile—— (*Waving hand with cigar in.*)

RUBY (*coldly*): Mind yer cigar!

ORMONROYD: In sickness and in health—rich or poor—still to-gether—side-by-side—hand-in-hand—through all life's sunshine and storms——

RUBY (*quickly*): You said that once.

ORMONROYD: Oh—yes—it's a wonderful—it's a bee-yutiful thing——

RUBY: What is?

ORMONROYD: *What is!* Lord help us—it's like talking to a little crocodile! I say—that it's a wonderful and bee-yutiful thing to go through good times and bad ones—always together—always with a loving smile——

RUBY: Side-by-side—an' 'and-in-'and——

ORMONROYD: Yes, and that's what I say.

RUBY: Then there must be summat wrong wi' me 'cos when I've tried goin' side-by-side an' 'and-in-'and even for twenty minutes I've 'ad more than I want.

ORMONROYD (*staring at her*): Extr'ord'n'ry! What's your name?

RUBY: It's still Ruby Birtle.

ORMONROYD: Well, haven't you had a home?

RUBY: Course I've 'ad a home. Why?

ORMONROYD: You talk as if you'd been brought up in a tramshed. No sentiment. No tender feeling. No—no—poetry——

RUBY (*indignantly*): Go on. I know Poetry. We learnt it at school. 'Ere——

RUBY *recites, as* ORMONROYD *sits.*

> They grew in beauty side by side,
>   They filled one home with glee;
> Their graves are severed, far an' wide,
>   By mount and stream and sea.
>
> The same fond mother bent at night
>   O'er each fair sleeping brow;
> She 'ad each folder flower in sight—
>   Where are those dreamers now?
>
> One 'midst the forest of the west,
>   By a dark stream is laid—
> The Indian knows his place of rest
>   Far——

RUBY *hesitates.* CLARA *enters quietly and stares at her in astonishment.* RUBY *gives her one startled look, then concludes hurriedly.*

> —Far in the cedar shade.

RUBY *hurries out.* CLARA *stands in* RUBY'S *place.* ORMONROYD, *who has turned away and closed his eyes, now turns and opens them, astonished to see* CLARA *there.*

ORMONROYD (*bewildered*): Now I call that most peculiar, *most* peculiar. I don't think I'm very well to-night——

CLARA (*same tone as* RUBY *used*): You're a bit tiddly, aren't you?

ORMONROYD: Things aren't rightly in their place, if you know what I mean. But I'll get it.

CLARA: Who are you, and what are you doing here?

ORMONROYD (*still dazed*): Henry Ormonroyd—*Yorkshire Argus*—take picture—silver wedding group——

CLARA (*firmly*): There's no silver wedding group 'll be taken *here* to-night.

ORMONROYD: Have I come to t' wrong house?

CLARA (*firmly*): Yes.

ORMONROYD: Excuse me. (*Moving to door, which opens to admit* ANNIE.)

ANNIE: Who's this?

ORMONROYD (*hastily confused*): Nobody, nobody—I'll get it all straightened out in a minute—now give me time——

ORMONROYD *goes out.*

ANNIE: Isn't he the *photographer*?

CLARA (*bitterly*): Yes, an' he's drunk, an' when I come in, Maria's servant's reciting poetry to him, an' God knows what's become of Herbert an' Albert an' that Mrs. Northrop an' (*angrily*) I'm fast losing my patience, I'm fast losing my patience——

ANNIE: Now, Clara——

MARIA *enters, rather wearily.*

MARIA: I can't knock any sense at all into Joe. Where's Herbert?

CLARA (*grimly*): Still looking for that Mrs. Northrop.

Front door bell rings.

Somebody else here now.

MARIA: Well, don't carry on like that, Clara. I didn't ask 'em to come, whoever it is.

CLARA: If you didn't, I'll bet Joe did. With his *Yorkshire Argus*!

RUBY *enters, rather mysteriously.*

MARIA: Well, Ruby, who is it?

RUBY (*lowering voice*): It's a woman.

CLARA (*hastily*): What woman?

MARIA: Now, Clara! (*To* RUBY) What sort of woman? Who is it?

RUBY (*coming in, confidentially*): I don't know. But she doesn't look up to much to me. Paint on her face. An' I believe her 'air's dyed.

The three women look at each other.

CLARA (*primly*): We don't want that sort o' woman here, Maria.

MARIA: Course we don't—but—— (*Hesitates.*)

ANNIE: You'll have to see what she wants, Maria. It might be something to do with—y'know—this business.

CLARA (*angrily*): How could it be?

ANNIE: Well, you never know, do yer?

CLARA: Let Joe see what she wants.

MARIA: Oh—no—state of mind Joe's in, *I'd* better see her. Ask her to come in, Ruby—and—er—you needn't bother Mr. Helliwell just now.

RUBY *goes out. The three women settle themselves, rather anxiously.* RUBY *ushers in* LOTTIE, *who enters smiling broadly.* MARIA *rises, the other two remaining seated.*

MARIA (*nervously*): Good evening.

LOTTIE: Good evening.

MARIA (*step down*): Did you want to see me?

LOTTIE (*coolly*): No, not particularly. (*She sits down, calmly, and looks about her.*)

The other three women exchange puzzled glances.

MARIA: Er—I don't think I got your name.

LOTTIE: No. You didn't get it because I didn't give it. But I'm Miss Lottie Grady.

MARIA (*with dignity*): And I'm Mrs. Helliwell.

LOTTIE (*shaking her head*): *No*, if we're all going to be on our dignity, let's get it *right*. You're not *Mrs. Helliwell*. You're Miss Maria Fawcett.

CLARA (*as* MARIA *is too stunned to speak*): Now just a minute——

LOTTIE (*turning to her, with mock sweetness*): Miss Clara Gawthorpe, isn't it? Gawthorpe's, Greengrocer's, corner of Park Road. (*Turning to* ANNIE) I'm afraid I don't know *your* maiden name——

ANNIE: I'm Mrs. Parker to you.

LOTTIE: Please yourself, I don't care. I'm *broadminded*. (*Surveying them with a smile.*)

CLARA (*angrily*): I suppose that Mrs. Northrop's been talking to you.

LOTTIE: Certainly. Met in the old *Hare and Hounds*, where I used to work. She's an old friend of mine.

CLARA (*angrily*): If you've come 'ere to get money out of us——

LOTTIE: Who said anything about money?

MARIA: Well, you must have some idea in coming to see us.

LOTTIE (*coolly*): Oh—I didn't come here to see any of you three.

ANNIE: Well, who did you come to see then?

LOTTIE (*smiling*): A gentleman friend, love.

CLARA (*angrily*): *Gentleman friend! You'll* find none o' your gentleman friends in *this house*, will she, Maria?

MARIA (*indignantly*): I should think not!

ANNIE: Just a minute, Clara. I'd like to hear a bit more about this.

LOTTIE: Very sensible of you. You see, if a gentleman friend gets fond of me—then tells me—more than once—that if he wasn't married already, he'd marry me——

CLARA (*grimly*): Well, go on.

LOTTIE: Well—then I suddenly find out that he isn't married already, after all, then you can't blame me—can you?—if I'd like to know if he's still in the same mind. (*Beams upon them, while they look at each other in growing consternation.*)

CLARA (*astounded*): Well, I'll be hanged.

ANNIE: Now we *are* getting to know something.

MARIA (*flustered*): Clara—Annie. (*Pause. Suddenly to* LOTTIE) Who was it?

Front door bell rings.

ANNIE: Just a minute, Maria, there's somebody else here now.

CLARA (*angrily*): Oh—for goodness' sake—can't you keep 'em out?

RUBY (*appearing, importantly*): The Rever-ent Clem-ent Mer-cer!

All three wives look startled, as MERCER, *a large grave clergyman, enters, and* RUBY *retires.*

MERCER (*sympathetically*): Mrs. Helliwell?

MARIA (*faintly*): Yes?

MERCER (*taking her hand a moment*): Now, Mrs. Helliwell, although you're not a member of my congregation, I want you to realise that I feel it my duty to give you any help I can.

MARIA (*confused*): I'm afraid—I don't understand—Mr. Mercer.

MERCER: Now, now, Mrs. Helliwell, don't worry. Let's take everything calmly. May I sit down? (*Takes chair and brings it down.*)

MERCER *sits down, smiling at them.* MARIA *sits.*

ANNIE: Did somebody ask you to come here?

MERCER: Yes, madam. A working man I know called Northrop

stopped me in the street and told me to go at once to Alderman Helliwell's house as a clergyman's presence was urgently required here. So here I am—entirely at your service.

> LOTTIE, *in danger of exploding, rises and goes quickly towards conservatory, where she stands with her back to the others.* MERCER *gives her a puzzled glance, then turns to the other three.*

Now what is it? Not, I hope, a really dangerous illness?

MARIA (*blankly*): No.

MERCER (*rather puzzled*): Ah!—I hurried because I thought there might be. But perhaps you feel some younger member of your family is in urgent need of spiritual guidance. An erring son or daughter?

> *A noise from* LOTTIE.

CLARA (*forcefully*): *No.*

MERCER (*puzzled*): I beg your pardon?

CLARA: I just said *No.* I mean, there aren't any erring sons and daughters. Just husbands, that's all.

MERCER (*rises*): Husbands?

> LOTTIE *suddenly bursts into a peal of laughter, turning towards them.* MERCER *looks puzzled at her.*

LOTTIE (*laughing*): You've got it all wrong.

MERCER (*rather annoyed*): Really! I don't see——

LOTTIE: I think they want you to marry 'em.

MERCER (*looking astounded*): *Marry them!*

ANNIE (*rising, with spirit*): 'Ere, Maria, come on, do something. (*To* MERCER) You'd better talk to Mr. Helliwell——

MARIA (*who has risen*): He's in the dining-room—just across—— (*Almost leading him out.*) Ask him if he thinks you can do anything for us—— (*Now outside room.*) Just in there—that's right——

CLARA (*to* LOTTIE): Which one was it?

> MARIA *returns, flustered, shutting door, as* LOTTIE *returns to her seat, still smiling.*

LOTTIE: I think you missed a chance there—at least, two of you did.

MARIA: Two of us!

LOTTIE: Well, you remember what I told you? (*Smiling reminiscently.*) I'd known him here in Cleckleywyke, but it was at Blackpool we really got going. He said he was feeling lonely—and you know what men are, when they think they're feeling lonely, specially at Blackpool.

CLARA (*hastily*): It couldn't have been Herbert. He's never been to Blackpool without me.

ANNIE: Yes, he has, Clara. Don't you remember—about four years since——?

CLARA (*thunderstruck*): And he said he hadn't a minute away from that Conference. I'll never believe another word he says. But your Albert was with him that time.

ANNIE (*grimly*): I know he was.

MARIA: So was Joe. Said he needed a change.

LOTTIE (*sweetly*): Well, we all like a change, don't we?

SOPPITT *enters, rather hesitantly.* CLARA *sees him first.*

CLARA (*sharply*): Now, Herbert Soppitt——

SOPPITT: Yes, Clara?

LOTTIE (*going to him*): Well, Herbert, how are you these days? (*Playfully.*) You haven't forgotten me, have you?

SOPPITT: Forgotten you? I'm afraid there's a mistake——

CLARA (*grimly*): Oh—there's a mistake all right.

MARIA: Now, Clara, don't be too hard on him. I expect it was only a bit o' fun.

SOPPITT: What is all this?

LOTTIE (*playfully*): Now, Herbert——

SOPPITT (*indignantly*): Don't call me Herbert.

CLARA (*angrily*): No, wait till I'm out o' t' way.

ANNIE: I expect he didn't mean it.

SOPPITT (*annoyed*): Mean *what?*

ALBERT PARKER *now enters, rather wearily.* SOPPITT *turns to him.*

I found that Mrs. Northrop, Albert.

LOTTIE: Oh—hello, Albert!

PARKER (*staring at her*): How d'you mean—*Hello, Albert!*

LOTTIE (*playfully*): Now, now—Albert!

PARKER *looks at her in astonishment, then at the three women, finishing with his wife.*

ANNIE (*bitterly*): Yes, you might well look at me, Albert Parker. You and your cheap holiday at Blackpool! I only hope you spent more on her than you've ever done on me.

PARKER (*vehemently*): Spent more on *her?* I've never set eyes on her before. *Who is she?*

ANNIE *and* CLARA *now look at one another, then at* MARIA, *who looks at them in growing consternation.*

MARIA: I don't believe it. I *won't* believe it.

RUBY *looks in, excitedly.*

RUBY: There's a motor-car stopping near t' front gate.

CLARA (*shouting as* RUBY *goes*): Well, tell it to go away again.

HELLIWELL *comes out of dining-room, bumping into* RUBY *as she goes out, and begins speaking early.*

HELLIWELL (*who is flustered*): What with a photographer who's drunk and a parson who's mad——! (*He sees* LOTTIE *now, and visibly wilts and gasps.*) Lottie!

MARIA (*furiously*): Lottie! So it was *you*, Joe Helliwell.

HELLIWELL: Me what?

MARIA: Who said you'd marry her——

HELLIWELL (*shouting desperately*): That was only a bit o' fun.

MARIA (*bitterly*): You and your bit o' fun!

RUBY (*importantly*): Mayor o' Cleckleywyke, *Yorkshire Argus, Telegraph and Mercury.*

MAYOR *enters, carrying case of fish slices, with* REPORTERS *behind.*

MAYOR (*pompously*): Alderman and Mrs. Helliwell, the Council and Corporation of Cleckleywyke offers you their heartiest congratulations on your Silver Wedding and with them this case of silver fish slices.

He is now offering the case to MARIA, *who has suddenly sunk down on the settee and is now weeping. She waves the case away, and the bewildered* MAYOR *now offers it to* HELLIWELL, *who has been looking in exasperation between his wife,* LOTTIE *and the* MAYOR. HELLIWELL *takes the case and opens it without thinking, then seeing what is in it, in his exasperation, shouts furiously:*

An' I told yer before, Fred—I don't like fish. (*Quick curtain.*)

END OF ACT TWO

ACT III

SCENE: *As before. About quarter of an hour later.* RUBY *is tidying up the room, and also eating a large piece of pasty. She continues with her work several moments after rise of curtain, then* NANCY *makes cautious appearance at conservatory, sees that nobody but* RUBY *is there, then turns to beckon in* GERALD, *and they both come into the room.*

NANCY: What's been happening, Ruby?

RUBY: What 'asn't been 'appening! Eee—we've had some trade on what wi' one thing an' another.

NANCY (*mischievous rather than reproachful*): You see what you've done, Gerald.

RUBY: What! He didn't start it, did he? 'Cos if he did, he's got summat to answer for.

NANCY: Did—anybody ask where I was, Ruby?

RUBY: No, an' I'll bet you could stop out all night and they'd neither know nor care.

GERALD: But what *has* been happening, Ruby?

RUBY (*confidentially*): Place 'as been like a mad-'ouse this last half-hour. To start with, mayor o' Cleckleywyke's been and gone——

NANCY: The mayor?

GERALD (*amused*): Why did they want to bring the mayor into it?

RUBY: Nobody brought him. He come of his own accord—with a case o' fish things an' wearing t' chain—like a chap in a pantymime. He soon took his 'ook. But reporters didn't——

GERALD: Reporters, eh?

RUBY: Ay, an' there were plenty of 'em an' all an' they didn't want to go, neither, not like t' mayor. So Mr. Helliwell an' Mr. Parker took 'em into t' kitchen an' give 'em bottled ale an' for all I know they may be there yet. Mrs. Helliwell's up in t' bedroom—feeling poorly—an' Mrs. Soppitt's with her. Mr. Soppitt an' Mrs. Parker's somewhere out in garden——

NANCY: I told you there was somebody there.

RUBY: Ah, but let me finish. Now there's a woman wi' dyed 'air washing herself in t' bathroom upstairs—an' nobody knows what she wants—beyond a good wash. Down in t' dining-room there's a photo-

191

grapher who's right tiddly tryin' to argue with gert big parson—an' I'll bet he's makin' a rare mess—an' that'll be to do next.

Exit RUBY.

GERALD: Sounds all very confused to me.

NANCY: Yes, and I'd better slip upstairs while nobody's about. Oh—Gerald.

GERALD: Nancy!

NANCY: Do you still love me?

GERALD: Yes, Nancy—still—even after a whole hour.

They kiss. Enter SOPPITT *and* ANNIE PARKER *from conservatory.*

SOPPITT: Here, I say! You two seem very friendly!

ANNIE: I believe you were the girl he was seen with.

SOPPITT: Were you?

NANCY: Yes. We're practically engaged, you know. Only—I was frightened of saying anything yet to Uncle Joe.

SOPPITT: Well, don't start to-night——

ANNIE: Why shouldn't she? He won't be quite so pleased with himself to-night as usual—just as I know another who won't.

NANCY: Good night.

ANNIE: Good night. Why don't you go outside and say good night properly? You're only young once.

NANCY *and* GERALD *exit to conservatory.*

ANNIE: Yes, you're only young once, Herbert. D'you remember that time, just after you'd first come to Cleckleywyke, when we all went on that choir trip to Barnard Castle?

SOPPITT: I do, Annie. As a matter of fact, I fancy I was a bit sweet on you then.

ANNIE: You fancy you were! I know you were, Herbert Soppitt. Don't you remember coming back in the wagonette?

SOPPITT: Ay!

ANNIE: Those were the days!

SOPPITT: Ay!

ANNIE: Is that all you can say—Ay?

SOPPITT: No. But I might say too much.

ANNIE: I think I'd risk it for once, if I were you.

SOPPITT: And what does that mean, Annie?

ANNIE: Never you mind. But you haven't forgotten that wagonette, have you?

SOPPITT: Of course I haven't.

He has his arm round her waist. Enter CLARA.

Hello, Clara.

CLARA: How long's this been going on?

ANNIE: Now, don't be silly, Clara.

CLARA: Oh—it's me that hasn't to be silly, is it? I suppose standing there with my 'usband's arm round you bold as brass, that isn't being silly, is it? I wonder what you call that sort of behaviour, then?

SOPPITT: It was only a bit of fun.

CLARA: Oh—an' how long have you been 'aving these bits o' fun —as you call them—Herbert Soppitt?

ANNIE: You've a nasty mind, Clara.

CLARA: Well—of all the cheek and impudence! Telling me I've got a nasty mind. You must have been at it some time getting Herbert to carry on like that with you. Don't tell me he thought of it himself, I know him too well.

ANNIE: Oh—don't be so stupid, Clara. I'm going into the garden. I want some fresh air.

She goes out.

CLARA: Well, Herbert Soppitt, why don't you follow her and get some fresh air, too? Go on, don't mind me. Come here.

SOPPITT *doesn't move.*

You 'eard me, come here!

SOPPITT: Why should I?

CLARA: Because I tell you to.

SOPPITT: I know. I heard you. But who do you think you are?

CLARA: Herbert Soppitt—you must have gone wrong in your head.

SOPPITT: No. Not me. I'm all right.

CLARA (*sharply*): You'd better go home now an' leave me to deal with this business here.

SOPPITT (*bravely*): Certainly not.

CLARA: In my opinion it's awkward with both of us here.

SOPPITT (*pause*): Well, *you* go home then!

CLARA: What did you say?

SOPPITT (*bravely*): I said, *you* go home. You are doing no good here.

Very angry now, she marches up to him and gives him a sharp slap on the cheek.

CLARA: Now then! (*Steps back and folds arms.*) Just tell me to go home again!

SOPPITT (*slowly, impressively, approaching her*): Clara, I always said that no matter what she did, I'd never lift a hand to my wife——

CLARA: I should think not indeed!

SOPPITT: But as you aren't my wife—what about this?

He gives her a sharp slap. She is astounded.

CLARA: Herbert!

SOPPITT (*commandingly*): Now sit down. (*Pointing.*)

She does not obey. In a tremendous voice of command.

Sit down!

She sits, staring at him. Then when she opens her mouth to speak:

Shut up! I want to think.

A silence, during which she still stares at him.

CLARA (*in a low voice*): I don't know what's come over you, Herbert Soppitt.

SOPPIT (*fiercely*): You don't, eh?

CLARA (*gaping at him*): No, I don't.

SOPPITT (*severely*): Well, you don't think I put up with women coming shouting and bawling at me and smacking my face, do you?

CLARA: Well—you've never gone on like this before.

SOPPITT: Yes, but then before you were my wife——

CLARA (*hastily*): I'm your wife now.

SOPPITT: Oh, no—you're not. (*Produces letter.*)

CLARA: Give me that letter!

SOPPITT: *Sit down*—and *shut up, woman!*

Enter ALBERT PARKER.

PARKER: Where's Annie?

SOPPITT: She's out there somewhere—why don't you look for her?

CLARA: Perhaps she's hiding her face—and if you'd seen what I'd seen to-night, Albert Parker——

SOPPITT: Hold your tongue before it gets you into mischief!

CLARA: I'm only——

SOPPITT: *Shut up.*

PARKER: Here, but wait a minute—I'd like to hear a bit more about this.

SOPPITT: Then you're going to be disappointed. (*To* CLARA) You get back to Maria Helliwell, go on!

PARKER: Here, Clara, you're not going to——

SOPPITT: YOU mind your own business! (*To* CLARA) Go on—sharp.

CLARA *exits.*

PARKER: Herbert, 'ave you been 'aving a lot to drink?

SOPPITT: I had a few, trying to find that Mrs. Northrop.

PARKER: I thought as much.

SOPPITT: And I may possibly have some more, but whether I do or not, I'll please myself—just for once—and if any of you don't like it, you can lump it.

PARKER: Where did you say my wife was?

SOPPITT: She's out there in the garden.

PARKER (*disapprovingly*): What—at this time o' night? (*Looking to garden.*)

SOPPITT: Yes—and why not?

PARKER (*with dignity*): I'll tell 'er that. I've no need to tell you. You're not my wife.

SOPPITT: No, and she isn't, either. Don't forget that.

PARKER *goes to the door and calls.*

PARKER: Annie! Hey—Annie!

SOPPITT: Why don't you go out and talk to her, instead o' calling her like that—as if she were a dog or something?

PARKER: 'Cos standing about in damp grass this time o' night is bad for me. I don't want to start a running cold on top of all this. (*Calls again.*) Hey—Annie! (*Turns to* SOPPITT.) I came in to 'ave a few words in private with her——

SOPPITT: Oh—I'll leave you.

PARKER: In my opinion, there's been a lot too much talk among us altogether, too much noisy 'anky-panky about this daft business. You might think we were a meeting o' t' gas committee way we've gone on so far. What's wanted is a few serious words i' private between us chaps an' our wives, an' less o' this public argy-bargy an' 'anky-panky.

ANNIE PARKER *enters through conservatory.*
Ah—so there y'are.

SOPPITT (*going*): Well, best o' luck, Annie!

PARKER (*suspiciously*): How d'you mean?

SOPPITT (*turning at door*): Hanky-panky!

He goes out.

PARKER: He's 'ad a drop too much, Herbert 'as! Comes of running round the town after that charwoman!

ANNIE (*amused*): Well, Albert?

PARKER (*pompously and complacently*): Well, Annie, I'm going to set your mind at rest.

ANNIE (*demurely*): Thank you, Albert.

PARKER (*pompously and complacently*): Yes, I don't want you to be worrying. Now I think you'll admit I've always tried to do my duty as a 'usband.

ANNIE: Yes, Albert, I think you've always tried.

PARKER (*suspiciously*): What do you mean?

ANNIE (*demurely*): Why—just what you mean, Albert.

PARKER (*after another suspicious glance, returns to former tone, and is insufferably patronising*): Of course, as nobody knows better than you, I'm in a different position altogether to what I was when I first married you——

ANNIE: When you *thought* you married me, Albert.

PARKER: Well, you know what I mean! In them days I was just plain young Albert Parker.

ANNIE: And now you're Councillor Albert Parker——

PARKER: Well, an' that's something, isn't it? And it isn't all, by a long chalk. I've got on i' business, made money, come to be a big man at chapel, vice-president o' t' Cricket League, on t' hospital committee, an' so forth—eh?

ANNIE: Yes, Albert, you've done very well.

PARKER (*complacently*): I know I 'ave. An' mind you, it's not altered me much. I'm not like some of 'em. No swank about me—no la-di-dah—*I'm a plain man.*

ANNIE (*rather sadly*): Yes, Albert, you are.

PARKER (*looking at her suspiciously*): Well, what's wrong wi' it? You're not going to tell me that at your time o' life——

ANNIE (*indignantly cutting in*): My time of life!

PARKER: Well, you're no chicken, are yer? And I say, you're not going to tell me now, at your time o' life, you'd like a bit o' swank an' la-di-dah!

ANNIE (*wistfully*): I've sometimes wondered——

PARKER (*brushing this aside*): Nay, nay, nay, nobody knows better than me what you'd like. An' you know very well what a good husband I've been: steady——

ANNIE (*rather grimly*): Yes, you've been steady all right, Albert.

PARKER (*complacently*): That's what I say. Steady. Reliable. Not silly wi' my money——

ANNIE (*same tone*): No, Albert, your worst enemy couldn't say you'd ever been silly with your money.

PARKER (*complacently*): And yet at the same time—not stingy. No, not stingy. Everything of the best—if it could be managed—everything of the best, within reason, y'know, within reason.

ANNIE: Yes, within reason.

PARKER (*in a dreamy ecstasy of complacency*): Always reasonable —and reliable. But all the time, getting on, goin' up i' the world, never satisfied with what 'ud do for most men—no, steadily moving on an' on, up an' up—cashier, manager, share in the business—councillor this year, alderman next, perhaps mayor soon—that's how it's been an' that's how it will be. Y'know, Annie, I've sometimes thought that right at first you didn't realise just what you'd picked out o' t' lucky bag. Ay! (*Contemplates his own greatness, while she watches him coolly.*)

ANNIE (*after a pause*): Well, Albert, what's all this leading up to?

PARKER (*recalled to his argument*): Oh!—Well, yer see, Annie, I was just saying that I thought I'd been a good husband to you. An', mind yer, I don't say you've been a bad wife—no, I don't——

ANNIE (*dryly*): Thank you, Albert.

PARKER (*with immense patronage*): So I thought I'd just set your mind at rest. Now don't you worry about this wedding business. If there's been a slip up—well, there's been a slip up. But I'll see you're all right, Annie. I'll see it's fixed up quietly, an' then we'll go an' get married again—properly. (*He pats her on the shoulder.*) I know my duty as well as t' next man—an' I'll see that you're properly married to me.

ANNIE: Thank you, Albert.

PARKER: That's all right, Annie, that's all right. I don't say every man 'ud see it as I do—but—never mind—I know what my duty is.

ANNIE: And what about me?

PARKER (*puzzled*): Well, I'm telling yer—you'll be all right.

ANNIE: How d'you know I will?

PARKER (*hastily*): Now don't be silly, Annie. If I say you'll be all right, you ought to know by this time yer *will* be all right.

ANNIE (*slowly*): But I don't think I want to be married to you.

PARKER (*staggered*): *What!*

ANNIE (*slowly*): You see, Albert, after twenty-five years of it, perhaps I've had enough.

PARKER (*horrified*): *'Ad enough!*

ANNIE: Yes, had enough. You talk about your duty. Well, for

twenty-five years I've done my duty. I've washed and cooked and cleaned and mended for you. I've pinched and scrimped and saved for you. I've listened for hours and hours to all your dreary talk. I've never had any thanks for it. I've hardly ever had any fun. But I thought I was your wife and I'd taken you for better or worse, and that I ought to put up with you——

PARKER (*staring, amazed*): *Put up with me!*

ANNIE (*coolly*): Yes, put up with you.

PARKER: But what's wrong with me?

ANNIE (*coolly*): Well, to begin with, you're very selfish. But then, I suppose most men are. You're idiotically conceited. But again, so are most men. But a lot of men at least are generous. And you're very stingy. And some men are amusing. But—except when you're being pompous and showing off—you're not at all amusing. You're just very dull and dreary——

PARKER: Never!

ANNIE (*firmly*): Yes, Albert. *Very* dull and *very, very* dreary and stingy.

PARKER (*staring at her as if seeing a strange woman*): 'As somebody put you up to this?

ANNIE: No, I've thought it for a long time.

PARKER: How long?

ANNIE: Nearly twenty-five years.

PARKER (*half dazed, half indignant*): Why—you—you—you little *serpent!*

ANNIE (*ignoring this*): So now I feel it's time I enjoyed myself a bit. I'd like to have *some* fun before I'm an old woman.

PARKER (*horrified*): Fun! Fun! What do you mean—fun?

ANNIE (*coolly*): Oh—nothing very shocking and terrible—just getting away from you, for instance——

PARKER (*in loud pained tone*): Stop it! Just stop it now! I think—Annie Parker—you ought to be ashamed of yourself.

ANNIE (*dreamily*): Well, I'm not. Bit of travel—and liveliness—and people that are amusing—and no wool business and town councillors and chapel deacons——

PARKER (*shouting angrily*): Why don't you dye your hair and paint your face and go on t' stage and wear tights——?

ANNIE (*wistfully*): I wish I could.

As PARKER *groans in despair at this*, RUBY *looks in*.

RUBY (*loudly and cheerfully*): Mr. Soppitt says if you haven't finished yet yer better 'urry up or go somewhere else to 'ave it out 'cos they're all coming in 'ere.

PARKER (*angrily*): Well, we 'aven't finished.

ANNIE (*coolly*): Yes, we have.

RUBY *nods and leaves the door open.*

PARKER (*loudly*): Now listen, Annie, let's talk a bit o' sense for a minute——

ANNIE: They'll all hear you—the door's open.

PARKER: Nay—damn it——!

Goes to shut door, but SOPPITT *and* CLARA *enter.*

SOPPITT (*amused*): Hello, Albert—what's made you look so flabbergasted?

PARKER (*annoyed*): If I want to look flabbergasted, then I'll look flabbergasted, without asking your advice, Herbert.

SOPPITT: Hanky-panky!

PARKER: Now shut up! 'Ere, Clara, yer wouldn't say I was stingy, would yer?

CLARA: Well, you've never been famous for getting your hand down, have you, Albert?

PARKER (*indignantly*): I've got my 'and down as well as t' next man. I've always paid my whack, let me tell yer. Call a chap stingy just because he doesn't make a big show—'cos he isn't—er——

ANNIE (*burlesqueing his accent, coolly*): La-di-dah!

SOPPITT: Now stop tormenting him, Annie.

PARKER (*indignantly*): Tormenting me! Nobody 'll torment me. And I like that coming from *you*, Herbert, when you've been a by-word for years.

CLARA (*angrily*): A by-word for what?

PARKER: For years.

CLARA: Yes, but a by-word for years for what?

PARKER: Oh! Hen-pecked! Ask anybody who wears trousers in your house!

ANNIE: Albert, don't be so vulgar!

PARKER: Why, a minute since you wanted to wear tights.

ANNIE: Only in a manner of speaking.

PARKER: How can it be in a manner of speaking?—'cos either you're wearing tights or you're not.

Enter LOTTIE *and* JOE HELLIWELL.

LOTTIE: What's this about tights?

PARKER: Now you'll clear out right sharp—if you'll take my tip.

LOTTIE: And I'll bet it's the only kind of tip you do give, too. (*To* ANNIE) He looks stingy to me!

PARKER: Stingy! If anyone says that again to me to-night—I'll—I'll give 'em jip.

Exit PARKER.

HELLIWELL: For two pins I'd either leave this house myself or else clear everybody else out. I've never seen such a place—there's folk nattering in every damn corner!

ANNIE: Where's poor Maria?

SOPPITT: Clara!

Exeunt SOPPITT, CLARA *and* ANNIE.

HELLIWELL: Now, Lottie, be reasonable. A bit o' devilment's all right, but I know you don't want to make real mischief——

LOTTIE: Where's the mischief come in? Didn't you say—more than once—that if you hadn't been married already——?

HELLIWELL (*urgently to her*): Now, you know very well that were only a bit o' fun. When a chap's on a 'oliday in a place like Blackpool an' gets a few drinks inside 'im, you know very well he says a lot o' damn silly things he doesn't mean——

LOTTIE (*indignantly*): Oh—I see. Just tellin' me the tale an' then laughing at me behind my back, eh?

HELLIWELL (*urgently*): No, I don't mean that, Lottie. Nobody admires you more than I do. You're a fine lass and a good sport. But you've got to be reasonable. Coming 'ere *like this*, when you know as well as I do, it were just a bit o' fun!

MARIA *enters. She is dressed to go out, and is carrying some housekeeping books, some keys, and several pairs of socks.*

MARIA (*at door, leaving it open; grimly*): Just a minute, Joe Helliwell!

HELLIWELL (*groaning*): Oh—Christmas! (*Then sees she has outdoor things on.*) 'Ere, Maria, where are yer going?

MARIA (*determined, but rather tearful*): I'm going back to me mother's.

HELLIWELL: *Your mother's!* Why, if you go to your mother in this state o' mind at this time o' night, you'll give her a stroke.

LOTTIE: That's right. She must be about ninety.

MARIA (*angrily*): She's seventy-two. (*Pauses.*) And mind your own *business*. I've got some of it 'ere *for you*.

LOTTIE: What do you mean?

MARIA (*indicating things she's carrying*): Some of your new business, an' see 'ow you like it. You'll find it a change from carrying on wi' men behind the bar.

HELLIWELL: What in the name o' thunder are you talking about?

MARIA: I'm talking about 'er. If she wants my job, she can 'ave it.

LOTTIE: ⎫ 'Ere, just a minute——
HELLIWELL: ⎭ Now listen, Maria——

MARIA (*silencing them by holding up keys and rattling*): There's all t' keys, an' you'd better start knowing where they fit. (*Puts them on table behind settee.*) An' don't forget charwoman's just been sacked, an' I don't expect Ruby'll stay. You'll have to manage by yourself a bit. An' greengrocer calls at ten and the butcher calls at half-past——

HELLIWELL (*shouting*): What does it matter when t' butcher calls?

MARIA (*calmly*): I'm talking to 'er, not to you. (*To* LOTTIE, *who looks astonished*) These is the housekeeping books an' you'll 'ave to 'ave 'em straight by Friday or he'll make a rumpus. 'Ere you are.

LOTTIE (*backing away*): I don't want 'em.

HELLIWELL (*harassed*): 'Course she doesn't——

MARIA: She can't run this house without 'em. You said so yourself. (*Throws books on to settee.*)

HELLIWELL: I know I did, but it's nowt to do with 'er.

MARIA: Then what did she come 'ere for? (*To* LOTTIE, *producing socks*) An' look, 'ere's five pairs of his socks and one pair of woollens (*hangs them on back of settee*) that wants darning, and you'd better get *started* on 'em. An' upstairs you'll find three shirts and two more pairs of woollens you'll 'ave to do to-morrow, an' you'd better be thinking o' to-morrow's dinner, 'cos he always wants something *hot* an' he's very *particular*—— (*Turns towards door.*)

LOTTIE (*aghast*): 'Ere, what do you think I am?

HELLIWELL: Now, Maria, you're getting it all wrong. Nobody knows better than me what a good wife you've been. Now 'ave a bit of sense, love. It's all a mistake.

MARIA: And there's a lot of other things you'll have to manage, but while you're trying to manage them and him, too, I'll be at Blackpool.

She goes, followed by HELLIWELL.

Enter ORMONROYD.

ORMONROYD: I know that face.

LOTTIE: Harry Ormonroyd.

Ormonroyd: Lottie, my beautiful Lottie. And you haven't forgotten me?

Lottie: Forgotten you! My word, if you're not off I'll saw your leg off. 'Ere, you weren't going to take their photos?

Ormonroyd: Yes, group for *Yorkshire Argus*. Make a nice picture—very nice picture.

Lottie: Nice picture! Don't you know? Haven't they told you? (*Roars with laughter*.)

Ormonroyd: Here now, stop it, stop it. Have a drink of port.

Lottie: Well, I suppose I might.

Ormonroyd: Certainly, certainly. Liberty 'All here to-night.

Lottie: Oh—it's Liberty Hall right enough. Chin—chin.

Ormonroyd: All the best, Lottie.

Lottie: Nice drop of port wine this. Joe Helliwell does himself very well here, doesn't he?

Ormonroyd: Oh, yes, Lottie, you'll find everything very comfortable here. 'Ere, somebody told me you were back at the Talbot.

Lottie: I was up to Christmas. Who told you? Anybody I know?

Ormonroyd (*solemnly*): Yes—now just a minute. You know him. I know him. We both know him. I have him here on the tip of my tongue. Er—— (*but can't remember*) no. But I'll get him, Lottie, I'll get him.

Lottie: Then I had to go home. Our Violet—you remember our Violet—she married a sergeant in the Duke of Wellington's—the dirty Thirty-Thirds—and now she's in India.

Ormonroyd (*remembering, triumphantly*): Tommy Toothill!

Lottie: What about him?

Ormonroyd (*puzzled by this*): Nay, weren't you asking about 'im?

Lottie: No, I've something better to do than to ask about Tommy Toothill.

Ormonroyd (*still bewildered*): Quite so, Lottie. But what were we talking about him for? Didn't you say he'd gone to India?

Lottie: No, you fathead, that's our Violet. Oh—I remember, it must have been Tommy Toothill 'at told you I was working at the *Talbot*—d'you see?

Ormonroyd (*still bewildered*): Yes, I know it was. But what of it, Lottie? Aren't you a bit argumentative to-night, love?

Lottie (*good-naturedly*): No, I'm not, but you've had a couple too many.

ORMONROYD: Nay, I'm all right, love. 'Ere, what's happened to your Violet?

LOTTIE (*impatiently*): She married a sergeant and went to India.

ORMONROYD (*triumphantly*): Of course she did. Somebody told me—just lately.

LOTTIE: I told you.

ORMONROYD (*reproachfully*): Yes, I know—I can 'ear. But so did somebody else. I know—Tommy Toothill!

LOTTIE: You've got him on the brain. Then at Whitsun—I took a job at Bridlington—but I only stuck it three weeks. No life at all —I told 'em, I says: "I don't mind work, but I do like a bit of life."

ORMONROYD: I'm just the same. Let's 'ave a bit of life, I say. An' 'ere we are, getting down in dumps, just because Tommy Toothill's gone to India.

LOTTIE: He hasn't, you piecan, that's our Violet. Nay, Harry, you're giving me the hump.

ORMONROYD: Well, play us a tune, just for old times' sake.

LOTTIE: Aaaa, you silly old devil, I'm right glad to see you.

ORMONROYD: Good old times, Lottie, good old times.

They sing. Interrupted by entrance of HELLIWELL, PARKER *and* SOPPITT.

HELLIWELL: Now what the hangment do you think this is—a tap-room? *Yorkshire Argus* wants you on telephone.

LOTTIE: Come on, love, I'll help you.

HELLIWELL: And then get off home.

ORMONROYD: See you later.

ORMONROYD *and* LOTTIE *exit.*

PARKER: Now, what's wanted now is a few serious words in private together.

HELLIWELL: Yes, yes, Albert. I know. But give a chap time to have a breather. I've just had to persuade Maria not to go back to her mother's.

PARKER: Why, what can her mother do?

HELLIWELL: Oh—don't start asking questions—just leave it, Albert, leave it, and let me have a breather.

Enter the three wives, all with hats and coats on.

ANNIE: Now then—Albert—Joe—Herbert——

HELLIWELL: What is this—an ultimatum?

MARIA: Joe Helliwell, I want you to answer one question.

HELLIWELL: Yes, Maria?

MARIA: Joe, do you love me?

HELLIWELL (*embarrassed*): Now what sort of a question is that to come and ask a chap—here? Why didn't you ask me upstairs?

MARIA (*solemnly*): Once and for all—do you or don't you?

HELLIWELL: Yes, of course I do, love.

MARIA: Then why didn't you say so before?

All three women sit down, take off hats.

PARKER (*as if beginning long speech*): And now we're all by ourselves it's about time we started to put our thinking caps on, 'cos we're not going to do any good running round the 'ouse argy-bargy-ing——

MARIA: That's right, Albert.

PARKER: Yes, but let me finish, Maria. We——

He is interrupted by RUBY *appearing round door.*

RUBY (*loudly, cheerfully*): She's back!

MARIA: Who is?

RUBY: That Mrs. Northrop. (*Withdraws, leaving door open.*)

HELLIWELL (*loudly, in despair*): Oh—Jerusalem—we don't want 'er 'ere.

MRS. NORTHROP (*appearing, still carrying bag, and flushed*): If you don't want me here why did you send 'im round chasing me and askin' me to come back? Yer don't know yer own minds two minutes together. (*To* MARIA) You 'aven't settled up wi' me yet, y'know.

HELLIWELL (*annoyed*): Outside!

PARKER (*hastily, anxiously*): Half a minute, Joe, we can't 'ave her telling all she knows—we'll be t'laughing stock of Cleckleywyke to-morrow.

MRS. NORTHROP (*contemptuously*): Yer've bin that for years, lad. I'd rather ha' Joe Helliwell nor you. Joe 'as 'ad a bit o'. fun in his time, but you've allus been too stingy.

PARKER (*the word again*): Stingy! If anybody says that again to me to-night, they'll get what for, an' I don't care who it is.

HELLIWELL (*to* MRS. NORTHROP): I told you—outside—sharp!

MRS. NORTHROP (*full of malice*): Suits me. I reckon naught o' this for a party. You can't frame to enjoy yourselves. But then there's one or two faces 'ere that'ud stop a clock, never mind a party. But wait till a few of 'em I know 'ears about it! You'll 'ear 'em laughing at back o' t'mill right up 'ere.

PARKER: Now we can't let her go i' that state o' mind.

CLARA: You ought to charge 'er with stealin'.

MRS. NORTHROP (*horrified*): Stealin'! Why—for two pins—I'll knock yer lying 'ead off, missis. Never touched a thing i' my life that wasn't me own!

RUBY *looks in, and* MRS. NORTHROP *sees her.*
What is it, love?

RUBY (*loudly, chiefly to* HELLIWELL): That photographer's asleep an' snoring be telephone.

HELLIWELL (*irritably*): Well, waken him up an' tell him to go home.

RUBY *withdraws.* MRS. NORTHROP *takes charge again.*

MRS. NORTHROP (*significantly*): An' I *could* keep me mouth shut if it were worth me while——

CLARA (*almost hissing*): That's blackmail!

SOPPITT (*hastily*): Shut up, Clara!

MRS. NORTHROP (*looking at him*): Hello, *you've* come to life, 'ave yer?

HELLIWELL (*to* MRS. NORTHROP): How much d'you want?

MARIA (*angrily*): I wouldn't give her a penny.

CLARA (*quickly*): Nor me, neither.

PARKER (*quickly*): Can we trust 'er—we've no guarantee?

SOPPITT (*quickly*): She could sign something.

ANNIE (*quickly*): That'ud be silly.

MARIA (*quickly*): Not one single penny!

HELLIWELL (*angrily*): Will you just let *me* get a word in—an' be quiet a minute? Now then——

RUBY (*looking in*): Mr. Helliwell!

HELLIWELL (*impatiently*): What?

RUBY: I wakened 'im an' told 'im to go 'ome. But 'e says 'e *is* at 'ome. (*Withdraws as* HELLIWELL *bangs and stamps in fury.*)

HELLIWELL (*at top of his voice*): What *is* this—a bloody mad-'ouse?

MERCER (*off, but approaching*): Mr. Helliwell! Please!

HELLIWELL (*groaning*): Oh!—Jehoshaphat!—another of 'em!

MERCER *enters.*

MERCER (*sternly*): Mr. Helliwell, I cannot allow you to use such language. It's quite unnecessary.

HELLIWELL (*protesting*): You wouldn't think so if——

MERCER (*cutting in*): *Quite* unnecessary. A little patience—a little quiet consideration—that's all that is needed.

HELLIWELL: What—with folk like her? (*Pointing to* MRS. NORTHROP.)

MERCER (*surprised and disapproving*): Mrs. Northrop! What are *you* doing here?

MARIA (*quickly*): Making trouble!

MERCER (*before* MRS. NORTHROP *can speak*): Making trouble? (*He stoops a little, near her.*) And you've been drinking again.

MRS. NORTHROP (*humble, crestfallen*): Only a drop or two—just because I was a bit upset——

MERCER (*accusingly*): And then you come and make a nuisance of yourself here. *T-t-t-t-t!* What's to be done with you? I am ashamed of you after all your promises.

MRS. NORTHROP (*humble and flattering*): Oh—Mr. Mercer—you're a wonderful man—an' you're t'only preacher i' Cleckleywyke worth listening to. (*To the others, roundly*) Aaaa!—he's a fine preacher is Mr. Mercer. Like—like a—gurt lion of a man! (*To* MERCER *admiringly*) Ay, y'are that an' all.

MERCER (*briskly, masterfully*): Now, Mrs. Northrop, flattery won't help. You've broken all your promises. I'm ashamed of you.

MRS. NORTHROP (*almost tearful now*): Nay—Mr. Mercer——

MERCER: Now—go home quietly——

MARIA (*quickly*): She'll tell all the town about us.

MERCER: We cannot allow that. Mrs. Northrop, you must make me a solemn promise.

MRS. NORTHROP (*looking up at him, humbly*): Yes, Mr. Mercer.

MERCER: Now promise me, solemnly, you will tell nobody what you've heard here to-night. Now promise me.

MRS. NORTHROP (*in solemn quavering tone*): I promise. (*Making suitable gestures.*) Wet or dry . . . may I die.

MERCER: T-t-t-t-t. But I suppose that will do. Now off you go, quietly home, and be a good woman. Good night, Mrs. Northrop.

MRS. NORTHROP (*humbly*): Good night, Mr. Mercer, and thank you very much. (*Turns at door to address the company.*) Aaaa!— he's a gurt lion of a man—— (*Fiercely, a parting shot*) Worth all you lot put together.

> *She goes.*

HELLIWELL (*with relief*): Well, we're rid o' one. (*To* MERCER) Now have you studied that letter, Mr. Mercer?

MERCER (*producing it*): I've considered it very carefully. (*Impressively*) And you know what I think?

SEVERAL OF THEM (*eagerly*): No. Tell us. (*Etc.*)

MERCER (*slowly*): This letter—in my opinion—is perfectly genuine.

HELLIWELL (*disgustedly*): I thought you were going to tell us summat we didn't know.

MERCER (*ignoring this*): I am sorry to say it—but—quite obviously —you are, none of you, really married.

PARKER (*bitterly*): 'Ere, don't rub it in. (*Hopefully*) Unless, of course, you're prepared to marry us yourself—quietly—now.

MERCER (*indignantly*): Certainly not. Quite impossible.

HELLIWELL (*impatiently*): Well—what the hangment are we going to do, then?

MERCER (*turning to him impressively*): My dear sir—— (*Then quickly*) I don't know.

HELLIWELL (*disgusted*): Oh—Christmas!

MERCER: But if you want my final opinion, I think that if there were less bad temper and bad language in this house, and a little more patience and quiet consideration, you would have a better chance of settling your affairs.

HELLIWELL (*exasperated*): And *I* think I'm getting a bit tired o' you, Mr. Mercer.

MERCER (*very angry, towering over* HELLIWELL): What! After wasting my time, you now have the audacity—— Here!

HELLIWELL *flinches, but it is the letter he is being given.* Good night, sir. Good night, ladies.

He marches out and bangs doors. HELLIWELL *breathes heavily and wipes his face.*

HELLIWELL: Well, that's another we're rid of.

PARKER (*beginning in his usual style*): And now what's wanted——

CLARA (*cutting in, mimicking him*): Is a few serious words. We know. But what's really wanted now is a bit o' brainwork, and where we're going to get it from I don't know.

HELLIWELL (*severely to* CLARA): You'll get it from me if you'll keep quiet a minute.

They concentrate hard, and now ORMONROYD, *still carrying a large glass of beer, comes in and sits down in the chair centre, while they stare at him in amazement and disgust.*

ORMONROYD (*cheerfully*): Now—let's see—what were we talking about?

PARKER (*angrily*): We weren't talking about anything to you.

ORMONROYD (*ignoring this*): I wouldn't object to a nice hand at cards. (*To* Helliwell, *who is looking exasperated*) I like a game o' solo, don't you?

Helliwell: No. And I told you to get off 'ome.

Ormonroyd (*reproachfully*): Nay, but you want your photo o' t'group, don't you?

Parker: You'll take no photos 'ere to-night.

Ormonroyd: Now it's a funny thing you should ha' said that. I'm a chap 'at notices things—I 'ave to be in my profession—an' I've been telling meself there's people 'ere in this 'ouse to-night who isn't easy in their minds. No, there's summat a bit off 'ere—just you see.

Clara: Oh—for goodness' sake——

Ormonroyd (*to* Helliwell): And people has to be easy in their minds to be photographed. Nobody ever comes with the toothache, y'know, to 'ave their photos taken.

Soppitt (*seriously*): No, I don't suppose they do. It never occurred to me—that.

Ormonroyd: Name, sir?

Soppitt: Soppitt.

Ormonroyd: Ormonroyd 'ere. There's thought in this face. I'd like to do it some time in a nice sepia finish. Remind me, Mr. Soppitt.

Lottie *enters.*

Ah, there y'are, Lottie. Join the company.

Maria (*to* Lottie): I thought you'd gone long since.

Helliwell: You know very well you promised to go, half an hour since.

Clara (*rises*): We ought to put police on you.

Ormonroyd: Now what's the idea of picking on Lottie? Why don't you live and let live? We're all in the same boat. We all come 'ere and we don't know why. We all go in our turn and we don't know where. If you are a bit better off, be thankful. An' if you don't get into trouble an' make a fool of yourself, well be thankful for that, 'cos you easily might. What I say is this—we're all human, aren't we?

Annie: Yes, and thank you, Mr. Ormonroyd.

Parker: What yer thanking him for? Who's he to start telling us what we ought to do?

Clara: Impudence, I call it. (*Telephone rings.*)

Ormonroyd: Oh, me? I'm nothing much. But in case you want to be nasty, Councillor Albert Parker, just remember though I may be nothing I 'appen to work for a newspaper. Behind me stands the

Press, don't forget that, an' the Press is a mighty power in the land to-day——

RUBY *enters.*

RUBY: Telephone went and when I says: "Who is it?" chap said: "*Yorkshire Argus*—is Ormonroyd, our photographer there?" an' when I says: "Yes, he's still 'ere," he says: "Well, tell him he's sacked." You're sacked. I'm sorry.

RUBY *exits.*

ORMONROYD (*suddenly crushed*): So am I, lass. I left a bag in 'ere somewhere.

LOTTIE: You must have left it down at *Lion*, lad.

PARKER: I thought 'e couldn't carry corn.

ANNIE: Shut up, Albert.

LOTTIE: Nay, Harry, you silly old devil, it's not so bad.

ORMONROYD: It's not so good. Hard to know where to turn.

LOTTIE: Come on, lad, never say die. We've seen a bit of life an' we'll see some more before they throw us on the muck heap. (*To others*) For two pins, I'd take him away now, and leave you to settle your own troubles—if you can.

HELLIWELL: Why—what's he got to do with our troubles?

LOTTIE: Plenty. Now, Harry, tell 'em where you were married.

ORMONROYD: Nay, Lottie, they don't want to hear about my bad luck.

PARKER: We've enough of our own, without his.

ANNIE: No, Albert. Come on, Mr. Ormonroyd.

LOTTIE: Tell 'em where you were married.

ORMONROYD: Lane End Chapel—five an' twenty years since.

HELLIWELL: 'Ere, he must be in t'same boat with us then.

ORMONROYD: Just another o' my bits of bad luck.

CLARA: We can understand that all right.

LOTTIE: Yes, but Harry 'ere had separated from his wife and they wanted to be free.

HELLIWELL: Well, what were they worrying for? They were free. Parson hadn't proper qualifications.

LOTTIE: Hold on a minute . . . go on, Harry.

ORMONROYD: I know he hadn't. Wife found that out. But what she'd forgotten, till I got a copy o' t'certificate, is that in them days —twenty-five years since—chapel wedding—registrar had to be there an' all—to sign certificate.

PARKER: Joe, he's right.

ORMONROYD: I know damn well I'm right. I've been carrying certificate for months trying to find a loophole in it—see for yourself.

CLARA: Are we married after all?

HELLIWELL: Yes, of course we are. If parson didn't tie us up, registrar did—all legal—as right as ninepence.

CLARA: Aaaaa, thank God!

MARIA: Mr. Ormonroyd, this is best night's work you ever did. Thank you.

LOTTIE: Now then, Harry, buck up, lad. Why don't you take that little photo shop in Blackpool again?

ORMONROYD: Nay, it 'ud cost me about a hundred pound to start it again—and I haven't a hundred shillings—an' I know you haven't.

LOTTIE: No, but there's folk here who'd never miss it.

PARKER: 'Ere, steady.

ANNIE: Albert, stingy again?

PARKER: Nay, never—if that's how you feel——

HELLIWELL: We'll soon fix you up, Ormonroyd lad, leave it to me. By gow, you've taken a load off my mind—— Aaaaa—— Now then, everybody, let's brighten up. (*At door.*) Who'll give us a song? Ruby . . . Ruby . . . bring some more drinks, lass. Owt you've got.

ANNIE: Let's sing a bit.

ORMONROYD: Lottie's the one. Come on, Lottie, play us a tune.

CLARA: Now then, Herbert Soppitt, you see, I am your wife after all.

SOPPITT: Yes, Clara, and I hope we'll be very happy. But we won't be if you don't drop that tone of voice. I don't like it.

CLARA: Yes, Herbert.

SOPPITT *begins to sing.*

PARKER: 'Ere, Joe, you wouldn't say I was dull and dreary, would you?

HELLIWELL: Ay, a bit, Albert.

PARKER: Well, that beats me. I've always seemed to myself an exciting sort of chap. (*To* ANNIE) Anyhow, stingy or whatever I am, I'm still your husband.

ANNIE: So it looks as if I'll have to make the best of you.

MARIA: We'll all have to make the best of each other. But then, perhaps it's what we're here for.

HELLIWELL: That's right, love.

PARKER: Well, we'd better see if we can have some of this fun of yours you talk about.

ANNIE: Aaaa, it doesn't matter, Albert.

PARKER: It does. I say we'll have some fun. (*Takes her hand and begins singing. They are all singing now.*)

ORMONROYD (*loudly*): All in your places. We'll have this group yet, and to hell with the *Yorkshire Argus!* Now, steady—steady—everybody.

    Enter RUBY. *The flashlight goes off and* RUBY *drops her tray. But they are all singing as curtain falls.*

END OF PLAY

THE LINDEN TREE

A Play in Two Acts

TO

J. P. MITCHELHILL

MY DEAR MITCH,

I hope you will accept, with my affectionate regards, the dedication of this play. You were enthusiastic about it from the first, and it took us back to the Duchess Theatre again, in the happiest circumstances, after an interval of nearly ten years, during which it looked as if we should never work together in the Theatre again. To have you on the management once more, together with my friends of the Westminster venture—and Dame Sybil and Sir Lewis Casson playing so beautifully —this has been happiness when I had almost ceased to dream of finding it in the Theatre. So far as the play itself has any virtue, it was a virtue plucked out of necessity. The heaviest snowfall the Isle of Wight had known for about a hundred years found me down at Billingham, in a house hard to warm and then desperately short of fuel. Besieged by this cruellest of Februarys, I ate, toiled and slept in one small room, and there the Lindens were born; and for ten days or so, while I worked at the play, they were almost my only company and the people I seemed to know best. And then—what luck!—I was back with you, back with the others, back at the Duchess, and all went miraculously well. So please accept the piece as a tribute to our friendship and your love of the Theatre.

Yours ever,

J. B. P.

"The Linden Tree" *was first produced at the Lyceum Theatre,* *Sheffield, on June 23rd, 1947, and subsequently at the Duchess Theatre,* *London, on August 15th, 1947, with the following cast:*

PROFESSOR ROBERT LINDEN	LEWIS CASSON
ISABEL LINDEN (his wife)	SYBIL THORNDIKE
REX LINDEN (his son)	JOHN DODSWORTH
DR. JEAN LINDEN (his eldest daughter)	FREDA GAYE
MARION DE SAINT VAURY (his daughter)	SONIA WILLIAMS
DINAH LINDEN (his youngest daughter)	TILSA PAGE
ALFRED LOCKHART (University Secretary)	J. LESLIE FRITH
EDITH WESTMORE (a student)	CARMEL MCSHARRY
BERNARD FAWCETT (a student)	TERENCE SOALL
MRS. COTTON (housekeeper)	EVERLEY GREGG

The play was produced by MICHAEL MACOWAN.

SYNOPSIS OF SCENES

The action takes place in Professor Linden's study, in the provincial city of Burmanley. Early spring, at the present time.

ACT I
Friday—
    SCENE I. Late afternoon.
    SCENE II. Two hours later.

ACT II
Saturday—
    SCENE I. Afternoon.
    SCENE II. Night, several hours later.

In each Act, between the Scenes, the curtain is lowered for a few moments only.

ACT 1

SCENE I

Professor Linden's study. It is a large room, clean but shabby. One door, preferably set obliquely and prominently between back and left (actors') walls. Big bay window on right wall. A companion window may be presumed to exist in fourth wall. Downstage L. is an anthracite stove. Back wall and all available R. and L. walls are covered with open bookshelves up to height of about five feet, with one or two tall filing cabinets for lecture MSS etc. A fairly large table, with papers, books, pipes, tobacco jar etc., rather downstage L. of centre. A small table on back wall near door with telephone on it. As this room is often used for seminars there are plenty of chairs about, mostly oldish upright chairs near walls but also several shabby comfortable easy chairs nearer centre. Down R. a globe on stand. A few good reproductions and perhaps an excellent original water-colour or two on the walls. No domestic ornaments, and general effect that of a scholarly, cheerful, untidy, and not well-to-do man.

It is afternoon in early spring, and rather coldish sunlight is coming through window R. and fourth wall, giving plenty of light in the room but not giving it any particular richness and warmth. At rise of curtain, stage is empty and then MRS. COTTON *shows in* ALFRED LOCKHART. MRS. C. *is the Lindens' woman-of-all-work and looks it. She is middle-aged and has a curious confused manner, which must be played seriously and not for laughs.* LOCKHART *is a precise, anxious, clerkly middle-aged man, soberly dressed. He wears a light overcoat and carries his hat.*

LOCKHART (*seeing where he is*): Oh—I say, is this right?

MRS. COTTON: Right? It's as right as we can make it. Nothing's right now, nor ever will be, if you ask me. Half the sitting-room ceiling come down yesterday—no warning—just come down in the night—and when I saw it, I stood there—ice-cold, turned to stone, I was—an' couldn't speak for ten minutes——

LOCKHART: I'm afraid I don't understand—I meant——

MRS. COTTON: It took me straight back—see? Lived in Croydon—an' went out one Saturday morning for a bit o' fish—and one o' them buzz-bombs came—and when I gets back—it's all over—finished for ever—all three of 'em—and the home of course——

215

Lockhart (*sympathetically*): Oh yes—I remember Mrs. Linden telling me. And so when you saw the sitting-room ceiling, it reminded you——

Mrs. Cotton (*cutting in, massively*): Turned to stone, I was—you could 'ave pushed a dozen pins into me, I wouldn't have known—couldn't speak for ten minutes. It's years since now—isn't it?—but sometimes I think to myself 'Suppose I'm still going for that fish'—I'm waiting outside Underwoods really an' just dreamin'—an' I'll go back an' everything'll be all right—Charlie an' Gladys an' little George—just waitin' for me—having a good laugh, I'll be bound——

Lockhart (*embarrassed by this*): Yes, I see what you mean. I——

Mrs. Cotton: No, you don't. Why should you? I don't blame you. (*More confidentially, and impressively.*) Sometimes I feel that if I could just turn a corner somewhere—or squeeze through a narrow gap—it'ud be all right again—an' I wouldn't be 'ere in Burmanley but in Croydon with everything all right—(*she points to the window*)—the sun's not the same now. Perhaps that would be different. (*With sudden change of manner, sensibly.*) But you'll 'ave to see Mrs. Linden in 'ere—'cos of the sitting-room ceiling, see?

Lockhart (*glad of this return*): That's what I meant. I was afraid you thought I'd come to see Professor Linden——

Mrs. Cotton: No, I 'eard you—Mrs. Linden, you said. Besides he's at the college on Friday afternoons, always—couldn't even meet the family this afternoon. They've just come in a big car—all the way from London. Plenty of petrol—money no object—that's the son, Rex——

Lockhart: Oh—is he here?

Mrs. Cotton: Yes, with his two sisters. All smart as paint. She's showing 'em their bedrooms. All excited. There'll be trouble 'ere this week-end. Ceilings comin' down—that's a start. You'll see. It's the Professor's birthday to-day. Watch out for that. Big changes comin'. I'll tell Mrs. Linden you're 'ere. (*Moves nearer door, then turns, confidentially.*) Don't believe all she says, she's too excited. 'Cos Rex is 'ere. I'd 'ave bin the same.

> *She goes out, leaving* Lockhart *bewildered. He stares about him a moment, tries a chair tentatively, then rises just before* Mrs. Linden *enters. She is a woman in her late fifties, not very smart but now dressed in her best, and with a brisk vivacious manner.*

Mrs. Linden: Oh—Mr. Lockhart, I hope you haven't been waiting long. Poor Mrs. Cotton isn't—well—you know—quite——

Lockhart: No, I gathered that.

MRS. LINDEN: Only at times, when things happen to upset her. We've had an accident to the drawing-room ceiling. This house is really in a shocking condition, and Robert won't make a fuss about it to the bursar—it's University property, you know—*your* property.

LOCKHART: Shall I say something to him?

MRS. LINDEN: I really don't think it matters now. Ten years ago was the time. But *do* sit down, Mr. Lockhart. So good of you to call so promptly when you're so busy.

LOCKHART: Not at all. I enjoyed the walk across. The early tulips are out on College Green. Very pleasant.

MRS. LINDEN: I've never cared for them. Tulips have never seemed like real flowers to me—more like something from a decorator's. All the children have just arrived, you know—Rex, Jean, and even Marion, who's come all the way from the very centre of France. Rex has just driven them down from London. So the whole family will be here this week-end—for the first time for years. Can you imagine what that means? No of course you can't—not really. Now—(*as she says this, confidentially, she sits fairly close to him and looks at him earnestly*)—I want you to consider this little talk of ours as being strictly between ourselves—very confidential. Even my husband doesn't know about it, and I'd much rather he didn't, if you don't mind.

LOCKHART: No—of course not—if you really think——

MRS. LINDEN: Yes, I do—most decidedly. It's about him, this little talk. And I'm appealing to you not simply as the secretary of the University but also as a friend. And Robert and I have always regarded you as a friend.

LOCKHART: I'm very glad, Mrs. Linden. And of course if there is anything I can do——

MRS. LINDEN: Poor Mr. Lockhart! How often have you to say that?

LOCKHART: About thirty times a day, at least. Including letters of course. But this time I mean it. Usually I don't.

MRS. LINDEN: Yes—well——

LOCKHART (*encouraging her*): Yes?

MRS. LINDEN (*plunging in*): Is there a definite retiring age for professors here at Burmanley?

LOCKHART: There *was*. Sixty-five.

MRS. LINDEN (*pleased*): Ah—I thought so.

LOCKHART: The late Vice-Chancellor ignored it. And of course during the war it was very convenient to keep on the older professors. But now——

MRS. LINDEN: Yes—now? What is the attitude of this new Vice-Chancellor—I never remember his name——

LOCKHART: Dr. Lidley.

MRS. LINDEN: Dr. Lidley. What's his attitude? He's not very old himself.

LOCKHART: About forty-five, I believe.

MRS. LINDEN: I'm sure *he* doesn't want old professors.

LOCKHART (*hesitantly*): Well—no—he doesn't.

MRS. LINDEN: He doesn't like my husband, does he?

As LOCKHART, *embarrassed, does not reply.*

Oh—I know. Robert doesn't like him. And you needn't look like that, Mr. Lockhart. I'm not talking to you now as the University official. You're here as a friend—and it's all in confidence. Dr. Lidley and my husband don't get on, do they?

LOCKHART: Well, of course they represent two different points of view—about the University, I mean. Totally opposed, really. Professor Linden left Oxford to come here—didn't he?

MRS. LINDEN (*emphatically*): He did—much to my disgust—though it's all a long time ago. And he promised we'd get back to Oxford some time—and look at us!—but go on.

LOCKHART: Well, he's always wanted Burmanley to be as like Oxford as possible. Dr. Lidley's quite different. He's been a very successful director of education in several cities. You might describe him as a high-pressure educationalist——

MRS. LINDEN (*quietly, but firmly*): Mr. Lockhart, frankly I don't care tuppence what Dr. Lidley is. The only time I met him he seemed to me one of those bright beaming bores. I hope I never see him again. And that's what I wanted to talk to you about.

LOCKHART: What—about not seeing the Vice-Chancellor again?

MRS. LINDEN: It amounts to that, really. My husband is sixty-five to-day. He ought not to stay here in Burmanley any longer. He's tired. He's been here far too long already. He'll never keep up with these new programmes of work you're introducing. (*She breaks off to look hard at him, then softly.*) Mr. Lockhart, I can tell by the look in your eye that already—and quite recently—you've heard somebody else say what I've just said about my husband.

LOCKHART (*embarrassed*): Really, Mrs. Linden, that's not fair——

MRS. LINDEN (*getting up*): Wives can't afford to be fair.

As LOCKHART *rises she regards him smilingly.*

I think you're fond of Robert, aren't you?

LOCKHART: Yes. Most of us are—I mean, the older lot here.

MRS. LINDEN (*very quietly, slowly*): Well then, if you want to do him a kindness, you won't oppose any attempt, by the other side, to get rid of him. He ought to go. And though he's obstinate, he won't stay where he's not wanted.

LOCKHART (*staggered, stammering*): But—but surely—if he himself——

MRS. LINDEN (*cutting in, hostess now*): Won't you have a cup of tea? It's here, I think.

LOCKHART: No, thank you. I must be getting back to my office.

MRS. COTTON *enters, either with a large tray or preferably pushing a trolley, with tea for five or six persons—bread and butter and cake on it.*

MRS. COTTON: Family's just coming. I've told 'em it's ready.

She goes out, leaving door open.

MRS. LINDEN: Well, just stay and say "How d'you do" to Rex and the girls.

Enter JEAN, MARION *and* REX. REX *is the eldest, about thirty-five, good-looking, cool, humorous, very self-confident, well-dressed in an easy fashion.* JEAN *is a trim handsome woman in her early thirties, a clear-cut and rather cold type at a first glance, very much the professional woman.* MARION *is a year or two younger, pretty, softer, very well-dressed in French clothes.*

REX (*to* LOCKHART): Hello! Remember me?

LOCKHART (*shaking hands*): Yes, of course, Rex. You're looking well.

REX: I'm feeling quite remarkable.

MRS. LINDEN (*to her daughters*): You remember Mr. Lockhart, the University Secretary, don't you?

As they smile, she turns to LOCKHART.

This is Jean—now *Dr.* Jean Linden, if you please, *and* on the staff of the North Middlesex Hospital. And this is Marion, who's come all the way from the centre of France, because now she's Madame de St. Vaury.

REX: Really an old-world French aristocrat who wonders what Burmanley is all about.

MARION (*not pleased at this*): Don't be an ape, Rex.

JEAN (*coldly*): I know what he means, though.

LOCKHART (*hastily*): It doesn't seem long since you were both schoolgirls—and now—well—makes me feel old. Wasn't there a René de St. Vaury up here just before the war?

MARION (*smiling*): Yes. Then I met him again in London, during the war, when he was with de Gaulle. And that's how it all began. We've been married four years—two children now——

LOCKHART: Splendid!

MRS. LINDEN: You're sure you won't stay to tea?

LOCKHART: No thank you. Well—nice to have seen you all again.

Smiles and nods, and they all murmur "Good afternoon" *or* "Good-bye" *and* MRS. LINDEN *takes him out. The other three look at each other.*

REX (*softly*): I'd say that mother's up to something with poor little Alf Lockhart. I saw it in her eye. What about some tea?

MARION: Mother'll want to pour out. (*Surveys tray with disgust.*) Just look at it—ugh!

JEAN: Yes, fairly sordid. But we're all used to that. And what can you expect?

MARION: Well, that's what I mean. If one of our maids brought in a tray looking like that, René or his mother would have a fit.

REX (*taking a piece of cake*): This is Labour England, ducky. Not your Catholic aristocratic old world, with a nice black market on the side. And not Jean's new world. (*He has been nibbling at the cake.*) If sawdust was easier to get, I'd say this cake was sawdust.

MRS. LINDEN *returns, smiling, closing door behind her.*

Well, Mother, what are you up to with poor little Alf Lockhart?

MRS. LINDEN: Just a little chat about your father. Now let's sit down and be cosy. You'd like some tea, wouldn't you, Rex?

REX: A cup, certainly.

JEAN: And so would Marion and I.

MRS. LINDEN: Naturally, dear. But men don't always want tea—that's why I asked. I'm afraid this cake won't be very nice.

REX: It isn't. I've tried it. Stick to the bread and butter.

MRS. LINDEN *is now pouring out;* JEAN *and* MARION *are sitting near her; and* REX *hands bread and butter and cups, etc., and throughout the following speeches they are having tea.*

MRS. LINDEN: Such a shame you couldn't bring the children, Marion.

MARION: It really wasn't possible. And Belle-Mère was quite furious even when I said I'd like to bring them.

MRS. LINDEN: She seems to forget they have another grand-mother——

MARION: No, that's not fair, Mother, when she and René are always suggesting that you should come and stay. We were talking about it one night last week when Father Honoré was dining with us—he's really very witty—and—— (*She breaks off.*)

MRS. LINDEN: Yes, dear?

MARION (*shortly*): I'll tell you later. Don't let's bother about it now.

MRS. LINDEN *looks from her to* JEAN *enquiringly.* REX, *who misses nothing, takes it up.*

REX: Marion's quite right, Mother. Only leads to trouble. She and Jean were at it on the way coming up in the car. And Father Who's-it is practically a detonator for Jean.

MRS. LINDEN: Well, really, Jean—if Marion wants to talk——

JEAN: I didn't stop her. And Rex is exaggerating—as usual.

MARION (*heatedly*): No, he's not. And if you're unhappy, Jean—it's not my fault is it?

JEAN (*coldly*): Unhappy? I'm not unhappy. What are you talking about?

MARION: Oh come off it. I'm not one of your hospital patients. Do you think I don't know you. You're miserable about something—I don't know what it is—so you're taking it out of me—or trying to do—just as you always did——

MRS. LINDEN: Now, Marion, you shouldn't talk like that.

MARION: But it's true, Mother. And as soon as I say anything that reminds her that I'm a Catholic now, she says something hateful and hurting. No, Rex, I'm not going to start arguing all over again. I agree with you—there's been too much already. I'm simply going to say this. I became a Catholic at first simply for René's sake. But now I'm more than glad I did. And the more I see of the rest of you—no, not you, Mother—and—of everything here—the more thankful I am that I am a Catholic—and—and have a Faith—and—and belong to a community that may be old-fashioned, as you call it, but is still civilised. (*Defiantly to* JEAN.) Now go on—call me a Fascist again——

JEAN (*coldly*): Why—do you enjoy it?

MRS. LINDEN: Now, stop it, both of you. If this is how you two go on, then I agree with Rex—there mustn't be any more of it.

MARION: I'm sorry, Mother. I've finished.

MRS. LINDEN: *Is* there something wrong, Jean? You're looking—well—rather strained, dear.

JEAN (*curtly*): I've been working too hard, that's all. We're all overworked at the North Middlesex. And we're terribly short of nurses—and domestic staff. Short of everything—except patients. Oh—forget it.

MRS. LINDEN: Couldn't you apply for some easier post somewhere?

JEAN: Not just now. But I'd like to find something not quite so futile. Half the people we try to patch up might as well be dead—they're only half alive——

MARION (*heatedly*): I call that wicked—yes, downright wicked——

JEAN: I wouldn't call it anything, if I were you, unless you're prepared to leave your delicious chateau and all your devoted peasants and take night duty for a few months.

MARION (*heatedly*): And that's——

REX (*cutting in, massively*): Girls, turn it up. We've had enough of it. We were asked up here for an urgent family reunion—business *and* pleasure, I hope. And the Catholic-Communist debate is now closed for the week-end.

MRS. LINDEN: Just what I was going to say, Rex. And Dinah and your father will be back soon——

REX: How is young Dinah—and why isn't she here?

MRS. LINDEN: She's practising with the orchestra this afternoon and nothing would induce her to stay away. She's very well and happy, really, but still the oddest child you ever knew. More tea, anybody? It isn't very nice, I know, but poor Mrs. Cotton, who likes nothing better than making tea all day long, really hasn't the least idea how to make it properly.

JEAN: Most of them haven't. They can't do anything properly.

REX: Don't care for the masses really, do you, Jeanie?

JEAN: No, of course not. That's why I want to see them turned into sensible civilised creatures.

The telephone rings. JEAN *starts up, but* REX, *already standing, forestalls her.*

REX (*as he goes*): I'll answer it. I'm expecting a call. (*At telephone.*) Hello! Yes, it is. Yes—speaking. Go ahead. . . . Yes, Fraser, Rex Linden here. . . . Yes, what did he say? . . . I see, well offer him twenty-five—cash down—as soon as he likes—if he walks straight out of the place, just taking his personal things and any sentimental bits and pieces, and leaves the rest. . . . Yes, twenty-five thousand—cold cash. . . . All right, ring me here later.

Comes away, looking pleased with himself, takes out cigarette-

case, offering it to his mother and MARION, *who shake their heads, then to* JEAN, *who takes one. He lights hers and his during following speeches.*

MRS. LINDEN: What was that about, dear? Some more of your mysterious business?

REX: No, not really. You remember my telling you about a nice little country place in Hampshire—small manor house with about ten acres, and all the comforts?

MRS. LINDEN (*excitedly*): You're going to buy it?

REX: You heard me. Twenty-five thousand, lock, stock and barrel Sir Charles walks out, Mr. Rex Linden walks in. I think he'll take it too, though he'd get far more if he auctioned everything. But he's in a hurry for the cash—wants to go to Africa.

MRS. LINDEN: But, Rex darling, that'll be wonderful. And—you know—just at the perfect time. Goodness—I hope you *do* get it.

REX: I'll lay ten to one I do—and to-night too. You'll see.

MARION: But—can you afford to put down twenty-five thousand pounds—just like that?

REX: Yes. And quite a good deal more, ducky. I sound a vulgar type, don't I? Perhaps I am. It's a solemn thought.

MARION: But how do you make all this money, Rex? I don't understand. What do you *do*? René was asking me that, the other day.

REX: I toil not neither do I spin.

JEAN (*dryly*): We know that.

REX: I live on my wits and gamble with the boys in the City. A kind of racketeer really—free of tax too. A de-luxe model Spiv.

MRS. LINDEN: Darling, nobody knows what you're talking about.

JEAN (*rising*): I do. And he's right. What about these tea things?

MRS. LINDEN (*rising*): We'll clear and wash up ourselves—I really can't ask Mrs. Cotton. I wish we could have gone out for dinner to-night, but really it's hopeless here.

They are now moving the trolley or tray and various tea things. As they move through door, front-door bell, not too close, is heard ringing.

MRS. LINDEN: Rex, would you mind seeing who that is?

Stage is empty for a moment or two. Then REX *returns with* EDITH WESTMORE, *a student, about twenty, carrying a cheap little case for books, note-books, etc. She wears spectacles, has untidy hair, rather shabby wrong clothes, but is not altogether unattractive and must not be grotesque or comic. She has a provincial accent, which must not be overdone, and has a strained manner, a mixture of shyness and defiance. Her general effect is likeable but rather pathetic. REX's manner with her has more charm than his lines might suggest.*

REX: You'll have to wait, I'm afraid. My father isn't back yet, though I gather he's expected at any moment.

EDITH: Yes, I was at his lecture. I—we—well, there's another student too—we always see him at this time every Friday—we write an essay for him every week——

REX (*smiling*): I know. Explain the Thirty Years War. Do sit down.

She does. He remains standing.

Good lecture?

EDITH (*with enthusiasm*): Oh—yes. Wonderful. He makes it all seem so clear—and so exciting—and it's hard to take notes—and then afterwards—somehow—— (*She hesitates.*)

REX: You can't remember a dam' thing.

EDITH: How do you know?

REX: I was a history student once. (*Produces his cigarette-case, a very expensive one.*) Have a cigarette while you're waiting.

EDITH (*hesitating*): Oh—well—thank you.

Takes one. He offers her a light. She smokes rather awkwardly. He looks at her quizzically.

REX: You're using the wrong shade of lipstick, y'know.

EDITH (*helplessly*): Oh—am I? Yes—I expect I am.

REX: You need a darker shade. Do you mind my talking like this?

EDITH (*rather dubiously*): No—not really. It's a bit—embarrassing —of course. You live in London, don't you?

REX: Yes, I'm a West End type now.

EDITH: Well, I haven't much time—to make myself look nice. And no money. I have a scholarship—and you can only just live on it, if you don't expect help from home—and I don't.

As he continues to regard her impersonally.

Well—what else is wrong? You seem a bit of an expert.

REX: I am. Now—suppose you take off your glasses——

She does.

and then pull your hair back—and then up—let me take your cigarette —no, not quite like that—further back—then up——

*He does, then, following his instructions, she pulls her hair back
in a much more becoming fashion. She now looks quite different,
quite attractive, and smiles at him uncertainly.*

Makes a tremendous difference. You'd be surprised. Now any
sensible young man would want to kiss you.

*She does not react to this, but still holds her face up, smiling
uncertainly.*

I mean more or less—like this.

*He bends down and kisses her, neatly and warmly but not
passionately. When he steps back again, she releases her hair,
gives a queer choking little sob, turns her face away, and fumbles
for a handkerchief.*

Oh I say. This is all wrong. I didn't mean——

EDITH (*cutting in, chokingly*): No, it's not you. . . . I didn't
mind . . . it's something quite different . . . suddenly I felt so
miserable . . . as if everything is so hopeless . . . oh where's my
rotten handkerchief?

REX (*offering his*): Take mine.

She does, and dabs at her eyes.

Why should you suddenly feel miserable—as if everything was
hopeless?

EDITH (*brokenly*): I don't know—I'm a silly fool—it's all so
muddled up——

REX: Never mind. What's the essay about this week?

EDITH (*still weepily*): Charles the Fifth.

REX: Here, try the cigarette again.

*Gives it to her. She puts it in her mouth and now puts her glasses
on again.*

Do you care about Charles the Fifth?

EDITH (*rather desperately*): No. I've tried—and Professor Linden's
so kind—and I must do well—they're all expecting me to, at home—
and my essay is so dull and stupid——

REX (*softly*): I'll tell you a secret about Charles the Fifth, if you
promise not to mention it to my father.

EDITH (*a mess of smoking, half crying and laughing*): All right.
What is it?

REX: Charles the Fifth doesn't matter a sausage. I haven't thought
about him for years, and I'm having a hell of a good time.

EDITH: Yes, but it's different for you. There's no money at home—
and I only just managed to get this scholarship——

REX: You stop worrying, and make the best of yourself and of everything else. What's your name?

EDITH: Edith Westmore.

REX: Well, Edith, that's my advice to you. Start living. There isn't much time.

EDITH: Isn't much time for what?

REX: For anything. And none for Charles the Fifth. He had his share. We'd better take ours while we can.

EDITH: It's all right talking like that. But I believe you're just making fun of me.

REX: I'm not. Never was more serious in my life. I tell you, there isn't much time.

There is a pause, while she looks at him dubiously and he stares quite sombrely at her. Then DINAH *enters, carrying a 'cello case and a pile of music and books. She is eighteen, and a young eighteen, and a very clear eager personality, quite different from anybody else in the play, as if she belonged to another race.*

DINAH: Rex!

REX (*who is clearly fond of her*): Hello, Dinah!

He goes up, kisses her on the cheek and rumples her hair, already untidy.

DINAH: Sorry I wasn't here when you came—did you bring Jean and Marion——?

REX: Yes.

DINAH: Good. Well, I just had to go to orchestra practice.

REX: And how was it?

DINAH: Gosh!—we were awful. (*She now notices* EDITH.) Hello!

EDITH (*subdued*): Hello!

DINAH: Isn't Daddy back yet? I think he's trying to buy some sherry. It's his birthday to-day and we're having a sort of family gathering.

EDITH: Perhaps I'd better go.

DINAH: I shouldn't, now you're here. Hang on a bit. Yes, we were quite peculiarly awful this afternoon. Were you ever in the orchestra, Rex?

REX: Yes, I played the triangle and the tambourine one term—about the time of the Great Depression. What is it murdering now?

DINAH: Dvorak's *New World*. And this afternoon we got all the parts boxed up, and one time Mary Stockfield—that's the other 'cello—and I were playing the third movement when everybody else had gone back to the first. I thought it sounded rather interesting—a bit like Bartok—but Old Nubby, who's our conductor, hated it and danced with rage. How are Jean and Marion?

REX: Inclined to be quarrelsome types. Partly ideology. In the car it was like giving a lift to Thomas Aquinas and Lenin. And then for a bonus you have to add feminine sniffiness and odd jealousies. They're much better apart, those girls.

DINAH: I must go and talk to them. I hope you brought Daddy a lovely present. After all, you're the rich one in this family.

REX: I am and I did. A case of pipes—very special. Took a lot of finding, let me tell you——

DINAH (*who is still near door*): Sh! I think he's here. (*Opens door and calls.*) Daddy, they're here.

REX (*going towards door, calling*): And this is me—Rex.

·REX *goes out, leaving door open.* DINAH *smiles at* EDITH, *who rises rather nervously.*

EDITH: I'm sure he won't want to bother with me to-night.

DINAH: Well, you can see—though it is all rather special to-night. Doesn't that gloomy boy usually come with you on Fridays?

EDITH: Yes. Bernard Fawcett. I don't know what's happened to him.

DINAH: Just brooding somewhere, I expect. Well, I must go and see my sisters. Haven't seen them for ages.

EDITH *takes her essay out of her case, still standing up. Then* PROFESSOR LINDEN *comes in. He is carelessly dressed but has a certain distinction. He looks his age and is obviously rather tired, yet there is a kind of youthfulness about him.*

PROFESSOR: Hello, Dinah! Good rehearsal?

DINAH: Awful!

DINAH *exits.*

PROFESSOR: I hope you haven't been waiting long, Miss Westmore. I hadn't forgotten, but I was held up. Do sit down. Where's Fawcett?

EDITH (*sitting down*): I don't know, Professor Linden. I haven't seen him this afternoon.

PROFESSOR (*filling a pipe*): Well, we'll have to do without him.

EDITH: Professor Linden, I thought—perhaps—as all your family are here—you probably wouldn't want to bother about us to-night.

PROFESSOR: No, no. But I won't keep you long, if you don't mind. Is that your paper? Thank you.

She *hands it over. He lights his pipe before looking at it, sitting on edge of arm-chair.*

EDITH (*timidly*): Can I say—Many Happy Returns——?

PROFESSOR (*smiling*): You can—and thank you very much. Sixty-five, you know. I ought to feel something special, and I've been trying all day and can't manage it. The last time I felt something quite definite was when I was forty—and I've never felt quite so old since. Now then——

He begins skimming through the essay with a practised eye, then breaks off to take up a portfolio and hand it to her.

You'll find some reproductions of old Peter Breughel in there. Have a look at 'em. He's a great favourite of mine. Earthy and elfish at the same time. Real life but with bits of magic starting to work. Look at the Winter and the Summer and the peasants boozing and romping.

As she does, there is a knock.

Come in.

BERNARD FAWCETT enters. He is a rather dour, aggressive youth, who has a cold. He is shabbily dressed and carries some books.

FAWCETT (*thick and sniffy*): I'm sorry I'm late. I went to the chemist's and couldn't get served.

PROFESSOR: I was late myself. And I'll have to cut you short to-night, I'm afraid. A family reunion here. Let's have your essay—and sit down.

FAWCETT hands over his paper, and sits down. PROFESSOR now glances quickly at this one, as he did at EDITH'S. After a moment or two of this, he glances at FAWCETT.

Dull, isn't it? (*Waving paper.*)

FAWCETT: I expect it is. When I have a cold I can't get interested somehow.

PROFESSOR: Miss Westmore couldn't either. All a long way off—and who cares?

EDITH (*looking up*): I'm sorry, Professor Linden.

PROFESSOR: How do you like those Breughels? Fascinating, aren't they?

EDITH: Yes—but I'd like to look at them a long time.

PROFESSOR: You can, if you like. Take 'em away with you. But the point is—that man was one of Charles the Fifth's subjects. And, allowing for old Breughel's temperament, you have to see Charles against that sort of background. Makes a difference, doesn't it?

EDITH (*impressed*): Why—yes—somehow I never thought——

PROFESSOR: No, you saw it as a lot of dim stuff in a book to be mugged up this week for Old Linden. So did Fawcett. Didn't you, Fawcett? With real life roaring all round you. Tell me—weren't you two both mixed up in that recent row about girl students at the Union?

EDITH (*eagerly*): Yes, I was. And I don't care what anybody says——

FAWCETT (*cutting in, alive now*): Wait a minute, before you start talking. I'll bet the Professor doesn't know——

EDITH (*cutting in, sharply*): Oh—I don't mind telling him how it all began. It wasn't our fault, not to begin with——

FAWCETT (*cutting in, louder*): Of course it was. If you girls hadn't insisted——

EDITH (*cutting in, louder*): We had a perfect right to insist. Look, Professor Linden, this is what happened——

PROFESSOR (*firmly*): Miss Westmore, I don't really want to know.

EDITH (*disappointed*): Oh—I thought you did.

PROFESSOR: No, I only wanted to show you both what history really is. And among other things—it's the row about the Union. And now it's come to life, hasn't it? It's important. It's serious. It's urgent. And each of you is ready to talk for the next hour about it at full speed. Now remember what you felt when you were writing these things—dead as mutton—(*indicates the two essays*). Let's forget about them, shall we?

Tears them up neatly and drops them into wastepaper basket. Then he rummages in his pockets, finally producing a square invitation card.

This—is a ticket—to admit two—to a meeting—probably an Indignation Meeting—of the Burmanley Citizens' Vigilant Society—to be held to-morrow afternoon in the Town Hall. Our friend Professor Crockett is among the speakers, and Crockett's always worth hearing. Now I suggest you go together, note-book in hand, to this meeting, and each write an essay for me—On the Influence of Tudor England upon the Burmanley Citizens' Vigilant Society.

FAWCETT (*astonished*): *Tudor* England?

PROFESSOR (*firmly*): Tudor England—and the Burmanley Citizens' etc., etc.

EDITH: But how can it? I mean, there won't be any possible connection between Tudor England—and—and this meeting——

PROFESSOR: Well, if there isn't, then say so. But I think there's sure to be. Even without going to the meeting, I can think of several possibly important links.

FAWCETT (*who has risen*): We can try anyhow. (*Hesitates*). Professor Linden, can I ask you something——?

PROFESSOR: Yes. Charles the Fifth?

FAWCETT: No, sir. What do you think's the best for a cold?

PROFESSOR: My dear chap, for sixty years I've been dosed with everything, beginning with eucalyptus and steadily progressing to sulphur drugs—M. and B.—this and that. I suggest prayer, fasting and patience—and don't encourage the wretched thing by *enjoying it*, so to speak. Try to think about something else—European History, for instance——

Enter MARION, *who stops when she sees the students.*

MARION: Oh—I'm sorry, Father.

PROFESSOR: No, come in, Marion. We've finished. I've cheated them out of fifty minutes to-night.

As MARION *comes forward.*

Two of my students—Miss Westmore—Mr. Fawcett—my daughter, Madame de Vaury.

They murmur "How d'you do's", *both students standing.*

Now—Fawcett—here's the ticket. To-morrow afternoon, both of you. And if my subject still doesn't make any sense to you, look in sometime after to-morrow afternoon and tell me about it. Borrow the portfolio if you like, Miss Westmore.

EDITH (*taking it, with her other things*): Thank you very much.

PROFESSOR: And the same time here next week, if you don't look in before—for help. (*He goes to door, holding it open for them smiling.*) And I liked your letter in the Rag, Fawcett. Quite wrong, every word of it, but I liked it. And keep taking a peep at Old Breughel, Miss Westmore. Good night. Good night!

EDITH and FAWCETT (*as they go*): Good night, Professor Linden.

They go out. He closes the door and smiles at MARION.

PROFESSOR: Well—now.

She kisses him on the cheek.

MARION: Many happy returns, Father.

PROFESSOR (*holding her arm*): Thank you, Marion.

MARION: And I've brought you a very nice present. Two bottles of very good Armagnac.

PROFESSOR (*delighted*): Armagnac! My dear girl, what a wonderful present. I haven't tasted any Armagnac for six or seven years at least. Every single sip will be a holiday in France.

MARION: It's hard to get even in France now. But René managed it. He sends his love. He couldn't possibly get away—he wanted to come, of course.

PROFESSOR: And the children?

MARION: Fat and flourishing. I've brought some photographs. You'll see.

PROFESSOR: Of course I shall see. (*Looks at her appraisingly.*) You're looking well, Marion. Happily settled there now? The truth, mind. Just between us.

MARION: Yes, I *am* happily settled now. It wasn't easy at first— harder than I made it out to be—they were all very kind but they made me feel a stranger—French people of that class are terribly clannish and close——

PROFESSOR: I know. It must have been like trying to push your way into a haystack. And René's mother looked a cast-iron Balzacian terror to me—a grenadier of the Old Guard.

MARION: Well, it's all right now. And the Church part of it has helped a lot. That and the children. So now I'm one of them.

PROFESSOR: I suppose that's possible, if it's what you want to be. And, I remember you always wanted something different—somewhere round the corner. And this must be it.

MARION: Yes, and I feel even better about it now that I've come back here. (*With sudden feeling.*) Oh—Dad, it's no use—I must tell you. I hate it here. It's so messy and drab and slovenly. I never liked it, but now it's much much worse. Look at those two who just went out—they were bad enough before the war, but they weren't as awful as that pair. I hate to think of you, being here, with that scruffy half-crazy Mrs. Cotton slouching about the house—and trying to teach history to dreary, shabby little half-baked students like those two. Just the very look of them——!

PROFESSOR (*mildly*): They're not my brightest. But they're better than they look. Perhaps we all are now. I know something about them—where they come from—how they struggled to get here—the odds against they're being any good at all—and—well, I can't agree, my dear. This is Burmanley, you know.

MARION: Yes, and I never want to see it again. No, never, never. You must come and stay with us from now on, Father. That's what René says too.

PROFESSOR: I'll try, though holidays abroad aren't easy.

MARION: But Daddy you look so tired—and——

PROFESSOR: And old. Go on, say it.

MARION (*gently*): Well, you do look much older, Dad—older than you ought to look. When I think of René's Uncle Gustave, who's years older than you really. It's coming from Vaury—and the life there—— (*She breaks off, looks at him uncertainly.*) Can I say this, Dad?

PROFESSOR: You can say anything you like, my dear.

MARION: Mother says you have some money coming to you now, from your endowment insurance. You could easily find some official excuse—health or a book or something—to drop everything here and come and live near us at Vaury.

PROFESSOR: And why should we do that, Marion?

MARION: Because it's a much better life than you find here. Better in every way. It's still part of the old civilised tradition, Father. Especially if you could do as I've done—and become a Catholic. I can see that Father Honoré was right—that's the secret—the Faith. That—and the land—and all the old tradition of living. (*Rather defiantly.*) I mean it, Father. At first I did it all for René, of course, but now I know it was worth doing for its own sake. I couldn't live any other way.

PROFESSOR (*easily but with some gravity*): That's your affair, Marion. I always said it was, and never tried to interfere, did I?

MARION: No. Mother did a bit, at first. But not you.

PROFESSOR: So if it's what you want, and it satisfies you——

MARION: More than that—makes me deeply happy——

PROFESSOR: Then that's all right. But you mustn't try to give it to me. Or to most of us. We tried it once—the peasants—the proprietors in their castles—the priests—the whole tradition—and then it didn't work. It doesn't work now, except in spots here and there. And those places really depend on other places, like Burmanley here, for instance. There's another side to the medal, Marion—a very dark side too. Sometimes as black as the shirts of Fascist bullies or the faces of the Moors let loose in Spain. You're living a very pleasant life, no doubt, my dear, but it can't solve a single major human problem——

MARION: It's solved mine.

PROFESSOR: But not mine—not ours—not the world's. No, my dear, I'd feel as if I were living in the Palm House at Kew. All right for a holiday—but——

JEAN *enters. He turns and sees her.*

Well, Jean!

JEAN: Hello, Father. Many happy returns!

They kiss.

I've brought you some books, I left them upstairs. Beckel's new social history is one of them.

PROFESSOR: Thank you, my dear. I'll enjoy disliking Beckel again—two parts Marx, one part Freud, a dash of Pavlov, and sprinkle well with sociological jargon. Now I spent half an hour this evening acquiring a bottle of what is probably not much better than cooking sherry. I'll go and uncork the muck for us.

He goes out. JEAN *goes down and sits.*

MARION (*after pause*): How do you think father is looking?

JEAN (*with professional calm*): Not too bad—he's sixty-five, you know.

MARION: You've seen him since I have. I had rather a shock. I think he looks tired—and older than he ought to look. I've just told him so.

JEAN: That must have cheered him up.

MARION (*bitterly*): I suppose he's probably another of the people you think might as well be dead.

JEAN (*angry, but calm*): Don't invent stupid insensitive things like that and then put them into my mouth. Though it's rather typical, that trick.

MARION: Typical of—what?

JEAN: Of you nice old-fashioned Christian souls. I've often noticed it.

They are silent for a·moment, angry with each other, glaring.

MARION: I believe the only explanation is, Jean, that you're jealous of me.

JEAN: What? René and your stuffy little chateau——

MARION: No. But jealous of what I'm feeling—my peace of mind.

JEAN: We've got bottles and bottles of your peace of mind in the dispensary. We inject it into the bad cases——

MARION (*losing her temper*): Oh—don't be such a conceited fool. *And* so childish!

JEAN (*angrily*): Well—really—after the infantilism you've treated me to, for the last eight hours——

MARION (*angrily*): Oh—shut up!

As they glare at each other, DINAH, *who now looks tidier, enters with a tray with small glasses on it.*

DINAH (*cheerfully*): What you two ought to do is to take some whacking great wallops at each other—and then you'd feel better.

JEAN: I don't say you're wrong, but for all that—don't be cheeky.

DINAH: All right, but don't go and muck up Daddy's birthday

between you. And, look here, what's the idea of everybody turning up for it this time?

MARION: Well, can't the family get together for once?

DINAH: Yes, of course. But there isn't somehow a nice Christmassy getting-togetherness about all this—it's more like business—like characters in old plays and novels all coming to hear the will of the late Sir Jasper read out by Mr. Groggins, the old family solicitor. So what's the idea?

MARION: It's to clear up one or two things. About Dad retiring— and so forth.

DINAH: He won't retire—and it looks like a plot to me. There's a plotty atmosphere about, particularly round Mother. (*She looks at them, and suddenly laughs.*)

JEAN: Now what is it?

DINAH: I suddenly remembered that time—oh, years ago when I was quite little—when we were staying in North Wales—and you two had a row about toothpaste or something.

MARION (*smiling*): It was cold cream stuff for sunburn—and we fought—do you remember, Jean?

JEAN: Yes—and the stuff came out and went over everything.

DINAH (*sitting on arm of chair*): That was a heavenly place—it smelt of whitewash and cows, and had gigantic fluffy brown hens— and I was just part of it—magic. That's what I don't like about growing up. You stop being part of places like that. You just look at them as if they were in a shop window. You're not swallowed up by them any more. And what do you get in exchange—by growing up?

JEAN: Consciousness—a more highly developed ego.

DINAH: I know. I can feel mine having growing pains. But I doubt if it's worth it. Marion, mother said if you really want to add a few fancy French tastings and touches to the dinner, now's the time. And Rex is messing about in there, trying to do something but I don't know what.

MARION (*rising*): I can't be worse than Rex.

She goes out.

JEAN (*rising*): Dinah, where's Dad?

DINAH: Trying to find the corkscrew. He always loses it.

JEAN (*quietly and quickly*): I want to put through a call to the hospital. If I can get through, will you please rush out and hold Dad up a minute or two until I've had my call?

DINAH: All right.

As JEAN *goes up to the telephone.*

I'll bet this isn't hospital work, though—but some love business—some man you're miserable about——

JEAN (*at telephone*): Is that Trunks? This is Burmanley—Two Five Eight One Three—and I want Northern—London—Five Four Eight Four. . . . Yes, I'll wait. . . .

DINAH: Isn't it?

JEAN: Yes, it is.

DINAH (*coolly*): I guessed it. I knew you were miserable anyhow. But this is more like Marion than you. I thought you considered this romantic sort of love a lot of silly old-fashioned rot.

JEAN: I do. But that doesn't make it any better does it?

DINAH: No, I suppose it might make it worse. Because you couldn't *enjoy* being miserable.

JEAN (*bitterly*): And might despise yourself too. (*To telephone.*) Is that the North Middlesex? Dr. Linden here—put me through to Dr. Shalgrove, please. . . . (*To* DINAH, *urgently.*) Go on, Dinah. Hurry—please!

DINAH, *who has wandered up towards door, hurries out.*

(*To telephone.*) Dr. Shalgrove, please. . . . Oh, Dorothy, this is Jean. Yes, I'm speaking from Burmanley. I must know about Arnold. Has he gone? (*With an effort.*) I see. And no message for me at all—not a word? . . . I see—just gone—like that. . . . No, I'm all right . . . to-morrow night, I hope. . . . (*With a greater effort.*) By the way, Dorothy, I forgot to leave a message to Crosfield —that he ought to look at that child in Five . . . yes, that's the one, and I'm not satisfied . . . yes . . . yes . . . good-bye, Dorothy.

She puts down the telephone slowly, and comes down rather blindly, fighting her emotions. She sits down, trembling, gives a choked kind of sob, clenching her fists, fighting hard.

PROFESSOR LINDEN *now enters carrying two different bottles, one of sherry, the other without a label. He gives a glance at* JEAN, *who has not looked round, and takes in her situation, so that we feel that his speech that follows is giving her a chance to recover. As he talks, he potters a bit with the bottles and glasses.*

PROFESSOR (*beginning as he enters*): Well, we've a choice of two aperitifs—my sherry, which may or may not be any good, and a mysterious concoction that Rex has brought, specially put up for him by one of his favourite barmen. It'll probably make us all roaring drunk. Except Rex of course, who probably has it for breakfast. (*He pours out a little, and sniffs it.*) It smells like something that probably goes with Big Business in Shanghai. We'd better try it, I suppose.

Slowly, while talking, he pours out several glasses of this stuff, of a dark amber shade.

It's a curious thing about Rex. He does, with complete ease, all the things I wouldn't know how to begin to do—such as compelling important West End barmen to mix bottles of this stuff—hob-nobbing with head-waiters—sitting up late with millionaires—and making money just by making it. All the things I've probably secretly wanted to do all my life. Rex is just busy representing my unconscious self. You too, in a way, Jean, for all that opening up of people, and cutting and stitching inside 'em, which you do without turning a hair is precisely what's awed and terrified me as long as I can remember. You and Rex—your'e the Lindens in reverse, so to speak. Not Marion —she's too completely feminine. But there's Dinah, though. Now she's unblushingly blazingly happy, which is something most of us older ones haven't dared to be for years and years and years. It's as if human nature, which doesn't propose to give in, is now producing a new race, like Dinah, who can't be downed by anything.

JEAN (*not turning, muffled*): There's a lot she doesn't know yet.

PROFESSOR: I don't believe it'll make any difference when she does.

Hands her a glass, holding one himself.

Now try this, my dear. And—your health, Dr. Linden. (*Drinking.*)

JEAN (*doing her best*): And yours—Professor. (*She takes a sip.*)

PROFESSOR: Got a warm disreputable flavour——

JEAN (*with an effort*): I've—had it before—once or twice. (*She gives a sort of gulp.*) Oh—damn! You know something's wrong, don't you?

PROFESSOR: Yes. Tell me if you want to.

JEAN (*turning now, urgently*): I can't. But I thought you guessed I wasn't feeling—very bright. Oh—I get so impatient with myself. Why can't we be as hard as steel?

PROFESSOR: Because it would do us more harm than good. The dinosaurs had that idea—it was probably the only idea they did have—and so they grew more and more armour, thicker and thicker scales, bigger and bigger claws and spikes—all to be hard and tough and safe—until they were like hundred-ton tanks—and couldn't move, couldn't feed themselves, couldn't mate—and were done for. Then came the turn of the soft little monkey people, who could adapt themselves—us.

JEAN: And are we going to manage it?

PROFESSOR: Probably touch-and-go. On the whole I think—Yes. But not by wanting to be as hard as steel. That's asking to be broken. (*He puts a hand on her shoulder.*) Jean, my dear—just take it easy.

Impulsively she turns and puts her cheek against his hand, and whispers.

JEAN: All right, Dad. I'll try. And—thank you.

Enter REX, carrying a handsome case of pipes.

REX (*holding out the case*): Here they are, Dad. And easily the pick of the market.

PROFESSOR (*who has turned, taking case*): Why—Rex, my boy— these are prodigious. Thank you—thank you. I didn't know there were such pipes any more.

REX (*taking glass*): There aren't. I had to comb London for 'em. Collectors' pieces really. Been in that case for years and years, the chap told me. Well, Dad—cheers for the Birthday. (*He drinks, then smacks his lips.*) Very fond of this stuff.

Enter MRS. LINDEN, MARION and DINAH.

MRS. LINDEN: Mrs. Cotton's just dishing up, but we've time for one of these drinks we've heard so much about.

REX (*gaily*): There's Dad's sherry—or the stuff I brought, *Later Than You Think.*

MRS. LINDEN: What do you mean, dear?

REX: That's the name I gave it—the barman couldn't think of one. From the old Chinese saying—"Enjoy yourself—it's later than you think."

MRS. LINDEN (*gaily*): I don't know what you're talking about, darling, but give me just a little—please.

MARION: And sherry for me, Rex.

DINAH: Me too, please.

REX *pours his stuff for his mother, while the* PROFESSOR *pours out sherry for the other two.* REX *then fills the glasses of* JEAN *and the* PROFESSOR *and his own again, throughout the following speeches.*

MRS. LINDEN (*happily*): Well now, I call this a thoroughly sensible way for a family to behave——

REX: You mean—all tippling, eh?

MRS. LINDEN (*beaming on him*): I mean, being all together under one roof—instead of scattered all over the place. Well—now—— (*preparing to drink*).

DINAH: We all drink to Daddy.

MARION: Yes, of course.

Rex (*grinning*): To the gnarled old trunk of the Linden tree!

Mrs. Linden: He's not gnarled. And anyhow—what about me?

Rex: You're not the trunk—you're the roots——

Mrs. Linden (*who has had a sip*): It's terribly strong—isn't it?

Jean (*standing now*): Yes, it always was. (*Drains her glass in one go.*

Mrs. Linden: Jean, are you all right?

Professor (*hastily*): Yes, she's all right. And I thank you for the Toast—(*burlesquing after-dinner speaker*) both for the terms in which it has been proposed and the way in which you have received it——

Rex (*similar burlesque*): Hear—hear!

> Mrs. Cotton, *wearing apron and looking hot and rather flustered appears at door.*

Mrs. Cotton: Well, I like to see everybody 'appy for a change— but you'd better go in an' eat that dinner 'cos it's in now an' getting cold——

> *She disappears, and laughing a little, the others all turn and move towards door, as* Curtain *comes down.*
>
> *This is the end of* Scene I.
>
> *House lights do not go up, and curtain remains down only long enough for bottles and glasses to be cleared, curtains drawn across window* R. *and lighting to be changed, for night.*

Scene II

> When Curtain *rises again, it is two hours later. Stage is empty a moment, then* Professor, *carrying tray with bottle of Armagnac and several glasses, enters with* Rex, *who is lighting a cigar. After* Professor *puts down tray—during first speeches—he lights one of his new pipes. There is an intimate after-dinner atmosphere between the two men.*

Professor: Rex, being a parent I have to pretend to understand you, but as a matter of fact I don't. What do you do and what are you up to?

Rex (*stretching out, comfortably*): It's so simple that hardly anybody believes me. First, what do I do? Well, I make money—by buying stocks and shares—and then selling them at a handsome profit —all for myself, not for other people. I'm not a broker.

Professor: You must have some kind of flair for it.

REX: I have. But it's easy, believe me. You work ten times as hard as I do. And now I'm worth—well, what do you think?

PROFESSOR: I've no idea. More than I am, certainly.

REX: At least a hundred and fifty thousand, at this minute.

PROFESSOR: Good God! It's incredible. But how have you managed it—in this short time?

REX: Jock Mitchell was killed by the same mortar that knocked me out in Italy. He was my best friend. When I came home I found he'd left me all he had—but you know all this. I came in for a nice little packet of stocks and shares that poor Jock hadn't bothered about. After I recovered and was sent to the War House, I began playing about with 'em. Made money. Made more money. Got in the know. Paid no taxes, don't forget. Lived well, but still piled it up. Every time some bit of news made the fools in the City feel shaky, I bought. The minute they felt better again, I sold.

PROFESSOR: It couldn't be as easy as that.

REX: It was. Plus some information and perhaps, as you say, a flair for it. As to what I'm up to—that's quite simple too—I'm enjoying myself—while there's time.

PROFESSOR: You don't see it lasting, you mean.

REX: I don't see anything lasting. If you ask me, we've had it. And you can take your choice between a lot of Trade Union officials giving themselves jobs and titles or Tory Big Business screaming to get back into the trough. All the same racket. Either way we've had it. We can't last. And anyhow when the atom bombs and rockets really start falling, whichever side sends 'em, it's about ten to one we'll be on the receiving end here. I've sometimes thought of clearing out— South America, for instance, or East Africa—but somehow I feel that wouldn't do. So I'll take what's coming. But before then I propose to enjoy myself.

PROFESSOR (*regarding him steadily*): I believe you're quite serious.

REX: Not a serious type as a rule—do a lot of clowning—but for once—and purely out of respect for you and this occasion—I'm in deadly earnest. What about some of Marion's Armagnac?

PROFESSOR: Sorry. I'd forgotten.

REX (*rising*): I'll do it. (*Goes to pour out brandy.*)

PROFESSOR: Thanks. I don't agree with you, of course.

REX: Naturally. I didn't expect you to.

PROFESSOR: But we won't argue. That's not the point. I simply want to understand. All this of course is a reaction, first, from what you were before the war, and then from soldiering—the usual dose of post-war cynicism.

REX (*handing brandy*): No doubt. But it's not a mood. It's permanent. For instance, not long ago, I broke with a young woman because she wanted us to marry and produce children. Nothing doing. So I broke it off—though I was very devoted to her. I wouldn't mention that to mother, by the way. She'd want to know all about it, and start worrying.

PROFESSOR: She would. And I could do a little worrying, myself. Doesn't it occur to you, by the way, that if we're drifting to disaster, you might try using some of your money and wits and energy in some kind of attempt to stop it.

REX (*after a sip*): Damned good brandy!

PROFESSOR (*who has also tried it*): Isn't it?

REX: You mean—politics, eh?

PROFESSOR: If necessary—yes.

REX (*feeling in his pockets*): The other night I was reading some of Waley's translations of old Chinese poems, and one of them particularly took my fancy so I copied it out. (*He has found it now, and reads it out.*) It's called *The Big Chariot.*

> "Don't help on the big chariot;
>   You will only make yourself dusty.
>   Don't think about the sorrows of the world;
>   You will only make yourself wretched.
>
>   Don't help on the big chariot;
>   You won't be able to see for dust.
>   Don't think about the sorrows of the world;
>   Or you will never escape from your despair."

(*Puts it away.*) And I couldn't agree with him more. I wish I could dig that poet out of his grave and ask him to stay with me at Huntingdon House for a few weeks—we'd laugh ourselves sick. Don't look so depressed, Dad. You're not responsible for me any more, and you did your best to turn me into a fine thoughtful public-spirited citizen.

PROFESSOR: Perhaps I did it the wrong way. That's what I'm wondering. I'm not depressed. I'm wondering. You've changed completely. What happened? That interests me.

REX: First, losing Jock—and some of the other chaps. Then that spell at the War House—and war-time London. But even then I was still ready to put my shoulder to one of the back wheels of the big chariot—and be as dusty as hell—if somebody big enough had shouted "Come on, chaps. Throw in everything you've got. Either we'll work miracles or go down fighting." Something like that. The words don't matter. But the mood does, and the inspiration—just to have one good crack at it before the bombs came again—or perhaps they would never come if we showed the world a great example— gave 'em all hope again. Look—I'm talking too much—and most of it bullsh, I suppose——

PROFESSOR: No, it makes sense to me. You were ready—if somebody gave you a lift——

REX: Yes. But not a sausage. So I said to myself "All right, Rex, you pack it up—earn some easy—and play." And I do enjoy myself— don't you believe those people who tell you that you can't nowadays— they don't know enough. Oh—you can't in Burmanley but you can where I live—if you know a few chaps and have the money.

Enter JEAN. REX *turns and sees her. Just in time for a little serious conversation.*

JEAN (*coming down*): There'll be some coffee in a minute.

PROFESSOR: Have some brandy, Jean?

JEAN: Not just now, thank you. Is Rex telling you how to make money without working for it?

PROFESSOR: No, he's been explaining why he believes in making money without working for it. Eh, Rex?

REX: Fair enough. Mine's the Spiv philosophy now—only mugs work. It's everybody for himself, isn't it? Nobody's shown me anything else for the last few years. Most of the place looking like a fourth-rate factory and a dingy fun-fair—a nasty little mess of silly cheap newspapers, greyhound tracks, football pools, squealing capitalists, trades unionists on the make, sleep-walking civil servants kids wanting to behave like touts or tarts——

PROFESSOR: Not much to enjoy then?

REX: Oh yes—if you just push it all away and forget about it. And that's where money comes in. You can buy a high wall or two—and bid for a little civilised amusement behind them. Look at Jean. I run into her now and again—with her boy friend—and they'd try to convert me. What's his name—I mean, the surgeon chap at your place?

JEAN (*very carefully*): Arnold French. He's just left, by the way.

REX (*looking at her curiously*): Has he now? I thought you and he——

PROFESSOR (*cutting in, deliberately*): Convert you to what?

REX (*grinning, to* JEAN): Tell him.

JEAN (*coldly*): It doesn't matter. I don't want to talk about it. And Rex wouldn't want to talk so much if he didn't know he was all wrong, with his delicious undergraduate's cynicism and Epicurean muck. We—I mean, I happen to believe in science and a properly planned community—and discipline—and work——

REX: And forced labour camps for anybody who won't join in——

JEAN (*coolly*): Yes—and why not? I've no use for people who won't face a few hard facts——

REX: You haven't much use for people of any kind, my dear Jean, except a few interesting patients—and your handsome Arnold——

JEAN (*suddenly furious*): Oh—for God's sake—shut up, you fool!

REX (*staring*): Look—Jeanie—I'm sorry. I didn't realise——

JEAN: Oh—drop it. (*She recovers herself by a great effort. Then speaks in a low, bitter tone.*) I'm just not going to run away and bawl in a bedroom.

PROFESSOR: There's probably something to be said for it, though. An old custom.

JEAN (*same tone*): I don't like old customs. And I hate all the idiotic feminine fusses and tantrums—and I've seen enough of them. And what's the use of asking for a disciplined scientific society, if I can't even discipline myself—a woman with a good scientific training?

PROFESSOR: All right, my dear. Only don't imagine that a scientific training turned you into somebody from another planet. You're still just one of us, you know—the same old muddled emotional gang, who've been here for a few hundred thousand years. And don't try to fight all your feminine ancestors—there are too many of them. Better to come to terms with 'em.

REX (*getting up*): And have some Armagnac now—do you good.

JEAN (*with a faint smile*): All right, Rex. And—sorry for the outburst.

He gets some brandy for her.

PROFESSOR: We have a new Vice-Chancellor here—a Dr. Lidley.

REX: I know. What's he like?

PROFESSOR (*gloomily*): He's an educationalist. He educationalises —in quite a big dashing sort of way. It's something quite different from educating people—newer and much better. They'll probably have machines to do it soon, when they can import them from America. Two of my oldest friends here—Tilley and Clark—have already resigned. I believe he's hoping I'll go next. I won't say I see it in his eye, because he always gives me the extraordinary impression that he has two glass eyes, which must be wrong. But there it is.

REX and JEAN exchange glances, which PROFESSOR notices at once. He continues calmly.

Fortunately you two haven't that kind of eye. Far more expressive. But what exactly did those glances mean?

JEAN: We were wondering—at least I know I was—why you should think it worth while going on here.

REX: Right. Dad, why not pack it up now?

PROFESSOR: We can't all pack it up, as you call it, Rex. And one packed-up man in a family is probably quite enough. As for you, Jean, who are not a packer-up, well, I'm surprised at *you*.

JEAN (*softly*): You're sixty-five now, Dad.

PROFESSOR: And one day, Jean, I hope, you'll be sixty-five—and then you may know what I'm feeling now——

JEAN (*contrite*): Dad, please, I didn't mean——

PROFESSOR (*cutting in, but gently*): I know you didn't, nobody does. They just say it, but don't mean what they think I think they mean. Mind you, I'll say this. Sixty-five is probably oldish for science. But history's different. You really know more about it—have the feel of it better—when you're sixty-five than when you're forty-five—or even twenty-five——

Enter DINAH, with a tray of cups filled with coffee.

Coffee, Dinah?

DINAH (*going to put tray down*): Coffee it is. And I made it myself while the others were finishing the washing-up—and all talking about babies. There must be something wrong with me—unwomanly or something—because I hate talk about babies. Mrs. Cotton told a mad *gruesome* story about a baby that turned blue in the blitz. Mrs. Cotton's never come out of the blitz really. In a kind of way she loves it. (*Looks at the three of them sharply.*) You've been quarrelling here, haven't you?

REX (*getting up to help with coffee*): No, we haven't.

DINAH: Well, that's what it feels like to me.

REX: You rather fancy yourself as the intuitive type, don't you?

DINAH (*coolly*): Yes, I do.

She takes a cup of coffee to JEAN, gives it to her, then impulsively bends down and kisses her on the cheek.

JEAN (*half-smiling*): But why, Dinah?

DINAH: I just felt like it, that's all. Don't you go and imagine—

just because you're a doctor now—you're high above all that sort of thing.

JEAN (*with a bitter smile*): It might be better if I did.

PROFESSOR: No, it wouldn't. Otherwise, in a few years you might easily go sour. I've known several good clever people who went sour. After forty's the danger. If you're a professor, you call it sound scholarship, integrity and fastidiousness—but really they're old skim milk turned green. And then they begin to hate ordinary stupid people.

JEAN: And is that such a bad thing?

PROFESSOR (*sipping his coffee now*): It's fatal. Even if we don't think we're ordinary stupid people ourselves—and we probably are—we're all rooted in ordinary stupid humanity. And try to cut your roots, and you're done for. Quite good coffee, Dinah.

DINAH (*solemnly*): I added a pinch of salt.

REX (*who has tried his coffee*): And a pretty big pinch too, young Dinah.

Enter MRS. LINDEN *and* MARION, *who are talking hard.*

MRS. LINDEN: Well, that's the trouble here now. Nobody cares how things are done—they just slop about and take the least possible trouble—and if you dare to complain, they don't hesitate to be rude at once—yes, at once.

MARION: I couldn't help noticing the difference, particularly this time. I don't say it's much better in the French cities, but in the country there's still a tradition—of taking trouble, and proper service, and politeness.

MRS. LINDEN: Well, it's quite hopeless here now.

DINAH (*handing cups*): I don't believe it *is* hopeless at all.

MRS. LINDEN: You don't know what we're talking about, child.

DINAH: I do. People in shops—and waitresses—and all that. And I think they're all right—nice and matey—considering.

MRS. LINDEN: You don't remember anything better.

MARION: Just what I was going to say. You're too young to be in this, Dinah.

PROFESSOR: I'm not, though. And I know what you mean. I remember when most of these people you're talking about were terrified that one or two complaints would throw 'em out into the street and back to the Labour Exchange. You could see that fear in their eyes, hear it in their apologetic voices, and I hated it so much that I never dared to make any complaints.

MRS. LINDEN: You were always much too easy-going.

PROFESSOR: No, no. But now I can grumble like mad, and they can grumble back at me, and I feel much better about it.

DINAH (*proudly*): Daddy had a blazing row with the man at the bookshop. Didn't you, Daddy?

PROFESSOR: Yes, but I thought he won on points. (*Catching his wife's eye.*) What is it, my dear?

MRS. LINDEN: Well, we're all here. I think we ought to talk about the money——

PROFESSOR: What money?

MRS. LINDEN: The endowment insurance. It was your idea. But Rex knows all about it, and perhaps it would be better if he explained to the others.

REX (*to his father*): I think it might, you know.

PROFESSOR: Well, you're the financial genius. Not that this needs one.

REX (*specially to* JEAN *and* MARION): No, it's as simple as pie. For years and years, ever since we were in the nursery in fact, Dad's been paying premiums on an endowment insurance. I don't know how he did it on his princely salary——

PROFESSOR: There were always extras—royalties on my two or three books—outside examination fees—that sort of thing. But never mind about that.

REX: All right. The point is—now that he's sixty-five the money's due to arrive any moment. And the parents agreed that this was really a family insurance, for all of us to have some share if we needed it. That's partly why we're here.

PROFESSOR (*with mild irony*): But we're quite glad to see you, even as shareholders——

MRS. LINDEN: Now, Robert—this is serious——

REX: It's serious you should feel like this. We appreciate it. But apart from that, really it's all nonsense, you know. This money's all yours. We don't want any part of it.

PROFESSOR: We realise that *you* don't, my boy. But there *are* others.

REX: Well, let's see. (*To* JEAN *and* MARION): What do you say, girls?

JEAN: You can count me out. You spent a lot on my education—and the least I can do is to say I don't need any more money, and of course I don't.

MARION: Neither do I. I wouldn't dream of taking a penny. René and I are better off than you are.

DINAH (*solemnly*): And I could probably manage somehow.

MRS. LINDEN (*hastily*): Don't be absurd, Dinah. We're not really talking to you.

DINAH: I don't see why not. A girl I know——

PROFESSOR (*cutting in, smiling*): Your offer is noted, Miss Linden, but not accepted. We shall be responsible for you for a few years yet, whether you like it or not. (*To the others.*) Now—are you three quite sure? Yes, you of course, Rex. But you two girls——

JEAN: Of course we are.

MARION: And you need every penny of it yourselves.

MRS. LINDEN: I knew that is what you'd all say.

PROFESSOR: Still, you had to be asked.

JEAN: You've your own future to consider. These are your savings —almost all you have—and you're sixty-five——

PROFESSOR (*rather sharply*): And still in full possession of my faculties, and still Professor of Modern History in the University of Burmanley.

MARION: Yes, but for how much longer?

PROFESSOR (*again, rather sharply*): Until I decide to resign the Chair.

There is a ring at the telephone. DINAH *runs to answer it.*

DINAH (*at telephone*): Hello! . . . What? . . . Oh yes he is— just a sec. . . . (*turns, holding receiver.*) It's for you, Rex. From London.

REX (*as he goes to telephone*): This'll be Fraser—about the place in Hampshire—you'll see. (*At telephone.*) Yes—Rex Linden here. . . . . I thought he would . . . probably to-morrow night. . . . On Monday if he likes. . . . Yes, I'll do all that . . . nice job, Fraser. . . . 'Bye. (*Puts down telephone, turns, smiling.*)

MRS. LINDEN (*excitedly*): Rex—you've bought it?

REX: I have. Behold the new owner and lord of the manor of Four Elms, Childing, Hants. Four recept., ten bed, four bath— billiard room, sun porch, hard tennis court, croquet lawn, large garden, ten acres, small dairy—and butter for tea. You're all invited.

DINAH: Gosh!—that's marvellous.

PROFESSOR: But you'll have to put some furniture and stuff into it.

MRS. LINDEN (*excitedly*): No—everything's there—isn't it, Rex?

REX: Ready to walk into—even a man and wife on the premises. It's a wonderful buy for twenty-five thousand, but I knew the chap would never resist an offer of cash down at once.

MARION: But it's wasted on a bachelor. You'll simply have to get married now, Rex.

REX: Never. So don't try putting any of your old girl chums on to me. There's nothing doing. Incidentally, I don't propose to live there —only week-ends and holidays and so on. I'm keeping on my flat in Huntingdon House.

DINAH: You sound so grand. I can't ever believe you lived here.

PROFESSOR: This one didn't. It's another Rex who lived here.

JEAN: And perhaps we prefer him.

MRS. LINDEN (*still excited*): Now don't be silly, you two. Rex has done wonderfully well, and I'm proud of him. (*Turning to* REX.) Now listen, darling—this settles it—you know?

REX: Yes, I think it does.

PROFESSOR: Settles what?

MRS. LINDEN (*gaily*): Shall we tell him? No, we'll wait a little while.

DINAH: There's plotting. I knew there was.

PROFESSOR: Well, I don't much like plotting.

MARION (*to* MRS. LINDEN): I know. And you might as well tell him now.

MRS. LINDEN (*hastily*): No, no, I have a special reason.

PROFESSOR (*lightly but with touch of gravity*): I don't like the sound of this.

DINAH: We're out of it.

JEAN: Well, don't look at me. I don't know what it's about.

MRS. LINDEN (*to* REX): It makes just the difference—and settles everything perfectly.

PROFESSOR (*to* JEAN): It's no use. Let's ignore them. Tell me, Dr. Linden, what are your impressions of Burmanley after your recent absence from our city?

JEAN (*same manner*): My immediate impression only confirms the opinion I have held for some time about your city—that it should be pulled down and then rebuilt, on some more civilised plan, as soon as possible.

The telephone rings. JEAN *jumps up.*
That may be for me. (*Goes to telephone.*)

DINAH: It won't be if you answer it. Somehow it never is.

JEAN (*at telephone*): Yes, yes. . . . Oh! Yes, she is. . . . (*Turning.*) For you, Mother. Mr. Lockhart.

MRS. LINDEN *rises hastily, going to telephone.*

PROFESSOR (*rising*): Lockhart? That'll be for me. It must be Alfred Lockhart—of the University.

JEAN (*now returning*): He said Mrs. Linden quite distinctly.

MRS. LINDEN: Yes?

PROFESSOR (*uncertainly, still standing*): Oh well—if that's the case——

MRS. LINDEN (*at telephone, eagerly*): Yes, Mr. Lockhart. . . . I see. . . . You're certain?

PROFESSOR (*going up and across*): Don't let him go.

MRS. LINDEN (*turning*): What? (*To telephone.*) No, I was speaking to my husband.

PROFESSOR (*firmly*): And I want to speak to him.

MRS. LINDEN (*turning*): Now, Robert——

PROFESSOR (*rather grimly*): When you've finished, Isabel.

MRS. LINDEN (*into telephone*): He wants to speak to you.

They look at each other for a moment as he takes the telephone. MRS. LINDEN *comes away but remains standing, looking rather tense.*

PROFESSOR (*into telephone*): Alfred—I don't want to know what you've been talking about to my wife—that's your business. But I'm wondering if you've anything you'd like me to know. . . . Never mind being delicate about it, Alfred. We've known each other too long for that. . . . No, I don't suppose you would choose this way of letting me know, but now I'm asking. . . . (*Now he listens very gravely.*) . . . I see. . . . No, no, I know that. . . . But I don't propose to accept this, you know. No, not for a moment. I'll see you in the morning. . . . By the way, was that what you were telling my wife. . . . Come on, now. . . . I thought as much. Well, you'll see me in the morning, Alfred—and I warn you, the fight's on. (*Puts down the telephone and looks hard at his wife.*) Isabel, I don't like the way that was done. Alfred Lockhart didn't sound happy about it either. Had you been speaking to him earlier?

MRS. LINDEN: There's no need—to look and talk like that, Robert. I did have a word with him, because I wanted to know what might happen.

PROFESSOR: Why?

MRS. LINDEN: Really, Robert—you needn't take that tone! I wanted to know if possible while the children were here—so that if any arrangements had to be made——

PROFESSOR (*harshly*): The only arrangements that have to be made are quite simple—I'm going to fight this decision by every possible means in my power.

MRS. LINDEN: But why—why?

PROFESSOR (*curtly*): Because there's work to be done here, and I'm still capable of doing it. (*Looks at the others, trying to smile.*) I've just been told that I shall be asked to resign my Chair. Officially because I've reached the official age limit, but we've had professors older than I am here for years now. Really, it's because I'm a nuisance. I'm too free-and-easy. I don't admire the mass-production and conveyor-belt system of education. I say *No* when important personages expect to hear *Yes*. And I propose to go on being a nuisance.

MARION: But, Dad, it simply isn't worth it—and if they don't want you, all right, what does it matter? You've done your share.

MRS. LINDEN: Of course he has—more than his share—hanging on for years in this miserable place——

PROFESSOR (*with some warmth*): You talk as if I were choosing a holiday resort. It's my life we're discussing. Or rather, we're not discussing—let's drop the subject. I'll go round in the morning, and point out that I still have a few friends round here.

REX: Now look, Dad——

PROFESSOR (*quietly*): Drop it, Rex. No more, to-night. I've had rather a long day, and I don't want to lose my temper (*trying to smile*). Besides, after all, it's my birthday.

DINAH (*eagerly*): Yes, it is. And I think we ought to play *Black Sam*. We haven't played it for years, and this family always used to play *Black Sam* on all holidays and special occasions.

MRS. LINDEN: Yes, dear, but now that everybody's grown up——

JEAN: No. I'd like to play *Black Sam* again.

REX: So would I. Though don't forget I nearly always win.

DINAH (*swiftly*): You used to cheat.

REX: Certainly. Cheating's part of it, after the first hour.

MARION: Have you still got the cards and counters?

MRS. LINDEN: They're about somewhere—but where, I can't imagine.

DINAH: The counters were up in somebody's bedroom the last time I saw them. Though I can't imagine why.

PROFESSOR: I think I know where the cards might be—at the back of one of the drawers in the dining-room.

DINAH: Well, you look for them, and I'll find the counters. You lot get the table ready.

She goes out with the PROFESSOR, *shutting door behind them.*
REX *and* MRS. LINDEN *begin clearing papers and books, etc.,*
off the study table throughout dialogue that follows. MARION
and JEAN *stand up and give them a hand too.*

MRS. LINDEN: I'm afraid your father's upset and annoyed—the
news coming like that—but it's a good thing really. I'll have to talk
him round, of course.

REX: Well, don't rush him. He's been here a long time——

MRS. LINDEN (*dryly*): Yes—and so have I.

REX: That's not the same thing.

JEAN: No, it isn't. But you seem to have settled something between
you—what is it?

MRS. LINDEN: To leave here at once—and stay with Rex. Your
father wouldn't want to stay in the London flat—but now he needn't.
He can stay in Rex's country house until perhaps later on, when we
find some little place of our own quite near.

JEAN: And what about Dinah?

REX: D'you know, I'd clean forgotten about young Dinah.

MRS. LINDEN: I hadn't. Dinah can stay on here in Burmanley
until the end of the summer term—I know several people who'd be
glad to let her have a room—and then she'd better try for Oxford or
Cambridge, unless she decides to go to the Royal College of Music.
And of course she'll be with us during part of her vacations, at least.

MARION: Well, it all sounds quite sensible to me. Though of course
you must come and stay with us sometimes.

MRS. LINDEN: Once we've left this wretched place, we can.

MARION: You've always hated it here, haven't you?

MRS. LINDEN: Always—always. I ought to have *made* your father
leave, years ago. He had several good opportunities. But then the
war came—and it didn't seem worth while going then. But now
Burmanley's finished with us—and we're done with Burmanley. This
time I really mean it.

MARION: Don't weaken on that, Mother.

MRS. LINDEN: Don't worry. I shan't. I'm getting older too—I'm
nearly fifty-nine—sixty soon—and I refuse to live any longer like
this. It isn't living. It hasn't been for years. Shabby, boring, dismal.
What is there here for me now?

MARION: Nothing—so far as I can see.

MRS. LINDEN: Rex agrees with me—don't you, darling?

REX: Absolutely. Pack it up, I say, and come and enjoy yourself
while there's still time. And you leave it to me, Mother.

He winks at her and she smiles at him fondly. JEAN *is looking gravely thoughtful.* MRS. LINDEN *notices this.*

MRS. LINDEN: Well, Jean? You agree, don't you?

JEAN (*slowly*): I don't know. I really don't know.

MRS. LINDEN: That's not like you.

MARION: No, Jean usually knows it all—right off—bang!

JEAN (*sharply*): Well, to-night for once, I don't. And it worries me. So just leave me out of it.

MRS. LINDEN (*sharply*): If it's your father you're thinking about, I'm just as anxious to get away for his sake as I am for my own. He's getting on—he's tired—most of his friends have gone——

MARION: And if his students are anything like the two specimens I saw here to-night, then they're not worth bothering about——

MRS. LINDEN: And the University doesn't even want him here any longer—(*specially to* JEAN)—so there you are.

JEAN: I'm not arguing against you.

MRS. LINDEN: No, but you're looking as if you might like to—as if —as if something was wrong, though you didn't quite know what.

JEAN: I've told you—this is one night when I don't find it easy to make up my mind—so leave me out of it.

REX (*who has been busy setting the table*): Well, that's all set. Dinah's right. What the Linden family needs is an hour or two of *Black Sam*—cheating and all. Where are these cards and counters? (*He begins to take one or two upright chairs to the table.*)

DINAH *now enters, carrying a box of counters, closing door behind her. She moves slowly and looks distressed.*

Well, here are the counters, eh?

DINAH: Yes.

MARION: Can't father find the cards?

DINAH (*tonelessly*): Yes, he's found them.

REX: What's the matter?

DINAH (*her face working, distressed*): I peeped into the dining-room as I came past. He didn't see me. He was just standing, holding the cards, staring at nothing. (*She gives a little sob. More distressed now.*) It was just as if I hadn't noticed him properly before. Suddenly —he looked so old—and tired—and so much by himself—as if everything was wrong and nobody cared—that I couldn't bear it—— (*She gives a sob.*)

MRS. LINDEN (*soothingly*): Now, Dinah——

DINAH (*urgently*): It isn't *Now Dinah* at all. Nothing to do with it.

MRS. LINDEN (*sharper now*): Now don't be stupid——

DINAH: I'm not being stupid. (*Looking at them, slowly.*) He's so sweet—and it's his birthday—and he was so pleased when he knew everybody was coming—(*with sudden anger*) and you're all whispering and plotting—and it seems so bloody mean——

MRS. LINDEN (*angrily*): Dinah, I won't have you talking like that.

JEAN (*very sharply*): Why shouldn't she if she feels like that?

MRS. LINDEN: Please mind your own business, Jean.

JEAN (*crossing to Dinah, who is crying*): This is my business.

Puts her arms round DINAH, who collapses against her.

All right, Dinah darling. You've said it now. All over.

DINAH (*muffled against JEAN*): I'm sorry. I don't know why I said it. But it was seeing him like that.

REX (*at table*): Look—turn this up, everybody. He'll be back any moment. Snap out of it, Dinah. Let's have the counters.

She gives them to him, and he pours them on the table, preparing to count them into heaps. With loud cheerful tone.

Do you remember that time up in Cumberland when the farmer came in from next door and we made him play *Black Sam* with us?

DINAH (*eagerly*): I can remember that, though I was too little to play. He had a huge whiskery sort of nose——

REX (*chuckling*): He was left with *Black Sam* every time——

MARION (*eagerly*): And he was so furious—do you remember, Jean?

JEAN (*beginning to laugh*): Yes, what did he use to say?

REX (*quoting, in Northern accent*): "Well, lay me aht an' bury me, Ah've got dom' thing again——"

DINAH (*laughing*): And then something happened to his collar, didn't it?

JEAN (*laughing*): Yes—yes—it suddenly *popped*——

MARION (*laughing*): I know—I nearly died—the stud went——

REX (*quoting again, uproariously*): And he said "Sitha, tha's Black Sammed me clean aht o' me collar——"

As they laugh, in the way families do at their special jokes, PROFESSOR enters, carrying box of playing cards. He lights up when he hears their laughter, which is reminiscent of their young days.

PROFESSOR (*smiling*): What's the joke?

REX (*still laughing*): That time—up in Cumberland—when the farmer played *Black Sam*——

PROFESSOR (*beginning to laugh*): Oh yes—Joe Sykes—and he burst out of his collar—and he swore to me afterwards that you were all cheating——

REX (*laughing harder than ever*): *But I was—I was——*

Here all the children give a yell. But suddenly MRS. LINDEN *has stopped laughing, and has turned her face away. As the laughter dies down.*

PROFESSOR (*to his wife*): What's the matter, my dear?

MRS. LINDEN (*turned away, muffled tone*): No—it's nothing—don't bother——

They have all stopped laughing now, and glance curiously at her,

PROFESSOR: All right. Well, let's play, shall we?

MRS. LINDEN: No. I mean—you all play, of course. But I don't want to.

MARION: What is it, Mother?

MRS. LINDEN: I suddenly felt awful—hearing you all laughing again—and remembering what fun we used to have. Oh—I went back long before that holiday in Cumberland—to other holidays and times—to when you were all very little—and before that—when everything was beginning for us. (*She looks rather defiantly at her husband.*) I don't know what you tell those students of yours, Robert. But I'd like to tell them something—the truth, for once—the real truth.

PROFESSOR (*gravely*): And what's that, Isabel?

MRS. LINDEN *now speaks with great sincerity and feeling, with a certain magnificence of manner.*

MRS. LINDEN: That everything just gets worse and worse—and it's time we stopped pretending it doesn't. Oh—I'm not just thinking about being short of things and having rations and queuing up. But when we were young—up to 1914—the world was sensible and safe and kind—and even if people didn't have much money, they had most of the things they wanted. They could be happy in a simple easy way—because life seemed good. Oh—the very roads and the grass and the trees and the lilac in spring were different then, and you could notice and enjoy everything, and be quiet and peaceful. And then afterwards—after those years of great black casualty lists every day—it was never the same again—never the same. But it wasn't too bad—we still didn't know all the horrors and the cruelties and the miseries—and you could go away for real holidays—and the children were such fun. But then everything got worse and worse—and look at us now, just look at us—with only a few years more and all the colour and fun and life gone for ever—I tell you, it's heart-breaking——

DINAH (*eagerly*): Oh, Mother, you're not fair. It's just because you're not interested, so you make it all seem dull and grey to yourself. It's all terribly exciting, really, and sometimes I lie awake at night—and think—and wonder—and can hardly bear it——

MRS. LINDEN (*harshly*): No, Dinah, you don't understand what I'm talking about—you're too young—much too young——

PROFESSOR: Yes, she's too young to understand what *you* feel. But she's given you the answer, just because she *is* young. And what am I to tell my students? That because I'm getting old and weary, they mustn't believe the very blood that's beating in their veins?

MARION: But there are such things as standards, Father. And mother's quite right——

JEAN (*contemptuously*): What—just because she's talking like any elderly member of a decayed middle class?

MRS. LINDEN (*angrily*): Oh—don't talk that pompous inhuman rubbish to me, Jean. I'm being real now. I'm not quoting books but talking about real life—and what I feel here—(*indicating her heart*).

PROFESSOR: Some things are worse, some things are better. And the sun will shine for Dinah to-morrow, my love, as it once shone for you, forty years ago—the same sun. And young families are still laughing somewhere at old farmers who burst their collars. And while there's time to lose the world, Rex, there's also time to save it—if we really want to save it. And there's also time—and of course it might be the last, you never know—for a Linden family game of *Black Sam*. Give us our counters, Rex—that's your job—(*He has now taken the cards out of the case*) while the old man, with his patience, shuffles the cards. Patience . . . patience . . . and shuffle the cards. . . .

> He is now shuffling the cards, REX is distributing the counters in heaps, while the others begin to sit round.

SLOW CURTAIN

ACT II

SCENE I

The scene as before, but it is afternoon again, with mild sunlight coming through the window. MARION, JEAN, EDITH WESTMORE *and* BERNARD FAWCETT *are all standing about, having a heated and noisy argument. Door is open and through it we hear* MRS. LINDEN *and* REX *occasionally calling to each other, with a good deal of movement and bumping, and also we can hear, fragmentarily,* DINAH *practising bits of the 'cello part of Elgar's 'Cello Concerto. It is altogether a noisy messy sort of scene.*

FAWCETT (*an aggressive debater*): How do you make that out? Just tell me that. How do you make that out?

EDITH (*heatedly*): It's your business to make it out, as you call it. Not ours. (*Appealing to* MARION, *her ally.*) Isn't it?

MARION (*nearly as heated as they are*): Of course it is. They think they can come along with any piffling little argument against religion, and that we have to reply, when the best minds of the last two thousand years——

JEAN (*cooler than the other three*): Wait a minute, Marion. We really can't swallow that.

FAWCETT (*disgusted*): Of course we can't. Lot o' tripe, that's all. Yes, tripe!

JEAN (*louder now*): The best minds have always been fighting the Churches tooth and nail. Just as they are to-day. And for the same old reason——

FAWCETT (*triumphantly*): Exactly—the same old reason——

REX (*off, but near door, calling*): What do you say, Mother? I know—but there's a hell of a row going on down here——

MRS. LINDEN (*off, distant, calling*): It's in the dining-room. *Din-ing Room!*

REX (*calling*): Okay! I'll go and look.

MARION: Yes, and what is the reason?

EDITH (*backing her up*): We know what it is. It's simply not to have any real moral responsibility——

MARION: To do what you like. And then you wonder why you're all so miserable——

255

Fawcett (*shouting*): Who said we're miserable? Were people any better off when they had Inquisitions and had to buy pardons and keep thousands of lazy priests and monks——

Edith: How do *you* know they were lazy?

Marion: And anyhow people *were* better off. First, the scientists want to be free of religion, and now when they've invented atom bombs and think we'll all blow ourselves to bits with them, they're telling us it's a pity there's no religion——

Jean: No, they're not, if they've any sense. What they're asking for is a properly planned and controlled world——

Fawcett: Which you lot couldn't give us anyhow, and have done your best to stop——

Marion: How can you plan and control without any real authority to guide you? That's where the Church comes in——

Edith: And if people don't worship God, then they'll worship the devil——

Fawcett (*jeering*): Superstition! Dope! That's all you're giving us.

Marion (*annoyed*): Don't be so loutish.

Fawcett (*to* Jean): There you are, you see. Bad temper now.

Edith (*angrily*): Well, you started it.

Rex (*calling, as before*): Are you sure it's a *brown* one. There's a *green* one here, that's all.

Mrs. Linden (*as before*): No, darling—the *brown* one.

Rex (*calling*): And what about this basket thing? Do you really want it?

Jean (*who apparently started earlier*): Just a little elementary psychology is what I'd suggest. And somatic medical treatment too.

Edith: What about them? Are they supposed to explain everything—what we're doing here at all, for instance——

Fawcett: Well, can you explain that?

Marion: We can make a better shot at it than you people can.

Jean: But don't you see that that kind of question is idiotic?

Edith: No, I don't. It's what I've always wanted to know—ever since I can remember——

Jean: Yes, of course it's a *child's* question—and that's all it is. We can explain how we came to be what we are—what physical and social forces——

Marion (*crossly*): Oh—never mind about physical and social

forces—they don't give the answer—they only explain how things work——

JEAN: Well, that's the only explanation that's sensible and necessary.

EDITH (*shouting*): No, it isn't.

JEAN (*haughtily*): I'll be much obliged if you won't shout at me like that.

FAWCETT: Can't face the argument. All alike.

EDITH (*to him*): Oh—you shut up! (*To* JEAN.) I'm sorry—I won't shout any more—but it always annoys me when people talk like that. Knowing how a thing works isn't knowing what it's for.

MARION: Exactly—and that's the mistake they all make——

JEAN: There's no *exactly* about it. Reality can't be *for* anything. It just *is*. You're talking out-of-date metaphysics—and don't even know it—that's your trouble.

MARION (*hotly*): And your trouble is—you're so ridiculously conceited——

FAWCETT (*insufferably*): Now—now—now—now!

MARION (*turning on him*): Really—you're *insufferable*. Please be quiet.

> *Enter* MRS. COTTON, *if anything odder than in the previous Act. She is smoking a cigarette and carrying a cup of tea.*

MRS. COTTON: 'Avin' a proper argy-bargy in 'ere, aren't you? Losing your tempers too, some of yer. (*To* JEAN *and* MARION.) Your tea'll be ready soon. Dining-room. Packed up to go?

MARION: Yes. At least I have.

JEAN: So have I.

MRS. COTTON: Your mother's makin' a proper job of it—an' keepin' Mr. Rex on the run all right. Yer'd think she was goin' for good, the way she's throwin' things about—never saw such a mess upstairs—every drawer out of every chest. All gone straight to 'er 'ead. Excitement. I knew it would. '*Im* comin'. I'd 'ave bin just the same.

> *Sits on edge of chair, takes a sip of tea, and looks at the others cynically.*

Well, get on with the argument. Don't let me stop yer. I like a bit of ding-dong.

MARION: No, I think we've had enough.

MRS. COTTON: My 'usband wouldn't say more than ten words for two or three days, then 'e'd 'ave two or three bottles o' stout an' argue the point about anything—shout you down too. I used to grumble but I wish to God 'e'd come in now an' start shoutin' me down again—an' you too——

FAWCETT (*grinning*): Perhaps we wouldn't let him.

MRS. COTTON (*with contempt*): 'E'd 'ave told you to run away an' play——

EDITH *giggles.* FAWCETT *is annoyed.*

FAWCETT: Here, wait a minute——

MRS. COTTON: What for? (*To* JEAN.) Who's this Cass Als?

JEAN: Cass Als?

MRS. COTTON: That's right. Dinah come 'ome like a mad thing early this afternoon an' she shouts "Mrs. Cotton. Isn't it wonderful? I met a man at my lesson who used to know Cass Als".

MARION: Oh—she means Casals—the great 'cellist——

MRS. COTTON: That'll be 'im. Nearly off 'er 'ead with excitement 'cos she'd met a man who knew 'im. What it is to be young an' silly. She started practisin' right off then. Proper mad thing. Not knowin' what's in store. I was the same about Fox Trots, years an' years ago, when they'd just started—mad on Fox Trots—couldn't think about work or eatin' or sleepin' for Fox Trots . . . even the name sounds dam' silly now. (*Suddenly, to* EDITH.) What are you mad on?

EDITH (*startled*): I don't know really——

MRS. COTTON: I'll bet yer don't. (*To* JEAN.) Well, what about gettin' on with the Brains Trust 'ere? Not quite time for your tea yet, even though yer are 'avin' it early. What's the subject?

JEAN (*amused*): A good old favourite. Science versus Religion.

MRS. COTTON: Never fancied either of 'em really. 'Ad a sister that went religious, chapel, and an uncle that was a bit on the scientific side—insecks, chiefly——

REX *appears at door. He is in his shirt-sleeves, carrying a suitcase in one hand, and a woman's coat and various oddments in the other. He has a cigarette, unlit, in his mouth, and looks rather ruffled.*

REX: Put a light to this cigarette, somebody, please.

FAWCETT *goes up to him, with lighter. He speaks now to* JEAN *and* MARION.

MARION: Well, we're not really debating chapels versus insects.

REX: Thanks, old boy. Helping mother pack is no joke. (*Looking at them all.*) You look a queer gang in here. Mrs. Cotton, do you know anything about a little travelling clock?

MRS. COTTON: No, I don't.

REX: Neither do I.

JEAN: I believe it's in my room. Shall I go——

REX: No, I'm going up——

Goes out. During all this scraps of 'cello playing, often repeating same passage, have been heard, with breaks. It continues now, though not heard above dialogue clearly.

EDITH (*rather shyly*): But—in a way—it *is* chapels versus insects. I mean, *they* (*indicating* JEAN *and* FAWCETT) talk as if we were only a superior sort of insect——

FAWCETT (*impatiently*): Oh—don't start all that old stuff. Nobody's ever said anything of the sort.

MARION: No, you don't *say* it. But that's what you mean.

JEAN: No, we don't. The point is, if we study insect life, we know *exactly* what we're doing——

EDITH (*sharply*): And we know what we're doing in chapels and churches——

MARION: We're behaving like spiritual beings——

FAWCETT: Or like superstitious savages——

EDITH (*angrily*): Do savages have chapels and churches?

MARION: It's just savages who don't. And now they're turning themselves into savages again——

JEAN: On the contrary, we're using our reason and knowledge of scientific method——

MARION (*loudly*): To blow everything and everybody to bits——

MRS. COTTON: 'Ere, 'ere.

JEAN (*to* MARION, *angrily*): Chiefly encouraged by *your* precious Church——

MARION (*angrily*): That's simply not true——

FAWCETT (*rudely*): Yes of course it is——

MARION (*angrily*): No it isn't—and I'm not talking to you——

FAWCETT (*loudly*): You can't reason with 'em. They won't listen to it.

MRS. COTTON (*top of her voice*): Go on, our side. Chapels versus Insecks (*she laughs*).

EDITH (*to* FAWCETT): If you'd just be quiet a minute and not interrupt——

FAWCETT (*overlapping with her*): Why should I be quiet? I've as much right to talk as you.

MARION (*angrily, overlapping too*): Because you don't understand what we're talking about. You're not arguing, you're just shouting——

260 J. B. PRIESTLEY

JEAN (*very loud, overlapping*): Well, I know what I'm talking about. I've had all this out years ago——

EDITH (*cutting in*): That doesn't make any difference. It doesn't prove you're right, does it?

JEAN (*together with* MARION, *as below*): I say, we used to talk this stuff for hours when I was in college, years ago——

MARION (*together with* JEAN, *as above*): No, but Jean always did know it all, and now she's a doctor, of course, naturally——

PROFESSOR LINDEN *has entered, and his voice cuts them off.*

PROFESSOR (*loudly*): Just a minute!

They are quiet, attentive to him. He speaks quietly now.

Listen to Dinah——

The door is open behind him, and now we hear quite clearly, though at some distance, the 'cello playing the rich melancholy second subject of the First Movement of the Elgar Concerto. They are all very still. The music dies away. Short pause.

MARION (*quietly*): What is that?

PROFESSOR: First Movement of the Elgar Concerto. I didn't know Dinah was doing the Elgar. She must have just started.

MRS. COTTON (*softly*): It sounds a sad piece.

PROFESSOR (*quietly*): Yes, it is. A kind of long farewell. An elderly man remembers his world before the war of 1914, some of it years and years before perhaps—being a boy at Worcester—or Germany in the 'Nineties—long days on the Malvern Hills—smiling Edwardian afternoons—Maclaren and Ranji batting at Lords, then Richter or Nikisch at the Queen's Hall—all gone, gone, lost for ever—and so he distils his tenderness and regret, drop by drop, and seals the sweet melancholy in a Concerto for 'cello. And he goes, too, where all the old green sunny days and the twinkling nights went—gone, gone. But then what happens? Why, a little miracle. You heard it.

JEAN (*softly*): Dinah playing?

PROFESSOR: Why yes. Young Dinah Linden, all youth, all eagerness, saying hello and not farewell to anything, who knows and cares nothing about Bavaria in the 'Nineties or the secure and golden Edwardian afternoons, here in Burmanley, this very afternoon, the moment we stop shouting at each other, unseals for us the precious distillation, uncovers the tenderness and regret, which are ours now as well as his, and our lives and Elgar's, Burmanley to-day and the Malvern Hills in a lost sunlight, are all magically intertwined. . . .

MRS. COTTON (*to the others, proudly*): When he likes, the Professor's a lovely talker.

PROFESSOR: That settles me. But that theme, you know—(*hums it a moment*) you can tell at once it's a farewell to long-lost summer afternoons. It's got a deep drowsy summerishness that belongs to everybody's youth—it's telling you quite plainly that now there aren't any such afternoons—the sun's never as hot, the grass as thick, the shade as deep and drowsy—and where are the bumble bees? God help me—I haven't seen a hammock for years and years and years. I must tell Dinah. (*Half turns, then checks himself.*) No, no, that'll keep. (*To the students.*) What are you two doing here? What about that meeting?

FAWCETT: We came to tell you. It's been cancelled.

EDITH: So as we had no other subject for this week's essay, we thought we'd better tell you at once.

PROFESSOR (*thoughtfully*): I see.

MARION (*to* MRS. COTTON): What about tea? I'll help.

MRS. COTTON: Come on then.

They go out together. PROFESSOR *looks at students.*

PROFESSOR: You're probably both going to the Union show to-night aren't you?

They nod and murmur "Yes".

Would it be a nuisance for you to slip in here afterwards? It wouldn't? Then do that, please. So off you go. And I'm sorry you had to wait.

PROFESSOR *goes to door,* FAWCETT *following. But* EDITH *looks at* JEAN.

EDITH (*humbly*): Dr. Linden—I hope I didn't sound rude when we were all arguing. Bernard always makes me lose my temper when he attacks religion.

JEAN (*smiling*): No, I didn't mind.

PROFESSOR (*as* EDITH *moves up*): High time you lost your temper, Miss Westmore. Pity I missed that. (*Confidentially.*) I lost my temper this morning, up at the University offices. Well, perhaps I shall see you to-night——

He is now ushering the students through the door. JEAN *lights a cigarette.* PROFESSOR *returns, closing door.*

JEAN: *Did* you lose your temper, this morning?

PROFESSOR (*with satisfaction*): I did. I raised merry hell. I told them they couldn't get rid of me simply by remembering we're supposed to have an age-limit.

JEAN: So you think it's all over and done with

PROFESSOR (*eyeing her*): Don't you?

JEAN (*softly*): No I don't.

Goes nearer to him.

PROFESSOR: I ought to write a letter or two.

JEAN (*now closer, softly*): They can wait a minute, Dad. And we're alone. Nobody listening. You can tell me. I'm not one of the *Get-Him-Out-Of-Here* party.

PROFESSOR: Who is—or are—members of it?

JEAN (*still softly*): Mother. Rex. Marion. Now confess, Dad, it's not all as easy as you pretended, is it?

PROFESSOR (*with elaborate whisper*): No—it isn't. Between ourselves, of course (*then in quite ordinary tone*). Nevertheless, I'll settle it all right. Actually the battle's not over—may be going on now. And I must write those notes—that wasn't an excuse not to talk. (*Going to desk or work table, to write.*) Lidley probably imagines from my grumpy manner that I haven't any friends round here. He's wrong. I still have a few. And his own position isn't as strong as he thinks, unless he has a string or two to pull that I don't know about. He may have, of course. (*Sitting down now, to begin writing.*) These notes are part of the campaign, otherwise I wouldn't bother about 'em now.

He begins writing swiftly. JEAN *watches him for a moment or two, very thoughtfully. She opens her mouth as if to speak, then checks herself.*

Yes?

JEAN: Nothing.

PROFESSOR (*still writing*): I thought you wanted to say something. If so, please say it. As Rex keeps telling us, there isn't much time.

JEAN (*after slight hesitation*): I may be conceited—people keep saying so—but—well, I know you're a very wise old bird, Dad, and you always understood me best. . . .

PROFESSOR (*looking up, putting pipe in*): So?

JEAN: What's the matter with me?

PROFESSOR (*lighting his pipe*): Not very much. Otherwise, you couldn't be doing the job you are doing.

JEAN: But there *is* something. *I* know that.

PROFESSOR (*coolly*): Feeling miserable, aren't you?

JEAN: Yes. And hating myself.

PROFESSOR (*calmly*): That's the trouble. You're resenting your own emotions. You're annoyed with yourself for being a woman. Quite wrong. After all, there's no escape from that. This man you're in love with.—Perhaps he isn't worth it. And you'll have to get over him. I don't know—and don't much want to. But just remember, you're a young woman, with a hundred thousand other women among your ancestors—and all the medical degrees in the world don't change that fact—and don't try to pretend to yourself you're a termite queen or a creature from Mars or something. Because you have to attend to bewildered sick women who perhaps enjoy their emotions— luxuriate in 'em—you refuse to give your own an inch of rope. And then they tear back at you like having a wounded cat inside you.

JEAN: Just about. But what can I do?

PROFESSOR: Buy a bottle of gin. Sit up with a girl friend. Split the bottle, tell everything, have a dam' good cry—and enjoy every minute of it. Then start again, on a better basis.

JEAN: For myself, you mean?

PROFESSOR: For yourself, and for the rest of us. Don't demand a world as efficient, sterilised and scientific as an operating theatre. We couldn't live in it if we got it. Don't confuse science with life. It's an abstraction—neat and quick, to get certain things done. That's all. Even if the bath water's distilled and heated to just the right temperature, it's still the baby that's important. Messy things too, babies. Always will be. You won't mind too much when it's yours.

JEAN: Let's have a long talk next time, Dad.

PROFESSOR (*beginning to write again, quickly*): Yes, come up here alone, as soon as you can.

JEAN: But, Dad—I think I ought to warn you.

PROFESSOR (*still writing*): Yes?

JEAN: Mother's more serious than you think.

PROFESSOR (*glancing up*): She needs a change badly, of course. Burmanley's been a bit too much for her lately, I know. Don't blame her.

JEAN: It's gone further than you think.

PROFESSOR (*looking at her now, quietly*): You believe that, do you?

Enter MARION, *holding door open.*

MARION: Tea's in.

JEAN (*moving*): I'm coming.

PROFESSOR (*writing*): Early, isn't it?

MARION: Yes, but we shall be starting soon. But mother said you needn't bother. She's having hers now, and she said she wanted to talk to you.

JEAN *has now gone.*

PROFESSOR: There—or here?

MARION: Here, I imagine. (*Hesitates a moment, drifting in a little.*) I hated that silly noisy argument we had this afternoon.

PROFESSOR (*still writing*): You made a hell of a row about it.

MARION: What's the matter with everybody here?

PROFESSOR: All kinds of things.

MARION: No, I mean—why are you all so completely materialistic now?

He looks up at her questioningly. She continues, with more warmth. As if nothing on earth mattered but production—and exports—and what people earned——

PROFESSOR (*mildly*): We have to live, you know. And being poorer than we used to be, it's more of a problem.

MARION: But that's not all there is in life.

PROFESSOR: Not a bit. Only the start of it. The mechanics so to speak.

MARION: But it's all you seem to care about now. No, not you—yourself.

PROFESSOR: I know. Not me, but everybody else. Remember the miracle of the loaves and fishes——?

MARION: Yes, of course.

PROFESSOR: Materialistic?

MARION: No, that's quite different.

PROFESSOR: The idea's the same. Spread it out and give everybody a fair share. It's never been done before, you know, not in a whole large society. Oh—there's been colour, grace, culture, philosophy, nobly spiritual lives—but always with a lot of poor devils, whole masses of people, left clean out, slogging away in the dark, ignored, forgotten. Is it materialistic and sordid not to ignore and forget them, to bring them all out into the light, to take their share?

MARION: Yes, but to talk and think about nothing else——

PROFESSOR (*jumping up*): Wrong, yes. I keep saying so. But give us a chance, my dear Marion. Call us drab and dismal, if you like, and tell us we don't know how to cook our food or wear our clothes—but for Heaven's sake, recognise that we're trying to do something that is as extraordinary and wonderful as it's difficult—to have a revolution for once without the Terror, without looting mobs and secret police, sudden arrests, mass suicides and executions, without setting in motion that vast pendulum of violence which can decimate three generations before it comes to a standstill. We're fighting in the last ditch of our civilisation. If we win through, everybody wins through. Why—bless my soul!—Marion——

He is leading her to the window now, then pointing:

Look—you see that flat-footed dough-faced fellow . . . slouching along there——

MARION (*half-laughing*): Yes. And I suppose he's the ordinary British citizen—the hero of the world——

PROFESSOR (*with sudden change of manner*): That's what I'd hoped, but actually I see it's poor Atherfield, our professor of physics, who took some bull-headed wrong line of his own upon the isotypes of uranium, or whatever it was—and so missed his place on the atomic band-wagon. If we're all blown to smithereens, he won't have contributed anything to the explosion—and the poor chap's heartbroken. But I must post my letters.

He hurries back to his desk or table and is putting letters in envelopes.

Enter MRS. LINDEN, *she is dressed ready for travelling, but not wearing a hat or heavy coat.*

MRS. LINDEN: Oh, there you are Marion. Do go and finish your tea. Rex wants to start in half an hour.

MARION: All right, Mother, don't fuss, I'm quite ready.

Exit MARION. MRS. LINDEN *looks at the* PROFESSOR *steadily. He looks at her, then slowly rises, the letters in his hand.*

MRS. LINDEN: Did you hear anything more this afternoon, Robert?

PROFESSOR: No, my love. I have an idea that Lidley's busy with my protest at this very moment. Alfred Lockhart told me there might be some sort of meeting this evening. So I might have news later to-night.

MRS. LINDEN (*gravely*): You know what I think about it.

PROFESSOR: Yes. That even if they wanted me to, I'd be a fool to stay on. And as some of 'em don't want me, as I have to fight to keep my job, I'm out of my senses to stay. Right?

MRS. LINDEN (*sits down*): Yes. And Rex—and Marion—and even Jean, I think—agree with me.

PROFESSOR (*easily*): Well, they could be wrong too. (*Pause, looks at her.*) I don't enjoy not having you on my side in this, you know, Isabel.

MRS. LINDEN (*sharply*): And do you think I enjoy it? I hate it. I hate it. But they never really liked you here—that's what you've never understood. It never was your place. I knew it—and you ought to have known it. All this is just another reason why I'm glad to go.

Professor (*lightly*): You've had a particularly difficult time lately, I know, my dear. A change will do you good. Rex, who understands these things much better than I do, will see that you enjoy yourself. I'm glad you're going. When you come back, my little quarrel with Lidley and his set will be over, I hope—and we'll try to find some more help for the house.

Mrs. Linden: I'm not coming back.

Professor (*stares at her*): You don't mean that.

Mrs. Linden: Robert, I mean every word of it. I'm not coming back. I'm leaving Burmanley for ever.

Professor: Never mind Burmanley. You're leaving *me*.

Mrs. Linden: I'm not leaving you. That's the point.

Professor: I don't see it.

Mrs. Linden (*with more urgency now*): It's quite simple, Robert. You ought to retire—and you've been told to. There's nothing to keep us here. We can live with Rex for a time—he's very anxious that we should, and he can well afford to have us as his guests. Afterwards, if necessary, we can find a little place of our own. Everybody agrees that this is what we ought to do. It's perfectly obvious. But suddenly you've decided to be obstinate. *You* want to stay on here. But what about me? Have you ever thought about me?

Professor: I tried to, Isabel. And I realise it's not easy for you——

Mrs. Linden (*urgently*): I never liked Burmanley from the first, but of course I put up with it—for your sake, always hoping that we'd soon be able to go somewhere else. During these last few years, with the older children away, with most of our friends dead or gone, with no proper help in the house, with all the rationing and queueing and drab misery, I've loathed every single day. And always I've been longing and praying for this time to come—when you'd have to retire—when we'd done with Burmanley for ever. Rex knew what I felt—he's always understood——

Professor (*lightly, but with underlying gravity*): Rex the Tempter—it's a part that suits him—offering you breakfast in bed at Huntingdon House—then Bond Street—a nice little lunch somewhere—a theatre —a little bridge——

Mrs. Linden (*warmly*): All right. And why not? Rex and I understand each other, always have done. And if he offers me those things—yes, and having my hair done properly—and looking at silly

illustrated weeklies—and having a good woman's gossip—and sometimes spending money foolishly—and being nicely looked after——

PROFESSOR (*not sneering*): Is that what you've always really wanted?

MRS. LINDEN: No, it isn't, except somewhere at the back of my
mind, like most women. What I've wanted is what I've had—looking
after you and the children—keeping this house going—trying to plan
good holidays for us all. And when it had to be done, I did it—and
did it gladly. But it hasn't to be done any more. And now I don't
want to spend another day in this hateful place——

PROFESSOR (*in wondering melancholy tone*): Hateful? Hateful? It's
just a city—full of people working, trying to get along—not very
different from us. Hateful?

MRS. LINDEN (*almost tearful now*): I don't mean I've never been
happy here. It was different at first. But it's hateful now—grey,
dismal—with a stupid shabby sort of life—all meaningless to me—so
that sometimes I've felt like a wretched ghost. You've had your work
—your students——

PROFESSOR: Yes, yes—I know it's easier for me—quite different.
But——

MRS. LINDEN (*tearful, though not crying*): And soon I shall be
sixty—all my life gone—Rex in London—Marion far away in France.
And I tell you I hate this drab gloomy world we've made. Rex is
right—the only thing to do is to laugh at it and then forget it. And
now he's been here again—and talked so much—Marion too—if they
went and left me here, I feel I'd die of misery——

As she almost breaks down, he crosses to comfort her.

PROFESSOR (*comfortably, as he crosses*): My dear, I'm sorry you
feel like this—I know it's been hard——

When he is about to touch her, she waves him away.

MRS. LINDEN (*checking her emotion*): No, Robert, please! Let
me say what I want to say. I'll be quite calm.

*She makes an effort. He steps back. Then she speaks fairly
quietly and firmly.*

No, I'm not leaving you. I'm leaving Burmanley. And I'm doing it
for your sake as well as for my own. I've tried to persuade you—so
have the children—and now I'm doing the only thing that I think
may make you behave sensibly. But I mean what I say. I'm going
and I'm not coming back. If you stay here, Robert, you'll stay here
alone—and I don't think you'll want to do that very long—thank
goodness!

As he stands stiffly, she pleads a little.

Robert, please! This isn't a quarrel. I'm not leaving *you*.

PROFESSOR (*gravely*): I think you are. A man stays where his work is, and the woman stays with the man.

MRS. LINDEN: And I did it for thirty-seven years. But you're no longer a man who has his work.

PROFESSOR (*bitterly*): That's the most damnably hurting thing you've ever said to me.

MRS. LINDEN: I'm sorry, Robert. I didn't say it to hurt you. But it's true—and you're hurting yourself because you won't admit it.

Enter REX, *wearing an overcoat but no hat. He looks sharply at his parents, but takes an easy tone.*

REX: Sorry to barge in. But I'd like to get off in about ten minutes. I've put most of the stuff in the car. Want to be alone?

MRS. LINDEN (*rather wearily*): No, it doesn't matter now. Come in, darling.

PROFESSOR *goes over to the window and looks out, standing stiffly.* REX *and* MRS. LINDEN *exchange a look, then she rises and they meet. He takes her arm and pats her hand with his other hand, affectionately. She smiles rather sadly at him.*

DINAH (*off, just outside, surprised*): But I didn't know you were going so soon.

MARION (*calling, further off*): In a few minutes.

DINAH (*off, as before*): Gosh!—I don't really know what's happening about this family.

JEAN (*further off, calling*): Has anybody seen my little red bag?

DINAH (*calling*): I'll have a look for it.

We hear her moving off whistling, the door being wide open. MRS. LINDEN *gently releases herself from* REX, *pulling herself together, but stands near him.* MARION *enters, ready to go, and looking very smart. She glances at her father's back, and then exchanges meaning glances with her mother and* REX.

MARION (*softly*): Dad—I hoped mother would have persuaded you to come with us.

PROFESSOR (*after turning, quietly*): Well, she hasn't, Marion. She tells me she's leaving Burmanley for good.

MARION: I know. And I think she's right. There's nothing for her here.

PROFESSOR: Except me. And some work still to be done.

MARION: I don't see that, Father. You needn't stay.

REX (*cheerfully*): They don't even want you to——

PROFESSOR (*sharply*): Rex—I've heard enough of that to-day.

REX (*who sees he is hurt*): Sorry, Dad. I didn't mean——

PROFESSOR (*cutting in, curtly*): All right.

MRS. LINDEN: If your father felt he was behaving sensibly, he wouldn't be so touchy. But he knows he isn't. I do think he's behaving with ridiculous obstinacy.

PROFESSOR: Quite possibly what I do may not be very important, but I want to keep straight on doing it. I don't believe this is simply personal vanity—an elderly man not wanting to be put on the shelf. Although even now I don't fancy being one of the passengers, I'd rather be with the crew.

REX: Is that one for me?

MARION: *And* me?

MRS. LINDEN: Well, if it is, it's absurd. Why shouldn't Rex——

PROFESSOR (*cutting in*): This isn't an attack on Rex. Or on anybody else. You all seem to think I'm unreasonable and I'm trying to explain myself. After all we've heard during the past twenty-four hours, we know by this time that Burmanley's a gloomy, shabby hole that nobody but an old fool would want to do any work in. And why work anyhow if you needn't? That's been the line. And it doesn't appeal to me. I don't like the sound of it. There's death in it, some-where. Down these fancy side turnings, although there seems more fun and colour and light that way, there are dead ends. I don't want to walk away from real life, give it up as a bad job. It's a pity just now that it's got a pinched look, frayed cuffs and down-at-heel shoes—whereas some coffins have satin linings—but I prefer to stay with it and help a bit if I can——

MARION: I don't see what this has got to do with anything we've said.

MRS. LINDEN: And neither do I. And I don't believe it has. Has it, Rex?

She looks appealingly at REX, *who does not reply but appears rather embarrassed.*

PROFESSOR (*grimly*): Well—Rex?

REX *finally shrugs his shoulders.*

My dear, your son is much too intelligent to reassure you.

MRS. LINDEN (*sharply*): Too good-mannered, you mean.

PROFESSOR (*sharply*): His manners are excellent. I wish mine were half as good. But—if you will have it—what I *do* mean is that the whole lot of you, except young Dinah, are now busy turning away from life, giving it up. The Lindens are leaving the mucky old high road. And somebody's got to stay.

Enter DINAH *and* JEAN. *The latter is ready for travelling.*

DINAH: Mrs. Cotton's *furious* because she says somebody's taken her tin of soap flakes.

PROFESSOR (*taking his letters*): I must post these at the corner.

DINAH: I'll take them.

PROFESSOR (*beginning to move*): No, thanks. I'm letting off steam. Better finish it off outside.

He goes out hastily. There is at once a certain slackening of tension.

JEAN (*to* REX): Have I time to telephone to London?

REX: You have, but I wouldn't advise it. We'll make a stop on the road.

MRS. LINDEN: Dinah darling, how would you like to come to London? We could probably arrange for you to go to the Royal College or the Academy of Music.

DINAH (*excited*): And concerts! Wow! Of course that would be marvellous! But what's happening? Are we all going now? I haven't packed—or anything.

JEAN (*rather heavily*): No, we're not. Dad isn't going. (*To her mother.*) Is he?

MRS. LINDEN (*rather sharply*): No, he's not. And I was just going to explain that, Jean, if you hadn't interrupted.

JEAN (*pointedly*): I'm glad.

MRS. LINDEN: Don't interfere, please Jean.

JEAN: I'm not going to.

REX: Look, chaps—drop this. We'll be off in a minute——

MRS. LINDEN (*turning to* DINAH): Your father's staying here—at least for the time being, though in my opinion he won't be here very long, even if the University doesn't insist upon his resignation. And I think they will, although he pretends they won't.

DINAH: Then I shall stay too. Daddy couldn't be here all by himself. Besides, I like it here, really. (*Looks at them all rather accusingly.*) What's been happening? Have you been saying things to him?

REX (*with grin*): No, he's been saying things to us.

DINAH: Oh—that's all right, then. (*Looks anxiously at her mother.*) Do you think I'll be able to manage Mrs. Cotton?

MRS. LINDEN: Well, I never could.

DINAH: No, I'm better at her than you.

MARION (*worried*): Mother—I know I agreed it was the best thing to do—but—well, Dinah and Mrs. Cotton—I can't help feeling worried, you know—now that——

JEAN (*cutting in*): I should think so, too.

MRS. LINDEN: If I thought for a moment it was going to last, of course I'd agree with you. But it won't. And it's the only way. I told him plainly what I felt—but in his present mood I was just wasting my time. It really is the only way.

DINAH: What is? What's this all about?

REX (*as his mother doesn't reply*): About Dad staying on here——

DINAH: Oh—we'll manage all right—you'll see——

> *Enter* MRS. COTTON, *in a grim searching mood.* DINAH *turns and sees her.*

Mrs. Cotton—you and I can manage this house somehow, can't we—and look after the Professor?

MRS. COTTON: Yes, we can. Manage better. (*Looks grim and searchingly at* MARION). Wasn't it you that was drying some smalls on the cistern this morning?

MARION (*taken aback*): No, it wasn't.

JEAN: They were mine—why?

MRS. COTTON (*grimly*): Well, it's a round biscuit-box really—with a dent in the lid and a picture of Clacton front round it—and full of my soap flakes——

JEAN: Well, I haven't seen it.

MRS. COTTON (*grimly*): That's what *you* say. One of you's taken it——

DINAH (*cheerfully*): No, they haven't. It's still here somewhere—and I'll find it. You know I can always find things. And I promise.

MRS. COTTON (*grumpily, going off*): All right, so long as you say so.

> *She goes.* REX *looks at his watch.*

REX: We ought to be going, you know. Is everything in the car?

JEAN: My case isn't. It's in the hall.

REX (*moving*): I'll put it in. Then we ought to get cracking. There isn't much time. There isn't much time.

> *Goes out. As he goes,* JEAN *goes nearer* DINAH.

JEAN: Dinah, if a telephone call comes for me, say I'm on my way back.

DINAH: All right.

JEAN: Say I ought to be up at the hospital about eight or half-past. Is it worth telling Mrs. Cotton? How is she about telephones?

DINAH: She answers it, but she hates it—and so she says anything she feels at the time. As if a nasty-looking stranger had popped into the house.

Enter PROFESSOR.

PROFESSOR: Rex says you ought to be off.

MARION (*moving*): We're coming now.

PROFESSOR: I'll be out in a minute.

MARION: Oh—dear!

DINAH (*moving with* JEAN): What's the matter?

MARION (*still moving*): I don't know. But I feel rather sad now.

They go out leaving PROFESSOR *and* MRS. LINDEN *alone, not far from door, ready to move out.*

MRS. LINDEN: Will you be in to-night, Robert?

PROFESSOR: Yes, unless there are dramatic developments over at the University.

MRS. LINDEN: You're too optimistic about this business.

PROFESSOR: Why do you say that?

MRS. LINDEN: I have a feeling they want to get rid of you—and that they will. So don't expect too much. I'll ring you up from Rex's flat.

PROFESSOR: Good!

MRS. LINDEN: But I meant every word I said, Robert. I'm not coming back. It's for your sake as much as mine. And this time you'll have to give in. (*As if about to break down.*) Oh—Robert—I hate this——

PROFESSOR: So do I, Isabel. It's all wrong.

He kisses her, lightly.

You think I'm making a mistake. I think you are. But don't let's make a quarrel out of it, not after all these years. You're my wife. I love you very dearly.

MRS. LINDEN (*as if about to change her mind*): Oh—Robert—I'll—— (*She hesitates.*)

PROFESSOR: Yes, my dear?

REX *can now be heard calling, through open door, impatiently but gaily.*

REX (*off*): Come on Mother. We're all set—the road's a-calling——

MRS. LINDEN (*calling*): I'm coming, darling. (*Changed again now, she looks sharply at* PROFESSOR.) I'll ring you to-night, Robert.

She turns and walks out, and, with something melancholy in the set of his back, he follows her. We then hear DINAH *calling.*

DINAH (*off*): Yes, she is. She's here now.

There is a pause of a moment or two, then the telephone bell rings sharply. Then it waits a moment, and rings sharply again. Again it waits, then continues ringing. MRS. COTTON, *smoking a cigarette and looking annoyed comes in to answer it.*

MRS. COTTON (*at telephone*): Yes?... Who? Doctor?... *Professor* Linden lives 'ere. . . . Oh—that one. No, she isn't . . . just gone. . . . . I don't know an' I don't care. . . . I sound bad-tempered 'cos I *am* bad-tempered.

As she bangs down the receiver, glares and blows smoke at it, the CURTAIN *is coming down for the end of Scene I. House lights stay down.*

SCENE II

When CURTAIN *rises, a minute later, for opening of Scene II, at night, several hours later, curtains are drawn across window and artificial lighting is on. This lighting should not be as general as it was in Act I, Scene II, but more intimate, perhaps making use of large standard lamp downstage L. Door is half-open.* DINAH *and* MRS. COTTON *are conferring.* DINAH *is holding several small shop-keeping books, while* MRS. COTTON *is perched on arm of chair, still smoking a cigarette and holding a cup of tea. We feel that this housekeeping conference, for that is what it is, has been on some time.* DINAH *is puzzling over one of the small books, which she holds open, frowning at it, and* MRS. COTTON *is watching her, and nothing is said for a few moments.*

DINAH: Oh—dear—this rationing's difficult, isn't it?

MRS. COTTON: 'Alf the time it isn't difficult—it's just bloody impossible. Minute I think o' them shops, up the language comes. I come out with it at Frost's, greengrocer's Tuesday mornin', an' 'e says "You're no lady to talk like that". An' I says "I know I'm not— but you're no greengrocer neither, though you've got it up outside you are", I says.

DINAH (*consulting book*): What's this about suet?

MRS. COTTON: I don't know—but try to get it, that's all. An' your pa likes a bit o' suety stuff—every proper man does——

Dinah: I do too. Steak pudding—and treacle roll——

Mrs. Cotton: That's 'cos you're young. Lies on my stomach like lead. But never mind what it says there about it. Just try to get some, that's all.

Dinah: Well, I will—but the trouble is, I haven't much time——

Mrs. Cotton: Don't be silly. I'll do it, same as I did for your Mum. Leave it to me——

Dinah: Well, I'd like to, Mrs. Cotton, because I don't really understand much about housekeeping, though I'll do my best——

Mrs. Cotton: Well, your best an' my best an' all the shops' best—won't make much dam' diff'rence, 'cos if we 'aven't got it, then we can't 'ave it. 'Cept on the Black Market touch, of course.

Dinah: If somebody offered me chocolate on the Black Market I'd take it.

Mrs. Cotton: So would I. Specially soft centres.

Dinah: Hard centres, I like. But then nobody ever does.

Mrs. Cotton: That's 'cos you're not in the know.

Dinah: Are you in the know, Mrs. Cotton?

Mrs. Cotton: Not up this way, I'm not. Might be at 'ome. But I'll bet I know one who is—an' that's your brother—that Rex. An' I'll bet he has your Mum all fixed up nice on Black Market tack—chickens an' cream an' eggs an' whisky——

Dinah: I don't think Mummie likes whisky——

Mrs. Cotton: I wish I didn't, 'cos I never see any, except that 'alf-bottle Bert sent me for Christmas.

Dinah (*with solemn air*): Well now, Mrs. Cotton, what about to-morrow——?

Mrs. Cotton: Sunday.

Dinah: Yes, I know. But I mean—meals an' things——

Mrs. Cotton: Don't you worry, we've enough stuff left over to do us nicely.

Dinah: Well, then, Monday——?

Mrs. Cotton: It's only Saturday now—you needn't bother your 'ead about Monday. Leave it to me. An' don't look so solemn about it—'cos it's no use—it's all 'it or miss, these days, an' mostly miss—an' if you start takin' it all serious, you'll soon be off your rocker. Matter of fact, 'alf the people nowadays *are* off their rockers, what with one thing an' another. Told you about my cousin, 'aven't I?

Dinah: You mean the one who's married to two different men?

Mrs. Cotton: No, that's poor Florrie—*she's* not all there neither.

But this is another one, Agnes, married to a baker. Know 'ow it takes 'er? (*In a loud whisper.*) Saves tissue paper. Collects it an' saves it. Go miles, for some. Smooths it out—irons it sometimes— an' puts it away all nice.—Got at least a cupboard full.

DINAH: But why?

MRS. COTTON (*same whisper*): Nobody knows. *She* doesn't know Bit mental. That's 'ow it takes 'er. I tell yer, ducks, there's more an' more goin' queer—mental. Man called at the back door, Thursday— clean-looking oldish man with a beard—spoke quite refined—an' said 'e'd bin sent by the Prophet Enoch——

DINAH (*astonished, half laughing*): The Prophet Enoch?

MRS. COTTON: True as I'm 'ere.

A distant ring, at front door.

DINAH: Somebody at the door. Do you think this might be one of them?

MRS. COTTON (*moving*): Might be. I'll go.

She goes out. DINAH gives the book in her hand a last puzzled look, then puts the book down. MRS. COTTON now reappears at doorway.

(*Grumpily.*) Student.

She shows in EDITH WESTMORE, then closes door as she goes.

EDITH: Professor Linden told us to call here to-night after the Union show——

DINAH: He's out but he'll be back any minute. Do sit down. Where's what's-his-name?

EDITH: Bernard Fawcett?

DINAH: Yes.

EDITH: He'll be coming along. But I didn't wait for him. He isn't a friend of mine—I don't like him much.

She is now sitting down—DINAH just perches casually.

DINAH: I don't know him really. He always looks as if something or somebody has just upset him.

EDITH: Usually they have. (*She laughs, then hesitates.*) Is your brother still staying here?

DINAH: No, he drove back to London this afternoon. Did you meet him?

EDITH: Just for a minute or two, yesterday. He's very attractive, isn't he?

DINAH: I don't know really.—Yes, I suppose he is.

EDITH: It's surprising he isn't married, isn't it?

DINAH: He's not the type. I think. He couldn't bother settling down with just one person.

EDITH: Still—a lot of men seem like that, don't they? And then they do marry after all.

DINAH: Yes. I suppose it could happen with Rex. Probably somebody terribly glamorous—like a film star, that he could show off in expensive places. Rex is very clever in a sharp sort of way. Do you know a game called *Black Sam*?

EDITH (*rather despondently*): No. We never played games at home.

DINAH: It's our Linden family game. We used to play it a lot. And last night we played it again. And it was just the same as it used to be. Rex won again. He always used to win. (*Begins laughing.*) And the whole last hour he was cheating, and we didn't know. He always did when we used to play it. And last night—Jean—that's my doctor sister, who's very serious and grown-up usually—was absolutely *furious* with him. People don't really change much, do they? Not inside themselves. And when they let themselves go again—when they're back with the family and are being silly—they're just the same as they always were.

EDITH: One of my brothers is quite different from what he was before the war. Now he won't look at you for a long time but then he suddenly stares—and laughs—in a meaningless sort of way. (*Hesitates a moment, then hesitantly.*) Do you think—this lipstick—suits me——?

DINAH (*rather astonished*): I don't know. I'm not good on lipstick. (*Goes closer to her, inspecting her.*) No. Much too dark.

EDITH (*miserably*): Oh dear! (*Then, bursting out.*) Sometimes I wish I weren't a girl. Don't you?

DINAH: I used to. But now I don't care—just don't bother about it.

MRS. COTTON *opens door. Same tone as before.*

MRS. COTTON: Another student.

BERNARD FAWCETT *enters, wearing a very shabby overcoat and a muffler, but with no hat.* MRS. COTTON *closes door.*

FAWCETT (*gloomily*): Hello!

DINAH: Hello! Father'll be back any minute. Won't you take off your overcoat?

FAWCETT (*gloomily*): No thanks.

DINAH: What's the matter?

FAWCETT (*irritably*): These dam' colds I get. I had a bad one yesterday—all the week, in fact. Then this afternoon I thought it had gone. Now it's come back again. Head aches and can't taste anything properly. But I'll smoke if it's all the same to you.

DINAH: Of course.

FAWCETT *pulls out a clumsy-looking cherrywood, of the type favoured by young students, and lights it rather awkwardly, then puffs out smoke gloomily.*

FAWCETT: That Union show was lousy.

EDITH (*mildly*): I rather liked it this time.

FAWCETT (*rudely*): You would!

EDITH (*sharply*): Don't be so rude.

FAWCETT (*astonished*): What?

EDITH (*still sharply*): I said *don't be so rude.*

FAWCETT: What's the matter with you?

EDITH: I don't know why you boys think you have to behave like—like louts—just because you've come to a university—because you're students. If you could only see what you looked like—in comparison—with—with—other kinds of men—you'd—you'd——

FAWCETT: Don't bother with it, Westmore. You sound to me as if you've fallen for somebody.

EDITH (*hastily*): I haven't—don't be stupid——

FAWCETT (*turning to* DINAH): What's this about your father?

DINAH (*alert at once*): What about him?

FAWCETT: Told another bloke who's taking history—chap called Thring—I was coming on here to get next week's essay subject—and he said I needn't bother. Because, he told me, there's a strong rumour going round that your father's retiring—right off——

DINAH (*sharply*): Well, it isn't true.

FAWCETT: Very strong rumour, he said. "Prof. Linden's had it" he said.

EDITH (*hastily*): Oh—for goodness sake, shut up.

FAWCETT: Why should I—(*he sneezes violently*). Oh—blast!

DINAH (*who has been rigid, fiercely*): And I hope it's 'flu—and the kind that gives you awful pains in your inside and they make you have castor oil——

She has now stalked out. FAWCETT *stares after her in astonishment, then looks at* EDITH.

FAWCETT: Did she say she hoped it was 'flu?

EDITH (*fiercely*): Yes. She was furious because you said that about her father. "Prof. Linden's had it"! What a way to talk! And what a thing to say to *her!*

FAWCETT (*patiently, misunderstood*): Look! Now what have I done? I meet a bloke called Thring——

EDITH (*angrily*): And I hope he has gastric 'flu too.

FAWCETT (*wrestling hard with his cold*): Women! Girls! Women! The more—more—more I see—(*another sneeze coming and he wrestles with it*).

> EDITH *begins laughing. He glares at her.*

How I admire your wonderful delicate sense of humour, Miss Westmore!

EDITH (*laughing*): If you only saw yourself. (*Laughs.*)

FAWCETT (*shouting*): I don't want to see myself——

> *Enter* PROFESSOR LINDEN.

PROFESSOR: Well, Fawcett, if you don't want to see yourself, there's no reason why you should, until you shave, to-morrow morning. Good evening, Miss Westmore. And I apologise once again for keeping you waiting.

EDITH: It's all right, Professor Linden.

PROFESSOR (*sitting down*): Thank you. What with my family coming and going—and other things—I seem to have completely lost my well-deserved reputation for punctuality. Well—this afternoon's meeting of the Burmanley Citizens' Vigilant Society was postponed—eh? And so, much to your relief, I imagine I'll have to find another subject for next week's essay.

FAWCETT: Yes.

EDITH (*timidly*): Professor Linden——?

PROFESSOR: Yes?

EDITH (*timidly*): We shall be coming to you next week—I mean——

PROFESSOR (*rather sharply*): I hope so. Why not?

> *They exchange glances, and he notices it. He gets up and moves a pace or two, impatiently, then more to himself than to them.*

Really—this is too bad. (*He turns to them.*) So you've heard rumours that I may not be here next week—eh?

FAWCETT: Yes. Only just to-night—at the Union.

PROFESSOR: I *see*. (*To* EDITH.) And you too?

EDITH (*unhappily*): Yes—I did hear—something.

PROFESSOR: You oughtn't to have done. But it only proves what I've said before—that a university is a mad village.

> *They stare at him for a moment, and there is a pause while he reflects. Then, with more decision:*

You two are pretty average Burmanley History students and here's a question I'd like to put to you, to be answered quite truthfully. If you're merely polite about it, then you'll make me sorry I asked it. (*Pauses, then quietly and impersonally.*) Would it really matter to you —if I wasn't here next week?

EDITH (*involuntarily*): Oh—dear!

PROFESSOR: A truthful impersonal answer mind. Fawcett?

FAWCETT (*steadily*): No, sir, it wouldn't—not really. I get on all right with Mr. Pearse and Mr. Saxon. I don't mean——

PROFESSOR (*quietly*): Never mind about what you don't mean. You gave me an honest answer. Now, Miss Westmore——

EDITH (*struggling*): Oh dear!—it's so difficult——

PROFESSOR: I could take that as an answer, if necessary.

EDITH (*struggling away*): No, I mean I enjoy your lectures more than anybody else's—and coming here for the essays—I don't understand you always as I do Mr. Pearse—but of course it would matter terribly if you went——

PROFESSOR (*quietly*): No, it wouldn't. You're giving me the same answer.

As she tries to apologise.

No, please, Miss Westmore. If you try to apologise to me, then I ought first to apologise to you—for asking such a question—and we might be at it all night. (*With an obvious effort.*) Well, that's that. But—because we don't know what's going to happen—that's no reason for not doing a bit of work, is it? So let's get back to the Sixteenth Century . . . the Sixteenth Century. . . . (*He moves about a little, trying to concentrate.*) Yes—well. Shakespeare's at the Globe Theatre, writing imperishable masterpieces. Suppose you try to trace the connection between that glorious fact and the rise of the Lombard cities and the development of the banking system.

FAWCETT (*dismayed*): The banking system?

PROFESSOR: Yes. You go back a century, of course. *Twelfth Night, Hamlet*—here—and there, the Italian cities and the banking system. Letters of credit and loans at five per cent, at one end of the chain, and at the other a crowded wooden theatre near the Thames and the afternoon fading and a player with a whitened face murmuring *Absent thee from felicity awhile.* That's all.

FAWCETT (*as they rise to go*): And if you're not here——

PROFESSOR (*rather sharply*): I've not been told yet that I shan't be, Fawcett. In fact, you may take it that I will be.

The telephone rings. PROFESSOR *goes to answer it.*

EDITH (*hissing at* FAWCETT): Idiot!

FAWCETT (*indignant whisper*): What for?

EDITH (*same*): Oh—shut up!

PROFESSOR (*at telephone*): Yes? . . . This is Professor Linden speaking . . . all right. . . . (*He turns to the students looking old and bleak now.*) This is a call from London and it may take some time, so would you mind letting yourselves out? And we meet here, I hope, next Friday at the usual time.

EDITH (*moving out*): Yes. Good night, Professor Linden.

FAWCETT (*moving out*): Good night.

PROFESSOR: Good night. . . .

They go out, leaving door ajar. He now answers telephone.

Yes, Isabel—Robert here. . . . Good. . . . No, no news at all, but rumours are flying round, of course . . . well, if it should be vanity, it's already receiving a shock or two . . . no, not worth talking about. . . . Do I? Well, you never did like my telephone voice, did you, my dear? And I may be rather tired. . . . Mrs. Cotton? I'll give her a shout, then we can go on talking. Just a minute.

Leaves telephone hastily and goes to door, calling "Mrs. Cotton—Mrs. Cotton—hurry!—telephone", and then goes back to telephone.

I've called her. . . . No, don't worry about us. Regarded from the splendours of Rex's flat, we probably seem worse off than we really are. . . . Certainly, why shouldn't you enjoy it, my dear. I'm glad. . . . Well, I was never good at sounding glad on a long-distance telephone late on Saturday night. . . . Yes, Isabel, I know, but that's how I feel and while I still live at all, I have to live with myself.

MRS. COTTON *now appears.*

. . . Let's leave it at that then, my dear—here's Mrs. Cotton.

He hands her the receiver, which MRS. COTTON *takes grimly, speaking into it in grim tone.*

MRS. COTTON (*at telephone*): This is Mrs. Cotton. . . . Yes, Mrs. Linden—well, you said that this morning . . . oh, we'll manage. . . . I'll tell 'em first thing Monday.—What? . . . Oh——

She glances at PROFESSOR, *who is standing not far away.*

A bit pinched, I'd say—as if it was a colder night than it is, if yer see what I mean. . . . Yes.—Oh, *she's* all right. . . . I tell yer, we'll manage. . . . To-morrow night, same time? I'll tell 'im. 'Bye. (*Puts down receiver as if she disliked it.*) She's goin' to ring yer same time to-morrow night. Money no object. Mr. Rex, I suppose. (*Sniffs dubiously.*) All this talkin' on telyphones—where's it get yer?

PROFESSOR (*rather despondently*): I don't know. I'm not good at it.

MRS. COTTON: Not yuman, that's what's wrong with it. Oh—there's a message for you.

PROFESSOR: Yes?

MRS. COTTON: Young woman—pal o' Miss Dinah's—brought 'er some gramyphone records—an' a message for you at the same time—works in 'is office, I think——

PROFESSOR: Whose office?

MRS. COTTON: That Mr. Lock'art. She said 'e's comin' to see yer to-night—might be any time now——

PROFESSOR (slowly, softly): I see. Well, Alfred Lockhart's an old friend of mine—and—(looking her in the eye) Mrs. Cotton—how much whisky is there left?

MRS. COTTON (with innocent air): Not much. Might be a couple o' pub doubles—and yer know what they are now——

PROFESSOR: There ought to be more than that.

MRS. COTTON: There isn't. Soon goes.

PROFESSOR (softly): It does. You couldn't—by any chance—have had any lately, could you?

MRS. COTTON (after giving him a nod): Just a nip—yesterday morning—when that ceiling come down—an' reminded me, you know—just 'ad to 'ave a nip.

PROFESSOR: Yes, fair enough. I'd have done the same.

MRS. COTTON: Ah—you an' me, Professor—we can get on all right—live an' let live—that's our motto.

PROFESSOR: Something like that. Well, bring what's left of the whisky and a couple of glasses for Mr. Lockhart and me. We've a ceiling coming down too.

Sound of gramophone, distant and behind closed door, comes through now.

MRS. COTTON: Right. 'Ear that? Music. She's at it. (*Smiles with some tenderness.*) Talked to me to-night in 'ere about 'ouse-keepin' an' shoppin' an' all that—wants to look after yer properly, she does—bless 'er!

PROFESSOR (gently): You must look after her, Mrs. Cotton. I know you're fond of her.

MRS. COTTON: As if she was my own. Kid got me from the first go off—one reason why I stayed. That Dinah, Professor—she's growin' up of course——

PROFESSOR: Yes, seventeen.

MRS. COTTON (*solemnly*): Eighteen. But she still lives in the land o' childhood, where you an' me's forgotten.

PROFESSOR (*astonished*): My dear Mrs. Cotton, it's true of course but what an extraordinary thing for you to say——

MRS. COTTON (*complacently*): 'Eard a chap say it top of a tram—one Easter Monday—an' it stuck in my mind. Crossin' the river we was—packed of course—an' it was rainin' a bit an' sun shinin' all at the same time—way it does about Easter—an' everything suddenly so bright an' shiny I could 'ave laughed an' cried. So when I 'eard 'im say that it stuck in my mind. Yer know?

PROFESSOR (*softly*): Yes. And perhaps, after all, we're not forgotten.

As if the door is now wide open, the gramophone can now be heard, clearly but still distantly. It is the Casals recording of the final movement of the Elgar 'Cello Concerto—the passage, before the very end, in which earlier themes are recalled poignantly. PROFESSOR *begins listening intently.*

MRS. COTTON (*quietly*): I'll get yer that whisky.

She goes, and as he listens near the open door, he is joined by DINAH, *in a fine state of excitement.*

DINAH (*in a loud whisper*): That's Casals. You didn't think it was me, did you?

PROFESSOR: I wondered, but I couldn't think how you'd got the B.B.C. symphony orchestra into the dining-room.

DINAH: Wouldn't it be marvellous if you could? Just pack them up in a magic little box?

PROFESSOR: They're in one now. Last movement, isn't it?

DINAH: Yes, and I'll never be able to play it properly for ages and ages—if ever. Listen—(*the music comes through poignantly*) he's remembering the earlier themes now, Daddy, and saying good-bye to them.

PROFESSOR (*quietly, almost to the music*): Wandering through the darkening house of life—touching all the things he loved—crying Farewell—for ever—for ever——

After a moment, there is heard a ring at the front door.

DINAH (*crossly*): Oh—bother! I'll go. (*Hurries out.*)

PROFESSOR (*going to doorway, calling*): If it's anybody but Alfred Lockhart, I can't see them. (*Going out to look.*) Oh—it *is* you, Alfred.

LOCKHART (*calling*): Yes.

PROFESSOR: Come up. Dinah, when you've finished with the gramophone, you'd better go to bed.

DINAH (*as she hurries past doorway*): All right, but I'm a bit excited.

PROFESSOR *now ushers in* LOCKHART, *who wears a dark overcoat and carries a dark hat. He looks grave.*

PROFESSOR (*still near door, not closed*): Alfred, you're wearing your undertaker's look to-night. Won't you take your coat off?

LOCKHART: No, thanks, Robert. I mustn't stay long.

MRS. COTTON *appears with a tray on which are two glasses, small jug of water, and whisky decanter with small amount of whisky in it.*

MRS. COTTON: 'Ere it is, what's left of it—so make the most of it, I say. (*Goes to put tray down.*)

PROFESSOR: Thank you, Mrs. Cotton. And there won't be anything else to-night. So—good-night.

MRS. COTTON (*moving out*): Good night. An' I'll try an' get that young madam off to bed too. (*She goes out and closes the door behind her.*)

PROFESSOR: A little whisky, Alfred?

LOCKHART (*gravely*): I'd rather get the official part of my visit over first, if you don't mind, Robert.

PROFESSOR: I thought there must be an official part.

They have now sat down.

LOCKHART: I'm not enjoying this. That's why I wanted to get it over to-night.

PROFESSOR: Go ahead.

LOCKHART (*steadily, impersonally*): I've been instructed by the Vice-Chancellor that in the circumstances he will not press for your immediate resignation—though he deplores—and he particularly asked me to tell you this—the attitude you have adopted and trusts you will reconsider your decision——

PROFESSOR (*cutting in*): Alfred, I can't listen to any more of this jargon or watch you pretending to be a Civil Service dummy. What have they agreed to? Do I stay as I am?

LOCKHART: No.

PROFESSOR (*shocked*): What?

LOCKHART: It's a compromise. I expected it, as I hinted this morning. You give up the Chair and most of the work but you can stay on an Emeritus level—no examining—off the Board of Studies— about half-salary—a little more perhaps——

PROFESSOR (*angrily*): God!—Alfred—it's an insult——

LOCKHART: It's what I expected.

PROFESSOR: But was there a proper meeting?

LOCKHART: Yes.

PROFESSOR: But what about Drury and Hamilton—and my lot——?

LOCKHART: They were there. Didn't like it. Hamilton said what he thought—he was pretty fierce. But they had to give in.

PROFESSOR (*quietly*): We'll have that whisky now, I think. (*Gets up and begins pouring it.*) And don't keep on being official, Alfred. You and I have known each other for over twenty years—skirmished and fought together—and tied up each other's wounds—eh?

LOCKHART (*calm and mild*): Yes. And I'm not being official any longer. To hell with 'em. And I'm sick of this job. I'll find a way out —and soon too.

Takes the glass PROFESSOR *gives him.*

Thanks, Robert. Can you spare it?

PROFESSOR: No, and neither can my housekeeper.

LOCKHART (*calmly*): It'll taste all the better. (*Looks solemnly over his glass.*) Skoal!

PROFESSOR (*raising his glass*): Salut!

They drink solemnly.

LOCKHART: I'll say what I tried to tell you this morning. You shouldn't have given them this chance. You should have walked out. Your wife was right——

PROFESSOR: You behaved badly there, Alfred, lending yourself to female intrigue. Isabel, by the way, has gone to live with Rex, and says she's never coming back here.

LOCKHART: Bad in theory, but right and sensible in practice— trying to force your hand. You ought to join her on Monday. Tell the V.C. he can keep his Emeritus nonsense. I'd enjoy taking him a message in your best style, Robert.

PROFESSOR: I'd two students here to-night, Alfred. Average types —Fawcett and the Westmore girl—so, like a fool, I did a Gallup Poll on them—would it really matter to them if I did go? I gathered it wouldn't. So far as they are concerned, I might as well be in Rex's super-flat to-night, swigging his excellent Black Market whisky.

LOCKHART: That's where I'd be.

PROFESSOR (*softly*): No, you wouldn't, Alfred you old liar. What about the job that Masterton, the motor chap offered you, last year, with an expense sheet as long as your arm? You turned it down— to toil on here.

LOCKHART: I was a fool.

PROFESSOR: I'm the same kind of fool. And insult or no insult, students or no students, wife or no wife, I'm staying——

LOCKHART (*rather angrily, for him*): But why? What in God's name do you think you can do here now?

PROFESSOR: Be an old nuisance. Make senile mischief. Throw large spanners into their Godless works. I'll grab the pick of the history honours people and show them what life's done so far with this gaudy little planet. I'll give lectures that have about as much to do with the syllabus as Brock's fireworks. I'll contradict every dreary little lie about humanity that Pearse and Saxon and the rest can cook up. I'll——

LOCKHART (*cutting in, rather sharply*): Don't go on, Robert. Because I think you're bluffing.

PROFESSOR, *who has been on his feet during his last speech, turns away, hurt, but not wanting* LOCKHART *to see he is hurt.* LOCKHART, *however, guesses this and rises, moving nearer* PROFESSOR. *The latter turns and looks at him, reproachfully.*

LOCKHART: I'm sorry. Even if I thought that, I oughtn't to have said it.

PROFESSOR: If you can think it, then you'd better say it—even to-night. But perhaps I was bluffing a bit—whistling in the dark perhaps. Let's put it like this, then. I've been here a long time—I like the glum mucky old place. And times are hard, Alfred—we've got to keep on if we can. And there might be something I could help to do here, before the light goes. A touch of colour. A hint of wonder. An occasional new glance at old stuff. A bit of insight. Or is it the characteristic vanity of the Emeritus type?

LOCKHART: No, it isn't. You've all that to give. If they'll let you.

PROFESSOR (*a trifle bleakly, at first*): Yes, there's that. And it's not so much men—as machines—that we have to beat. The new educational machine here, for instance. And generally—the capital-industrial machine—and now the Trade Union machine and the Civil Service machine.

LOCKHART: Right.

PROFESSOR: I was telling my family, who don't care a damn, that we're trying to do a wonderful thing here. And so we are. But somehow not in a wonderful way. There's a kind of grey chilly hollowness inside, where there ought to be gaiety, colour, warmth, vision. Sometimes our great common enterprise seems only a noble skeleton, as if the machines had already sucked the blood and marrow out of it. My wife and family tell me to go away and enjoy myself. Doing what? Watching the fire die out of the heart, and never even stooping to blow? Here in Burmanley—with Dinah and her kind—and a few friends and allies—I can still blow a little—brighten an ember or two.

LOCKHART: The young and the old are the best now, Robert. There's a lot of rotten dead stuff in the middle——

PROFESSOR: But perhaps there always was, and the young and the old were always the best. Nearer the door in and the door out, and with more spirit to spare. The world's too much with the middles, who are busy looking for promotion and a seat on the Board.

LOCKHART: Robert—you look tired—cold too. Go to bed and don't bother seeing me out——

PROFESSOR (*exasperated*): Damn it, man, I'm sixty-five—not eighty-five——

LOCKHART (*moving rapidly, decisively*): Good night.

He is out before PROFESSOR *can get near him. As* PROFESSOR *is at door, we hear a rather desolate door-slam off.* PROFESSOR *now comes down and may here make change to more intimate lighting still, with most of stage in shadow.* PROFESSOR *moves slowly and wearily, and now for first time looks really dispirited. He sits down in light, rather heavily, puts a pipe in his mouth but does not smoke it, but stares rather desolately, perhaps with his head in his hands.* DINAH, *now in pyjamas, slippers, thick dressing-gown, enters very quietly, closing door softly behind her, and looking concerned at sight of her father brooding there, slowly comes down.*

DINAH (*softly*): Daddy!

PROFESSOR (*looking up*): Hello, Dinah. Thought you'd gone to bed.

DINAH: I started—but—(*lets this trail off. Then softly.*) You looked so miserable sitting there——

PROFESSOR (*neither denying nor agreeing*): I was brooding a bit. There *are* times—— (*He breaks off.*)

DINAH (*encouragingly*): Yes?

PROFESSOR (*with a sheepish grin*): Well—let's say—there are times. Leave it at that.

She glances with concern at him, then settles in large arm-chair, not far from where he is sitting, preferably up at desk or table.

Here, young woman—settling down?

DINAH: Will you do something specially to please me?

PROFESSOR: I might.

DINAH: Do you remember—you read us once—a bit of that book on history you started writing? Will you read some of it again—the beginning——

PROFESSOR: You don't want that stuff.

DINAH: I do. I *need* it. *You* need it. And if we don't have it, I'll go to bed and be miserable—and you'll go on being broody and lonely down here. So—please!

PROFESSOR (*in pretence of grumbling tone*): All right then—if I can find the thing——

She settles back, as he brings the MS. out of drawer, puts on a pair of spectacles, and then begins to read—quietly but impressively.

"History, to be worthy of the name, should bring us a stereoscopic view of man's life. Without that extra dimension, strangely poignant as well as vivid, it is flat, and because it is flat it is false. There are two patterns, endlessly being superimposed on one another. The first pattern is that of man reproducing himself, finding food and shelter, tilling the land, building cities, crossing the seas. It is the picture we understand now with ease, perhaps too easily. For the other pattern is still there, waiting to be interpreted. It is the record of man as a spiritual creature, with a whole world of unknown continents and strange seas, gardens of Paradise and cities lit with hell-fire, within the depths of his own soul. History that ignores the god and the altar is as false as history that could forget the sword and the wheel. Nor does the former belong only to the first youth of a civilisation——" (*Breaks off to say quietly, glancing up.*) I don't like "former"—can't imagine—(*his voice gets softer and slower*) how I came to write it. . . .

For now standing up, quietly, he sees that DINAH is fast asleep. He looks down smilingly for a moment. As he quietly sits down again, takes out a pen and crosses out a word or two in the MS. the CURTAIN *is slowly descending.*

END OF PLAY

AN INSPECTOR CALLS

A Play in Three Acts

TO
MICHAEL MACOWAN

"An Inspector Calls" was first produced at *The New Theatre in October,* 1946, *with the following cast:*

ARTHUR BIRLING	JULIEN MITCHELL
GERALD CROFT	HARRY ANDREWS
SHEILA BIRLING	MARGARET LEIGHTON
SYBIL BIRLING	MARIAN SPENCER
EDNA	MARJORIE DUNKELS
ERIC BIRLING	ALEC GUINNESS
INSPECTOR GOOLE	RALPH RICHARDSON

The play produced by BASIL DEAN

ACTS

All three acts, which are continuous, take place in the dining-room of the Birlings' house in Brumley, an industrial city in the North Midlands. It is an evening in spring, 1912.

ACT I

*The dining-room of a fairly large suburban house, belonging to a pro-
sperous manufacturer. It has good solid furniture of the period.
The general effect is substantial and heavily comfortable, but not
cosy and homelike. (If a realistic set is used, then it should be
swung back, as it was in the Old Vic production at the New Theatre.
By doing this, you can have the dining-table centre downstage
during Act I, when it is needed there, and then, swinging back, can
reveal the fireplace for Act II, and then for Act III can show a small
table with telephone on it, downstage of fireplace; and by this time
the dining-table and its chairs have moved well upstage. Producers
who wish to avoid this tricky business, which involves two re-
settings of the scene and some very accurate adjustments of the
extra flats necessary, would be well advised to dispense with an
ordinary realistic set, if only because the dining-table becomes a
nuisance. The lighting should be pink and intimate until the
INSPECTOR arrives, and then it should be brighter and harder.)*

*At rise of curtain, the four BIRLINGS and GERALD are seated at the table,
with ARTHUR BIRLING at one end, his wife at the other, ERIC downstage, and SHEILA and GERALD seated upstage. EDNA, the parlour-
maid, is just clearing the table, which has no cloth, of dessert plates
and champagne glasses, etc., and then replacing them with decanter
of port, cigar box and cigarettes. Port glasses are already on the
table. All five are in evening dress of the period, the men in tails and
white ties, not dinner-jackets. ARTHUR BIRLING is a heavy-looking,
rather portentous man in his middle fifties with fairly easy
manners but rather provincial in his speech. His wife is about fifty, a
rather cold woman and her husband's social superior. SHEILA is a
pretty girl in her early twenties, very pleased with life and rather
excited. GERALD CROFT is an attractive chap about thirty, rather
too manly to be a dandy but very much the easy well-bred young
man-about-town. ERIC is in his early twenties, not quite at ease,
half shy, half assertive. At the moment they have all had a good
dinner, are celebrating a special occasion, and are pleased with
themselves.*

BIRLING: Giving us the port, Edna? That's right. (*He pushes it
towards* ERIC.) You ought to like this port, Gerald. As a matter of
fact, Finchley told me it's exactly the same port your father gets from
him.

GERALD: Then it'll be all right. The governor prides himself on being a good judge of port. I don't pretend to know much about it.

SHEILA (*gaily, possessively*): I should jolly well think not, Gerald. I'd hate you to know all about port—like one of these purple-faced old men.

BIRLING: Here, I'm not a purple-faced old man.

SHEILA: No, not yet. But then you don't know all about port—do you?

BIRLING (*noticing that his wife has not taken any*): Now then, Sybil, you must take a little to-night. Special occasion, y'know, eh?

SHEILA: Yes, go on, Mummy. You must drink our health.

MRS. BIRLING (*smiling*): Very well, then. Just a little, thank you. (*To* EDNA, *who is about to go, with tray.*) All right, Edna. I'll ring from the drawing-room when we want coffee. Probably in about half an hour.

EDNA (*going*): Yes, ma'am.

> EDNA *goes out. They now have all the glasses filled.* BIRLING *beams at them and clearly relaxes.*

BIRLING: Well, well—this is very nice. Very nice. Good dinner too, Sybil. Tell cook from me.

GERALD (*politely*): Absolutely first-class.

MRS. BIRLING (*reproachfully*): Arthur, you're not supposed to say such things——

BIRLING: Oh—come, come—I'm treating Gerald like one of the family. And I'm sure he won't object.

SHEILA (*with mock aggressiveness*): Go on, Gerald—just you object!

GERALD (*smiling*): Wouldn't dream of it. In fact, I insist upon being one of the family now. I've been trying long enough, haven't I? (*As she does not reply, with more insistence.*) Haven't I? You know I have.

MRS. BIRLING (*smiling*): Of course she does.

SHEILA (*half serious, half playful*): Yes—except for all last summer, when you never came near me, and I wondered what had happened to you.

GERALD: And I've told you—I was awfully busy at the works all that time.

SHEILA (*same tone as before*): Yes, that's what *you* say.

MRS. BIRLING: Now, Sheila, don't tease him. When you're married you'll realise that men with important work to do sometimes have to spend nearly all their time and energy on their business. You'll have to get used to that, just as I had.

SHEILA: I don't believe I will. (*Half playful, half serious, to* GERALD.) So you be careful.

GERALD: Oh—I will, I will.

ERIC *suddenly guffaws. His parents look at him.*

SHEILA (*severely*): Now—what's the joke?

ERIC: I don't know—really. Suddenly I felt I just had to laugh.

SHEILA: You're squiffy.

ERIC: I'm not.

MRS. BIRLING: What an expression, Sheila! Really, the things you girls pick up these days!

ERIC: If you think that's the best she can do——

SHEILA: Don't be an ass, Eric.

MRS. BIRLING: Now stop it, you two. Arthur, what about this famous toast of yours?

BIRLING: Yes, of course. (*Clears his throat.*) Well, Gerald, I know you agreed that we should only have this quiet little family party. It's a pity Sir George and—er—Lady Croft can't be with us, but they're abroad and so it can't be helped. As I told you, they sent me a very nice cable—couldn't be nicer. I'm not sorry that we're celebrating quietly like this——

MRS. BIRLING: Much nicer really.

GERALD: I agree.

BIRLING: So do I, but it makes speech-making more difficult——

ERIC (*not too rudely*): Well, don't do any. We'll drink their health and have done with it.

BIRLING: No, we won't. It's one of the happiest nights of my life. And one day, I hope, Eric, when you've a daughter of your own, you'll understand why. Gerald, I'm going to tell you frankly, without any pretences, that your engagement to Sheila means a tremendous lot to me. She'll make you happy, and I'm sure you'll make her happy. You're just the kind of son-in-law I always wanted. Your father and I have been friendly rivals in business for some time now—though Crofts Limited are both older and bigger than Birling and Company— and now you've brought us together, and perhaps we may look forward to the time when Crofts and Birlings are no longer competing but are working together—for lower costs and higher prices.

GERALD: Hear, hear! And I think my father would agree to that.

MRS. BIRLING: Now, Arthur, I don't think you ought to talk business on an occasion like this.

SHEILA: Neither do I. All wrong.

BIRLING: Quite so, I agree with you. I only mentioned it in passing. What I did want to say was—that Sheila's a lucky girl—and I think you're a pretty fortunate young man too, Gerald.

GERALD: I know I am—this once anyhow.

BIRLING (*raising his glass*): So here's wishing the pair of you—the very best that life can bring. Gerald and Sheila.

MRS. BIRLING (*raising her glass, smiling*): Yes, Gerald. Yes, Sheila darling. Our congratulations and very best wishes!

GERALD: Thank you.

MRS. BIRLING: Eric!

ERIC (*rather noisily*): All the best! She's got a nasty temper sometimes—but she's not bad really. Good old Sheila!

SHEILA: Chump! I can't drink to this, can I? When do I drink?

GERALD: You can drink to me.

SHEILA (*quiet and serious now*): All right then. I drink to you, Gerald.

> For a moment they look at each other.

GERALD (*quietly*): Thank you. And I drink to you—and hope I can make you as happy as you deserve to be.

SHEILA (*trying to be light and easy*): You be careful—or I'll start weeping.

GERALD (*smiling*): Well, perhaps this will help to stop it. (*He produces a ring case.*)

SHEILA (*excited*): Oh—Gerald—you've got it—is it the one you wanted me to have?

GERALD (*giving the case to her*): Yes—the very one.

SHEILA (*taking out the ring*): Oh—it's wonderful! Look—Mummy —isn't it a beauty? Oh—darling—— (*She kisses GERALD hastily.*)

ERIC: Steady the Buffs!

SHEILA (*who has put ring on, admiringly*): I think it's perfect. Now I really feel engaged.

MRS. BIRLING: So you ought, darling. It's a lovely ring. Be careful with it.

SHEILA: Careful! I'll never let it go out of my sight for an instant.

MRS. BIRLING (*smiling*): Well, it came just at the right moment. That was clever of you, Gerald. Now, Arthur, if you've no more to say, I think Sheila and I had better go into the drawing-room and leave you men——

BIRLING (*rather heavily*): I just want to say this. (*Noticing that

SHEILA *is still admiring her ring*.) Are you listening, Sheila? This concerns you too. And after all I don't often make speeches at you——

SHEILA: I'm sorry, Daddy. Actually I was listening.

She looks attentive, as they all do. He holds them for a moment before continuing.

BIRLING: I'm delighted about this engagement and I hope it won't be too long before you're married. And I want to say this. There's a good deal of silly talk about these days—*but*—and I speak as a hard-headed business man, who has to take risks and know what he's about—I say, you can ignore all this silly pessimistic talk. When you marry, you'll be marrying at a very good time. Yes, a very good time—and soon it'll be an even better time. Last month, just because the miners came out on strike, there's a lot of wild talk about possible labour trouble in the near future. Don't worry. We've passed the worst of it. We employers at last are coming together to see that our interests—and the interests of Capital—are properly protected. And we're in for a time of steadily increasing prosperity.

GERALD: I believe you're right, sir.

ERIC: What about war?

BIRLING: Glad you mentioned it, Eric. I'm coming to that. Just because the Kaiser makes a speech or two, or a few German officers have too much to drink and begin talking nonsense, you'll hear some people say that war's inevitable. And to that I say—fiddlesticks! The Germans don't want war. Nobody wants war, except some half-civilised folks in the Balkans. And why? There's too much at stake these days. Everything to lose and nothing to gain by war.

ERIC: Yes, I know—but still——

BIRLING: Just let me finish, Eric. You've a lot to learn yet. And I'm talking as a hard-headed, practical man of business. And I say there isn't a chance of war. The world's developing so fast that it'll make war impossible. Look at the progress we're making. In a year or two we'll have aeroplanes that will be able to go anywhere. And look at the way the automobile's making headway—bigger and faster all the time. And then ships. Why, a friend of mine went over this new liner last week—the *Titanic*—she sails next week—forty-six thousand eight hundred tons—forty-six thousand eight hundred tons—New York in five days—and every luxury—and unsinkable, absolutely unsinkable. That's what you've got to keep your eye on, facts like that, progress like that—and not a few German officers talking nonsense and a few scaremongers here making a fuss about nothing. Now you three young people, just listen to this—and remember what I'm telling you now. In twenty or thirty years' time—let's say, in 1940

—you may be giving a little party like this—your son or daughter might be getting engaged—and I tell you by that time you'll be living in a world that'll have forgotten all these Capital versus Labour agitations and all these silly little war scares. There'll be peace and prosperity and rapid progress everywhere—except of course in Russia, which will always be behindhand, naturally.

MRS. BIRLING: Arthur!

As MRS. BIRLING *shows signs of interrupting.*

BIRLING: Yes, my dear, I know—I'm talking too much. But you youngsters just remember what I said. We can't let these Bernard Shaws and H. G. Wellses do all the talking. We hard-headed practical business men must say something sometime. And we don't guess— we've had experience—and we *know*.

MRS. BIRLING (*rising. The others rise*): Yes, of course, dear. Well— don't keep Gerald in here too long. Eric—I want you a minute.

She and SHEILA *and* ERIC *go out.* BIRLING *and* GERALD *sit down again.*

BIRLING: Cigar?

GERALD: No, thanks. Can't really enjoy them.

BIRLING (*taking one himself*): Ah, you don't know what you're missing. I like a good cigar. (*Indicating decanter.*) Help yourself.

GERALD: Thank you.

BIRLING *lights his cigar and* GERALD, *who has lit a cigarette, helps himself to port then pushes decanter to* BIRLING.

BIRLING: Thanks. (*Confidentially.*) By the way, there's something I'd like to mention—in strict confidence—while we're by ourselves. I have an idea that your mother—Lady Croft—while she doesn't object to my girl—feels you might have done better for yourself socially——

GERALD, *rather embarrassed, begins to murmur some dissent, but* BIRLING *checks him.*

No, Gerald, that's all right. Don't blame her. She comes from an old county family—landed people and so forth—and so it's only natural. But what I wanted to say is—there's a fair chance that I might find my way into the next Honours List. Just a knighthood, of course.

GERALD: Oh—I say—congratulations!

BIRLING: Thanks. But it's a bit too early for that. So don't say anything. But I've had a hint or two. You see, I was Lord Mayor here two years ago when Royalty visited us. And I've always been regarded as a sound useful party man. So—well—I gather there's a very good chance of a knighthood—so long as we behave ourselves, don't get into the police court or start a scandal—eh? (*Laughs complacently.*)

GERALD (*laughs*): You seem to be a nice well-behaved family——

BIRLING: We think we are——

GERALD: So if that's the only obstacle, sir, I think you might as well accept my congratulations now.

BIRLING: No, no, I couldn't do that. And don't say anything yet.

GERALD: Not even to my mother? I know she'd be delighted.

BIRLING: Well, when she comes back, you might drop a hint to her. And you can promise her that we'll try to keep out of trouble during the next few months.

They both laugh. ERIC *enters.*

ERIC: What's the joke? Started telling stories?

BIRLING: No. Want another glass of port?

ERIC (*sitting down*): Yes, please. (*Takes decanter and helps himself.*) Mother says we mustn't stay too long. But I don't think it matters. I left 'em talking about clothes again. You'd think a girl had never had any clothes before she gets married. Women are potty about 'em.

BIRLING: Yes, but you've got to remember, my boy, that clothes mean something quite different to a woman. Not just something to wear—and not only something to make 'em look prettier—but—well, a sort of sign or token of their self-respect.

GERALD: That's true.

ERIC (*eagerly*): Yes, I remember—— (*but he checks himself.*)

BIRLING: Well, what do you remember?

ERIC (*confused*): Nothing.

BIRLING: Nothing?

GERALD (*amused*): Sounds a bit fishy to me.

BIRLING (*taking it in same manner*): Yes, you don't know what some of these boys get up to nowadays. More money to spend and time to spare than I had when I was Eric's age. They worked us hard in those days and kept us short of cash. Though even then—we broke out and had a bit of fun sometimes.

GERALD: I'll bet you did.

BIRLING (*solemnly*): But this is the point. I don't want to lecture you two young fellows again. But what so many of you don't seem to understand now, when things are so much easier, is that a man has to make his own way—has to look after himself—and his family too, of course, when he has one—and so long as he does that he won't come to much harm. But the way some of these cranks talk and write now, you'd think everybody has to look after everybody else, as if we were all mixed up together like bees in a hive—community and all that nonsense. But take my word for it, you youngsters—and I've learnt in the good hard school of experience—that a man has to mind his own business and look after himself and his own—and——

We hear the sharp ring of a front door bell. BIRLING *stops to listen.*

ERIC: Somebody at the front door.

BIRLING: Edna'll answer it. Well, have another glass of port, Gerald—and then we'll join the ladies. That'll stop me giving you good advice.

ERIC: Yes, you've piled it on a bit to-night, Father.

BIRLING: Special occasion. And feeling contented, for once, I wanted you to have the benefit of my experience.

EDNA *enters.*

EDNA: Please, sir, an inspector's called.

BIRLING: An inspector? What kind of inspector?

EDNA: A police inspector. He says his name's Inspector Goole.

BIRLING: Don't know him. Does he want to see me?

EDNA: Yes, sir. He says it's important.

BIRLING: All right, Edna. Show him in here. Give us some more light.

EDNA *does, then goes out.*

I'm still on the Bench. It may be something about a warrant.

GERALD (*lightly*): Sure to be. Unless Eric's been up to something. (*Nodding confidentially to* BIRLING.) And that would be awkward, wouldn't it?

BIRLING (*humorously*): Very.

ERIC (*who is uneasy, sharply*): Here, what do you mean?

GERALD (*lightly*): Only something we were talking about when you were out. A joke really.

ERIC (*still uneasy*): Well, I don't think it's very funny.

BIRLING (*sharply, staring at him*): What's the matter with *you?*

ERIC (*defiantly*): Nothing.

EDNA (*opening door, and announcing*): Inspector Goole.

The INSPECTOR *enters, and* EDNA *goes, closing door after her. The* INSPECTOR *need not be a big man but he creates at once an impression of massiveness, solidity and purposefulness. He is a man in his fifties, dressed in a plain darkish suit of the period. He speaks carefully, weightily, and has a disconcerting habit of looking hard at the person he addresses before actually speaking.*

INSPECTOR: Mr. Birling?

BIRLING: Yes. Sit down, Inspector.

INSPECTOR (*sitting*): Thank you, sir.

BIRLING: Have a glass of port—or a little whisky?

INSPECTOR: No, thank you, Mr. Birling. I'm on duty.

BIRLING: You're new, aren't you?

INSPECTOR: Yes, sir. Only recently transferred.

BIRLING: I thought you must be. I was an alderman for years—and Lord Mayor two years ago—and I'm still on the Bench—so I know the Brumley police officers pretty well—and I thought I'd never seen you before.

INSPECTOR: Quite so.

BIRLING: Well, what can I do for you? Some trouble about a warrant?

INSPECTOR: No, Mr. Birling.

BIRLING (*after a pause, with a touch of impatience*): Well, what is it then?

INSPECTOR: I'd like some information, if you don't mind, Mr. Birling. Two hours ago a young woman died in the Infirmary. She'd been taken there this afternoon because she'd swallowed a lot of strong disinfectant. Burnt her inside out, of course.

ERIC (*involuntarily*): My God!

INSPECTOR: Yes, she was in great agony. They did everything they could for her at the Infirmary, but she died. Suicide of course.

BIRLING (*rather impatiently*): Yes yes. Horrible business. But I don't understand why you should come here, Inspector——

INSPECTOR (*cutting through, massively*): I've been round to the room she had, and she'd left a letter there and a sort of diary. Like a lot of these young women who get into various kinds of trouble, she'd used more than one name. But her original name—her real name—was Eva Smith.

BIRLING (*thoughtfully*): Eva Smith?

INSPECTOR: Do you remember her, Mr. Birling?

BIRLING (*slowly*): No—I seem to remember hearing that name—Eva Smith—somewhere. But it doesn't convey anything to me. And I don't see where I come into this.

INSPECTOR: She was employed in your works at one time.

BIRLING: Oh—that's it, is it? Well, we've several hundred young women there, y'know, and they keep changing.

INSPECTOR: This young woman, Eva Smith, was a bit out of the ordinary. I found a photograph of her in her lodgings. Perhaps you'd remember her from that.

INSPECTOR takes a photograph, about postcard size, out of his pocket and goes to BIRLING. *Both* GERALD *and* ERIC *rise to have a look at the photograph, but the* INSPECTOR *interposes himself between them and the photograph. They are surprised and rather annoyed.* BIRLING *stares hard, and with recognition, at the photograph, which the* INSPECTOR *then replaces in his pocket.*

GERALD (*showing annoyance*): Any particular reason why I shouldn't see this girl's photograph, Inspector?

INSPECTOR (*coolly, looking hard at him*): There might be.

ERIC: And the same applies to me, I suppose?

INSPECTOR: Yes.

GERALD: I can't imagine what it could be.

ERIC: Neither can I.

BIRLING: And I must say, I agree with them, Inspector.

INSPECTOR: It's the way I like to go to work. One person and one line of enquiry at a time. Otherwise, there's a muddle.

BIRLING: I see. Sensible really. (*Moves restlessly, then turns.*) You've had enough of that port, Eric.

The INSPECTOR *is watching* BIRLING *and now* BIRLING *notices him.*

INSPECTOR: I think you remember Eva Smith now, don't you, Mr. Birling?

BIRLING: Yes, I do. She was one of my employees and then I discharged her.

ERIC: Is that why she committed suicide? When was this, Father?

BIRLING: Just keep quiet, Eric, and don't get excited. This girl left us nearly two years ago. Let me see—it must have been in the early autumn of nineteen-ten.

INSPECTOR: Yes. End of September, nineteen-ten.

BIRLING: That's right.

GERALD: Look here, sir. Wouldn't you rather I was out of this?

BIRLING: I don't mind your being here, Gerald. And I'm sure you've no objection, have you, Inspector? Perhaps I ought to explain first that this is Mr. Gerald Croft—the son of Sir George Croft—you know, Crofts Limited.

INSPECTOR: Mr. Gerald Croft, eh?

BIRLING: Yes. Incidentally we've been modestly celebrating his **engagement** to my daughter, Sheila.

INSPECTOR: I see. Mr. Croft is going to marry Miss Sheila Birling?

GERALD (*smiling*): I hope so.

INSPECTOR (*gravely*): Then I'd prefer you to stay.

GERALD (*surprised*): Oh—all right.

BIRLING (*somewhat impatiently*): Look—there's nothing mysterious —or scandalous—about this business—at least not so far as I'm concerned. It's a perfectly straightforward case, and as it happened more than eighteen months ago—nearly two years ago—obviously it has nothing whatever to do with the wretched girl's suicide. Eh, Inspector?

INSPECTOR: No, sir. I can't agree with you there.

BIRLING: Why not?

INSPECTOR: Because what happened to her then may have determined what happened to her afterwards, and what happened to her afterwards may have driven her to suicide. A chain of events.

BIRLING: Oh well—put like that, there's something in what you say. Still, I can't accept any responsibility. If we were all responsible for everything that happened to everybody we'd had anything to do with, it would be very awkward, wouldn't it?

INSPECTOR: Very awkward.

BIRLING: We'd all be in an impossible position, wouldn't we?

ERIC: By Jove, yes. And as you were saying, Dad, a man has to look after himself——

BIRLING: Yes, well, we needn't go into all that.

INSPECTOR: Go into what?

BIRLING: Oh—just before you came—I'd been giving these young men a little good advice. Now—about this girl, Eva Smith. I remember her quite well now. She was a lively good-looking girl— country-bred, I fancy—and she'd been working in one of our machine shops for over a year. A good worker too. In fact, the foreman there told me he was ready to promote her into what we call a leading operator—head of a small group of girls. But after they came back from their holidays that August, they were all rather restless, and they suddenly decided to ask for more money. They were averaging about twenty-two and six, which was neither more nor less than is paid generally in our industry. They wanted the rates raised so that they could average about twenty-five shillings a week. I refused, of course.

INSPECTOR: Why?

BIRLING (*surprised*): Did you say "Why?"?

INSPECTOR: Yes. Why did you refuse?

BIRLING: Well, Inspector, I don't see that it's any concern of yours how I choose to run my business. Is it now?

INSPECTOR: It might be, you know.

BIRLING: I don't like the tone.

INSPECTOR: I'm sorry. But you asked me a question.

BIRLING: And you asked me a question before that, a quite unnecessary question too.

INSPECTOR: It's my duty to ask questions.

BIRLING: Well, it's my duty to keep labour costs down, and if I'd agreed to this demand for a new rate we'd have added about twelve per cent to our labour costs. Does that satisfy you? So I refused. Said I couldn't consider it. We were paying the usual rates and if they didn't like those rates, they could go and work somewhere else. It's a free country, I told them.

ERIC: It isn't if you can't go and work somewhere else.

INSPECTOR: Quite so.

BIRLING (to ERIC): Look—just you keep out of this. You hadn't even started in the works when this happened. So they went on strike. That didn't last long, of course.

GERALD: Not if it was just after the holidays. They'd be all broke— if I know them.

BIRLING: Right, Gerald. They mostly were. And so was the strike, after a week or two. Pitiful affair. Well, we let them all come back— at the old rates—except the four or five ringleaders, who'd started the trouble. I went down myself and told them to clear out. And this girl, Eva Smith, was one of them. She'd had a lot to say—far too much— so she had to go.

GERALD: You couldn't have done anything else.

ERIC: He could. He could have kept her on instead of throwing her out. I call it tough luck.

BIRLING: Rubbish! If you don't come down sharply on some of these people, they'd soon be asking for the earth.

GERALD: I should say so!

INSPECTOR: They might. But after all it's better to ask for the earth than to take it.

BIRLING (staring at the INSPECTOR): What did you say your name was, Inspector?

INSPECTOR: Goole. G. double O—L—E.

BIRLING: How do you get on with our Chief Constable, Colonel Roberts?

INSPECTOR: I don't see much of him.

BIRLING: Perhaps I ought to warn you that he's an old friend of mine, and that I see him fairly frequently. We play golf together sometimes up at the West Brumley.

INSPECTOR (*dryly*): I don't play golf.

BIRLING: I didn't suppose you did.

ERIC (*bursting out*): Well, I think it's a dam' shame.

INSPECTOR: No, I've never wanted to play.

ERIC: No. I mean about this girl—Eva Smith. Why shouldn't they try for higher wages? We try for the highest possible prices. And I don't see why she should have been sacked just because she'd a bit more spirit than the others. You said yourself she was a good worker. I'd have let her stay.

BIRLING (*rather angrily*): Unless you brighten your ideas, you'll never be in a position to let anybody stay or to tell anybody to go. It's about time you learnt to face a few responsibilities. That's something this public-school-and-Varsity life you've had doesn't seem to teach you.

ERIC (*sulkily*): Well, we don't need to tell the Inspector all about that, do we?

BIRLING: I don't see we need to tell the Inspector anything more. In fact, there's nothing I can tell him. I told the girl to clear out, and she went. That's the last I heard of her. Have you any idea what happened to her after that? Get into trouble? Go on the streets?

INSPECTOR (*rather slowly*): No, she didn't exactly go on the streets.

SHEILA *has now entered.*

SHEILA (*gaily*): What's this about streets? (*Noticing the* INSPECTOR.) Oh—sorry. I didn't know. Mummy sent me in to ask you why you didn't come along to the drawing-room.

BIRLING: We shall be along in a minute now. Just finishing.

INSPECTOR: I'm afraid not.

BIRLING (*abruptly*): There's nothing else, y'know. I've just told you that.

SHEILA: What's all this about?

BIRLING: Nothing to do with you, Sheila. Run along.

INSPECTOR: No, wait a minute, Miss Birling.

BIRLING (*angrily*): Look here, Inspector, I consider this uncalled-for and officious. I've half a mind to report you. I've told you all I know—and it doesn't seem to me very important—and now there isn't the slightest reason why my daughter should be dragged into this unpleasant business.

SHEILA (*coming further in*): What business? What's happening?

INSPECTOR (*impressively*): I'm a police inspector, Miss Birling. This afternoon a young woman drank some disinfectant, and died, after several hours of agony, to-night in the Infirmary.

SHEILA: Oh—how horrible! Was it an accident?

INSPECTOR: No. She wanted to end her life. She felt she couldn't go on any longer.

BIRLING: Well, don't tell me that's because I discharged her from my employment nearly two years ago.

ERIC: That might have started it.

SHEILA: Did you, Dad?

BIRLING: Yes. The girl had been causing trouble in the works. I was quite justified.

GERALD: Yes, I think you were. I know we'd have done the same thing. Don't look like that, Sheila.

SHEILA (*rather distressed*): Sorry! It's just that I can't help thinking about this girl—destroying herself so horribly—and I've been so happy to-night. Oh I wish you hadn't told me. What was she like? Quite young?

INSPECTOR: Yes. Twenty-four.

SHEILA: Pretty?

INSPECTOR: She wasn't pretty when I saw her to-day, but she had been pretty—very pretty.

BIRLING: That's enough of that.

GERALD: And I don't really see that this enquiry gets you any-where, Inspector. It's what happened to her since she left Mr. Birling's works that is important.

BIRLING: Obviously. I suggested that some time ago.

GERALD: And we can't help you there because we don't know.

INSPECTOR (*slowly*): Are you sure you don't know?

He looks at GERALD, *then at* ERIC, *then at* SHEILA.

BIRLING: And are you suggesting now that one of them knows something about this girl?

INSPECTOR: Yes.

BIRLING: You didn't come here just to see me then?

INSPECTOR: No.

The other four exchange bewildered and perturbed glances.

BIRLING (*with marked change of tone*): Well, of course, if I'd known that earlier, I wouldn't have called you officious and talked about reporting you. You understand that, don't you, Inspector? I thought that—for some reason best known to yourself—you were making the most of this tiny bit of information I could give you. I'm sorry. This makes a difference. You sure of your facts?

INSPECTOR: Some of them—yes.

BIRLING: I can't think they can be of any great consequence.

INSPECTOR: The girl's dead though.

SHEILA: What do you mean by saying that? You talk as if we were responsible——

BIRLING (*cutting in*): Just a minute, Sheila. Now, Inspector, perhaps you and I had better go and talk this over quietly in a corner——

SHEILA (*cutting in*): Why should you? He's finished with you. He says it's one of us now.

BIRLING: Yes, and I'm trying to settle it sensibly for you.

GERALD: Well, there's nothing to settle as far as I'm concerned. I've never known an Eva Smith.

ERIC: Neither have I.

SHEILA: Was that her name? Eva Smith?

GERALD: Yes.

SHEILA: Never heard it before.

GERALD: So where are you now, Inspector?

INSPECTOR: Where I was before, Mr. Croft. I told you—that like a lot of these young women, she'd used more than one name. She was still Eva Smith when Mr. Birling sacked her—for wanting twenty-five shillings a week instead of twenty-two and six. But after that she stopped being Eva Smith. Perhaps she'd had enough of it.

ERIC: Can't blame her.

SHEILA (*to* BIRLING): I think it was a mean thing to do. Perhaps that spoilt everything for her.

BIRLING: Rubbish! (*To* INSPECTOR.) Do you know what happened to this girl after she left my works?

INSPECTOR: Yes. She was out of work for the next two months. Both her parents were dead, so that she'd no home to go back to. And she hadn't been able to save much out of what Birling and Company had paid her. So that after two months, with no work, no money coming in, and living in lodgings, with no relatives to help her, few friends, lonely, half-starved, she was feeling desperate.

SHEILA (*warmly*): I should think so. It's a rotten shame.

INSPECTOR: There are a lot of young women living that sort of existence in every city and big town in this country, Miss Birling. If there weren't, the factories and warehouses wouldn't know where to look for cheap labour. Ask your father.

SHEILA: But these girls aren't cheap labour—they're *people*.

INSPECTOR (*dryly*): I've had that notion myself from time to time. In fact, I've thought that it would do us all a bit of good if sometimes we tried to put ourselves in the place of these young women counting their pennies in their dingy little back bedrooms.

SHEILA: Yes, I expect it would. But what happened to her then?

INSPECTOR: She had what seemed to her a wonderful stroke of luck. She was taken on in a shop—and a good shop too—Milwards.

SHEILA: Milwards! We go there—in fact, I was there this afternoon—— (*archly to* GERALD) for *your* benefit.

GERALD (*smiling*): Good!

SHEILA: Yes, she was lucky to get taken on at Milwards.

INSPECTOR: That's what she thought. And it happened that at the beginning of December that year—nineteen-ten—there was a good deal of influenza about, and Milwards suddenly found themselves short-handed. So that gave her her chance. It seems she liked working there. It was a nice change from a factory. She enjoyed being among pretty clothes, I've no doubt. And now she felt she was making a good fresh start. You can imagine how she felt.

SHEILA: Yes, of course.

BIRLING: And then she got herself into trouble there, I suppose?

INSPECTOR: After about a couple of months, just when she felt she was settling down nicely, they told her she'd have to go.

BIRLING: Not doing her work properly?

INSPECTOR: There was nothing wrong with the way she was doing her work. They admitted that.

BIRLING: There must have been something wrong.

INSPECTOR: All she knew was—that a customer complained about her—and so she had to go.

SHEILA (*staring at him, agitated*): When was this?

INSPECTOR (*impressively*): At the end of January—last year.

SHEILA: What—what did this girl look like?

INSPECTOR: If you'll come over here, I'll show you.

He moves nearer a light—perhaps standard lamp—and she crosses to him. He produces the photograph. She looks at it closely, recognises it with a little cry, gives a half-stifled sob, and then runs out. The INSPECTOR *puts the photograph back into his pocket and stares speculatively after her. The other three stare in amazement for a moment.*

BIRLING: What's the matter with her?

ERIC: She recognised her from the photograph, didn't she?

INSPECTOR: Yes.

BIRLING (*angrily*): Why the devil do you want to go upsetting the child like that?

INSPECTOR: I didn't do it. She's upsetting herself.

BIRLING: Well—why—why?

INSPECTOR: I don't know—yet. That's something I have to find out.

BIRLING (*still angrily*): Well—if you don't mind—I'll find out first.

GERALD: Shall I go to her?

BIRLING (*moving*): No, leave this to me. I must also have a word with my wife—tell her what's happening. (*Turns at door, staring at* INSPECTOR *angrily*.) We were having a nice little family celebration to-night. And a nasty mess you've made of it now, haven't you?

INSPECTOR (*steadily*): That's more or less what I was thinking earlier to-night, when I was in the Infirmary looking at what was left of Eva Smith. A nice little promising life there, I thought, and a nasty mess somebody's made of it.

BIRLING *looks as if about to make some retort, then thinks better of it, and goes out, closing door sharply behind him.* GERALD *and* ERIC *exchange uneasy glances. The* INSPECTOR *ignores them.*

GERALD: I'd like to have a look at that photograph now, Inspector.

INSPECTOR: All in good time.

GERALD: I don't see why——

INSPECTOR (*cutting in, massively*): You heard what I said before, Mr. Croft. One line of enquiry at a time. Otherwise we'll all be talking at once and won't know where we are. If you've anything to tell me, you'll have an opportunity of doing it soon.

GERALD (*rather uneasily*): Well, I don't suppose I have——

ERIC (*suddenly bursting out*): Look here, I've had enough of this.

INSPECTOR (*dryly*): I dare say.

ERIC (*uneasily*): I'm sorry—but you see—we were having a little party—and I've had a few drinks, including rather a lot of champagne —and I've got a headache—and as I'm only in the way here—I think I'd better turn in.

INSPECTOR: And I think you'd better stay here.

ERIC: Why should I?

INSPECTOR: It might be less trouble. If you turn in, you might have to turn out again soon.

GERALD: Getting a bit heavy-handed, aren't you, Inspector?

INSPECTOR: Possibly. But if you're easy with me, I'm easy with you.

GERALD: After all, y'know, we're respectable citizens and not criminals.

INSPECTOR: Sometimes there isn't as much difference as you think. Often, if it was left to me, I wouldn't know where to draw the line.

GERALD: Fortunately, it isn't left to you, is it?

INSPECTOR: No, it isn't. But some things are left to me. Enquiries of this sort, for instance. (*Enter* SHEILA, *who looks as if she's been crying.*) Well, Miss Birling?

SHEILA (*coming in, closing door*): You knew it was me all the time, didn't you?

INSPECTOR: I had an idea it might be—from something the girl herself wrote.

SHEILA: I've told my father—he didn't seem to think it amounted to much—but I felt rotten about it at the time and now I feel a lot worse. Did it make much difference to her?

INSPECTOR: Yes, I'm afraid it did. It was the last real steady job she had. When she lost it—for no reason that she could discover—she decided she might as well try another kind of life.

SHEILA (*miserably*): So I'm really responsible?

INSPECTOR: No, not entirely. A good deal happened to her after that. But you're partly to blame. Just as your father is.

ERIC: But what did Sheila do?

SHEILA (*distressed*): I went to the manager at Milwards and I told him that if they didn't get rid of that girl, I'd never go near the place again and I'd persuade mother to close our account with them.

INSPECTOR: And why did you do that?

SHEILA: Because I was in a furious temper.

INSPECTOR: And what had this girl done to make you lose your temper?

SHEILA: When I was looking at myself in the mirror I caught sight of her smiling at the assistant, and I was furious with her. I'd been in a bad temper anyhow.

INSPECTOR: And was it the girl's fault?

SHEILA: No, not really. It was my own fault. (*Suddenly, to* GERALD) All right, Gerald, you needn't look at me like that. At least, I'm trying to tell the truth. I expect you've done things you're ashamed of too.

GERALD (*surprised*): Well, I never said I hadn't. I don't see why——

INSPECTOR (*cutting in*): Never mind about that. You can settle that between you afterwards. (*To* SHEILA.) What happened?

SHEILA: I'd gone in to try something on. It was an idea of my own —mother had been against it, and so had the assistant—but I insisted. As soon as I tried it on, I knew they'd been right. It just didn't suit me at all. I looked silly in the thing. Well, this girl had brought the dress up from the workroom, and when the assistant—Miss Francis—had asked her something about it, this girl, to show us what she meant, had held the dress up, as if she was wearing it. And it just suited her. She was the right type for it, just as I was the wrong type. She was a very pretty girl too—with big dark eyes—and that didn't make it any better. Well, when I tried the thing on and looked at myself and knew that it was all wrong, I caught sight of this girl smiling at Miss Francis —as if to say: "Doesn't she look awful"—and I was absolutely furious. I was very rude to both of them, and then I went to the manager and told him that this girl had been very impertinent—and— and—— (*She almost breaks down, but just controls herself.*) How could I know what would happen afterwards? If she'd been some miserable plain little creature, I don't suppose I'd have done it. But she was very pretty and looked as if she could take care of herself. I couldn't be sorry for her.

INSPECTOR: In fact, in a kind of way, you might be said to have been jealous of her.

SHEILA: Yes, I suppose so.

INSPECTOR: And so you used the power you had, as a daughter of a good customer and also of a man well-known in the town, to punish the girl just because she made you feel like that?

SHEILA: Yes, but it didn't seem to be anything very terrible at the time. Don't you understand? And if I could help her now, I would——

INSPECTOR (*harshly*): Yes, but you can't. It's too late. She's dead.

ERIC: My God, it's a bit thick, when you come to think of it——

SHEILA (*stormily*): Oh shut up, Eric. I know, I know. It's the only time I've ever done anything like that, and I'll never, never do it again to anybody. I've noticed them giving me a sort of look sometimes at Milwards—I noticed it even this afternoon—and I suppose some of them remember. I feel now I can never go there again. Oh—why had this to happen?

INSPECTOR (*sternly*): That's what I asked myself to-night when I was looking at that dead girl. And then I said to myself: "Well, we'll try to understand why it had to happen." And that's why I'm here, and why I'm not going until I know *all* that happened. Eva Smith lost her job with Birling and Company because the strike failed and they were determined not to have another one. At last she found another job—under what name I don't know—in a big shop, and had to leave there because you were annoyed with yourself and passed the annoyance on to her. Now she had to try something else. So first she changed her name to Daisy Renton——

GERALD (*startled*): What?

INSPECTOR (*steadily*): I said she changed her name to Daisy Renton.

GERALD (*pulling himself together*): D'you mind if I give myself a drink, Sheila?

      SHEILA *merely nods, still staring at him, and he goes across to the tantalus on the sideboard for a whisky.*

INSPECTOR: Where is your father, Miss Birling?

SHEILA: He went into the drawing-room, to tell my mother what was happening here. Eric, take the Inspector along to the drawing-room. (*As* ERIC *moves, the* INSPECTOR *looks from* SHEILA *to* GERALD, *then goes out with* ERIC.) Well, Gerald?

GERALD (*trying to smile*): Well what, Sheila?

SHEILA: How did you come to know this girl—Eva Smith?

GERALD: I didn't.

SHEILA: Daisy Renton then—it's the same thing.

GERALD: Why should I have known her?

SHEILA: Oh don't be stupid. We haven't much time. You gave yourself away as soon as he mentioned her other name.

GERALD: All right. I knew her. Let's leave it at that.

SHEILA: We can't leave it at that.

GERALD (*approaching her*): Now listen, darling——

SHEILA: No, that's no use. You not only knew her but you knew her very well. Otherwise, you wouldn't look so guilty about it. When did you first get to know her? (*He does not reply.*) Was it after she left Milwards? When she changed her name, as he said, and began to lead a different sort of life? Were you seeing her last spring and summer, during that time when you hardly came near me and said you were so busy? Were you? (*He does not reply but looks at her.*) Yes, of course you were.

GERALD: I'm sorry, Sheila. But it was all over and done with, last summer. I hadn't set eyes on the girl for at least six months. I don't come into this suicide business.

SHEILA: I thought I didn't, half an hour ago.

GERALD: You don't. Neither of us does. So—for God's sake—don't say anything to the Inspector.

SHEILA: About you and this girl?

GERALD: Yes. We can keep it from him.

SHEILA (*laughs rather hysterically*): Why—you fool—*he knows.* Of course he knows. And I hate to think how much he knows that we don't know yet. You'll see. You'll see.

She looks at him almost in triumph He looks crushed. The door slowly opens and the INSPECTOR *appears, looking steadily and searchingly at them.*

INSPECTOR: Well?

END OF ACT ONE

ACT II

At rise, scene and situation are exactly as they were at end of Act I.

The INSPECTOR *remains at the door for a few moments looking at* SHEILA *and* GERALD. *Then he comes forward, leaving door open behind him.*

INSPECTOR (*to* GERALD): Well?

SHEILA (*with hysterical laugh, to* GERALD): You see? What did I tell you?

INSPECTOR: What did you tell him?

GERALD (*with an effort*): Inspector, I think Miss Birling ought to be excused any more of this questioning. She's nothing more to tell you. She's had a long, exciting and tiring day—we were celebrating our engagement, you know—and now she's obviously had about as much as she can stand. You heard her.

SHEILA: He means that I'm getting hysterical now.

INSPECTOR: And are you?

SHEILA: Probably.

INSPECTOR: Well, I don't want to keep you here. I've no more questions to ask you.

SHEILA: No, but you haven't finished asking questions—have you?

INSPECTOR: No.

SHEILA (*to* GERALD): You see? (*To* INSPECTOR.) Then I'm staying.

GERALD: Why should you? It's bound to be unpleasant and disturbing.

INSPECTOR: And you think young women ought to be protected against unpleasant and disturbing things?

GERALD: If possible—yes.

INSPECTOR: Well, we know one young woman who wasn't, don't we?

GERALD: I suppose I asked for that.

SHEILA: Be careful you don't ask for any more, Gerald.

GERALD: I only meant to say to you—— Why stay when you'll hate it?

SHEILA: It can't be any worse for me than it has been. And it might be better.

GERALD (*bitterly*): I see.

SHEILA: What do you see?

GERALD: You've been through it—and now you want to see somebody else put through it.

SHEILA (*bitterly*): So that's what you think I'm really like. I'm glad I realised it in time, Gerald.

GERALD: No, no, I didn't mean——

SHEILA (*cutting in*): Yes, you did. And if you'd really loved me, you couldn't have said that. You listened to that nice story about me. I got that girl sacked from Milwards. And now you've made up your mind I must obviously be a selfish, vindictive creature.

GERALD: I neither said that nor even suggested it.

SHEILA: Then why say I want to see somebody else put through it? That's not what I meant at all.

GERALD: All right then, I'm sorry.

SHEILA: Yes, but you don't believe me. And this is just the wrong time not to believe me.

INSPECTOR (*massively taking charge*): Allow me, Miss Birling. (*To* GERALD.) I can tell you why Miss Birling wants to stay on and why she says it might be better for her if she did. A girl died to-night. A pretty, lively sort of girl, who never did anybody no harm. But she died in misery and agony—hating life——

SHEILA (*distressed*): Don't please—I know, I know—and I can't stop thinking about it——

INSPECTOR (*ignoring this*): Now Miss Birling has just been made to understand what she did to this girl. She feels responsible. And if she leaves us now, and doesn't hear any more, then she'll feel she's entirely to blame, she'll be alone with her responsibility, the rest of to-night, all to-morrow, all the next night——

SHEILA (*eagerly*): Yes, that's it. And I know I'm to blame—and I'm desperately sorry—but I can't believe—I won't believe—it's simply my fault that in the end she—she committed suicide. That would be too horrible——

INSPECTOR (*sternly to them both*): You see, we have to share something. If there's nothing else, we'll have to share our guilt.

SHEILA (*staring at him*): Yes. That's true. You know. (*She goes closer to him, wonderingly.*) I don't understand about you.

INSPECTOR (*calmly*): There's no reason why you should.

He regards her calmly while she stares at him wonderingly and dubiously. Now MRS. BIRLING *enters, briskly and self-confidently, quite out of key with the little scene that has just passed.* SHEILA *feels this at once.*

MRS. BIRLING (*smiling, social*): Good evening, Inspector.

INSPECTOR: Good evening, madam.

MRS. BIRLING (*same easy tone*): I'm Mrs. Birling, y'know. My husband has just explained why you're here, and while we'll be glad to tell you anything you want to know, I don't think we can help you much.

SHEILA: No, Mother—please!

MRS. BIRLING (*affecting great surprise*): What's the matter, Sheila?

SHEILA (*hesitantly*): I know it sounds silly——

MRS. BIRLING: What does?

SHEILA: You see, I feel you're beginning all wrong. And I'm afraid you'll say something or do something that you'll be sorry for afterwards.

MRS. BIRLING: I don't know what you're talking about, Sheila.

SHEILA: We all started like that—so confident, so pleased with ourselves until he began asking us questions.

MRS. BIRLING *looks from* SHEILA *to the* INSPECTOR.

MRS. BIRLING: You seem to have made a great impression on this child, Inspector.

INSPECTOR (*coolly*): We often do on the young ones. They're more impressionable.

He and MRS. BIRLING *look at each other for a moment. Then* MRS. BIRLING *turns to* SHEILA *again.*

MRS. BIRLING: You're looking tired, dear. I think you ought to go to bed—and forget about this absurd business. You'll feel better in the morning.

SHEILA: Mother, I couldn't possibly go. Nothing could be worse for me. We've settled all that. I'm staying here until I know why that girl killed herself.

MRS. BIRLING: Nothing but morbid curiosity.

SHEILA: No it isn't.

MRS. BIRLING: Please don't contradict me like that. And in any case I don't suppose for a moment that we can understand why the girl committed suicide. Girls of that class——

SHEILA (*urgently, cutting in*): Mother, don't—please don't. For your own sake, as well as ours, you mustn't——

MRS. BIRLING (*annoyed*): Mustn't—what? Really, Sheila!

SHEILA (*slowly, carefully now*): You mustn't try to build up a kind of wall between us and that girl. If you do, then the Inspector will just break it down. And it'll be all the worse when he does.

MRS. BIRLING: I don't understand you. (*To* INSPECTOR.) Do you?

INSPECTOR: Yes. And she's right.

MRS. BIRLING (*haughtily*): I beg your pardon!

INSPECTOR (*very plainly*): I said Yes—I do understand her. And she's right.

MRS. BIRLING: That—I consider—is a trifle impertinent, Inspector. (SHEILA *gives short hysterical laugh.*) Now, what is it, Sheila?

SHEILA: I don't know. Perhaps it's because *impertinent* is such a silly word.

MRS. BIRLING: In any case . . .

SHEILA: But, Mother, do stop before it's too late.

MRS. BIRLING: If you mean that the Inspector will take offence——

INSPECTOR (*cutting in, calmly*): No, no. I never take offence.

MRS. BIRLING: I'm glad to hear it. Though I must add that it seems to me that we have more reason for taking offence.

INSPECTOR: Let's leave *offence* out of it, shall we?

GERALD: I think we'd better.

SHEILA: So do I.

MRS. BIRLING (*rebuking them*): *I'm* talking to the Inspector now, if you don't mind. (*To* INSPECTOR, *rather grandly.*) I realise that you may have to conduct some sort of enquiry, but I must say that so far you seem to be conducting it in a rather peculiar and offensive manner. You know of course that my husband was Lord Mayor only two years ago and that he's still a magistrate——

GERALD (*cutting in, rather impatiently*): Mrs. Birling, the Inspector knows all that. And I don't think it's a very good idea to remind him——

SHEILA (*cutting in*): It's crazy. Stop it, please, Mother.

INSPECTOR (*imperturbable*): Yes. Now what about Mr. Birling?

MRS. BIRLING: He's coming back in a moment. He's just talking to my son, Eric, who seems to be in an excitable silly mood.

INSPECTOR: What's the matter with him?

MRS. BIRLING: Eric? Oh—I'm afraid he may have had rather too much to drink to-night. We were having a little celebration here——

INSPECTOR (*cutting in*): Isn't he used to drinking?

MRS. BIRLING: No, of course not. He's only a boy.

INSPECTOR: No, he's a young man. And some young men drink far too much.

SHEILA: And Eric's one of them.

MRS. BIRLING (*very sharply*): Sheila!

SHEILA (*urgently*): I don't want to get poor Eric into trouble. He's probably in enough trouble already. But we really must stop these silly pretences. This isn't the time to pretend that Eric isn't used to drink. He's been steadily drinking too much for the last two years.

MRS. BIRLING (*staggered*): It isn't true. You know him, Gerald—and you're a man—you must know it isn't true.

INSPECTOR (*as* GERALD *hesitates*): Well, Mr. Croft?

GERALD (*apologetically, to* MRS. BIRLING): I'm afraid it is, y'know. Actually I've never seen much of him outside this house—but—well, I have gathered that he does drink pretty hard.

MRS. BIRLING (*bitterly*): And this is the time you choose to tell me.

SHEILA: Yes, of course it is. That's what I meant when I talked about building up a wall that's sure to be knocked flat. It makes it all the harder to bear.

MRS. BIRLING: But it's you—and not the Inspector here—who's doing it——

SHEILA: Yes, but don't you see? *He hasn't started on you yet.*

MRS. BIRLING (*after pause, recovering herself*): If necessary I shall be glad to answer any questions the Inspector wishes to ask me. Though naturally I don't know anything about this girl.

INSPECTOR (*gravely*): We'll see, Mrs. Birling.

Enter BIRLING, *who closes door behind him.*

BIRLING (*rather hot, bothered*): I've been trying to persuade Eric to go to bed, but he won't. Now he says you told him to stay up. Did you?

INSPECTOR: Yes, I did.

BIRLING: Why?

INSPECTOR: Because I shall want to talk to him, Mr. Birling.

BIRLING: I can't see why you should, but if you must, then I suggest you do it now. Have him in and get it over, then let the lad go.

INSPECTOR: No, I can't do that yet. I'm sorry, but he'll have to wait.

BIRLING: Now look here, Inspector——

INSPECTOR (*cutting in, with authority*): He must wait his turn.

SHEILA (*to* MRS. BIRLING): You see?

MRS. BIRLING: No, I don't. And please be quiet, Sheila.

BIRLING (*angrily*): Inspector, I've told you before, I don't like your tone nor the way you're handling this enquiry. And I don't propose to give you much more rope.

INSPECTOR: You needn't give me any rope.

SHEILA (*rather wildly, with laugh*): No, he's giving us rope—so that we'll hang ourselves.

BIRLING (*to* MRS. BIRLING): What's the matter with that child?

MRS. BIRLING: Over-excited. And she refused to go. (*With sudden anger, to* INSPECTOR.) Well, come along—what is it you want to know?

INSPECTOR (*coolly*): At the end of January, last year, this girl Eva Smith had to leave Milwards, because Miss Birling compelled them to discharge her, and then she stopped being Eva Smith, looking for a job, and became Daisy Renton, with other ideas. (*Sharply turning on him.*) Mr. Croft, when did you first get to know her?

An exclamation of surprise from BIRLING *and* MRS. BIRLING.

GERALD: Where did you get the idea that I did know her?

SHEILA: It's no use, Gerald. You're wasting time.

INSPECTOR: As soon as I mentioned the name Daisy Renton, it was obvious you'd known her. You gave yourself away at once.

SHEILA (*bitterly*): Of course he did.

INSPECTOR: And anyhow I knew already. When and where did you first meet her?

GERALD: All right, if you must have it. I met her first, sometime in March last year, in the stalls bar at the Palace. I mean the Palace music hall here in Brumley——

SHEILA: Well, we didn't think you meant Buckingham Palace.

GERALD (*to* SHEILA): Thanks. You're going to be a great help, I can see. You've said your piece, and you're obviously going to hate this, so why on earth don't you leave us to it?

SHEILA: Nothing would induce me. I want to understand exactly what happens when a man says he's so busy at the works that he can hardly ever find time to come and see the girl he's supposed to be in love with. I wouldn't miss it for worlds——

INSPECTOR (*with authority*): Yes, Mr. Croft—in the stalls bar at the Palace Variety Theatre . . .

GERALD: I happened to look in, one night, after a rather long dull day, and as the show wasn't very bright, I went down into the bar for a drink. It's a favourite haunt of women of the town——

MRS. BIRLING: Women of the town?

BIRLING: Yes, yes. But I see no point in mentioning the subject—especially—— (*indicating* SHEILA.)

Mrs. Birling: It would be much better if Sheila didn't listen to this story at all.

Sheila: But you're forgetting I'm supposed to be engaged to the hero of it. Go on, Gerald. You went down into the bar, which is a favourite haunt of women of the town.

Gerald: I'm glad I amuse you——

Inspector (*sharply*): Come along, Mr. Croft. What happened?

Gerald: I didn't propose to stay long down there. I hate those hard-eyed dough-faced women. But then I noticed a girl who looked quite different. She was very pretty—soft brown hair and big dark eyes—— (*breaks off*) My God!

Inspector: What's the matter?

Gerald (*distressed*): Sorry—I—well, I've suddenly realised—taken it in properly—that she's dead——

Inspector (*harshly*): Yes, she's dead.

Sheila: And probably between us we killed her.

Mrs. Birling (*sharply*): Sheila, don't talk nonsense.

Sheila: You wait, Mother.

Inspector (*to* Gerald): Go on.

Gerald: She looked young and fresh and charming and altogether out of place down there. And obviously she wasn't enjoying herself. Old Joe Meggarty, half-drunk and goggle-eyed, had wedged her into a corner with that obscene fat carcase of his——

Mrs. Birling (*cutting in*): There's no need to be disgusting. And surely you don't mean Alderman Meggarty?

Gerald: Of course I do. He's a notorious womaniser as well as being one of the worst sots and rogues in Brumley——

Inspector: Quite right.

Mrs. Birling (*staggered*): Well, really! Alderman Meggarty! I must say, we *are* learning something to-night.

Sheila (*coolly*): Of course we are. But everybody knows about that horrible old Meggarty. A girl I know had to see him at the Town Hall one afternoon and she only escaped with a torn blouse——

Birling (*sharply, shocked*): Sheila!

Inspector (*to* Gerald): Go on, please.

Gerald: The girl saw me looking at her and then gave me a glance that was nothing less than a cry for help. So I went across and told Joe Meggarty some nonsense—that the manager had a message for him or something like that—got him out of the way—and then told the girl that if she didn't want any more of that sort of thing, she'd better let me take her out of there. She agreed at once.

INSPECTOR: Where did you go?

GERALD: We went along to the County Hotel, which I knew would be quiet at that time of night, and we had a drink or two and talked.

INSPECTOR: Did she drink much at that time?

GERALD: No. She only had a port and lemonade—or some such concoction. All she wanted was to talk—a little friendliness—and I gathered that Joe Meggarty's advances had left her rather shaken—as well they might——

INSPECTOR: She talked about herself?

GERALD: Yes. I asked her questions about herself. She told me her name was Daisy Renton, that she'd lost both parents, that she came originally from somewhere outside Brumley. She also told me she'd had a job in one of the works here and had had to leave after a strike. She said something about the shop too, but wouldn't say which it was, and she was deliberately vague about what happened. I couldn't get any exact details from her about her past life. She wanted to talk about herself—just because she felt I was interested and friendly—but at the same time she wanted to be Daisy Renton—and not Eva Smith. In fact, I heard that name for the first time to-night. What she did let slip—though she didn't mean to—was that she was desperately hard up and at that moment was actually hungry. I made the people at the County find some food for her.

INSPECTOR: And then you decided to keep her—as your mistress?

MRS. BIRLING: What?

SHEILA: Of course, Mother. It was obvious from the start. Go on, Gerald. Don't mind Mother.

GERALD (steadily): I discovered, not that night but two nights later, when we met again—not accidentally this time of course—that in fact she hadn't a penny and was going to be turned out of the miserable back room she had. It happened that a friend of mine, Charlie Brunswick, had gone off to Canada for six months and had let me have the key of a nice little set of rooms he had—in Morgan Terrace—and had asked me to keep an eye on them for him and use them if I wanted to. So I insisted on Daisy moving into those rooms and I made her take some money to keep her going there. (Carefully, to the INSPECTOR) I want you to understand that I didn't install her there so that I could make love to her. I made her go to Morgan Terrace because I was sorry for her, and didn't like the idea of her going back to the Palace bar. I didn't ask for anything in return.

INSPECTOR: I see.

Sheila: Yes, but why are you saying that to him? You ought to be saying it to me.

Gerald: I suppose I ought really. I'm sorry, Sheila. Somehow I——

Sheila (*cutting in, as he hesitates*): I know. Somehow he makes you.

Inspector: But she became your mistress?

Gerald: Yes. I suppose it was inevitable. She was young and pretty and warm-hearted—and intensely grateful. I became at once the most important person in her life—you understand?

Inspector: Yes. She was a woman. She was lonely. Were you in love with her?

Sheila: Just what I was going to ask?

Birling (*angrily*): I really must protest——

Inspector (*turning on him sharply*): Why should you do any protesting? It was you who turned the girl out in the first place.

Birling (*rather taken aback*): Well, I only did what any employer might have done. And what I was going to say was that I protest against the way in which my daughter, a young unmarried girl, is being dragged into this——

Inspector (*sharply*): Your daughter isn't living on the moon. She's here in Brumley too.

Sheila: Yes, and it was I who had the girl turned out of her job at Milwards. *And* I'm supposed to be engaged to Gerald. And I'm not a child, don't forget. I've a right to know. *Were* you in love with her, Gerald?

Gerald (*hesitatingly*): It's hard to say. I didn't feel about her as she felt about me.

Sheila (*with sharp sarcasm*): Of course not. You were the wonderful Fairy Prince. You must have adored it, Gerald.

Gerald: All right—I did for a time. Nearly any man would have done.

Sheila: That's probably about the best thing you've said to-night. At least it's honest. Did you go and see her every night?

Gerald: No. I wasn't telling you a complete lie when I said I'd been very busy at the works all that time. We were very busy. But of course I did see a good deal of her.

Mrs. Birling: I don't think we want any further details of this disgusting affair——

Sheila (*cutting in*): I do. And, anyhow, we haven't had any details yet.

GERALD: And you're not going to have any. (*To* MRS. BIRLING.) You know, it wasn't disgusting.

MRS. BIRLING: It's disgusting to me.

SHEILA: Yes, but after all, you didn't come into this, did you, Mother?

GERALD: Is there anything else you want to know—that you ought to know?

INSPECTOR: Yes. When did this affair end?

GERALD: I can tell you exactly. In the first week of September. I had to go away for several weeks then—on business—and by that time Daisy knew it was coming to an end. So I broke it off definitely before I went.

INSPECTOR: How did she take it?

GERALD: Better than I'd hoped. She was—very gallant—about it.

SHEILA (*with irony*): That was nice for you.

GERALD: No, it wasn't. (*He waits a moment, then in low, troubled tone.*) She told me she'd been happier than she'd ever been before—but that she knew it couldn't last—hadn't expected it to last. She didn't blame me at all. I wish to God she had now. Perhaps I'd feel better about it.

INSPECTOR: She had to move out of those rooms?

GERALD: Yes, we'd agreed about that. She'd saved a little money during the summer—she'd lived very economically on what I'd allowed her—and didn't want to take any more from me, but I insisted on a parting gift of enough money—though it wasn't so very much—to see her through to the end of the year.

INSPECTOR: Did she tell you what she proposed to do after you'd left her?

GERALD: No. She refused to talk about that. I got the idea, once or twice from what she said, that she thought of leaving Brumley. Whether she did or not—I don't know. Did she?

INSPECTOR: Yes. She went away for about two months. To some seaside place.

GERALD: By herself?

INSPECTOR: Yes. I think she went away—to be alone, to be quiet, to remember all that had happened between you.

GERALD: How do you know that?

INSPECTOR: She kept a rough sort of diary. And she said there that she had to go away and be quiet and remember "just to make it last longer". She felt there'd never be anything as good again for her—so she had to make it last longer.

GERALD (*gravely*): I see. Well, I never saw her again, and that's all I can tell you.

INSPECTOR: It's all I want to know from you.

GERALD: In that case—as I'm rather more—upset—by this business than I probably appear to be—and—well, I'd like to be alone for a little while—I'd be glad if you'd let me go.

INSPECTOR: Go where? Home?

GERALD: No. I'll just go out—walk about—for a while, if you don't mind. I'll come back.

INSPECTOR: All right, Mr. Croft.

SHEILA: But just in case you forget—or decide not to come back, Gerald, I think you'd better take this with you. (*She hands him the ring.*)

GERALD: I see. Well, I was expecting this.

SHEILA: I don't dislike you as I did half an hour ago, Gerald. In fact, in some odd way, I rather respect you more than I've ever done before. I knew anyhow you were lying about those months last year when you hardly came near me. I knew there was something fishy about that time. And now at least you've been honest. And I believe what you told us about the way you helped her at first. Just out of pity. And it was my fault really that she was so desperate when you first met her. But this has made a difference. You and I aren't the same people who sat down to dinner here. We'd have to start all over again, getting to know each other——

BIRLING: Now, Sheila, I'm not defending him. But you must understand that a lot of young men——

SHEILA: Don't interfere, please, Father. Gerald knows what I mean, and you apparently don't.

GERALD: Yes, I know what you mean. But I'm coming back—if I may.

SHEILA: All right.

MRS. BIRLING: Well, really, I don't know. I think we've just about come to an end of this wretched business——

GERALD: I don't think so. Excuse me.

He goes out. They watch him go in silence. We hear the front door slam.

SHEILA (*to* INSPECTOR): You know, you never showed him that photograph of her.

INSPECTOR: No. It wasn't necessary. And I thought it better not to.

MRS. BIRLING: You have a photograph of this girl?

INSPECTOR: Yes. I think you'd better look at it.

MRS. BIRLING: I don't see any particular reason why I should——

INSPECTOR: Probably not. But you'd better look at it.

MRS. BIRLING: Very well. (*He produces the photograph and she looks hard at it.*)

INSPECTOR (*taking back the photograph*): You recognise her?

MRS. BIRLING: No. Why should I?

INSPECTOR: Of course she might have changed lately, but I can't believe she could have changed so much.

MRS. BIRLING: I don't understand you, Inspector.

INSPECTOR: You mean you don't choose to do, Mrs. Birling.

MRS. BIRLING (*angrily*): I meant what I said.

INSPECTOR: You're not telling me the truth.

MRS. BIRLING: I beg your pardon!

BIRLING (*angrily, to* INSPECTOR): Look here, I'm not going to have this, Inspector. You'll apologise at once.

INSPECTOR: Apologise for what—doing my duty?

BIRLING: No, for being so offensive about it. I'm a public man——

INSPECTOR (*massively*): Public men, Mr. Birling, have responsibilities as well as privileges.

BIRLING: Possibly. But you weren't asked to come here to talk to me about my responsibilities.

SHEILA: Let's hope not. Though I'm beginning to wonder.

MRS. BIRLING: Does that mean anything, Sheila?

SHEILA: It means that we've no excuse now for putting on airs and that if we've any sense we won't try. Father threw this girl out because she asked for decent wages. I went and pushed her further out, right into the street, just because I was angry and she was pretty. Gerald set her up as his mistress and then dropped her when it suited him. And now you're pretending you don't recognise her from that photograph. I admit I don't know why you should, but I know jolly well you did in fact recognise her, from the way you looked. And if you're not telling the truth, why should the Inspector apologise? And can't you see, both of you, you're making it worse?

She turns away. We hear the front door slam again.

BIRLING: That was the door again.

MRS. BIRLING: Gerald must have come back.

INSPECTOR: Unless your son has just gone out.

BIRLING: I'll see.

He goes out quickly. INSPECTOR *turns to* MRS. BIRLING.

INSPECTOR: Mrs. Birling, you're a member—a prominent member—of the Brumley Women's Charity Organisation, aren't you?

MRS. BIRLING *does not reply.*

SHEILA: Go on, Mother. You might as well admit it. (*To* IN-SPECTOR.) Yes, she is. Why?

INSPECTOR (*calmly*): It's an organisation to which women in distress can appeal for help in various forms. Isn't that so?

MRS. BIRLING (*with dignity*): Yes. We've done a great deal of useful work in helping deserving cases.

INSPECTOR: There was a meeting of the interviewing committee two weeks ago?

MRS. BIRLING: I dare say there was.

INSPECTOR: You know very well there was, Mrs. Birling. You were in the chair.

MRS. BIRLING: And if I was, what business is it of yours?

INSPECTOR (*severely*): Do you want me to tell you—in plain words?

Enter BIRLING, *looking rather agitated.*

BIRLING: That must have been Eric.

MRS. BIRLING (*alarmed*): Have you been up to his room?

BIRLING: Yes. And I called out on both landings. It must have been Eric we heard go out then.

MRS. BIRLING: Silly boy! Where can he have gone to?

BIRLING: I can't imagine. But he was in one of his excitable queer moods, and even though we don't need him here——

INSPECTOR (*cutting in, sharply*): We do need him here. And if he's not back soon, I shall have to go and find him.

BIRLING *and* MRS. BIRLING *exchange bewildered and rather frightened glances.*

SHEILA: He's probably just gone to cool off. He'll be back soon.

INSPECTOR (*severely*): I hope so.

MRS. BIRLING: And why should you hope so?

INSPECTOR: I'll explain why when you've answered my questions, Mrs. Birling.

BIRLING: Is there any reason why my wife should answer questions from you, Inspector?

INSPECTOR: Yes, a very good reason. You'll remember that Mr. Croft told us—quite truthfully, I believe—that he hadn't spoken to or seen Eva Smith since last September. But Mrs. Birling spoke to and saw her only two weeks ago.

SHEILA (*astonished*): Mother!

BIRLING: Is this true?

MRS. BIRLING (*after a pause*): Yes, quite true.

INSPECTOR: She appealed to your organisation for help?

MRS. BIRLING: Yes.

INSPECTOR: Not as Eva Smith?

MRS. BIRLING: No. Nor as Daisy Renton.

INSPECTOR: As what then?

MRS. BIRLING: First, she called herself Mrs. Birling——

BIRLING (*astounded*): *Mrs. Birling!*

MRS. BIRLING: Yes. I think it was simply a piece of gross impertinence—quite deliberate—and naturally that was one of the things that prejudiced me against her case.

BIRLING: And I should think so! Damned impudence!

INSPECTOR: You admit being prejudiced against her case?

MRS. BIRLING: Yes.

SHEILA: Mother, she's just died a horrible death—don't forget.

MRS. BIRLING: I'm very sorry. But I think she had only herself to blame.

INSPECTOR: Was it owing to your influence, as the most prominent member of the committee, that help was refused the girl?

MRS. BIRLING: Possibly.

INSPECTOR: Was it or was it not your influence?

MRS. BIRLING (*stung*): Yes, it was. I didn't like her manner. She'd impertinently made use of our name, though she pretended afterwards it just happened to be the first she thought of. She had to admit, after I began questioning her, that she had no claim to the name, that she wasn't married, and that the story she told at first—about a husband who'd deserted her—was quite false. It didn't take me long to get the truth—or some of the truth—out of her.

INSPECTOR: Why did she want help?

MRS. BIRLING: You know very well why she wanted help.

INSPECTOR: No, I don't. I know why she *needed* help. But as I wasn't there, I don't know what she asked from your committee.

MRS. BIRLING: I don't think we need discuss it.

INSPECTOR: You have no hope of *not* discussing it, Mrs. Birling.

MRS. BIRLING: If you think you can bring any pressure to bear upon me, Inspector, you're quite mistaken. Unlike the other three, I did nothing I'm ashamed of or that won't bear investigation. The girl asked for assistance. We are asked to look carefully into the claims made upon us. I wasn't satisfied with this girl's claim—she seemed to me to be not a good case—and so I used my influence to have it refused. And in spite of what's happened to the girl since, I consider I did my duty. So if I prefer not to discuss it any further, you have no power to make me change my mind.

INSPECTOR: Yes I have.

MRS. BIRLING: No you haven't. Simply because I've done nothing wrong—and you know it.

INSPECTOR (*very deliberately*): I think you did something terribly wrong—and that you're going to spend the rest of your life regretting it. I wish you'd been with me to-night in the Infirmary. You'd have seen——

SHEILA (*bursting in*): No, no, please! Not that again. I've imagined it enough already.

INSPECTOR (*very deliberately*): Then the next time you imagine it, just remember that this girl was going to have a child.

SHEILA (*horrified*): No! Oh—horrible—horrible! How could she have wanted to kill herself?

INSPECTOR: Because she'd been turned out and turned down too many times. This was the end.

SHEILA: Mother, you must have known.

INSPECTOR: It was because she was going to have a child that she went for assistance to your mother's committee.

BIRLING: Look here, this wasn't Gerald Croft——

INSPECTOR (*cutting in, sharply*): No, no. Nothing to do with him.

SHEILA: Thank goodness for that! Though I don't know why I should care now.

INSPECTOR (*to* MRS. BIRLING): And you've nothing further to tell me, eh?

MRS. BIRLING: I'll tell you what I told her. Go and look for the father of the child. It's his responsibility.

INSPECTOR: That doesn't make it any the less yours. She came to you for help, at a time when no woman could have needed it more. And you not only refused it yourself but saw to it that the others refused it too. She was here alone, friendless, almost penniless, desperate. She needed not only money, but advice, sympathy, friendliness. You've had children. You must have known what she was feeling. And you slammed the door in her face.

SHEILA (*with feeling*): Mother, I think it was cruel and vile.

BIRLING (*dubiously*): I must say, Sybil, that when this comes out at the inquest, it isn't going to do us much good. The Press might easily take it up——

MRS. BIRLING (*agitated now*): Oh, stop it, both of you. And please remember before you start accusing me of anything again that it wasn't I who had her turned out of her employment—which probably began it all. (*Turning to* INSPECTOR) In the circumstances I think I was justified. The girl had begun by telling us a pack of lies. Afterwards, when I got at the truth, I discovered that she knew who the father was, she was quite certain about that, and so I told her it was her business to make him responsible. If he refused to marry her—and in my opinion he ought to be compelled to—then he must at least support her.

INSPECTOR: And what did she reply to that?

MRS. BIRLING: Oh—a lot of silly nonsense!

INSPECTOR: What was it?

MRS. BIRLING: Whatever it was, I know it made me finally lose all patience with her. She was giving herself ridiculous airs. She was claiming elaborate fine feelings and scruples that were simply absurd in a girl in her position.

INSPECTOR (*very sternly*): Her position now is that she lies with a burnt-out inside on a slab. (*As* BIRLING *tries to protest, turns on him.*) Don't stammer and yammer at me again, man. I'm losing all patience with you people. *What did she say?*

MRS. BIRLING (*rather cowed*): She said that the father was only a youngster—silly and wild and drinking too much. There couldn't be any question of marrying him—it would be wrong for them both. He had given her money but she didn't want to take any more money from him.

INSPECTOR: Why didn't she want to take any more money from him?

MRS. BIRLING: All a lot of nonsense—I didn't believe a word of it.

INSPECTOR: I'm not asking you if you believed it. I want to know what she said. Why didn't she want to take any more money from this boy?

MRS. BIRLING: Oh—she had some fancy reason. As if a girl of that sort would ever refuse money!

INSPECTOR (*sternly*): I warn you, you're making it worse for yourself. What reason did she give for not taking any more money?

MRS. BIRLING: Her story was—that he'd said something one night, when he was drunk, that gave her the idea that it wasn't his money.

INSPECTOR: Where had he got it from then?

MRS. BIRLING: He'd stolen it.

INSPECTOR: So she'd come to you for assistance because she didn't want to take stolen money?

MRS. BIRLING: That's the story she finally told, after I'd refused to believe her original story—that she was a married woman who'd been deserted by her husband. I didn't see any reason to believe that one story should be any truer than the other. Therefore, you're quite wrong to suppose I shall regret what I did.

INSPECTOR: But if her story was true, if this boy had been giving her stolen money, then she came to you for help because she wanted to keep this youngster out of any more trouble—isn't that so?

MRS. BIRLING: Possibly. But it sounded ridiculous to me. So I was perfectly justified in advising my committee not to allow her claim for assistance.

INSPECTOR: You're not even sorry now, when you know what happened to the girl?

MRS. BIRLING: I'm sorry she should have come to such a horrible end. But I accept no blame for it at all.

INSPECTOR: Who is to blame then?

MRS. BIRLING: First, the girl herself.

SHEILA (*bitterly*): For letting Father and me have her chucked out of her jobs!

MRS. BIRLING: Secondly, I blame the young man who was the father of the child she was going to have. If, as she said, he didn't belong to her class, and was some drunken young idler, then that's all the more reason why he shouldn't escape. He should be made an example of. If the girl's death is due to anybody, then it's due to him.

INSPECTOR: And if her story is true—that he was stealing money——

MRS. BIRLING (*rather agitated now*): There's no point in assuming that——

INSPECTOR: But suppose we do, what then?

MRS. BIRLING: Then he'd be entirely responsible—because the girl wouldn't have come to us, and have been refused assistance, if it hadn't been for him——

INSPECTOR: So he's the chief culprit anyhow.

MRS. BIRLING: Certainly. And he ought to be dealt with very severely——

SHEILA (*with sudden alarm*): Mother—stop—stop!

BIRLING: Be quiet, Sheila!

SHEILA: But don't you see——

MRS. BIRLING (*severely*): You're behaving like an hysterical child to-night. (SHEILA *begins crying quietly.* MRS. BIRLING *turns to* INSPECTOR.) And if you'd take some steps to find this young man and then make sure that he's compelled to confess in public his responsibility—instead of staying here asking quite unnecessary questions—then you really would be doing your duty.

INSPECTOR (*grimly*): Don't worry, Mrs. Birling. I shall do my duty. (*He looks at his watch.*)

MRS. BIRLING (*triumphantly*): I'm glad to hear it.

INSPECTOR: No hushing up, eh? Make an example of the young man, eh? Public confession of responsibility—um?

MRS. BIRLING: Certainly. I consider it your duty. And now no doubt you'd like to say good night.

INSPECTOR: Not yet. I'm waiting.

MRS. BIRLING: Waiting for what?

INSPECTOR: To do my duty.

SHEILA (*distressed*): Now, Mother—don't you see?

MRS. BIRLING (*understanding now*): But surely . . . I mean . . . it's ridiculous . . .

She stops, and exchanges a frightened glance with her husband.

BIRLING (*terrified now*): Look, Inspector, you're not trying to tell us that—that my boy—is mixed up in this——?

INSPECTOR (*sternly*): If he is, then we know what to do, don't we? Mrs. Birling has just told us.

BIRLING (*thunderstruck*): My God! But—look here——

MRS. BIRLING (*agitated*): I don't believe it. I *won't* believe it . . .

SHEILA: Mother—I begged you and begged you to stop——

INSPECTOR *holds up a hand. We hear the front door. They wait, looking towards door.* ERIC *enters, looking extremely pale and distressed. He meets their enquiring stares.*

Curtain falls quickly.

END OF ACT TWO

ACT III

Exactly as at end of Act II. ERIC *is standing just inside the room and the others are staring at him.*

ERIC: You know, don't you?

INSPECTOR (*as before*): Yes, we know.

ERIC *shuts the door and comes further in.*

MRS. BIRLING (*distressed*): Eric, I can't believe it. There must be some mistake. You don't know what we've been saying.

SHEILA: It's a good job for him he doesn't, isn't it?

ERIC: Why?

SHEILA: Because mother's been busy blaming everything on the young man who got this girl into trouble, and saying he shouldn't escape and should be made an example of——

BIRLING: That's enough, Sheila.

ERIC (*bitterly*): You haven't made it any easier for me, have you. Mother?

MRS. BIRLING: But I didn't know it was *you*—I never dreamt, Besides, you're not that type—you don't get drunk——

SHEILA: Of course he does. I told you he did.

ERIC: *You* told her. Why, you little sneak!

SHEILA: No, that's not fair, Eric. I could have told her months ago, but of course I didn't. I only told her to-night because I knew everything was coming out—it was simply bound to come out to-night—so I thought she might as well know in advance. Don't forget—I've already been through it.

MRS. BIRLING: Sheila, I simply don't understand your attitude.

BIRLING: Neither do I. If you'd had any sense of loyalty——

INSPECTOR (*cutting in, smoothly*): Just a minute, Mrs. Birling. There'll be plenty of time, when I've gone, for you all to adjust your family relationships. But now I must hear what your son has to tell me. (*Sternly, to the three of them*) And I'll be obliged if you'll let us get on without any further interruptions. (*Turning to* ERIC) Now then.

ERIC (*miserably*): Could I have a drink first?

BIRLING (*explosively*): No.

332

INSPECTOR (*firmly*): Yes. (*As* BIRLING *looks like interrupting explosively*) I know—he's your son and this is your house—but look at him. He needs a drink now just to see him through.

BIRLING (*to* ERIC): All right. Go on.

> ERIC *goes for a whisky. His whole manner of handling the decanter and then the drink shows his familiarity with quick heavy drinking. The others watch him narrowly.*

(*Bitterly*) I understand a lot of things now I didn't understand before.

INSPECTOR: Don't start on that. I want to get on. (*To* ERIC.) When did you first meet this girl?

ERIC: One night last November.

INSPECTOR: Where did you meet her?

ERIC: In the Palace bar. I'd been there an hour or so with two or three chaps. I was a bit squiffy.

INSPECTOR: What happened then?

ERIC: I began talking to her, and stood her a few drinks. I was rather far gone by the time we had to go.

INSPECTOR: Was she drunk too?

ERIC: She told me afterwards that she was a bit, chiefly because she'd not had much to eat that day.

INSPECTOR: Why had she gone there——?

ERIC: She wasn't the usual sort. But—well, I suppose she didn't know what to do. There was some woman who wanted her to go there. I never quite understood about that.

INSPECTOR: You went with her to her lodgings that night?

ERIC: Yes, I insisted—it seems. I'm not very clear about it, but afterwards she told me she didn't want me to go in but that—well, I was in that state when a chap easily turns nasty—and I threatened to make a row.

INSPECTOR: So she let you in?

ERIC: And that's when it happened. And I didn't even remember—that's the hellish thing. Oh—my God!—how stupid it all is!

MRS. BIRLING (*with a cry*): Oh—Eric—how could you?

BIRLING (*sharply*): Sheila, take your mother along to the drawing-room——

SHEILA (*protesting*): But—I want to——

BIRLING (*very sharply*): You heard what I said. (*Gentler*) Go on, Sybil.

> He goes to open the door while SHEILA *takes her mother out. Then he closes it and comes in.*

INSPECTOR: When did you meet her again?

ERIC: About a fortnight afterwards.

INSPECTOR: By appointment?

ERIC: No. And I couldn't remember her name or where she lived. It was all very vague. But I happened to see her again in the Palace bar.

INSPECTOR: More drinks?

ERIC: Yes, though that time I wasn't so bad.

INSPECTOR: But you took her home again?

ERIC: Yes. And this time we talked a bit. She told me something about herself and I talked too. Told her my name and what I did.

INSPECTOR: And you made love again?

ERIC: Yes. I wasn't in love with her or anything—but I liked her—she was pretty and a good sport——

BIRLING (*harshly*): So you had to go to bed with her?

ERIC: Well, I'm old enough to be married, aren't I, and I'm not married, and I hate these fat old tarts round the town—the ones I see some of your respectable friends with——

BIRLING (*angrily*): I don't want any of that talk from you——

INSPECTOR (*very sharply*): I don't want any of it from either of you. Settle it afterwards. (*To* ERIC.) Did you arrange to see each other after that?

ERIC: Yes. And the next time—or the time after that—she told me she thought she was going to have a baby. She wasn't quite sure. And then she was.

INSPECTOR: And of course she was very worried about it?

ERIC: Yes, and so was I. I was in a hell of a state about it.

INSPECTOR: Did she suggest that you ought to marry her?

ERIC: No. She didn't want me to marry her. Said I didn't love her—and all that. In a way, she treated me—as if I were a kid. Though I was nearly as old as she was.

INSPECTOR: So what did you propose to do?

ERIC: Well, she hadn't a job—and didn't feel like trying again for one—and she'd no money left—so I insisted on giving her enough money to keep her going—until she refused to take any more——

INSPECTOR: How much did you give her altogether?

ERIC: I suppose—about fifty pounds all told.

BIRLING: Fifty pounds—on top of drinking and going round the town! Where did you get fifty pounds from?

As ERIC *does not reply,*

INSPECTOR: That's my question too.

ERIC (*miserably*): I got it—from the office——

BIRLING: *My* office?

ERIC: Yes.

INSPECTOR: You mean—you stole the money?

ERIC: Not really.

BIRLING (*angrily*): What do you mean—*not really?*

ERIC *does not reply because now* MRS. BIRLING *and* SHEILA *come back.*

SHEILA: This isn't my fault.

MRS. BIRLING (*to* BIRLING): I'm sorry, Arthur, but I simply couldn't stay in there. I had to know what's happening.

BIRLING (*savagely*): Well, I can tell you what's happening. He's admitted he was responsible for the girl's condition, and now he's telling us he supplied her with money he stole from the office.

MRS. BIRLING (*shocked*): Eric! You stole money?

ERIC: No, not really. I intended to pay it back.

BIRLING: We've heard that story before. How could you have paid it back?

ERIC: I'd have managed somehow. I had to have some money——

BIRLING: I don't understand how you could take as much as that out of the office without somebody knowing.

ERIC: There were some small accounts to collect, and I asked for cash——

BIRLING: Gave the firm's receipt and then kept the money, eh?

ERIC: Yes.

BIRLING: You must give me a list of those accounts. I've got to cover this up as soon as I can. You damned fool—why didn't you come to me when you found yourself in this mess?

ERIC: Because you're not the kind of father a chap could go to when he's in trouble—that's why.

BIRLING (*angrily*): Don't talk to me like that. Your trouble is—you've been spoilt——

INSPECTOR (*cutting in*): And my trouble is—that I haven't much time. You'll be able to divide the responsibility between you when I've gone. (*To* ERIC.) Just one last question, that's all. The girl discovered that this money you were giving her was stolen, didn't she?

ERIC (*miserably*): Yes. That was the worst of all. She wouldn't take any more, and she didn't want to see me again. (*Sudden startled tone*) Here, but how did you know that? Did she tell you?

INSPECTOR: No. She told me nothing. I never spoke to her.

SHEILA: She told mother.

MRS. BIRLING (*alarmed*): Sheila!

SHEILA: Well, he has to know.

ERIC (*to* MRS. BIRLING): She told you? Did she come here—but then she couldn't have done, she didn't even know I lived here. What happened? (MRS. BIRLING, *distressed, shakes her head but does not reply.*) Come on, don't just look like that. Tell me—tell me—what happened?

INSPECTOR (*with calm authority*): I'll tell you. She went to your mother's committee for help, after she'd done with you. Your mother refused that help.

ERIC (*nearly at breaking point*): Then—you killed her. She came to you to protect me—and you turned her away—yes, and you killed her —and the child she'd have had too—my child—your own grandchild— you killed them both—damn you, damn you——

MRS. BIRLING (*very distressed now*): No—Eric—please—I didn't know—I didn't understand——

ERIC (*almost threatening her*): You don't understand anything. You never did. You never even tried—you——

SHEILA (*frightened*): Eric, don't—don't——

BIRLING (*furious, intervening*): Why, you hysterical young fool— get back—or I'll——

INSPECTOR (*taking charge, masterfully*): Stop! (*They are suddenly quiet, staring at him.*) And be quiet for a moment and listen to me. I don't need to know any more. Neither do you. This girl killed herself—and died a horrible death. But each of you helped to kill her. Remember that. Never forget it. (*He looks from one to the other of them carefully.*) But then I don't think you ever will. Remember what you did, Mrs. Birling. You turned her away when she most needed help. You refused her even the pitiable little bit of organised charity you had in your power to grant her. Remember what you did——

ERIC (*unhappily*): My God—I'm not likely to forget.

INSPECTOR: Just used her for the end of a stupid drunken evening, as if she was an animal, a thing, not a person. No, you won't forget. (*He looks at* SHEILA.)

SHEILA (*bitterly*): I know. I had her turned out of a job. I started it·

INSPECTOR: You helped—but didn't start it. (*Rather savagely, to* BIRLING.) You started it. She wanted twenty-five shillings a week instead of twenty-two and sixpence. You made her pay a heavy price for that. And now she'll make you pay a heavier price still.

BIRLING (*unhappily*): Look, Inspector—I'd give thousands—yes, thousands——

INSPECTOR: You're offering the money at the wrong time, Mr. Birling. (*He makes a move as if concluding the session, possibly shutting up notebook, etc. Then surveys them sardonically.*) No, I don't think any of you will forget. Nor that young man, Croft, though he at least had some affection for her and made her happy for a time. Well, Eva Smith's gone. You can't do her any more harm. And you can't do her any good now, either. You can't even say "I'm sorry, Eva Smith."

SHEILA (*who is crying quietly*): That's the worst of it.

INSPECTOR: But just remember this. One Eva Smith has gone—but there are millions and millions and millions of Eva Smiths and John Smiths still left with us, with their lives, their hopes and fears, their suffering, and chance of happiness, all intertwined with our lives, with what we think and say and do. We don't live alone. We are members of one body. We are responsible for each other. And I tell you that the time will soon come when, if men will not learn that lesson, then they will be taught it in fire and blood and anguish. Good night.

He walks straight out, leaving them staring, subdued and wondering. SHEILA *is still quietly crying.* MRS. BIRLING *has collapsed into a chair.* ERIC *is brooding desperately.* BIRLING, *the only active one, hears the front door slam, moves hesitatingly towards the door, stops, looks gloomily at the other three, then pours himself out a drink, which he hastily swallows.*

BIRLING (*angrily to* ERIC): You're the one I blame for this.

ERIC: I'll bet I am.

BIRLING (*angrily*): Yes, and you don't realise yet all you've done. Most of this is bound to come out. There'll be a public scandal.

ERIC: Well, I don't care now.

BIRLING: You! You don't seem to care about anything. But I care. I was almost certain for a knighthood in the next Honours List——

ERIC *laughs rather hysterically, pointing at him.*

ERIC (*laughing*): Oh—for God's sake! What does it matter now whether they give you a knighthood or not?

BIRLING (*stormily*): It doesn't matter to you. Apparently nothing matters to you. But it may interest you to know that until every penny of that money you stole is repaid, you'll work for nothing. And there's going to be no more of this drinking round the town—and picking up women in the Palace bar——

Mrs. Birling (*coming to life*): I should think not. Eric, I'm absolutely ashamed of you.

Eric: Well, I don't blame you. But don't forget I'm ashamed of you as well—yes, both of you.

Birling (*angrily*): Drop that. There's every excuse for what both your mother and I did—it turned out unfortunately, that's all——

Sheila (*scornfully*): *That's all.*

Birling: Well, what have you to say?

Sheila: I don't know where to begin.

Birling: Then don't begin. Nobody wants you to.

Sheila: I behaved badly too. I know I did. I'm ashamed of it. But now you're beginning all over again to pretend that nothing much has happened——

Birling: Nothing much has happened! Haven't I already said there'll be a public scandal—unless we're lucky—and who here will suffer from that more than I will?

Sheila: But that's not what I'm talking about. I don't care about that. The point is, you don't seem to have learnt anything.

Birling: Don't I? Well, you're quite wrong there. I've learnt plenty to-night. And you don't want me to tell you what I've learnt, I hope. When I look back on to-night—when I think of what I was feeling when the five of us sat down to dinner at that table——

Eric (*cutting in*): Yes, and do you remember what you said to Gerald and me after dinner, when you were feeling so pleased with yourself? You told us that a man has to make his own way, look after himself and mind his own business, and that we weren't to take any notice of these cranks who tell us that everybody has to look after everybody else, as if we were all mixed up together. Do you remember? Yes—and then one of those cranks walked in—the Inspector. (*Laughs bitterly.*) I didn't notice you told him that it's every man for himself.

Sheila (*sharply attentive*): Is that when the Inspector came, just after Father had said that?

Eric: Yes. What of it?

Mrs. Birling: Now what's the matter, Sheila?

Sheila (*slowly*): It's queer—very queer—— (*she looks at them reflectively.*)

Mrs. Birling (*with some excitement*): I know what you're going to say. Because I've been wondering myself.

Sheila: It doesn't much matter now, of course—but *was* he really a police inspector?

BIRLING: Well, if he wasn't, it matters a devil of a lot. Makes all the difference.

SHEILA: No, it doesn't.

BIRLING: Don't talk rubbish. Of course it does.

SHEILA: Well, it doesn't to me. And it oughtn't to you, either.

MRS. BIRLING: Don't be childish, Sheila.

SHEILA (*flaring up*): I'm not being. If you want to know, it's you two who are being childish—trying not to face the facts.

BIRLING: I won't have that sort of talk. Any more of that and you leave this room.

ERIC: That'll be terrible for her, won't it?

SHEILA: I'm going anyhow in a minute or two. But don't you see, if all that's come out to-night is true, then it doesn't much matter who it was who made us confess. And it *was* true, wasn't it? You turned the girl out of one job, and I had her turned out of another. Gerald kept her—at a time when he was supposed to be too busy to see me. Eric—well, we know what Eric did. And mother hardened her heart and gave her the final push that finished her. That's what's important —and not whether a man is a police inspector or not.

ERIC: He was our police inspector all right.

SHEILA: That's what I mean, Eric. But if it's any comfort to you— and it isn't to me—I have an idea—and I had it all along vaguely— that there was something curious about him. He never seemed like an ordinary police inspector——

BIRLING (*rather excited*): You're right. I felt it too. (*To* MRS. BIRLING.) Didn't you?

MRS. BIRLING: Well, I must say his manner was quite extra-ordinary; so—so rude—and assertive——

BIRLING: Then look at the way he talked to me. Telling me to shut up—and so on. He must have known I was an ex-Lord Mayor and a magistrate and so forth. Besides—the way he talked—you remember. I mean, they don't *talk* like that. I've had dealings with dozens of them.

SHEILA: All right. But it doesn't make any real difference, y'know.

MRS. BIRLING: Of course it does.

ERIC: No, Sheila's right. It doesn't.

BIRLING (*angrily*): That's comic, that is, coming from you. You're the one it makes *most* difference to. You've confessed to theft, and now he knows all about it, and he can bring it out at the inquest, and then if necessary carry it to court. He can't do anything to your mother and Sheila and me—except perhaps make us look a bit ashamed of ourselves in public—but as for you, he can ruin you. You know.

SHEILA (*slowly*): We hardly ever told him anything he didn't know. Did you notice that?

BIRLING: That's nothing. He had a bit of information, left by the girl, and made a few smart guesses—but the fact remains that if we hadn't talked so much, he'd have had little to go on. (*Looks angrily at them.*) And really, when I come to think of it, why you all had to go letting everything come out like that, beats me.

SHEILA: It's all right talking like that now. But he made us confess.

MRS. BIRLING: He certainly didn't make me *confess*—as you call it. I told him quite plainly that I thought I had done no more than my duty.

SHEILA: Oh—Mother!

BIRLING: The fact is, you allowed yourselves to be bluffed. Yes—bluffed.

MRS. BIRLING (*protesting*): Now really—Arthur.

BIRLING: No, not you, my dear. But these two. That fellow obviously didn't like us. He was prejudiced from the start. Probably a Socialist or some sort of crank—he talked like one. And then, instead of standing up to him, you let him bluff you into talking about your private affairs. You ought to have stood up to him.

ERIC (*sulkily*): Well, I didn't notice you standing up to him.

BIRLING: No, because by that time you'd admitted you'd been taking money. What chance had I after that? I was a fool not to have insisted upon seeing him alone.

ERIC: That wouldn't have worked.

SHEILA: Of course it wouldn't.

MRS. BIRLING: Really, from the way you children talk, you might be wanting to help him instead of us. Now just be quiet so that your father can decide what we ought to do. (*Looks expectantly at* BIRLING.)

BIRLING (*dubiously*): Yes—well. We'll have to do something—and get to work quickly too. (*As he hesitates there is a ring at the front door. They look at each other in alarm.*) Now who's this? Had I better go?

MRS. BIRLING: No. Edna'll go. I asked her to wait up to make us some tea.

SHEILA: It might be Gerald coming back.

BIRLING (*relieved*): Yes, of course. I'd forgotten about him.

EDNA *appears.*

EDNA: It's Mr. Croft.

GERALD appears, and EDNA *withdraws.*

GERALD: I hope you don't mind my coming back?

MRS. BIRLING: No, of course not, Gerald.

GERALD: I had a special reason for coming. When did that Inspector go?

SHEILA: Only a few minutes ago. He put us all through it——

MRS. BIRLING (*warningly*): Sheila!

SHEILA: Gerald might as well know.

BIRLING (*hastily*): Now—now—we needn't bother him with all that stuff.

SHEILA: All right. (*To* GERALD.) But we're all in it—up to the neck. It got worse after you left.

GERALD: How did he behave?

SHEILA: He was—frightening.

BIRLING: If you ask me, he behaved in a very peculiar and suspicious manner.

MRS. BIRLING: The rude way he spoke to Mr. Birling and me—it was quite extraordinary!

GERALD: Hm—hm!

They all look enquiringly at GERALD.

BIRLING (*excitedly*): You know something. What is it?

GERALD (*slowly*): That man wasn't a police officer.

BIRLING (*astounded*): What?

MRS. BIRLING: Are you certain?

GERALD: I'm almost certain. That's what I came back to tell you.

BIRLING (*excitedly*): Good lad! You asked about him, eh?

GERALD: Yes. I met a police sergeant I know down the road. I asked him about this Inspector Goole and described the chap carefully to him. He swore there wasn't any Inspector Goole or anybody like him on the force here.

BIRLING: You didn't tell him——

GERALD (*cutting in*): No, no. I passed it off by saying I'd been having an argument with somebody. But the point is—this sergeant was dead certain they hadn't any inspector at all like the chap who came here.

BIRLING (*excitedly*): By Jingo! A fake!

MRS. BIRLING (*triumphantly*): Didn't I tell you? Didn't I say I couldn't image a real police inspector talking like that to us?

Gerald: Well, you were right. There isn't any such inspector. We've been had.

Birling (*beginning to move*): I'm going to make certain of this.

Mrs. Birling: What are you going to do?

Birling: Ring up the Chief Constable—Colonel Roberts.

Mrs. Birling: Careful what you say, dear.

Birling (*now at telephone*): Of course. (*At telephone.*) Brumley eight seven five two. (*To others as he waits.*) I was going to do this anyhow. I've had my suspicions all along. (*At telephone.*) Colonel Roberts, please. Mr. Arthur Birling here. . . . Oh, Roberts—Birling here. Sorry to ring you up so late, but can you tell me if an Inspector Goole has joined your staff lately . . . Goole. G-O-O-L-E . . . a new man . . . tall, clean-shaven. (*Here he can describe the appearance of the actor playing the* Inspector.) I see . . . yes . . . well, that settles it. . . . No, just a little argument we were having here. . . . Good night. (*He puts down the telephone and looks at the others.*) There's no Inspector Goole on the police. That man definitely wasn't a police inspector at all. As Gerald says—we've been had.

Mrs. Birling: I felt it all the time. He never talked like one. He never even looked like one.

Birling: This makes a difference, y'know. In fact, it makes *all* the difference.

Gerald: Of course!

Sheila (*bitterly*): I suppose we're all nice people now.

Birling: If you've nothing more sensible than that to say, Sheila, you'd better keep quiet.

Eric: She's right, though.

Birling (*angrily*): And *you*'d better keep quiet anyhow. If that *had* been a police inspector and he'd heard you confess——

Mrs. Birling (*warningly*): Arthur—careful!

Birling (*hastily*): Yes, yes.

Sheila: You see, Gerald, you haven't to know the rest of our crimes and idiocies.

Gerald: That's all right, I don't want to. (*To* Birling.) What do you make of this business now? Was it a hoax?

Birling: Of course. Somebody put that fellow up to coming here and hoaxing us. There are people in this town who dislike me enough to do that. We ought to have seen through it from the first. In the ordinary way, I believe I would have done. But coming like that, bang on top of our little celebration, just when we were all feeling so pleased with ourselves, naturally it took me by surprise.

MRS. BIRLING: I wish I'd been here when that man first arrived. I'd have asked *him* a few questions before I allowed him to ask us any.

SHEILA: It's all right saying that now.

MRS. BIRLING: I was the only one of you who didn't give in to him. And now I say we must discuss this business quietly and sensibly and decide if there's anything to be done about it.

BIRLING (*with hearty approval*): You're absolutely right, my dear. Already we've discovered one important fact—that that fellow was a fraud and we've been hoaxed—and that may not be the end of it by any means.

GERALD: I'm sure it isn't.

BIRLING (*keenly interested*): You are, eh? Good! (*To* ERIC, *who is restless.*) Eric, sit down.

ERIC (*sulkily*): I'm all right.

BIRLING: All right? You're anything but all right. And you needn't stand there—as if—as if——

ERIC: As if—what?

BIRLING: As if you'd nothing to do with us. Just remember your own position, young man. If anybody's up to the neck in this business, you are, so you'd better take some interest in it.

ERIC: I do take some interest in it. I take too much, that's my trouble.

SHEILA: It's mine too.

BIRLING: Now listen, you two. If you're still feeling on edge, then the least you can do is to keep quiet. Leave this to us. I'll admit that fellow's antics rattled us a bit. But we've found him out—and all we have to do is to keep our heads. Now it's our turn.

SHEILA: Our turn to do—what?

MRS. BIRLING (*sharply*): To behave sensibly, Sheila—which is more than you're doing.

ERIC (*bursting out*): What's the use of talking about behaving sensibly? You're beginning to pretend now that nothing's really happened at all. And I can't see it like that. This girl's still dead, isn't she? Nobody's brought her to life, have they?

SHEILA (*eagerly*): That's just what I feel, Eric. And it's what they don't seem to understand.

ERIC: Whoever that chap was, the fact remains that I did what I did. And Mother did what she did. And the rest of you did what you did to her. It's still the same rotten story whether it's been told to a police inspector or to somebody else. According to you, I ought to feel a lot better—— (*To* GERALD.) I stole some money, Gerald, you might as well know—— (*As* BIRLING *tries to interrupt*) I don't care, let him know. The money's not the important thing. It's what happened to the girl and what we all did to her that matters. And I still feel the same about it, and that's why I don't feel like sitting down and having a nice cosy talk.

SHEILA: And Eric's absolutely right. And it's the best thing any one of us has said to-night and it makes me feel a bit less ashamed of us. You're just beginning to pretend all over again.

BIRLING: Look—for God's sake!

MRS. BIRLING (*protesting*): Arthur!

BIRLING: Well, my dear, they're so damned exasperating. They just won't try to understand our position or to see the difference between a lot of stuff like this coming out in private and a downright public scandal.

ERIC (*shouting*): And I say the girl's dead and we all helped to kill her—and that's what matters——

BIRLING (*also shouting, threatening* ERIC): And I say—either stop shouting or get out. (*Glaring at him but in quiet tone*) Some fathers I know would have kicked you out of the house anyhow by this time. So hold your tongue if you want to stay here.

ERIC (*quietly, bitterly*): I don't give a damn now whether I stay here or not.

BIRLING: You'll stay here long enough to give me an account of that money you stole—yes, and to pay it back too.

SHEILA: But that won't bring Eva Smith back to life, will it?

ERIC: And it doesn't alter the fact that we all helped to kill her.

GERALD: But is it a fact?

ERIC: Of course it is. You don't know the whole story yet.

SHEILA: I suppose you're going to prove now you didn't spend last summer keeping this girl instead of seeing me, eh?

GERALD: I did keep a girl last summer. I've admitted it. And I'm sorry, Sheila.

SHEILA: Well, I must admit you came out of it better than the rest of us. The Inspector said that.

BIRLING (*angrily*): He wasn't an Inspector.

SHEILA (*flaring up*): Well, he inspected us all right. And don't let's start dodging and pretending now. Between us we drove that girl to commit suicide.

GERALD: Did we? Who says so? Because I say—there's no more

real evidence we did than there was that that chap was a police inspector.

SHEILA: Of course there is.

GERALD: No, there isn't. Look at it. A man comes here pretending to be a police officer. It's a hoax of some kind. Now what does he do? Very artfully, working on bits of information he's picked up here and there, he bluffs us into confessing that we've all been mixed up in this girl's life in one way or another.

ERIC: And so we have.

GERALD: *But how do you know it's the same girl?*

BIRLING (*eagerly*): Now wait a minute! Let's see how that would work. Now—— (*hesitates*) no, it wouldn't.

ERIC: We all admitted it.

GERALD: All right, you all admitted something to do with a girl. But how do you know it's the same girl?

> *He looks round triumphantly at them. As they puzzle this out, he turns to* BIRLING, *after pause.*

Look here, Mr. Birling. You sack a girl called Eva Smith. You've forgotten, but he shows you a photograph of her and then you remember. Right?

BIRLING: Yes, that part's straightforward enough. But what then?

GERALD: Well, then he happens to know that Sheila once had a girl sacked from Milwards shop. He tells us that it's this same Eva Smith. And he shows her a photograph that she recognises.

SHEILA: Yes. The same photograph.

GERALD: How do you know it's the same photograph? Did you see the one your father looked at?

SHEILA: No, I didn't.

GERALD: And did your father see the one he showed you?

SHEILA: No, he didn't. And I see what you mean now.

GERALD: We've no proof it was the same photograph and therefore no proof it was the same girl. Now take me. I never saw a photograph, remember. He caught me out by suddenly announcing that this girl changed her name to Daisy Renton. I gave myself away at once because I'd known a Daisy Renton.

BIRLING (*eagerly*): And there wasn't the slightest proof that this Daisy Renton was really Eva Smith. We've only his word for it, and we'd his word for it that he was a police inspector, and we know now he was lying. So he could have been lying all the time.

GERALD: Of course he could. Probably was. Now what happened after I left?

MRS. BIRLING: I was upset because Eric had left the house, and this man said that if Eric didn't come back, he'd have to go and find him. Well, that made me feel worse still. And his manner was so severe and he seemed so confident. Then quite suddenly he said I'd seen Eva Smith only two weeks ago.

BIRLING: Those were his exact words.

MRS. BIRLING: And like a fool I said Yes I had.

BIRLING: I don't see now why you did that. She didn't call herself Eva Smith when she came to see you at the committee, did she?

MRS. BIRLING: No, of course she didn't. But, feeling so worried, when he suddenly turned on me with those questions, I answered more or less as he wanted me to answer.

SHEILA: But, Mother, don't forget that he showed you a photograph of the girl before that, and you obviously recognised it.

GERALD: Did anybody else see it?

MRS. BIRLING: No, he showed it only to me.

GERALD: Then, don't you see, there's still no proof it was really the same girl. He might have showed you the photograph of any girl who applied to the committee. And how do we know she was really Eva Smith or Daisy Renton?

BIRLING: Gerald's dead right. He could have used a different photograph each time and we'd be none the wiser. We may all have been recognising different girls.

GERALD: Exactly. Did he ask you to identify a photograph, Eric?

ERIC: No. He didn't need a photograph by the time he'd got round to me. But obviously it must have been the girl I knew who went round to see mother.

GERALD: Why must it?

ERIC: She said she had to have help because she wouldn't take any more stolen money. And the girl I knew had told me that already.

GERALD: Even then, that may have been all nonsense.

ERIC: I don't see much nonsense about it when a girl goes and kills herself. You lot may be letting yourselves out nicely, but I can't. Nor can mother. We did her in all right.

BIRLING (*eagerly*): Wait a minute, wait a minute! Don't be in such a hurry to put yourself into court. That interview with your mother could have been just as much a put-up job, like all this police inspector business. The whole damned thing can have been a piece of bluff.

ERIC (*angrily*): How can it? The girl's dead, isn't she?

GERALD: What girl? There were probably four or five different girls.

ERIC: That doesn't matter to me. The one I knew is dead.

BIRLING: Is she? *How do we know she is?*

GERALD: That's right. You've got it. How do we know any girl killed herself to-day?

BIRLING (*looking at them all, triumphantly*): Now answer that one. Let's look at it from this fellow's point of view. We're having a little celebration here and feeling rather pleased with ourselves. Now he has to work a trick on us. Well, the first thing he has to do is to give us such a shock that after that he can bluff us all the time. So he starts right off. A girl has just died in the Infirmary. She drank some strong disinfectant. Died in agony——

ERIC: All right, don't pile it on.

BIRLING (*triumphantly*): There you are, you see. Just repeating it shakes you a bit. And that's what he had to do. Shake us at once— and then start questioning us—until we didn't know where we were. Oh—let's admit that. He had the laugh of us all right.

ERIC: He could laugh his head off—if I knew it really was all a hoax.

BIRLING: I'm convinced it is. No police enquiry. No one girl that all this happens to. No scandal——

SHEILA: And no suicide?

GERALD (*decisively*): We can settle that at once.

SHEILA: How?

GERALD: By ringing up the Infirmary. Either there's a dead girl there or there isn't.

BIRLING (*uneasily*): It will look a bit queer, won't it—ringing up at this time of night——

GERALD: I don't mind doing it.

MRS. BIRLING (*emphatically*): And if there isn't——

GERALD: Anyway we'll see. (*He goes to telephone and looks up number. The others watch tensely.*) Brumley eight nine eight six. . . . Is that the Infirmary? This is Mr. Gerald Croft—of Crofts Limited. . . . Yes. . . . We're rather worried about one of our employees. Have you had a girl brought in this afternoon who committed suicide by drinking disinfectant—or any like suicide? Yes, I'll wait.

> As he waits, the others show their nervous tension. BIRLING *wipes his brow,* SHEILA *shivers,* ERIC *clasps and unclasps his hand, etc.*

Yes? . . . You're certain of that. . . . I see. Well, thank you very much. . . . Good night. (*He puts down telephone and looks at them.*) No girl has died in there to-day. Nobody's been brought in after drinking disinfectant. They haven't had a suicide for months.

BIRLING (*triumphantly*): There you are! Proof positive. The whole story's just a lot of moonshine. Nothing but an elaborate sell! (*He produces a huge sigh of relief.*) Nobody likes to be sold as badly as that —but—for all that—— (*he smiles at them all*) Gerald, have a drink.

GERALD (*smiling*): Thanks, I think I could just do with one now.

BIRLING (*going to sideboard*): So could I.

MRS. BIRLING (*smiling*): And I must say, Gerald, you've argued this very cleverly, and I'm most grateful.

GERALD (*going for his drink*): Well, you see, while I was out of the house I'd time to cool off and think things out a little.

BIRLING (*giving him a drink*): Yes, he didn't keep you on the run as he did the rest of us. I'll admit now he gave me a bit of a scare at the time. But I'd a special reason for not wanting any public scandal just now. (*Has his drink now, and raises his glass.*) Well, here's to us. Come on, Sheila, don't look like that. All over now.

SHEILA: The worst part is. But you're forgetting one thing I still can't forget. Everything we said had happened really had happened. If it didn't end tragically, then that's lucky for us. But it might have done.

BIRLING (*jovially*): But the whole thing's different now. Come, come, you can see that, can't you? (*Imitating* INSPECTOR *in his final speech.*) *You all helped to kill her.* (*Pointing at* SHEILA *and* ERIC, *and laughing.*) And I wish you could have seen the look on your faces when he said that. (SHEILA *moves towards door.*) Going to bed, young woman?

SHEILA (*tensely*): I want to get out of this. It frightens me the way you talk.

BIRLING (*heartily*): Nonsense! You'll have a good laugh over it yet. Look, you'd better ask Gerald for that ring you gave back to him hadn't you? Then you'll feel better.

SHEILA (*passionately*): You're pretending everything's just as it was before.

ERIC: I'm not!

SHEILA: No, but these others are.

BIRLING: Well, isn't it? We've been had, that's all.

SHEILA: So nothing really happened. So there's nothing to be sorry for, nothing to learn. We can all go on behaving just as we did.

MRS. BIRLING: Well, why shouldn't we?

SHEILA: I tell you—whoever that Inspector was, it was anything but a joke. You knew it then. You began to learn something. And now you've stopped. You're ready to go on in the same old way.

BIRLING (*amused*): And you're not, eh?

SHEILA: No, because I remember what he said, how he looked, and what he made me feel. Fire and blood and anguish. And it frightens me the way you talk, and I can't listen to any more of it.

ERIC: And I agree with Sheila. It frightens me too.

BIRLING: Well, go to bed then, and don't stand there being hysterical.

MRS. BIRLING: They're over-tired. In the morning they'll be as amused as we are.

GERALD: Everything's all right now, Sheila. (*Holds up the ring.*) What about this ring?

SHEILA: No, not yet. It's too soon. I must think.

BIRLING (*pointing to* ERIC *and* SHEILA): Now look at the pair of them—the famous younger generation who know it all. And they can't even take a joke——

The telephone rings sharply. There is a moment's complete silence. BIRLING *goes to answer it.*

Yes? . . . Mr. Birling speaking. . . . *What?*—Here——

But obviously the other person has rung off. He puts the telephone down slowly and looks in a panic-stricken fashion at the others.

BIRLING: That was the police. A girl has just died—on her way to the Infirmary—after swallowing some disinfectant. And a police inspector is on his way here—to ask some—questions——

As they stare guiltily and dumbfounded, the curtain falls.

END OF PLAY

DANGEROUS CORNER

A Play in Three Acts

Produced in May, 1932, at the Lyric Theatre, London, with the following cast:

ROBERT CAPLAN	RICHARD BIRD
FREDA CAPLAN	MARIE NEY
BETTY WHITEHOUSE	ISLA BEVAN
GORDON WHITEHOUSE	WILLIAM FOX
OLWEN PEEL	FLORA ROBSON
CHARLES TREVOR STANTON	FRANK ALLENBY
MAUD MOCKRIDGE	ESME CHURCH

Produced by TYRONE GUTHRIE

SCENE: Drawing-room of the Caplan's house at Chantbury Close After dinner.

ACTS II and III same as ACT I.

ACT I

The curtain rises on a stage in darkness. There is a sound of a revolver shot, somewhat muffled, followed by a woman's scream, a moment's silence. After a small interval of silence, FREDA says, with a touch of irony, "There!" and switches on the lights at mantelpiece.

She is revealed as a handsome and vivacious woman of about thirty.

She remains standing by the mantelpiece for a second or two.

OLWEN, *a dark, distinguished creature,* FREDA'S *contemporary, is discovered sitting in a chair near the fireplace.*

BETTY, *a very pretty young thing, is lounging on a settee, and* MISS MOCKRIDGE, *who is your own idea of what a smart middle-aged woman novelist should be, is seated securely in the middle of the room.*

They are all in evening dress, and have obviously been listening to the wireless—from the cabinet on the table, and waiting for the men to join them. FREDA *starts to move across to switch off the set when the wireless announcer, speaking in the accents of his kind, begins:*

ANNOUNCER: You have just been listening to a play in eight scenes, specially written for Broadcasting, by Mr. Humphrey Stoat, called "The Sleeping Dog."

FREDA (*crossing slowly to radio*): And that's that. I hope it didn't bore you, Miss Mockridge?

MISS M.: Not in the least.

BETTY: I don't like the plays and the stuffy talks. I like the dance music and so does Gordon.

FREDA (*switching off the wireless*): You know, Miss Mockridge, every time my brother Gordon comes here he annoys us by fiddling about trying to get dance music.

BETTY: I *adore* switching off the solemn pompous lecturers—just extinguishing them.

MISS M.: What did they call that play?

OLWEN: "The Sleeping Dog."

MISS M.: Why the sleeping dog?

BETTY: Because you had to let him lie.

FREDA: Let who lie?

353

BETTY: Well, they were all telling lies, weren't they? Or they had been.

MISS M.: How many scenes did we miss?

OLWEN: Five, I think.

MISS M.: I suppose they must have been telling a lot of lies in those scenes. That's why that man was so angry—the husband, I mean.

BETTY: But which was the husband? Was it the one with the adenoidy voice?

MISS M. (*briskly*): Yes, the one with the adenoidy voice, and he went and shot himself. Very pathetic, I'm sure.

FREDA: Rather too many adenoids.

MISS M.: They're rather pathetic, too.

They laugh, and then there comes a subdued burst of laughter from the men in the dining-room.

BETTY: Listen to the men.

MISS M.: They're probably laughing at something very improper.

BETTY: No, just gossip. Men gossip like anything.

FREDA: Of course they do.

MISS M.: Quite right. People who don't like gossip aren't interested in their fellow creatures. I insist upon my publishers gossiping.

BETTY: Yes, but the men pretend it's business.

FREDA: They've got a marvellous excuse now that they're all three directors of the firm.

MISS M.: Yes, of course. Miss Peel, I think you ought to marry Mr. Stanton.

OLWEN: Oh, why should I?

MISS M.: To complete the pattern here. Then there'd be three pairs of adoring husbands and wives. I was thinking so all through dinner.

FREDA: There you are, Olwen.

MISS M.: I'm almost prepared to marry Charles Stanton myself to be one of your charmed circle. What a snug little group you are.

FREDA: Are we?

MISS M.: Well, aren't you?

FREDA (*giving the tiniest laugh*): Snug little group. How awful.

MISS M.: Not awful at all. I think it's charming.

FREDA (*smiling*): It sounds disgusting.

BETTY: Yes. Like Dickens or a Christmas card.

MISS M.: And very nice things to be. In these days almost too good to be true.

FREDA (*apparently amused*): Oh, why should it be?

OLWEN: I didn't know you were such a pessimist, Miss Mockridge.

MISS M.: Didn't you? Then you don't read the reviews of my books—and you ought to, you know, being an employee of my publishers. I shall complain of that to my three directors when they come in. (*Gives a slight laugh.*) Certainly I'm a pessimist. But I didn't mean it that way, of course. I think it's wonderful.

FREDA: It *is* rather nice here. We've been lucky.

OLWEN: Enchanting. I hate to leave it. (*To* MISS M.) You know I'm in the town office now—not down here at the press—but I come back as often as I can.

MISS M.: I'm sure you do. It must be so comforting to be all so settled.

BETTY: Pretty good.

MISS M. (*to* FREDA): But I suppose you all miss your brother-in-law. He used to be down here with you too, didn't he?

FREDA (*who obviously does not like this*): You mean Robert's brother, Martin.

MISS M.: Yes, Martin Caplan. I was in America at the time and never quite understood what happened. Something rather dreadful, wasn't it? (*There is a pause and* BETTY *and* OLWEN *look at* FREDA. MISS M. *looks from one to the other.*) Oh, have I dropped a brick? I always am dropping bricks.

FREDA (*very quietly*): No, not at all. It was distressing for us at the time, but it's all right now. Martin shot himself. It happened nearly a year ago—last June, in fact—not here, but at Fallows End, about twenty miles away. He'd taken a cottage there.

MISS M.: Oh, yes—dreadful business, of course. I only met him twice, I think. I remember I thought him very amusing and charming. He was very handsome, wasn't he?

> *Enter* STANTON *and* GORDON. STANTON *is a man about forty, with a rather studied and slightly sardonic manner.* GORDON *is in his earlier twenties, and an attractive if somewhat excitable youngster.*

OLWEN: Yes, very handsome.

STANTON (*with jovial condescension*): Who's very handsome?

FREDA: Not you, Charles.

STANTON: May we know or is it some grand secret between you?

GORDON (*taking* BETTY's *hand*): They were talking about me. Betty, why do you allow them all to talk about your husband in this fulsome fashion. Have you no shame, girl?

BETTY (*holding his hand*): Darling, I'm sure you've had too much manly gossip and old brandy. You're beginning to look purple in the face and bloated—a typical financier.

    Enter ROBERT. *He is in his early thirties and is a good specimen. You might not always respect his judgment, but you cannot help liking him.*

ROBERT: Sorry to be so late, Freda—but it's that wretched puppy of yours.

FREDA: Oh, what's it been doing now?

ROBERT: It was eating the script of Sonia William's new novel, and I thought it might make him sick. You see, Miss Mockridge, how we talk of you novelists.

MISS M.: Yes, I heard you. I've just been saying what a charming cosy little group you've made here, all of you.

ROBERT: I'm glad you think so.

MISS M.: I think you've all been lucky.

ROBERT: I agree, we have.

STANTON: It's not all luck, Miss Mockridge. You see, we all happen to be nice easy-going people.

ROBERT (*playfully, perhaps too playfully*): Except Betty—she's terribly wild.

STANTON: That's only because Gordon doesn't beat her often enough—yet.

MISS M.: You see, Miss Peel, Mr. Stanton is still the cynical bachelor—I'm afraid he rather spoils the picture.

STANTON: Miss Peel can't afford to talk—she's transferred herself to the London office and deserted us.

OLWEN: I come back here as often as I'm asked.

GORDON: But whether it's to see me or Robert, we can't yet decide. Anyhow, our wives are getting jealous.

BETTY (*laughing*): Oh, frightfully.

GORDON (*beginning to fiddle about with wireless*): What's disturbing the ether to-night? Anybody know?

FREDA: Oh, Gordon, don't start it again. We've only just turned it off.

GORDON: What did you hear?

FREDA: The last half of a play.

OLWEN: It was called "The Sleeping Dog."

STANTON: Why?

MISS M.: We're not sure—something to do with lies, and a gentleman shooting himself.

STANTON: What fun they have at the B.B.C.

OLWEN (*who has been thinking*): You know, I believe I understand that play now. The sleeping dog was the truth, do you see, and that man—the husband—insisted upon disturbing it.

ROBERT: He was quite right to disturb it.

STANTON: Was he? I wonder. I think it a very sound idea—the truth as a sleeping dog.

MISS M. (*who doesn't care*): Of course we do spend too much of our time telling lies and acting them.

BETTY (*in her best childish manner*): Oh, but one has to. I'm always fibbing. I do it all day long.

GORDON (*still fiddling with the wirless*): You do, darling, you do.

BETTY: It's the secret of my charm.

MISS M. (*rather grimly*): Very likely. But we meant something much more serious.

ROBERT: Serious or not, I'm all for it coming out. It's healthy.

STANTON: I think telling the truth is about as healthy as skidding round a corner at sixty.

FREDA (*who is being either malicious or enigmatic*): And life's got a lot of dangerous corners—hasn't it, Charles?

STANTON (*a match for her or anybody else present*): It can have—if you don't choose your route well. To lie or not to lie—what do you think, Olwen? You're looking terribly wise.

OLWEN (*very seriously*): I agree with you. I think telling everything is dangerous. The point is, I think—there's truth *and* truth.

GORDON: I always agree to that. Something *and* something.

STANTON: Shut up, Gordon. Go on, Olwen.

MISS M.: Yes—go on.

OLWEN (*thoughtfully*): Well—the real truth—that is, every single little thing, with nothing missing at all, wouldn't be dangerous. I suppose that's God's truth. But what most people mean by truth, what that man meant in the wireless play, is only half the real truth. It doesn't tell you all that went on inside everybody. It simply gives you a lot of facts that happened to have been hidden away and were perhaps a lot better hidden away. It's rather treacherous stuff.

GORDON: Yes, like the muck they drag out of everybody in the law courts. Where were you on the night of the 27th of November last? Answer yes or no.

MISS M. (*who obviously likes a discussion*): I'm not convinced, Miss Peel. I'm ready to welcome what you call half the truth—the facts.

ROBERT: So am I. I'm all for it.

FREDA (*enigmatically*): You would be, Robert.

ROBERT: What do you mean by that, Freda?

FREDA (*nonchalantly*): Anything, nothing. Let's talk about something more amusing. Who wants a drink? Drinks, Robert. And cigarettes.

ROBERT (*examining cigarette box on table*): There aren't any here.

FREDA: There are some in this one. (*Taking up musical cigarette box from table.*) Miss Mockridge, Olwen—a cigarette? (*Offering the box.*)

OLWEN (*looking at the box*): Oh, I remember that box. It plays a tune at you, doesn't it. I remember the tune. Yes, it's the Wedding March, isn't it? (*She opens the box, taking a cigarette, and the box plays its own charming tinkly version of the Wedding March.*)

ROBERT: Good, isn't it?

FREDA (*shutting the box*): It can't have been this box you remember. This is the first time I've had it out. It belonged to—someone else.

OLWEN: It belonged to Martin, didn't it? He showed it to me.

There is a tiny silence. The two women look at one another steadily.

FREDA: He couldn't have shown it to you, Olwen. He hadn't got it when you saw him last.

STANTON: How do you know he hadn't got it, Freda?

FREDA: That doesn't matter. I do know. Martin couldn't have· shown you this box, Olwen.

OLWEN: Couldn't he? (*Looks at* FREDA *significantly for a second, then makes a quick change of manner.*) No, perhaps he couldn't. I suppose I got mixed up. I must have seen a box like this somewhere else, and then pushed it on to poor Martin because he was always so fond of things like this.

FREDA *moves away.*

ROBERT: Olwen, I'm going to be rather rude, but I know you won't mind. You know *you* suddenly stopped telling the truth *then*, didn't you? You're absolutely positive that this is the box Martin showed you, just as Freda is equally positive it isn't.

OLWEN: Well, does that matter?

GORDON (*fiddling with wireless*): Not a hoot. I'm trying to find some dance music, but this thing has suddenly decided not to function.

ROBERT (*with irritation*): Then don't fiddle about with it.

BETTY: Don't bully Gordon.

ROBERT: Well, you stop him. No, I don't suppose it does matter, Olwen, but after what we'd been saying, I couldn't help thinking that it was rather an odd provoking situation.

MISS M. (*anxious to be entertained*): Just what I was thinking. It's all terribly provoking. More about the cigarette box, please.

FREDA: It's all perfectly simple——

OLWEN: Wait a minute, please, Freda. I don't think it is all perfectly simple, but I can't see that it matters now.

FREDA: I don't understand you.

ROBERT: Neither do I. First you say that it can't have been the same box and now you say it's not all perfectly simple and begin to hint at grand mysteries. I believe you're hiding something, Olwen, and that isn't like you. Either that box you saw was Martin's or it wasn't——

STANTON (*with his own blend of good humour and brutality*): Oh, damn the box.

BETTY: ⎰ Oh, but Charles—we'd like to hear——
MISS M.: ⎱ But Mr. Stanton——

STANTON: Sorry—but I hate a box that plays tunes at you like that anyway. Let's forget it.

GORDON (*with a sudden touch of bitterness*): Yes, and Martin too. He's not here—and we are, all warm and cosy—such a charming group.

ROBERT: Shut up, Gordon.

GORDON: Don't let's mention Martin or think about him. Bad form. He's dead.

FREDA: Well, there's no need to be hysterical about it, Gordon. One would think you owned Martin, to hear you talk.

BETTY: Instead of which, nobody owned Martin. He belonged to himself. He'd some sense.

ROBERT (*who is rapidly getting out of his depth*): What does all that mean, Betty?

BETTY (*with a laugh*): It means that I'm being rather stupid and that you're all talking a lot of rot and I think I'm going to have a headache any minute.

ROBERT: Is that all?

BETTY: Isn't that quite enough? (*She smiles at him.*)

ROBERT: Go on, Freda.

FREDA: I wish you wouldn't be so absurdly persistent, Robert. But it's quite simple about the cigarette box. It came to us with some other of Martin's things from the cottage. I put it away and this is the first time it's been out here. Now the last time Olwen was at the Fallows End cottage was that Saturday when we all went over—you remember, at the very beginning of June.

GORDON (*with an undercurrent of real emotion*): Gosh—yes. What a day that was. And a marvellous night, wasn't it? That was the time when we all sat out in the garden for hours and Martin told us all about those ridiculous people he'd stayed with in Cornwall—the handwoven people——

BETTY: Yes—and the long, long, thin woman who always said: "Do you belong?"

GORDON (*who means it*): I don't think I ever had a better day We'll never have another like that.

ROBERT: Yes, it was a good day. Though I'd no idea you'd been so excited about it, Gordon.

FREDA: Neither had anybody else. Gordon seems to have decided that he ought to be hysterical every time Martin is mentioned.

BETTY: I suspect it's Robert's old brandy. And those enormous glasses. They go to his head.

GORDON: Well, where do you want them to go to?

ROBERT (*to* FREDA): The point is, then, that that first Saturday in June was the last time Olwen was at Martin's cottage.

FREDA: Yes, and I know that he hadn't got this cigarette box then.

ROBERT: No, he'd have shown it to us if he'd had it then. As a matter of fact, I never remember seeing the thing at the cottage. So there you are, Olwen.

OLWEN (*with an uncertain smile*): There I am.

ROBERT: Yes, but—hang it all—where are you?

OLWEN (*smiling at him affectionately*): You *are* a baby, Robert. I don't know where I am. Out of the dock or the witness box, I hope.

MISS M.: Oh no, please. That would be too disappointing.

BETTY (*who has been thinking*): You know, that *wasn't* the last time you were at the cottage, Olwen. Don't you remember, you and I ran over the next Sunday afternoon, to see Martin about those little etchings?

OLWEN: Yes.

ROBERT: Yes, that's true.

BETTY: But I don't remember him showing us this cigarette box. In fact, I've never seen it before.

STANTON: I've never seen it before, and I don't think I ever want to see it again. I never heard such a lot of fuss about nothing.

FREDA: I wouldn't be too sure about that, Charles. But I may as well tell you—if only to have done with it—that Martin couldn't have shown you the box that Sunday anyhow, because he hadn't got it then.

STANTON (*not without malice*): You seem to know a lot about that box, Freda.

GORDON: That's just what I was going to say. Why are you so grand and knowing about it?

BETTY (*pointing triumphantly*): I know why. You gave it to him.

They all looked at FREDA.

ROBERT: Did you, Freda?

FREDA (*calmly*): Yes, I gave it to him.

ROBERT: That's queer. I don't mean it's queer your giving him the cigarette box—why shouldn't you? But it's queer your never mentioning it. When did you give it to him? Where did you pick it up?

FREDA (*still mistress of the situation*): That's all quite simple too. You remember the day before that awful Saturday. You were staying up in town, and I came up for the day. Well, I happened to see the cigarette box at Calthrop's. It was amusing and rather cheap, so I bought it for Martin.

ROBERT: And Calthrop's sent it to Martin, down at Fallows End, so that he never got it until that last Saturday?

FREDA: Yes.

ROBERT: Well, that's that.

GORDON: I'm sorry, Freda, but it's not quite so simple as all that. You mustn't forget that I was with Martin at the cottage that very Saturday morning.

ROBERT: Well, what about it?

GORDON: Well, I was there when the parcel post came, with the letters in the morning. I remember Martin had a parcel of books from Jack Brookfield—I don't forget anything about that morning, and neither would you if you'd been dragged into that hellish inquest as I was. But he didn't have that cigarette box.

FREDA: I suppose it must have arrived by the afternoon post then. What does it matter?

GORDON: It doesn't matter at all, Freda darling, except that at Fallows End parcels are never delivered by the afternoon post.

FREDA: Yes they are.

GORDON: No.

FREDA (*sharply*): How do you know?

GORDON: Because Martin used to grumble about it and say that he always got books and manuscripts a day late. That cigarette box didn't arrive in the morning, because I saw the post opened, and it couldn't have been delivered in the afternoon. Freda, I don't believe those shop people in town ever *sent* the box. You *took* it to Martin yourself. You did, didn't you?

FREDA (*with a sudden rush of temper*): You are a fool, Gordon.

GORDON: Possibly. But remember I didn't start all this. You did take it to Martin, didn't you?

ROBERT: Did you?

FREDA (*hastily composing herself*): Well, if you must know—I did.

ROBERT: Freda!

GORDON: I thought so.

ROBERT (*amazed*): But, Freda, if you went to the cottage to give Martin the box after Gordon had left, you must have seen Martin later than anybody, only a few hours before he—before he shot himself.

FREDA: I did. I saw him between tea and dinner.

ROBERT: But why have you never said anything about it? Why didn't you come forward at the inquest? You could have given evidence.

FREDA: I could, but why should I? What good would it have done? It was bad enough Gordon having to do it——

GORDON: It was hell.

FREDA: If it could have helped Martin, I'd have gone. But it couldn't have helped anybody.

STANTON: That's true. You were quite right.

ROBERT: Yes, I can understand that. But why didn't you tell *me*? Why did you keep it to yourself, why have you kept it to yourself all this time? You were the very last person to talk to Martin.

FREDA: Was I the last person?

ROBERT: You must have been.

FREDA: Then what about Olwen?

ROBERT: Olwen—Oh—the cigarette box.

FREDA: Yes, of course—the cigarette box. Martin didn't get that box until after tea on that Saturday afternoon, and Olwen admitted that he showed it to her.

BETTY (*who obviously doesn't like all this*): No, she didn't. She said it was some other box, and I vote we believe her and have done with it.

MISS M.: No. No, Mrs. Whitehouse——

BETTY: Yes, I do. It's all wrong going on and on like this.

STANTON: And I second that.

ROBERT: And I don't.

BETTY: Oh, but Robert——

ROBERT: I'm sorry, Betty—though after all you don't come into this and it can't hurt you. But Martin was my brother and I don't like all these mysteries and I've a right to know.

OLWEN: All right, Robert. But must you know now?

FREDA (*coldly*): I don't see the necessity. But then I didn't see the necessity why I should have been cross-examined, with the entire approval of the company apparently. But now that it's your turn, Olwen, I've no doubt that Robert will relent.

ROBERT: I don't see why you should say that, Freda.

OLWEN: I'm sure you don't, Robert.

FREDA (*her turn now*): You might as well admit it, Olwen. Martin showed you that box, didn't he? So you must have seen him, you must have been to the cottage that Saturday night.

OLWEN: Yes, he did show me the box. That was after dinner—about nine o'clock—on that Saturday night.

ROBERT (*completely astounded*): You were there too? But this is crazy. First Freda—then you. And neither of you has said a word about it.

OLWEN: I'm sorry, Robert. I just couldn't.

ROBERT: But what were you doing there?

OLWEN: I'd been worried about—something—something that I'd heard—it had been worrying me for days, and at last I couldn't stand it any longer. I felt I had to see Martin to ask him about it. So I ran over to Fallows End. I had some dinner on the way, and got to the cottage just before nine. Nobody saw me go and nobody saw me leave—you know how quiet it was there. Like Freda, I thought it wouldn't serve any good purpose to come forward at the inquest—so I didn't. That's all.

ROBERT: But you can't dismiss it like that. You must have been the very last person to talk to Martin. You must know something about it.

OLWEN (*wearily*): It's all over and done with. Let's leave it alone. Please, Robert. (*With change of manner.*) Besides, I'm sure we must be boring Miss Mockridge with all this stuff.

MISS M. (*briskly*): Oh no, I'm enjoying it—very much.

OLWEN: We don't mean to discuss it, do we, Freda? There's nothing to discuss. All over.

ROBERT (*who has been brooding. Emphatically*): But look here, Olwen, you must tell me this. Had your visit to Martin that night anything to do with the firm? You say you'd been worried about something.

FREDA: Oh, Robert, please.

ROBERT: I'm sorry, but I must know this. Was that *something* to do with that missing five hundred pounds?

GORDON (*excitedly*): Oh—for God's sake—don't drag that money into it. We don't want all that all over again. Martin's gone. Leave him alone, can't you, and shut up about the rotten money.

FREDA: Gordon, be quiet. You're behaving like an hysterical child to-night. (*To* MISS M.) I'm so sorry.

GORDON (*mumbling*): Oh, so am I. I beg your pardon, Miss Mockridge.

MISS M. (*rising*): Not at all. But I think—if you don't mind—it must be getting late.

FREDA: Oh, no.

ROBERT: It's early yet.

MISS M.: The Pattersons said they'd send their car over for me to take me back. Has it arrived yet, do you know?

ROBERT (*going to the door*): Yes, I heard it arrive when we left the dining-room and I told the man to wait in the kitchen. I'll get hold of him for you.

FREDA (*aware of the irony of this*): Oh, must you really go?

MISS M.: Yes, I really think I ought. It's at least half an hour's run to the Pattersons', and I don't suppose they like their car and chauffeur to be kept out too late. (*Shaking hands with* FREDA.) Thank you so much. (*Shakes hands with* OLWEN.) It's been so delightful seeing you all again—such a charming group you make here. (*Shakes hands with* BETTY.) Good-bye, Mrs. Whitehouse, good-bye. (*Shaking hands with* STANTON.)

FREDA (*going to door*): I think you left your wrap in my room. I'll get it for you.

MISS M. (*at the door*): Good-bye.

ALL: Good-bye.

FREDA (*going out*): I hear you had a very good time in America. . . .

> *Both women go out and door is shut.* OLWEN *looks at the books on shelves.* BETTY *moves up to the bay of piano and takes a cigarette.*

STANTON, *after a sigh of relief, pours out a drink.*

GORDON: For this relief, much thanks.

BETTY: Good Lord—yes. I'm sorry, but I can t bear that woman. She reminds me too much of a geometry mistress we used to have at Lorsdale.

STANTON: I've always suspected your geometry, Betty. Drink, Gordon?

GORDON: No thanks.

STANTON: It's very rum—but nevertheless she's not at all a bad novelist. I don't mean she's just a good seller, but she's a goodish novelist too. Why is it there seems to be always something rather unpleasant about good novelists?

GORDON: I give it up. But I don't call Maud Mockridge a good novelist, Stanton.

BETTY: I bet she's a gossiper.

STANTON: She is. She's notorious for it. That's why they ought to have shut up. She'll embroider that cigarette box story and have it all round London within a week. The Pattersons will have it to-night, to begin with. It must have been agony for her to go away and not hear any more.

GORDON: She wouldn't have gone if she'd thought she'd have heard any more. But she's got something to be going on with. (*With a chuckle.*) She'll probably start a new novel in the morning and we'll all be in it.

BETTY (*bravely*): Well, she'll have to use her imagination a bit about me.

STANTON: And me. Perhaps she'll invent the most frightful vices for us, Betty.

BETTY (*with a laugh*): She can't really do much with what she's just heard, you know. After all, why shouldn't Freda have taken Martin a cigarette box, and why shouldn't Olwen have gone to see him?

OLWEN (*looking at book, idly*): Yes, why not?

BETTY: Oh—I'd forgotten you were there, Olwen. Can I ask you something? After all I don't think I've asked anybody anything, so far, have I?

OLWEN: You can ask. I don't promise to answer.

BETTY: I'll risk it then. Were you in love with Martin, Olwen?

OLWEN (*steadily*): Not in the least.

BETTY: I thought you weren't.

OLWEN: As a matter of fact, to be absolutely candid, I rather disliked him.

BETTY: Yes, I thought so.

GORDON: Oh—rot. I'll never believe that, Olwen. You *couldn't* dislike Martin. Nobody could. I don't mean he hadn't any faults or anything, but with him they just didn't matter. He was one of those people. You had to like him. He was Martin.

BETTY: In other words—your god. You know, Gordon literally adored him. Didn't you, darling?

STANTON: Well, he could be fascinating. And he was certainly very clever. I must admit the firm's never been the same without him.

GORDON: I should think not.

BETTY (*mockingly*): How could it be?

OLWEN *puts book back. Enter* ROBERT *who goes to table, pours out drink, followed by* FREDA *who takes a cigarette.*

ROBERT: Now we can thrash this out.

OLWEN: Oh no, please Robert.

ROBERT: I'm sorry, Olwen. But I want to know the truth now. There's something very queer about all this. First Freda going to see Martin, and never saying a word about it. And then you going to see him too, Olwen, and never saying a word about it either. It's not good enough. You've both been hiding this all along. You may be hiding other things too. It seems to me it's about time some of us began telling the truth—for a change.

FREDA: Do you always tell the truth, Robert?

ROBERT: I try to.

STANTON (*with irony*): Noble fellow. But don't expect too much of us ordinary mortals. Spare our weaknesses.

FREDA (*suddenly mischievous*): What weaknesses?

STANTON (*shrugging his shoulders*): Anything you like, my dear Freda. Buying musical cigarette boxes, for instance. I'm sure that's a weakness.

FREDA (*significantly*): Or making rather too much use of one's little country cottage. I think that, too, in certain circumstances might be described as a weakness.

STANTON: Do you mean Martin's cottage? I hardly ever went there.

FREDA: No, I wasn't thinking of Martin's. I must have been thinking of another one—perhaps your own.

STANTON (*looking at her steadily*): I'm afraid I don't understand.

ROBERT (*exasperated*): Look here, what's all this about? Are *you* starting now, Stanton?

STANTON: Certainly not. (*Laughs.*)

ROBERT: Well, I want to get to the bottom of this Martin business. And I want to do it now.

GORDON: Oh Lord, is this going to be another inquest?

ROBERT: Well, it wouldn't be necessary if we'd heard more of the truth perhaps when there was an inquest. And it's up to you, Olwen. You were the last to see Martin. Why did you go to see him like that? Was it about the missing money?

OLWEN: Yes, it was.

ROBERT: Did you know then that Martin had taken it?

OLWEN: No.

ROBERT: But you thought he had?

OLWEN: I thought there was a possibility he had.

GORDON (*bitterly*): You were all damned ready to think that.

BETTY (*urgently*): Gordon, I want to go home now.

ROBERT: So soon, Betty?

BETTY: I'm going to have an awful headache if I stay any longer. I'm going home—to bed.

GORDON: All right. Just a minute.

STANTON: I'll take you along, Betty, if Gordon wants to stay on.

BETTY (*going to* GORDON): No, I want Gordon to come along too.

GORDON: All right. (*Rising.*) I'll come along. But hang on a minute.

BETTY (*with sudden hysterical scream*): I tell you I want to go now. Take me home.

ROBERT: Why, what's the matter, Betty?

BETTY: I don't know. I'm stupid, I suppose.

GORDON: All right. We'll go. (*Follows her.* FREDA *rises.*)

STANTON: I'll come along too.

ROBERT: But, Betty, I'm awfully sorry if all this stuff has upset you. I know it's nothing to do with you, anyhow——

BETTY (*pushing him aside and running to the door*): Oh, don't go on and on about it. Why can't you leave things alone?

She rushes out and slams the door.

GORDON (*at the door*): Well, good night everybody.

STANTON (*going to door*): I'll see these infants home and then turn in myself.

OLWEN (*with irony*): Very good of you.

STANTON (*smiling grimly*): Good night.

After he goes out, the three who are left drift nearer the fire and one another, and the room has a nice intimate atmosphere.

ROBERT: And now, Olwen, you can tell me exactly why you rushed to see Martin like that about the missing money.

OLWEN: We're all being truthful now, are we?

ROBERT: I want to be.

OLWEN: What about you, Freda?

FREDA (*rather wearily*): Yes, yes, yes, I don't care. What does it matter?

ROBERT (*puzzled again*): Queer way of putting it.

FREDA: Is it? Well sometimes, Robert, I'm rather a queer woman. You'd hardly know me.

OLWEN: You started all this, you know, Robert. Now it's your turn. Will you be truthful with me?

ROBERT: Good God! Yes—of course I will. I loathe all these silly mysteries. But it's not my turn. I asked you a question that you haven't answered yet.

OLWEN: I know you have. But I'm going to ask you one before I do answer yours. I've been wanting to do it for some time but I've never had the chance or never dared. Now, I don't care. It might as well come out. Robert—did you take that money?

ROBERT (*amazed*): Did I take the money?

OLWEN: Yes.

ROBERT: Of course not. You must be crazy, Olwen. (OLWEN *gives a laugh of great relief*.) Do you think, even if I had taken it, I'd have let poor Martin shoulder the blame like that? But Martin took it, of course. We all know that.

OLWEN: Oh, what a fool I've been.

ROBERT: I don't understand. Surely you must have known that Martin took it. You can't have been thinking all this time that I did.

OLWEN: Yes, I have. And I've not been thinking it—I've been torturing myself with it.

ROBERT: But why, why? Damn it all—it doesn't make sense. I might have taken the money—I suppose we're all capable of that, under certain circumstances—but never on earth could I have let somebody else—and especially Martin—take the blame for it. How could you think me capable of such a thing! I thought you were a friend of mine, Olwen—one of my best and oldest friends.

FREDA (*calmly and boldly*): You might as well know, Robert——

OLWEN (*greatly agitated*): Oh no, Freda. Please. Please.

FREDA (*calmly and taking* OLWEN's *arm*): Why not? What does it matter? You might as well know, Robert—and how you can be so dense baffles me—that Olwen is not a friend of yours.

ROBERT: Of course she is.

FREDA: She's not. She's a woman who's in love with you—a very different thing. She's been in love with you for ages.

OLWEN (*in great distress*): Freda, that's damnably unfair. It's cruel, cruel.

FREDA: It's not going to hurt you. And he wanted the truth. Let him have it.

ROBERT: I'm terribly sorry, Olwen. I suppose I've been stupid. We've always been very good friends and I've always been very fond of you.

OLWEN: Stop, stop. Oh, Freda, that was unforgivable. You'd no right to say that.

FREDA: But it's true, isn't it. You wanted the truth, Robert, and here it is—some of it. Olwen's been in love with you for ages. I don't know exactly how long, but I've been aware of it for the last eighteen months. Wives always are aware of these things, you know. And not only that, I'll tell you now what I've longed to tell you for some time—that I think you're a fool for not being aware of it yourself, for not having responded to it, for not having done something drastic about it long before this. If somebody loves you like that, for God's sake enjoy it, make the most of it, hold on to it, before it's too late.

OLWEN (*staring at her*): Freda, I understand now.

FREDA: Understand what?

OLWEN: About you. I ought to have understood before.

ROBERT: If you mean by that, that you understand now that Freda doesn't care for me very much—you're right. We've not been very happy together. Somehow our marriage hasn't worked. Nobody knows——

FREDA: Of course they know.

ROBERT: Do you mean you've told them?

FREDA: No, of course I haven't told them. If you mean by *they* the people we know intimately—our own group here—they didn't need to be told.

ROBERT: But Olwen here has just said she understood about it for the first time.

OLWEN (*gently*): No, I knew about that before, Robert. It was something else I've just——

ROBERT: Well, what is it?

OLWEN: I'd rather not explain. (*Looking away.*)

FREDA: Being noble now, Olwen? You needn't, you know. We're past that.

OLWEN (*in distress*): No, it's not that. It's—it's because I couldn't talk about it. There's something horrible to me about it. And I can't tell you why.

FREDA (*staring at her*): Something horrible?

OLWEN: Yes, something really horrible. Don't let's talk about that side of it.

FREDA: But, Olwen——

OLWEN: I'm sorry I said I understood. It slipped out. Please——

FREDA: Very well. But you've got to talk about that money now. You said you believed all along that Robert had taken it?

OLWEN: It looked to me as if he must have done.

ROBERT: But if you believed that, why didn't you say something?

FREDA: Oh, Robert—can't you see why she couldn't?

ROBERT: You mean—she was shielding me?

FREDA: Yes, of course.

ROBERT: Olwen—I'm terribly sorry. I'd no idea. Though it's fantastic, I must say, that you could think I was that kind of man and yet go on caring enough not to say anything.

FREDA
      (*together*):
OLWEN
{ But it's not fantastic at all.
That's why I said I'd been torturing myself with it.

FREDA (*emphatically*): If you're in love with somebody, you're in love with them, and they can do all sorts of things, be as mean as hell, and you'll forgive them or just not bother about it. At least, some women will.

ROBERT: I don't see you doing it, Freda.

FREDA (*recovering her normal self*): Don't you? But there are a lot of things about me you don't see. But this is what I wanted to say, Olwen. If you thought that Robert had taken that money, then you knew that Martin hadn't?

OLWEN: Yes, I was sure—after I had talked to him that last night—that Martin hadn't taken it.

FREDA (*bitterly*): But you let us all think he had.

OLWEN: I know. I know. But it didn't seem to matter then. It couldn't hurt Martin any more. He wasn't there to be hurt. And I felt I had to keep quiet.

ROBERT: Because of me?

OLWEN: Yes, because of you, Robert.

ROBERT: But Martin *must* have taken it.

OLWEN: No.

ROBERT: That's why he did what he did. He thought he'd be found out. He was terribly nervy—always was, poor chap. And he simply couldn't face it.

OLWEN: No, it wasn't that at all. You *must* believe me. I'm positive that Martin never *touched* that money.

FREDA (*eagerly*): I've always thought it queer that he should. It wasn't Martin's style at all that—doing some sneaky work with a cheque. I know he could be wild—and rather cruel sometimes. But he couldn't be a cautious cunning little sneak-thief. It wasn't his style at all. And he didn't care enough about money.

ROBERT: He spent enough of it. He was badly in debt, you know.

FREDA: Yes, but that's just the point. He didn't mind being in debt. He could have cheerfully gone on being in debt. Money simply didn't matter. Now *you* loathe being in debt. You're entirely different.

OLWEN: Yes, that was one of the reasons, I thought that you——

ROBERT: Yes, I see that. Though I think those fellows who don't care about money, who don't mind being in debt, are just the sort of fellows who help themselves to other people's.

FREDA: Yes, but not in a cautious sneaky way. That wasn't like Martin at all.

ROBERT (*pausing and thinking*): I wonder—Olwen, where did you get the idea that I'd taken it?

OLWEN: Why, because Martin himself was sure that you had taken it. He told me so.

ROBERT (*amazed*): Martin told you so?

OLWEN: Yes. That was the first thing we talked about.

ROBERT: Martin thought I had taken it! But he knew me better than that. Why should he have thought that?

FREDA: You thought he'd been the thief. You didn't know him any better, it seems.

ROBERT: Yes, but that's different. There were special circumstances. And I'd been told something. Besides, I wasn't at all sure. It wasn't until after he shot himself that I felt certain.

OLWEN (*with growing excitement*): You say you'd been told something? But then Martin had been told something too. He'd practically been told that you'd taken that cheque.

ROBERT (*staring at her*): My God!

OLWEN: And do you know who told him that you'd taken the cheque?

ROBERT: I can guess now.

FREDA: Who?

ROBERT (*fiercely*): Stanton, wasn't it?

OLWEN: Yes, Stanton.

ROBERT: But Stanton told me that Martin had taken that cheque.

FREDA ⎧ Oh, but he——

  (*together*): ⎨

OLWEN ⎩ My God, he——

ROBERT: He practically proved it to me. He said he didn't want Martin given away—said we'd all stand in together, all that sort of thing.

OLWEN: But don't you see—he told Martin all that too. And Martin would never have told me if he hadn't known—well, that I would never give you away.

ROBERT (*brooding*): Stanton.

FREDA (*with decision*): Then it was Stanton himself who got that money?

OLWEN: It looks like it.

FREDA (*now counsel for the prosecution*): I'm sure it was. And he's capable of it. You see, he played Martin and Robert off against one another. Could you have anything more vile?

ROBERT (*thoughtfully*): You know, it doesn't follow that Stanton himself was the thief.

FREDA: Of course he was.

ROBERT: Wait. Let's get this clear. Old Slater wanted some money and Mr. Whitehouse signed a bearer cheque for five hundred. Slater always insisted on bearer cheques—though God knows why. The cheque was on Mr. Whitehouse's desk. Slater didn't turn up the next morning, as he said he would, and when he did turn up, three days afterwards, the cheque wasn't there. Meanwhile it had been taken to the bank and cashed. And the bank wasn't the firm's usual place, because the cheque was on Mr. Whitehouse's private account. Only Stanton, Martin or I could have got at the cheque—except dear old Watson, who certainly didn't take it. And—this is the point—none of us was known at this branch at all, but they said the fellow who cashed the cheque was about Martin's age or mine. They were rather vague, I gathered, but what they did remember of him certainly ruled out Stanton himself.

OLWEN: Mr. Whitehouse wouldn't have you identified at the bank, I remember.

FREDA: No, he was too fond of them all, and too hurt. He wasn't well at the time either.

ROBERT: I understood that he simply wanted the one who had taken the money to confess and then go.

OLWEN: He told me that too.

FREDA: Me too. Father was like that, of course. But what made you believe Martin had taken the cheque?

ROBERT: The evidence pointed to Martin and me, and I knew I hadn't taken it.

FREDA (*slowly*): And Stanton told you——?

ROBERT: Stanton told me he'd seen Martin coming out of your father's room.

OLWEN: Stanton told Martin he'd seen *you* coming out of that room.

FREDA (*very emphatically*): Stanton took that money himself.

ROBERT (*fiercely*): Whether he took the money or not, Stanton's got to explain this. (*Moves to door, opens it and snatches up the telephone receiver.*) No wonder he didn't approve of this business and was glad to get out of it. He's got too much to hide.

OLWEN (*sadly*): We'd all got too much to hide.

ROBERT: Then we'll let some daylight into it for once, if it kills us. Stanton's got to explain this. (*Telephoning.*) *Chantbury one two.*

FREDA: When?

ROBERT: To-night.

FREDA: Are you going to get them all back, Robert?

ROBERT: Yes. (*Telephoning.*) Hello, is that you, Gordon? . . . He is, is he? Well, I want you both to come back here. . . . Yes, more and more of it. . . . It's *damned* important. . . . Yes, we're all in it. Oh, no, of course not. We can keep Betty out of it. (FREDA *and* OLWEN *exchange glances.*) All right then. Be as quick as you can. (*Puts back receiver on table in hall, closes the door, switches on the light at doorway and says:* "They're coming back," *as the curtain begins to fall.*)

END OF ACT ONE

ACT II

ROBERT, FREDA *and* OLWEN *are discovered in exactly the same positions as they were at the end of* ACT I.

ROBERT: They're coming back.

FREDA: All of them?

ROBERT: No, not Betty. She's going to bed.

OLWEN (*with a touch of bitterness*): Wise little Betty.

ROBERT: I don't see why you should use that tone of voice, Olwen—as if Betty was cleverly dodging something. You know very well she's not mixed up in this business.

OLWEN: Do I?

ROBERT (*alarmed*): Well, don't you?

FREDA (*grimly amused*): Poor Robert, look at him now. This is *really* serious he's saying to himself. How we give ourselves away. It's a wonder we have any secrets at all.

ROBERT: No, but—hang it all, Olwen—you've no right to sneer at Betty like that. You know very well it's better to keep her out of all this.

OLWEN: No, we mustn't soil her pure young mind.

ROBERT: Well, after all, she's younger than we are—and she's terribly sensitive. You saw what happened to her just before they went. She couldn't stand the atmosphere of all this.

OLWEN: But that wasn't——

ROBERT: Obviously you dislike her, Olwen. I can't imagine why. She's always had a great admiration for you.

OLWEN (*frankly, not maliciously*): Well, I'm sorry, Robert, but I can't return her admiration—except for her looks. I don't dislike her. But—well, I can't be as sorry for her as I'd like to be or ought to be.

ROBERT (*annoyed by this*): You can't be sorry for her. Is it necessary for you or anybody else to be sorry for her? You're talking wildly now, Olwen.

FREDA (*in her best form*): I suspect not, Robert. And anyhow it seems to be our evening for talking wildly. Also, I'm now facing a most urgent problem, the sort of problem that only women have to face. If a man has been dragged back to your house to be told he's a

374

liar and a cad and a sneak and a possible thief, oughtn't you to make a few sandwiches for him?

ROBERT (*heavily*): He'll get no sandwiches from me.

FREDA (*mocking him*): No sincerity, no sandwiches—that's your motto, is it? No? Oh dear—how heavy we are without Martin. And how he would have adored all this. He'd have invented the most extravagant and incredible sins to confess to. Oh, don't look so dreadfully solemn, you two. You might be a bit brighter—just for a minute.

ROBERT (*heavily*): I'm afraid we haven't got your light touch, my dear Freda.

FREDA: I suppose I feel like this because, in spite of everything, I feel like a hostess expecting company, and I can't help thinking about bright remarks and sandwiches.

A bell rings out in the hall.

FREDA: And there they are. You'll have to let them in yourself, Robert.

ROBERT *goes out. As soon as the two women are left together the atmosphere changes. They speak in quick whispers.*

OLWEN: Have you really known a long time?

FREDA: Yes. More than a year. I've often wanted to say something to you about it.

OLWEN: What would you have said?

FREDA: I don't quite know. Something idiotic. But friendly, very friendly. (*Taking both her hands.*)

OLWEN: And I only guessed about you to-night, Freda. And now it all seems so obvious. I can't think why I never guessed before.

FREDA: Neither can I.

OLWEN: This is quite mad, isn't it?

FREDA: Quite mad. And rapidly getting madder. I don't care. Do you? It's rather a relief.

OLWEN: Yes it is—in a way. But it's rather frightening too. Like being in a car when the brakes are gone.

FREDA: And there are cross roads and corners ahead.

Noise of men outside. STANTON *enters first.*

STANTON (*as he enters*): I can't see why. I'm sorry about this, Freda, but it's Robert's doing. He insisted on our coming back.

FREDA (*coldly*): Well, I think Robert was right.

GORDON (*who has gone straight to settee and sprawled on it*): That's a change, anyhow. Well, what's it all about?

ROBERT: Chiefly about that money.

GORDON (*disgusted*): Oh—hell—I thought as much. Why can't you leave poor Martin alone?

ROBERT: Wait a minute, Gordon. Martin didn't take that cheque.

GORDON (*leaping to his feet*): What. Is that true? Are you sure?

FREDA: Yes.

GORDON: You know, I never could understand that. It wasn't *like* Martin.

STANTON (*to* FREDA *and* ROBERT): Do you really believe that Martin didn't get that money? If he didn't, who did? And if he didn't, why did he shoot himself?

ROBERT (*very deliberately*): Stanton, we don't know. But we're hoping that you'll tell us.

STANTON (*with raised eyebrows*): Being funny, Robert?

ROBERT: Not a bit. I wouldn't have dragged you back here to be funny. You told me—didn't you—that you were practically certain that Martin took that cheque?

STANTON: Certainly I did. And I told you why I thought so. All the evidence pointed that way. And what happened afterwards proved that I was right.

ROBERT: Did it?

STANTON: Well, didn't it?

FREDA (*in a sudden flare of passion*): If it did, then why did you tell Martin that you thought Robert had done it?

STANTON (*uneasy*): Don't be ridiculous, Freda. Why should I tell Martin that I thought Robert had done it?

FREDA: Yes, why should you? That's what we want to know.

STANTON: But of course I didn't.

OLWEN (*quietly*): Yes, you did.

STANTON (*turning to her, despairingly*): Olwen! Are you in this too?

OLWEN: Yes, I'm in it too. Because you lied like that to Martin, telling him you were sure Robert took the cheque, you've given me hours and hours and hours of misery.

STANTON: But I never meant to, Olwen. How could I know that you would go and see Martin and that he would tell you?

OLWEN: It doesn't matter whether you knew or not. It was a mean vile lie. After this I feel that I never want to speak to you again.

STANTON: I'm sorry, Olwen. I'd rather anything had have happened than that. You do believe that, don't you? (*Looks at her appealingly but gets no response.*)

FREDA (*coldly, cuttingly*): Apparently the rest of us don't matter very much. But you owe us a few explanations.

ROBERT: You'd better stop lying now, Stanton. You've done enough. Why did you play off Martin and me against each other like that?

FREDA: There can only be one explanation. Because he took that cheque himself.

GORDON (*fiercely*): My God—you didn't, did you, Stanton?

STANTON: Yes, I did.

GORDON (*excitedly, and rushing over to* STANTON *with threatening gestures*): Then you're a rotten swine, Stanton. I don't care about the money. But you let Martin take the blame. You let everybody think he was a thief.

STANTON: Don't be such a hysterical young fool. (*Pushing* GORDON *away.*)

ROBERT: Shut up, Gordon.

STANTON: Keep quiet and stop waving your hands at me. We don't want this to develop into a free fight.

GORDON: But you let——

STANTON: I didn't let Martin take the blame, as you call it. He wasn't the sort to take the blame, and you ought to know that. It happened that in the middle of all the fuss about this money, he went and shot himself. You all jumped to the conclusion that it was because he had taken the money and was afraid of being found out. I let you go on thinking it, that's all. You might as well think he shot himself for that as for anything else. And anyhow he was done with it, out of it. Besides—where he's gone to, it doesn't matter a damn whether people here think you've stolen five hundred pounds or not.

ROBERT: But you deliberately tried to fasten the blame on to Martin or me.

FREDA: Of course he did. That's what makes it so foul.

STANTON: Not really. I'd not the least intention of letting anybody else be punished for what I'd done. I was only playing for time. I took that cheque because I'd got to have some money quickly and I didn't know where to turn. I knew I could square it up in a week, and I knew too that if necessary I could make it all right with old Slater, who's a sportsman. But when it all came out, I'd got to play for time, and that seemed to me the easiest way of doing it.

ROBERT: But you couldn't have cashed the cheque at the bank yourself?

STANTON: No, I got somebody else to do that—a fellow who could keep his mouth shut. It was pure coincidence that he was a fellow about the same age and build as you and Martin. Don't go thinking there was any deep laid plot. There wasn't. There never is in real life. It was all improvised and haphazard and damned stupid.

ROBERT: Why didn't you confess to this before?

STANTON (*turning to him*): Why the devil should I?

FREDA: If you can't understand why, it's hopeless for us to try and show you. But there's such a thing as common honesty and decency.

STANTON (*himself again now*): Is there? I wonder. Don't forget—before you become too self-righteous—that you happen to be taking the lid off me. It might be somebody else's turn before we've finished.

ROBERT: Possibly. But that doesn't explain why you've kept so quiet about all this.

STANTON: I should have thought it did. Martin's suicide put *paid* to the whole thing. Nobody wanted to talk about it after that. Dear Martin must have done it, so we won't mention it. That was the line. It wasn't the five hundred. I'd have been glad to replace that. But I knew damned well that if I confessed the old man would have had me out of the firm in two minutes. I wasn't one of his pets like you and Martin. I'd had to work myself up from nothing in the firm. I hadn't been brought in because I had the right university and social back-grounds. If the old man had thought for a minute that I'd done it, there'd have been none of this hush-hush business. He'd have felt like calling in the police. Don't forget, I'd been a junior clerk in the office. You fellows hadn't. It makes a difference, I can tell you.

FREDA: But my father's been retired from the firm for six months.

STANTON: Well, what if he has? The whole thing was over and done with. Why open it up again? It might never have been mentioned if you hadn't started on this damn fool inquisition to-night. Robert, Gordon and I were all working well together in the firm. What would have happened if I'd confessed? Where are we? Who's better off because of this?

FREDA: You're not, it's true. But Martin is. And the people who cared about Martin.

STANTON: Are they?

FREDA: Of course they are.

STANTON: Don't be too sure.

FREDA: At least we know now that he wasn't a mean thief.

STANTON: And that's all you do know. But for all that he went and shot himself. And you don't suppose he did it for fun, do you?

FREDA (*terribly hurt*): Oh—you—you—— (*Turns away.*)

GORDON (*furious, rising and taking a step forward*): You are a rotter, Stanton.

ROBERT: Drop that sort of talk, Stanton.

These last three lines are spoken together.

STANTON (*turning on them*): Why should I? You wanted the truth, and now you're getting it. I didn't want to come back here and be put in the witness box. It's your own doing. I'll say what I damn well like. Martin shot himself, and he did it knowing that he'd never touched the money. So it must have been something else. Well, what was it? You see what you've started now.

FREDA (*coldly*): Well, what have we started? You're talking now as if you knew a lot more about Martin than we did.

STANTON: What I *do* know is that he must have had some reason for doing what he did, and that if it wasn't the money, it must have been something else. You're probably a lot better off for not knowing what that something is, just as you'd have been a lot better off if you'd never started poking about and prying into all this business.

ROBERT (*thoughtfully*): Perhaps he did it because he thought I'd taken the money.

STANTON (*sardonically*): And then again—perhaps not. If you think that Martin would have shot himself because he thought you'd taken some money—then you didn't know your own brother. Why he laughed when I told him. It amused him. A lot of things amused that young man.

OLWEN (*wearily*): That's true, I know. He didn't care. He didn't care at all.

ROBERT: Look here—do you know why Martin did shoot himself?

STANTON: No. How should I?

FREDA (*with rising temper*): You talk as if you do.

STANTON: I can imagine reasons.

FREDA (*very sharply*): What do you mean by that?

STANTON: I mean he was that sort of chap. He'd got his life into a mess.

ROBERT: Well, I don't think it's——

STANTON: I don't blame him.

FREDA (*furious*): You don't blame him. Who are you to blame him or not to blame him? You're not fit to mention his name. You hung your mean little piece of thieving round his neck, tried to poison our memory of him, and now when you're found out and Martin's name is clear of it, you want to begin all over again and start hinting that he was a criminal or a lunatic or something.

ROBERT: That's true. The less you say now, the better.

STANTON (*harshly*): The less we all say, the better. You should have thought of that before. I told you as much before you began dragging all this stuff out. Like a fool, you wouldn't leave well alone.

ROBERT: Anyway, I've cleared Martin's name.

STANTON: You've cleared nothing yet, and if you'd a glimmer of sense you'd see it. But now I don't give a damn. You're going to get all you ask for.

FREDA (*still furious*): One of the things we shall ask for is to be rid of you.

GORDON: Do you think you'll stay on with the firm after this?

STANTON: I don't know and I don't care.

FREDA: You did a year ago.

STANTON: Yes, but now I don't. I can get along better now without the firm than they can without me.

GORDON: Well, after this, at least it will be a pleasure to try. You always hated Martin, and I knew it.

STANTON: I had my reasons. Unlike the Whitehouse family— father, daughter and son—who all fell in love with him.

ROBERT (*slowly*): Does that mean anything, Stanton? If it doesn't, just take it back—now. If it does, you'll kindly explain yourself.

STANTON: I'll take nothing back.

OLWEN (*coming between them*): Stanton—please. Don't let's have any more of this. We've all said too much already.

STANTON (*turning to her*): I'm sorry, Olwen. But you can't blame me.

ROBERT (*with cold deliberation*): I'm waiting for your explanation.

FREDA: Don't you see, it's me he's getting at.

ROBERT: Is that true, Stanton?

STANTON: I'm certainly not leaving her out.

ROBERT: Be careful.

STANTON: It's too late to be careful. Why do you think Freda's been so angry with me? There's only one reason, and I've known it for a long time. She was in love with Martin.

>   FREDA *gives a cry.* ROBERT *stares at* FREDA, *then at* STANTON, *then at her again.*

ROBERT (*going to* FREDA *and standing behind her*): Is that true, Freda? I must know, because if it isn't I'm going to kick Stanton out of this house.

STANTON: Don't talk like a man in a melodrama, Caplan. I wouldn't have said it if I hadn't known it was true. Whether she admits it or not is another matter. But even if she doesn't admit it, you're not going to kick me out of the house. I'll go in the ordinary way, thank you.

ROBERT: Freda, is it true?

FREDA (*her last defence gone*): Yes.

ROBERT (*who speaks as if they were alone*): Has that been the trouble all along?

FREDA: Yes. All along.

ROBERT: When did it begin?

FREDA: A long time ago. Or it seems a long time ago. Ages.

ROBERT: Before we were married?

FREDA: Yes. I thought I could—break it—then. I did for a little time. But it came back, worse than ever.

ROBERT: I wish you'd told me. Why didn't you tell me?

FREDA: I wanted to. Hundreds of times I seem to have tried to. I've said the opening words to myself—you know—and sometimes I've hardly known whether I didn't actually say them out loud to you.

ROBERT: I wish you had, I wish you had. But why didn't I see it for myself? It seems plain enough now. I must have been a fool. I know now when it began. It was when we were all down at Tintagel that summer.

FREDA: Yes, it began then. Tintagel, that lovely, lovely summer. Nothing's ever been quite real since then.

ROBERT: Martin went away walking, and you said you'd stay a few days with the Hutchinsons. Was that——?

FREDA (*very quietly*): Yes, Martin and I spent that little time together, of course. It was the only time we did really spend together. It didn't mean much to him—a sort of experiment, that's all.

ROBERT: But didn't Martin care?

FREDA (*in great distress*): No, not really. If he had have done, it would have been all so simple. That's why I never told you. And I thought when we were married, it would be—different. It wasn't fair to you, I know, but I thought it would be all right. And so did Martin. But it wasn't. You know that too. It was hopeless. But you don't know how hopeless it was—for me.

ROBERT: But why didn't Martin himself tell me? He knew how unhappy I was.

FREDA: He couldn't. He was rather afraid of you.

ROBERT: Martin afraid of me!

GORDON: Yes, he was.

ROBERT: Nonsense. He wasn't afraid of anybody—and certainly not of me.

FREDA: Yes, he was, in some queer way.

OLWEN (*very gently*): That's true, Robert. He was. I knew that.

GORDON: So did I. He told me that when you're really angry, you'll stop at nothing.

ROBERT (*brooding*): Queer. I never knew Martin felt like that. And it was he who—I wonder why? What was it? (*To* FREDA.) It couldn't have been—this——

FREDA: No, no. He didn't care. (*Breaks down completely.*) Oh, Martin, Martin——

OLWEN (*going to* FREDA *and putting her arms round her*): Freda, Freda—don't.

STANTON (*while* OLWEN *is still comforting* FREDA): That's how it goes on, you see, Caplan. A good evening's work this.

ROBERT: I'm not regretting it. I'm glad all this has come out. I wish to God I'd known earlier, that's all.

STANTON: What difference would it have made? You couldn't have done anything.

ROBERT: To begin with, I'd have known the truth. And then something might have been done about it. I wouldn't have stood in their way.

STANTON (*sardonically*): You didn't stand in their way.

GORDON (*on whom all this is having a very bad effect*): No, it was Martin himself, you see. He didn't care, as Freda says. I knew. He told me about it. (*At* FREDA.)

ROBERT (*turning, and incredulously*): He told you?

GORDON: Yes.

ROBERT: Freda's brother?

FREDA (*pushing* OLWEN *aside and looking up*): Gordon, I don't believe you.

GORDON (*hotly*): Why should I lie about it? Martin told me. He used to tell me everything.

FREDA: Rubbish. He thought you were a little nuisance—always hanging about him.

GORDON: That's not true.

FREDA: It is. He told me so, that—that very last Saturday, when I took him the cigarette box. He told me then, you'd stayed the night before at the cottage and that he'd had to do everything he could to get rid of you.

GORDON (*plunging now into a quarrel*): Freda—you're making this up, every word about me, I know you are. Martin would never have said that about me. He knew how fond I was of him, and he was fond of me too, in his own way.

FREDA: He wasn't.

GORDON: You're just saying this because you're jealous.

FREDA: I'm not.

GORDON: You've always been jealous of Martin's interest in me.

FREDA (*hotly*): Gordon, that's simply a disgusting lie.

GORDON: It isn't.

FREDA: It is. He told me himself how tired he was of your hanging about him and suddenly becoming hysterical. I see what he meant now. Every time he's been mentioned to-night, you've been hysterical. What are you trying to persuade me into believing you are? (*Putting her hands to her head and turning away.*)

ROBERT (*sharply*): Freda, you're mad.

GORDON (*shrilly, in a rage and turning to* ROBERT): It's all jealousy, jealousy. If he'd thought I was a nuisance, Martin wouldn't have kept asking me down to the cottage. (*Turning to* FREDA.) But he was tired of *you*, pestering him and worrying him all the time. He didn't care for women. He was sick of them. He told me so. He wanted me to tell you, so that you'd leave him alone.

FREDA (*wildly*): You're making me feel sick.

GORDON: Well, you just leave me——

OLWEN (*distressed and pushing* GORDON *away*): Stop it. Stop it, both of you.

STANTON (*grimly*): Let them have it out. They might as well, now they've started.

GORDON (*to* FREDA): And I was going to tell you too. Only then— he killed himself.

FREDA: I don't believe it. I don't believe it. Martin couldn't have been so cruel.

GORDON (*close to her*): Couldn't he? What did he say to you that afternoon when you took him the cigarette box?

FREDA: What does it matter what he said? You're just making up these abominable lies——

ROBERT (*roughly*): Look here, I'm not having any more of this. You're like a pair of lunatics—screaming at each other like that over a dead man. I understand about you, Freda, and I'm sorry—but for God's sake keep quiet about it now. I can't stand any more. As for you, Gordon—you must be tight or something——

GORDON (*sulking*): I'm not. I'm as sober as you are.

ROBERT: Well, behave as if you were. You're not a child. I know Martin was a friend of yours——

GORDON (*turning on* ROBERT *hotly and scornfully*): Friend of mine! He wasn't a friend of mine. You talk like a fish. Martin was the only person on earth I really cared about. I couldn't help it. There it was. I'd have done anything for him. Five hundred pounds. My God, I'd have stolen five thousand pounds from the firm if Martin had asked me to. He was the most marvellous person I'd ever known. Sometimes I tried to hate him. Sometimes he gave me a hell of a time. But it didn't really matter. He was Martin, and I'd rather be with him, even if he was just jeering at me all the time, than be with anybody else I've ever known. I'm like Freda—since he died, I haven't really cared a damn, I've just been passing the time. He didn't really care for women at all. He tried to amuse himself with them, but he really distrusted them, disliked them. He told me so, many a time. Martin told me everything. And that was the finest thing that ever happened to me. And now you can call me any name you like, I don't care.

There is a silence, and he looks at them all defiantly.

ROBERT: But what about Betty?

GORDON (*sullenly*): You can leave her out of this.

ROBERT: I want to. But I can't help thinking about her.

GORDON: Well, you needn't. She can look after herself.

ROBERT: That's just what she can't do and she oughtn't to have to do. You ought to see that.

GORDON: Well, I don't see it. And I know Betty better than you do.

FREDA (*bitterly*): You know everybody better than anybody else does, don't you?

GORDON: You would say that, wouldn't you? I can't help it if Martin liked me better than he liked you.

FREDA: How do you know that he——

OLWEN: Oh, stop that. Stop it, both of you. Can't you see that Martin was making mischief, just to amuse himself?

GORDON (*sulkily*): No, I can't. He wasn't like that.

STANTON (*with irony*): Oh no. Not at all like that. You couldn't ask for a quiet, simpler, more sincere fellow.

FREDA (*hotly*): Nobody's going to pretend he was that. But at least he didn't steal money and then try to put the blame on other people.

STANTON: We could all start talking like that, you know, Freda. Just throwing things at each other's heads. But I suggest we don't.

OLWEN: I agree. But I do want Freda and Gordon to understand that it's simply madness quarrelling over anything Martin ever said to them. He was a born mischief-maker and as cruel as a cat. That's one of the reasons why I disliked him so much.

ROBERT: Disliked him?

OLWEN: Yes, I'm sorry, Robert, but I didn't like Martin. I detested him. You ought to have seen that.

STANTON: I saw it. And you were quite right. I'm afraid you always are, OLWEN.

OLWEN: No, I'm not.

STANTON: I'd trust your judgment.

ROBERT: So would I, for that matter.

OLWEN: No. No.

STANTON: And you're the only one of us who will come out of this as sound as you went in.

OLWEN (*embarrassed and a little alarmed*): No, that's not true.

GORDON: No—it was Olwen and that damned cigarette box that began the whole business.

STANTON: Oh, that was nothing. I knew about that all along.

OLWEN: You knew about what?

STANTON: I knew you'd been to see Martin Caplan that Saturday night.

OLWEN (*alarmed*): You knew?

STANTON: Yes.

OLWEN: But how could you? I don't understand.

STANTON: I was spending that week-end at my own cottage. You remember that garage, where the road forks? You stopped there that night for some petrol.

OLWEN (*remembering*): Yes, I believe I did.

STANTON: They told me, and said you'd taken the Fallows End road, and so I knew you must have been going to see Martin. You couldn't have been going anywhere else, could you? Quite simple.

OLWEN (*staring at him*): And you've known all this time?

STANTON: Yes. All this time.

ROBERT (*rather bitterly*): I suppose, Stanton, it's no use asking *you* why you've never said a word about it?

STANTON (*coolly*): I'm afraid not. I think I've done my share in the confession box to-night.

GORDON: Well, I wish I'd known a bit more, that's all. There was I dragged into that foul inquest. Did I know this? Did I know that? My God—and all the time I wasn't the last person he'd talked to at all. Freda had been there some time in the afternoon, And Olwen was there that very night, at the very moment—for all we know.

STANTON: Don't talk rubbish.

GORDON: Well, is it rubbish? (*Indicating* OLWEN, *who turns away and moves up to the window.*) After all, what do we know? What was Olwen doing there?

ROBERT: She's told us that. She was there to talk to Martin about the money.

GORDON: And how far does that take us?

STANTON: What do you mean by that?

FREDA: He means—I imagine—that Olwen hasn't told us very much so far. We know she went to Martin to talk to him about the missing money. And we know that Martin thought Robert had taken it and that she thought so too. And that's all we do know.

GORDON: Yes, we don't know how long she was there or what Martin said to her, or anything. It's a good job *she* wasn't pushed in front of that coroner or they'd have had it out of her in no time. (*Turning round to* OLWEN.) I think it's up to *her* to tell us a little more.

STANTON: Well, there's no need to sound so damned vindictive about it.

OLWEN, *who has just looked out through the window, pulling the curtain back a little, suddenly starts back and gives a little scream.*

ROBERT ⎫
STANTON ⎭ (*together*): Hello, what's the matter?

ROBERT *goes up to window, looks out, and* FREDA *rises and turns to window.*

ROBERT (*still looking out*): There's nobody there now.

OLWEN: No, they darted away. But I'll swear there was somebody. They'd been listening.

STANTON (*who has remained seated. Grimly*): Well, they couldn't have chosen a better night for it.

ROBERT: It's impossible, Olwen. And there isn't a sign of anybody.

GORDON: Thank the Lord for that.

They all start to move forward and as they move, there are several short rings of a door bell heard from off. They all stop and look at one another in surprise and consternation.

ROBERT: Who on earth can this be?

FREDA: Don't ask me. I haven't the least idea. Go and see.

ROBERT: Yes, I know. But we don't want anybody interrupting us now.

FREDA: Well, don't let them interrupt us, whoever they are. But you'll have to see who it is.

The bells rings again and ROBERT *goes out. While he is away, nobody speaks and they all look somewhat constrained.*

Then the voices of ROBERT *and* BETTY *can be heard.*

ROBERT (*heard outside*): But we haven't, I tell you. You've never been mentioned.

BETTY (*outside*): I know you have. I can feel it. That's why I had to come back.

ROBERT (*outside*): I tell you we haven't.

ROBERT *opens the door and* BETTY *is seen in front of him.*

GORDON: I thought you'd gone to bed, Betty. What's the matter?

BETTY (*just inside the door*): You're talking about me, all of you. (*Looking round at them all.*) I know you are. I wanted to go to bed. I started to go. And then I couldn't. I knew you were all talking about me. I couldn't stand it. I had to come back.

FREDA (*coldly*): Well, you were wrong. As a matter of fact, you're the one person we *haven't* been talking about.

BETTY (*looking at* GORDON, STANTON *and then* ROBERT): Is that true?

ROBERT: Yes, of course.

OLWEN: You were outside just now, weren't you? Outside the window, listening.

BETTY (*confused*): No, I wasn't listening. I was trying to peep in, to see exactly who was here and what you all looked like. You see, I was sure you were all saying things about me. And I meant to go to bed and I was tired but I felt too excited inside to sleep and so I took three of those tablets I have to make me sleep and now I feel absolutely dopey. God knows what I shall be saying in a minute. You mustn't mind me. (*Sinks into the chair.*)

ROBERT (*leaning over her*): I'm so sorry, Betty. Can I get you anything? (*As she shakes her head.*) Sure? (*She shakes her head again.*) And not a word's been said about you. In fact, we all wanted to keep you out of this. It's all rather unpleasant.

Freda (*with irony*): But seeing that Betty has married into one of the families concerned, I think she ought not to be too carefully protected from the sordid truth.

Robert (*losing his temper*): Oh shut up, Freda.

Freda: I won't. Why should I? I thought we should see a different Robert now.

Robert: After what you've said to night, I can't see that it matters much to you how different I may be.

Freda: Perhaps not, but I still like reasonably decent manners.

Robert: Then set us an example.

Gordon: Oh, shut up, both of you.

Betty: But what have you been talking about then?

Gordon: It began about the money.

Betty: You mean that Martin took?

Gordon: Martin didn't take it. We know that now. Stanton took that money. He's admitted it.

Betty *gives a short cry.*

Betty: Admitted it. Stanton? Oh surely—it's impossible.

Stanton (*sardonically*): It sounds impossible, doesn't it, Betty, but it isn't. I'm sorry to go down with such a bump in your estimation, my dear Betty, but this is our night for telling the truth, and I've had to admit that I took the money. Terrible, isn't it?

Stanton *looks at* Betty *and she avoids his glance, uncomfortably.* Robert *looks from one to the other of them.*

Robert: What did you mean by that, Stanton?

Stanton: I meant what I said. I nearly always do.

Robert: Why did you use that tone of voice to Betty?

Stanton: Perhaps—because I think that Betty has not a very high opinion of me—and so need not have sounded so surprised and shocked.

Robert (*slowly*): I don't quite understand that.

Freda (*sarcastically*): I'm sure you don't, Robert.

Robert (*turning on her sharply*): Do you?

Freda (*sweetly*): Yes, I think so.

Betty: But if Martin didn't take the money—then why—why—did he shoot himself?

Gordon: That's what we want to know. Olwen saw him last of all, that very evening, and she knew he hadn't taken the money, but that's all she's told us.

Olwen: I've told you that he thought Robert had taken the money.

ROBERT: And that was enough—in the state he was in then—to throw him clean off his balance. All that stuff about his merely being amused is nonsense. That was just his bluff. Martin hated anybody to think he was really moved or alarmed by anything.

GORDON: That's true.

ROBERT (*with growing excitement*): And he depended on me. He used to laugh a lot at me, but that was nothing. He depended on me. You've told me yourselves—that he was secretly rather frightened of me. It was because Martin had a respect for me. He thought I was the solid steady one. I was one of the very few people he had a respect for. I tell you, it must have been a hell of a shock to poor Martin.

OLWEN: I don't think it was, Robert.

STANTON: Neither do I.

ROBERT: But neither of you knew him as I did. What's the good of talking. He was in a wretched state, all run down and neurotic, and when he heard that I'd taken the cheque he must have felt that there was nobody left he could depend on, that I'd let him down. He'd probably been brooding over it day and night—he was that sort. He wouldn't let you see it, Olwen. But it would be there all the time, giving him hell. Oh, what a fool I was.

GORDON: You!

ROBERT: Yes, of course. I ought to have gone straight to Martin and told him what Stanton had told me.

GORDON: If this is true, then the person really responsible is Stanton.

FREDA: Yes.

STANTON: Rubbish.

FREDA: It isn't. Don't you see what you did?

STANTON: No, because I don't believe it.

GORDON: No, because you don't choose to, that's all.

STANTON: Oh, talk sense. Can't you see Martin had his own reasons?

ROBERT: No. What drove Martin to suicide was my stupidity and your damned lying, Stanton.

BETTY (*bursting into tears*): Oh!

ROBERT: Oh, sorry, Betty—but this has got to be settled, once and for all.

STANTON (*grimly*): You're none of you in a state to settle anything.

ROBERT: Listen to me, Stanton——

STANTON: Oh, drop it, man.

GORDON: You've got to answer.

ROBERT: I'll never forgive you for telling Martin what you did—by God, I won't!

STANTON: You've got it all wrong.

GORDON: They haven't, you rotten liar. (*Moves as if to strike him.*)

STANTON (*pushing him aside*): Oh, get out.

GORDON (*shouting and about to go for him again*): You made Martin shoot himself.

OLWEN: Wait a minute, Gordon. (*Everybody turns and looks at her.*) Martin didn't shoot himself.

END OF ACT TWO

ACT III

All are discovered in exactly the same positions as they were in at the end of ACT II.

OLWEN: Martin didn't shoot himself.

FREDA: Martin didn't——

OLWEN: Of course he didn't. I shot him.

BETTY *gives a little scream, the others gasp and stare.*

ROBERT: That's ridiculous, Olwen. You couldn't have done.

GORDON: Is this your idea of a joke?

OLWEN: I wish it was. (*Suddenly sits down and buries her face in her hands. She does not make any sound, however.*)

GORDON: Olwen!

ROBERT (*with lowered voice*): She must be hysterical or something. I believe people often confess to all sorts of mad things in that state, things they could not possibly have done.

STANTON (*shaking his head*): Olwen's not hysterical. She means it.

BETTY (*in a whisper*): But she can't mean—she *murdered* him. Can she?

STANTON (*gently*): You might as well tell us exactly what happened now, Olwen, if you can stand it. And I might as well tell you—before you begin—that I'm not at all surprised. I suspected it was you at the first.

OLWEN (*staring at him*): You suspected I'd done it? But why?

STANTON: For three reasons. The first was that I couldn't understand why Martin should shoot himself. You see, I knew he hadn't taken the money, and though he was in every kind of mess, he didn't seem to me the sort of chap who'd get out of it that way. Then I knew you'd been with him quite late, because—as I said before—I'd been told you'd gone that way. And the third reason—well, that'll keep. You'd better tell us what happened now. It was an accident, wasn't it?

OLWEN (*in a low, strained voice*): Yes, it was really an accident. I'll tell you what happened, but I can't go into details. It's all too muddled and horrible. But I'll tell you the complete truth. I won't hide anything more, I promise you. I think we'd all better tell everything we know now, really speak our minds.

ROBERT (*also in a low voice*): I agree.

STANTON: Wait a minute, Olwen. Will you have a drink before you begin?

OLWEN: I'll just have a little soda water, if you don't mind.
He pours out drink and gives it to her.

ROBERT: Sit here.

OLWEN (*to* STANTON): Thank you. (*Sips drink.*) (*To* ROBERT) No, I'll sit by the fire.

OLWEN: I went to see Martin that Saturday night, as you know, to talk to him about the missing money. Mr. Whitehouse had told me about it. He thought that either Martin or Robert must have taken it. I gathered it was more likely Robert. So I went to see Martin. I didn't like Martin and he knew it, but he knew, too, what I felt about Robert, and after all, he was Robert's brother. He believed that Robert had taken the money, and he wasn't a bit worried about it. I'm sorry, Robert, but he wasn't. I hated him for that, too. He was rather maliciously amused. The good brother fallen at last—that sort of thing.

FREDA (*in a low, bitter voice*): I can believe that. I hate to, but I know he could be like that sometimes. He was that day.

OLWEN (*gently*): You found that, too, that day?

FREDA: Yes, he was in one of his worst moods. He could be cruel— torturing—sometimes.

OLWEN: I've never seen him as bad as he was that night. He wasn't really sane.

ROBERT (*shocked*): Olwen!

OLWEN (*very gently*): I'm sorry, Robert. I didn't want you to know all this, but there's no help for it now. You see, Martin had been taking some sort of drug——

ROBERT: Drug? Do you mean dope stuff?

OLWEN: Yes. He'd had a lot of it.

ROBERT: Are you sure? I can't believe it.

STANTON: It's true, Caplan. I knew it.

GORDON: So did I. He made me try some once, but I didn't like it. It just made me feel rather sick.

ROBERT: When was this?

GORDON: You remember when he went to Berlin and how nervy he was just then?

STANTON: Yes, I remember.

GORDON: Well, a fellow he met there put him on to it—some new drug that a lot of the literary and theatrical set were doping themselves with——

FREDA: But did Martin——

GORDON: Yes. He liked it and took more and more of it.

ROBERT: But where did he get it?

GORDON: Through some German he knew in town. When he couldn't get it, he was pretty rotten. Not so bad as those dope fiends one reads about, you know, but nevertheless pretty rotten.

STANTON: But didn't you try to stop him?

GORDON: Of course—but he only laughed. I don't blame him really. None of you can understand what life was like to Martin—he was so sensitive and nervy. He was one of those people who are meant to be happy.

STANTON (*grimly*): We're all those people who are meant to be happy. Martin's no exception.

ROBERT: Yes, that's true. But I know what Gordon means.

FREDA: You couldn't help knowing what he means, if you knew Martin. There was no sort of middle state, no easy jog-trot with him. Either he had to be gay—and when he was gay, he was gayer than anybody else in the world—or he was intensely miserable.

BETTY (*impulsively*): I'm like that. Everybody is—aren't they?—except old and stuffy people.

ROBERT: But what about this drug, Olwen?

OLWEN: He took some—it was in little white tablets—while I was there, and it had a horrible effect on him. It gave him a sort of devilish gaiety. I can see him now. His eyes were queer. Oh—he really wasn't sane. (*Stops.*)

ROBERT: What happened?

OLWEN (*quiet, but very agitated*): It's horrible to talk about. I've tried not to think about it. He knew I disliked him, but he couldn't believe I *really* disliked him. He was frightfully conceited about himself. He seemed to think that everybody young, male or female, ought to be falling in love with him. He saw himself as a sort of Pan, you know.

FREDA (*in a low voice*): Yes, he did. And he'd every reason to.

OLWEN: He began taunting me. He thought of me—or pretended to—as a priggish spinster, full of repressions, who'd never really lived. All rubbish, because I'm really not that type at all. But he pretended to think I was, and kept telling me that my dislike of him showed that I was trying to repress a great fascination he had for me. And of course that all these repressions were bad for me. I'd never lived, never

would live, and all the rest of it. He talked a lot about that. I ought to
have run out and left him, but I felt I couldn't while he was in that
state. In a way I was sorry for him, because really he was ill, sick in
mind and body, and I thought perhaps I could calm him down. I
might dislike him, but after all he wasn't a stranger. He was one of our
own set, mixed up with most of the people I liked best in the world. I
tried hard to stop him. But everything I said seemed to make him
worse. I suppose it would when he was in that excited, abnormal state.
Well, he talked about my repressions, and when I pretended to laugh
at him, he got more and more excited. And then he tried to show me
some beastly foul drawings he had—horrible, obscene things by some
mad Belgian artist——

FREDA (*swaying*): Oh—my God! (*Sobs.*)

OLWEN (*going to her*): Oh, Freda, I'm so sorry. Please forgive me.
I know how this must be hurting you.

FREDA (*distraught*): Martin. Martin.

OLWEN: Don't listen to any more. I'll stop if you like. Or go and lie
down.

FREDA: I couldn't. Oh—he wasn't like that really. If you'd known
him as I'd known him—before.

OLWEN: I know that. We all do. He was different. He was ill.

FREDA (*in a muffled tone*): Go on, Olwen.

ROBERT: Yes, Olwen. You can't stop now.

OLWEN: There isn't a lot to tell now. When I pushed his beastly
drawings away and was rather indignant about them, he got still more
excited, completely unbalanced, and shouted out things about my
repressions. And then I found he was telling me to take my clothes
off. I told him not to be a fool and that I was going. But then he stood
between me and the door. And he had a revolver in his hand and was
shouting something about danger and terror and love. He wasn't
threatening me with it or himself. He was just waving it about—being
dramatic. I didn't even believe it was loaded. But by this time I'd had
more than enough of him—I couldn't be sorry for him any more—and
I told him to get out of the way. When he wouldn't, I tried to push
him out of the way. And then we had a struggle. (*She is distressed now
and a trifle incoherent.*) He tried to tear my clothes. We really fought
one another. It was horrible. He wasn't any stronger than I was.
(*Illustrating this by grabbing her own wrist and slowly turning it.*) I'd
grabbed the hand with the revolver in it. I'd turned the revolver
towards him. His finger must have been on the trigger. I must have
given it a jerk. (*Covers her face with her hands.*) The revolver went off.
Oh—horrible—horrible! I've tried and tried to forget that. If he'd just

been wounded, I'm sure I would have stopped with him—even though I was in such a panic. But he wasn't. He was dead.

ROBERT: Yes, we understand that. You needn't tell us.

OLWEN: When I realised what had happened I rushed out in a dreadful panic and sat in my car outside for I don't know how long. I couldn't move a finger. There was nobody about. It was fairly late and you know how lonely that cottage was. I just sat on and on in the car, shivering, and it was so quiet in the cottage, so horribly quiet. I've gone through that over and over again. (*Buries her face in her hands and sobs soundlessly.*)

BETTY (*in a whisper and turning her head away*): God!

ROBERT: You can't be blamed, Olwen.

STANTON (*decisively, and rising*): Of course she can't be blamed. And there must never be a word spoken about this—not to anybody. We must all promise that.

They all nod or murmur their assent.

GORDON (*bitterly*): It's a pity we can't all be as cool and business-like about this as you are, Stanton.

STANTON: I don't feel very cool and business-like about it. But you see, it's not as big a surprise to me as it is to you people. I guessed long ago that something like this had happened.

ROBERT: But it looked so much like suicide that nobody bothered to suggest it wasn't. It never seemed to me to be anything else. All the evidence pointed that way. I can't think how you could have guessed even though you knew Olwen had been there.

STANTON: I told you I had a third reason. I was over fairly early next morning—the postmistress at Fallows End rang me up—and I was there before anybody but the village constable and the doctor. And I spotted something on the floor that the village bobby had missed, and I picked it up when he wasn't looking. I've kept it in my pocket-book ever since. (*Brings out pocket-book and produces from it a small square of patterned silk.*) I'm rather observant about such things.

OLWEN: Let me see. (*Examines it.*) Yes, that's a piece of the dress I was wearing. It was torn in the struggle we had. So that's how you knew?

STANTON (*dropping piece of silk in the fireplace*): That's how I knew.

OLWEN: But why didn't you say anything?

GORDON (*bitterly*): I can tell you that. He didn't say anything because he wanted everybody to think that Martin had shot himself. You see, that meant that Martin must have taken the money.

ROBERT (*wearily*): That's about it, I suppose. It falls into line with everything we've heard from him to-night.

STANTON: No, there happened to be another reason, much more important. I knew that if Olwen had had a hand in Martin's death, then something like that must have happened, and so Olwen couldn't be blamed. I knew her better than any of you—or I felt I did. And I trusted her. She's about the only person I would trust. She knows all about that. I've told her often enough. She's not interested, but there it is.

OLWEN (*wonderingly*): And you never even hinted to me that you knew.

STANTON: Surprising, isn't it? What a chance I missed to capture your interest for a few minutes. But I couldn't take that line with you. I suppose even nowadays, when we're all so damned tough, there has got to be one person that you behave to always as if you were Sir Roger de Coverly, and with me you've been that person for a long time now. And I knew all along that you were saying nothing because you thought Robert here had taken the money and that he was safe after everybody put it down to Martin. And that didn't always make it any easier for me.

BETTY (*with shrill irony*): No? What a shame! But what a fine romantic character you are, aren't you?

ROBERT (*gently*): Steady, Betty. You don't understand.

FREDA (*bitterly*): How could she?

BETTY (*indignantly, and turning to* FREDA): Why do you say that—in that tone of voice?

FREDA (*wearily*): Why does one say anything—in any tone of voice?

OLWEN (*to* STANTON): You know, I nearly did take you into my confidence. And that might have made a difference. But I chose a bad moment.

STANTON (*eagerly*): Why? When was this? Tell me.

OLWEN: I told you I sat in my car that night for some time not able to do anything. But then, when I felt a little better, I felt I had to tell somebody, and you were the nearest person——

STANTON (*alarmed*): But you didn't go there—that night?

OLWEN (*quietly*): Yes, I did. I drove over to your cottage at Church Marley that very Saturday night. I got there about eleven o'clock or just afterwards. I left my car at the bottom of that tiny narrow lane and walked up to your cottage. And then—I walked back again.

STANTON: You walked up to the cottage?

OLWEN: Yes, yes—don't be stupid about it, please, Stanton. I walked right up to your cottage and saw enough to set me walking straight back again.

STANTON: So that's when you came. After that, it was hopeless, I suppose.

OLWEN: Quite hopeless. I think that added the last touch to that night. I don't think I've ever felt the same about people—not just here, but everybody, even the people who walk into the office or sit opposite one in buses and trains—since that night. I know that's stupid, but I couldn't help it. And (*forcing a smile*) you must all have noticed that I've been completely off country cottages.

FREDA (*maliciously*): Yes, even Betty's noticed that.

BETTY *bursts into tears and bangs her head.*

ROBERT: Why, what's the matter, Betty?

GORDON: What a little liar you are, Betty.

BETTY (*in muffled voice*): Haven't we all been liars?

ROBERT (*puzzled*): But you haven't, Betty.

GORDON: Oh, don't be a fool, Robert. Of course she has. She's lied like fury.

ROBERT: What about?

FREDA: Why don't you ask her?

OLWEN (*wearily*): Oh, what does it matter. Leave the child alone.

BETTY: I'm not a child. That's the mistake you've all made.

ROBERT (*who has been thinking*): Not you—and Stanton? (*A pause. She does not reply.*) Is that what they mean? (BETTY *just keeps still and looks defiant.*) Why don't you tell them it's ridiculous?

FREDA (*contemptuously*): How can she? Don't be absurd.

OLWEN (*gently*): You see, Robert, I saw them both in Stanton's cottage that night.

ROBERT: I'm sorry, Olwen, but I won't take even your word for this. Besides, there are other possible explanations.

STANTON: Oh, drop this, Caplan. We've had too much of it already. I'm going.

ROBERT (*ferociously turning on him*): You're not going.

STANTON: Don't be a fool. It's no business of yours.

FREDA (*maliciously*): That's where you're wrong, Stanton. This is where Robert's business really begins.

ROBERT: I'm waiting for an answer, Betty.

BETTY (*frightened*): What do you want me to say?

ROBERT: Were you with Stanton at his cottage?

BETTY (*whispers*): Yes.

ROBERT: Were you his mistress?

BETTY: Yes. (*Turns away and drops her head.*)

ROBERT (*quietly but with great passion. Turning to* STANTON): My God, I could—— (*A pause, then turns to* BETTY, *in extreme agitation.*) But why—why—in God's name—why? How could you? How could you?

BETTY (*suddenly stung into life*): How could I? Because I'm not a child and I'm not a little stuffed doll, that's why. You would drag all this out and now you can damned well have it. Yes, I stayed with Stanton that night, and I've stayed with him other nights. And he's not in love with me and I know it, and I'm not in love with him. I wouldn't marry him if I could. But I'd got to make something happen. Gordon was driving me mad. If you want to call someone a child, then call him one, for that's all he is. This damned marriage of ours that you all got so sentimental about is the biggest sham there's ever been. It isn't a marriage at all. It's just nothing—pretence, pretence, pretence. Betty darling and Gordon darling, when all the time he's mooning over his Martin and the very sight of him makes me want to scream. (*Her voice now had become a shriek.*)

FREDA: Betty, you mustn't go——

BETTY: It's not my fault. I was in love with him when we were married, and I thought everything was going to be marvellous. I wouldn't have looked at anybody else if he'd been—real. But he just isn't there. He can't even *talk* to me.

GORDON: For God's sake, shut up, Betty.

BETTY (*with shrill emphasis*): I won't shut up. They want to know the truth, and they can have it. I don't care. I've had nothing, nothing out of my marriage but shame and misery.

OLWEN: Betty, that's simply nonsense.

BETTY: If I were the nice little doll you all thought me, perhaps it wouldn't have mattered. But I'm not. I'm not a child either. I'm a woman. And Stanton was the one person who guessed what was happening and treated me like a woman.

GORDON (*scornfully*): I wouldn't have blamed you if you'd gone and fallen in love properly with someone, but this was just a low sordid intrigue, a dirty little affair, not worth all your silly lies. I suppose Stanton was the rich uncle in America who kept giving you all those fine presents?

BETTY: Yes, he was. You couldn't even be generous though you'd have given your precious Martin everything we'd got. I knew Stanton didn't really care for me, so I got what I could out of him. (STANTON *turns to her and gives an amused grin mixed with surprise.*) It served you right. Men who say they're in love with one woman and keep spending their week-ends with another deserve all they get.

FREDA (*to* STANTON): Is that why you suddenly found yourself so short of money that you had to have that five hundred pounds?

STANTON: Yes. Queer how it works out, isn't it?

GORDON: Then Betty is responsible for everything, for all this misery, for Martin.

BETTY (*turning round to them*): You see? Always Martin. If I was responsible for all that, then it's your fault really, Gordon. Because you're responsible for everything that happened to me. You ought never to have married me.

GORDON: I didn't know. It was a mistake.

FREDA (*bitterly*): We seem to make that kind of mistake in our family.

BETTY (*moving down to end of piano*): I ought to have left you long before this. That was *my* mistake—staying on—trying to make the best of it—pretending to be married to somebody who wasn't there, simply dead.

GORDON: Yes, I think I am dead. I think I died last summer. Olwen shot me.

OLWEN: Gordon, I think that's unfair and also rather stupid and affected.

GORDON (*quietly*): It may have sounded like that, but it wasn't. I meant it, Olwen.

ROBERT (*who has just had half a glass of whisky*): I began this, didn't I? Well, I'll finish it. I'll say something now. Betty, I worshipped you, I suppose you knew that?

FREDA: If she didn't, she must have been very dense.

ROBERT (*turning on* FREDA. *He is not drunk but speaks in a thick voice and is a trifle wild in manner*): I'm talking to Betty now. You might leave us alone for a minute. (*Turning to* BETTY.) Did you realise that I felt like that, Betty?

BETTY: Yes. But I didn't care very much.

ROBERT (*bitterly*): No, why should you?

BETTY: No, it isn't that. But I knew you weren't in love with me. You didn't know me. You were only worshipping somebody you'd invented, who looked like me. And that's not the same thing at all.

ROBERT: I didn't do much about it. I couldn't, you see. I thought that you and Gordon were reasonably happy together——

BETTY: Yes, we put up a good show, didn't we?

ROBERT: You did. (*Goes for another drink.*)

GORDON: Yes, we did. What would have happened if we'd gone on pretending like hell to be happy together?

BETTY: Nothing.

GORDON (*thinking it out*): No. If we'd gone on pretending long enough, I believe we might have *been* happy together, sometimes. It often works out like that.

BETTY: Never.

OLWEN: Yes, it does. That's why all this is so wrong really. The *real* truth is something so deep you can't get at it this way, and all this half truth does is to blow everything up. It isn't *civilised*.

STANTON: I agree.

ROBERT (*after another drink, cynically*): *You* agree!

STANTON: You'll get no sympathy from me, Caplan.

ROBERT: Sympathy from you! I never want to set eyes on you again, Stanton. You're a thief, a cheat, a liar, and a dirty cheap seducer.

STANTON: And you're a fool, Caplan. You look solid, but you're not. You've a good deal in common with that cracked brother of yours. You won't face up to real things. You've been living in a fool's paradise, and now, having got yourself out of it by to-night's efforts—all your doing—you're busy building yourself a fool's hell to live in.

ROBERT (*picking up the glass that* STANTON *had left*): I think this was your glass, Stanton. (*Moves up to window and throws it out.*) And now take yourself after it. Get out. (*Pours out another drink for himself.*)

STANTON: Good night, Olwen. I'm sorry about all this.

OLWEN: So am I. (*Offers him her hand. He takes it.*) Good night.

STANTON: Good night, Freda.

FREDA: Good night.

STANTON (*turning at door. To* BETTY *and* GORDON): I suppose you're coming along?

GORDON: Not with you, I'm afraid. And don't forget, Stanton, you owe the firm five hundred pounds—and a resignation.

STANTON: Oh, you're going to take it that way, are you?

GORDON: Yes, I'm going to take it that way.

STANTON: You'll regret it. Good night. (*With ironical politeness.*) No, don't trouble. I can find my way out. (*He goes out.*)

OLWEN: Don't be too hasty, Gordon. Whatever his faults Stanton's a first-class man at his job. If he goes, the firm will suffer.

GORDON: I can't help it. I couldn't work with him after this. The firm will have to suffer, that's all.

ROBERT: Don't worry. It's not a case of the firm suffering. The firm's smashed to hell *now*.

FREDA: Nonsense.

ROBERT: Is it? I don't think so.

GORDON (*bitterly*): Well, Betty darling, I think we'd better return to our happy little home, our dear little nest——

BETTY: Oh, don't, Gordon.

FREDA (*going out with* GORDON): I'll let you out.

ROBERT (*as* BETTY *turns to move off*): Good-bye. (*Staring at her.*)

BETTY: Why do you look like that?

ROBERT: I'm not saying good-bye to *you*. I don't know you. I never did, it seems. I'm saying good-bye to this. (*Indicates her face and body.*) That's all. (*Turns away abruptly, and goes up for another drink.*)

BETTY *stares for a second and then goes quickly out.*

OLWEN (*distressed*): Robert, please don't drink any more to-night. I know how you feel, but it'll only make you worse—really it will.

ROBERT: What does it matter? I'm through, anyway.

OLWEN: Robert, I can't bear seeing you like this. You don't know how it hurts me.

ROBERT: I'm sorry, Olwen, I really am sorry. You're the only one who's really come out of this. I know that. Strange, isn't it—that you should have been feeling like that about me all the time?

OLWEN: Yes, all the time.

ROBERT: I'm sorry.

OLWEN: I'm not. I mean about myself. I suppose I ought to be, but I'm not. It's hurt like anything sometimes, but it's kept me going too.

ROBERT: I know. And you see, now I've stopped going. Something's broken—inside.

OLWEN: It won't seem bad to-morrow. It never does.

ROBERT: All this isn't going to seem any better to-morrow, Olwen.

OLWEN: Freda will help too. After all, Robert, she's fond of you.

ROBERT: No, not really. It isn't that she dislikes me steadily, but every now and then she hates me—and now I see why, of course. She

402 J. B. PRIESTLEY

hates me because I'm Robert Caplan and not Martin, because he's dead and I'm alive.

OLWEN: She may feel differently—after to-night.

ROBERT: She may. I doubt it. She doesn't change easily—that's the trouble. And then again, you see, I don't care any more. That's the point. Whether she changes or doesn't change I don't care now.

OLWEN (*with deep feeling*): And you know there's nothing I wouldn't do, Robert. I'll—— (*She gives a little laugh.*) I'll run away this very minute with you if you like.

ROBERT (*simply*): I'm terribly grateful, Olwen. But nothing happens here—inside. That's the damned awful cruel thing. Nothing happens. All hollow, empty.

FREDA *enters and shuts the door.*

FREDA: I'm sure it's not at all the proper thing to say at such a moment, but the fact remains that I feel rather hungry. What about you, Olwen? You, Robert? Or have you been drinking too much?

ROBERT: Yes, I've been drinking too much.

FREDA: Well, it's very silly of you.

ROBERT (*wearily*): Yes. (*Buries his face in his hands.*)

FREDA: And you did ask for all this.

ROBERT (*half looking up*): I asked for it. And I got it.

FREDA: Though I doubt if you minded very much until it came to Betty.

ROBERT: That's not true. But I can understand your thinking so. You see, as more and more of this rotten stuff came out, so more and more I came to depend on my secret thoughts of Betty—as someone who seemed to me to represent some lovely quality of life.

FREDA: I've known some time, of course, that you were getting very sentimental and noble about her. And I've known some time, too, all about Betty, and I've often thought of telling you.

ROBERT: I'm not sorry you didn't.

FREDA: You ought to be.

ROBERT: Why?

FREDA: That kind of self-deception's rather stupid.

ROBERT: What about you and Martin?

FREDA: I didn't deceive myself. I knew everything—or nearly everything—about him. I wasn't in love with somebody who really wasn't there, somebody I'd made up.

ROBERT: I think you were. Probably we always are.

OLWEN: Then it's not so bad. You can always build up another image for yourself to fall in love with.

ROBERT: No, you can't. That's the trouble. You lose the capacity for building. You run short of the stuff that creates beautiful illusions, just as if a gland had stopped working.

OLWEN: Then you have to learn to live without illusions.

ROBERT: Can't be done. Not for us. We started life too early for that. Possibly they're breeding people now who can live without illusions. I hope so. But I can't do it. I've lived among illusions——

FREDA (*grimly*): You have.

ROBERT (*with growing excitement*): Well, what if I have? They've given me hope and courage. They've helped me to live. I suppose we ought to get all that from faith in life. But I haven't got any. No religion or anything. Just this damned farmyard to live in. That's all. And just a few bloody glands and secretions and nerves to do it with. But it didn't look too bad. I'd my little illusions, you see.

FREDA (*bitterly*): Then why didn't you leave them alone, instead of clamouring for the truth all night like a fool?

ROBERT (*terribly excited now*): Because I *am* a fool. Stanton was right. That's the only answer. I had to meddle, like a child with a fire. I began this evening with something to keep me going. I'd good memories of Martin. I'd a wife who didn't love me, but at least seemed too good for me. I'd two partners I liked and respected. There was a girl I could idealise. And now——

OLWEN (*distressed*): No, Robert—please. We know.

ROBERT (*in a frenzy*): But you don't know, you *can't* know—not as I know—or you wouldn't stand there like that, as if we'd only just had some damned silly little squabble about a hand at bridge.

OLWEN: Freda, can't you——

ROBERT: Don't you see, we're not living in the same *world* now. Everything's gone. My brother was an obscene lunatic——

FREDA (*very sharply*): Stop that!

ROBERT: And my wife doted on him and pestered him. One of my partners is a liar and a cheat and a thief. The other—God knows what he is—some sort of hysterical young pervert—— (*Both women try to check and calm him.*) And the girl's a greedy little cat on the tiles——

OLWEN (*half screaming*): No, Robert, no. This is horrible, mad. Please, please don't go on. (*Quieter.*) It won't seem like this to-morrow.

ROBERT (*crazy now*): To-morrow. *To-morrow.* I tell you, I'm through. I'm through. There can't be a to-morrow. (*He goes swaying to the door.*)

FREDA (*screaming, moves to* OLWEN *and grips her arm*): He's got a revolver in his bedroom.

OLWEN (*screaming and running to the door*): Stop, Robert! Stop! Stop!

> *For the last few seconds the light has been fading, now it is completely dark. There is a revolver shot, a woman's scream, a moment's silence, then the sound of a woman sobbing, exactly as at the beginning of* ACT I.

OLWEN (*in the darkness, with great emphasis but with a certain hysterical quality*): It can't happen. It *shan't* happen.

> *And now* MISS MOCKRIDGE'S *voice can be heard faintly, and the lights come up slowly, showing the four women in just the same places as they were at the beginning of* ACT I.

MISS MOCKRIDGE: How many scenes did we miss ?

OLWEN: Five, I think.

> FREDA *goes to wireless and switches it off.*

MISS M.: I suppose they must have been telling a lot of lies in those scenes. That's why that man was so angry—the husband, I mean.

> *There is a subdued burst of laughter from the men in the dining-room.*

BETTY: Listen to the men.

MISS M.: They're probably laughing at something very improper.

BETTY: No, just gossip. Men gossip like anything.

FREDA: Of course they do. And they've got a marvellous excuse now that they're all three directors of the firm.

MISS M.: What a snug little group you are.

FREDA (*making a face*): Snug little group. It sounds disgusting.

OLWEN: Enchanting. I hate to leave it.

MISS M.: I should think you do. It must be so comforting to be all so settled.

BETTY: Pretty good.

MISS M. (*to* FREDA): But I suppose you all miss your brother-in-law. He used to be down here with you too, didn't he?

FREDA: You mean Robert's brother, Martin.

> OLWEN, BETTY *and* FREDA *exchange glances, and there is a pause.*

MISS M.: I say, have I dropped a brick? I always am dropping bricks.

FREDA (*very quietly*): No, not at all. It was very distressing at the time, but it's all right now. Martin shot himself.

MISS M.: Oh, yes—dreadful business, of course. He was very handsome, wasn't he?

Enter STANTON, *followed by* GORDON, *who goes to front of settee and takes* BETTY's *hand.*

OLWEN: Yes, very handsome.

STANTON (*with jovial condescension*): Who's very handsome? May we know?

BETTY: Not you, Charles.

GORDON: They were talking about me. Betty, why do you allow them to talk about your husband in this fulsome fashion. Have you no shame, girl?

BETTY (*taking his hand*): Darling, I'm sure you've had too much manly gossip and old brandy.

ROBERT *enters.*

ROBERT: Sorry to be so late, Freda—but it's that wretched puppy of yours.

FREDA: Oh, what's he been doing now?

ROBERT: He was trying to eat the script of Sonia William's new novel. I was afraid it might make him sick. You see, Miss Mockridge, how we talk of you novelists.

MISS M.: Yes, I hear you. I've just been saying what a charming, cosy little group you've made here. I think you've been lucky.

STANTON: It's not all luck, Miss Mockridge. You see, we all happen to be nice easy-going people.

ROBERT: Except Betty, she's terribly wild.

STANTON: That's only because Gordon doesn't beat her often enough—yet.

MISS M.: You see, Miss Peel, Mr. Stanton is still the cynical bachelor, I'm afraid he rather spoils the picture.

GORDON: What's disturbing the ether to-night? Anybody know? (*Beginning to fiddle with the wireless set.*)

FREDA: Oh, Gordon, don't start it again. We've only just turned it off.

GORDON: What did you hear?

FREDA: The last half of a play.

OLWEN: It was called "The Sleeping Dog."

STANTON: Why?

Miss M.: We're not sure, but it ends with a gentleman shooting himself.

Stanton: What fun they have at B.B.C.

Freda: Yes. Shots and things.

Olwen: I think I understand that play now. The sleeping dog was the truth, do you see, and that man, the husband, insisted upon disturbing it.

Robert: He was quite right to disturb it.

Stanton: Was he? I wonder. I think telling the truth is about as healthy as skidding at sixty round a corner.

Freda: And life's got lots of dangerous corners, hasn't it, Charles?

Stanton: It can have if you don't choose your route well.

Freda (*nonchalantly*): Let's talk about something else. Who wants a drink? Drinks, Robert, and cigarettes.

Robert (*examining box on table*): There aren't any here.

Freda: There are some in this one. (*Coming forward with musical cigarette box.*) Miss Mockridge, Olwen, a cigarette? (*Offers box to them.*)

Olwen (*looking at the box*): Oh, I remember that box. It plays a tune at you, doesn't it? I remember the tune. Yes, it's the Wedding March. (*Opens box, and it plays.*)

Gordon (*who has been fiddling with the wireless*): Wait a minute. Listen to this.

"*Can't we talk it over*" *gradually fades in on the wireless set.*

Betty (*rising*): Oh, I adore that tune.

Stanton: What is it?

Betty: "Can't we talk it over".

Miss M.: What?

Gordon: "Can't we talk it over".

On this Robert *pulls back the chair that* Miss M. *has been sitting in.* Freda *moves the table back to window.*

Stanton *asks* Miss M. *to dance. She declines.*

Olwen *crosses to* Robert *and they dance.*

They are all very gay and the music gets louder and louder as the curtain falls.

End of Act Three